Legacies of the War on Poverty

Legacies of the War on Poverty

Edited by Martha J. Bailey and Sheldon Danziger

The National Poverty Center Series on Poverty and Public Policy

Russell Sage Foundation ♦ New York

The Russell Sage Foundation

The Russell Sage Foundation, one of the oldest of America's general purpose foundations, was established in 1907 by Mrs. Margaret Olivia Sage for "the improvement of social and living conditions in the United States." The Foundation seeks to fulfill this mandate by fostering the development and dissemination of knowledge about the country's political, social, and economic problems. While the Foundation endeavors to assure the accuracy and objectivity of each book it publishes, the conclusions and interpretations in Russell Sage Foundation publications are those of the authors and not of the Foundation, its Trustees, or its staff. Publication by Russell Sage, therefore, does not imply Foundation endorsement.

Library of Congress Cataloging-in-Publication Data

Legacies of the War on Poverty / Martha J. Bailey and Sheldon Danziger, editors.
   pages cm. — (National poverty series on poverty and public policy)
   Includes bibliographical references and index.
   ISBN 978-0-87154-007-2 (pbk. : alk. paper) — ISBN 978-1-61044-806-2 (ebook)   1. Public welfare—United States.   2. Poverty—Government policy—United States.   3. United States—Social policy.   4. United States—Economic policy.   I. Bailey, Martha J., 1974— II. Danziger, Sheldon.
   HV95.L44 2013
   362.5'560973—dc23   2013009876

RUSSELL SAGE FOUNDATION
112 East 64th Street, New York, New York 10065
10 9 8 7 6 5 4 3 2 1

To our children, Eve and Ella, and grandchildren, Hazel and Minna.

Contents

Contents

Tables and Figures

About the Authors

MARTHA J. BAILEY is associate professor in the Department of Economics at the University of Michigan, faculty affiliate of the National Poverty Center, research associate of the Population Studies Center, and faculty research fellow at the National Bureau of Economic Research.

SHELDON DANZIGER is H. J. Meyer Distinguished University Professor of Public Policy and director of the National Poverty Center at the Gerald R. Ford School of Public Policy, University of Michigan.

ELIZABETH CASCIO is associate professor in the Department of Economics at Dartmouth College, faculty research fellow at the National Bureau of Economic Research, and research fellow at the Institute for the Study of Labor.

CHLOE GIBBS is assistant professor of public policy and education at the University of Virginia's Batten School of Leadership and Public Policy.

HARRY J. HOLZER is professor of public policy at Georgetown University, an institute fellow at the American Institutes of Research, and a former Chief Economist for the U.S. Department of Labor.

BRIDGET TERRY LONG is Xander Professor of Education at the Harvard Graduate School of Education and research associate of the National Bureau of Economic Research.

JENS LUDWIG is the McCormick Foundation Professor of Social Service Administration, Law, and Public Policy and director of the Crime Lab at the University of Chicago.

KATHLEEN MCGARRY is professor and chair in the Department of Economics at the University of California, Los Angeles, and research associate at the National Bureau of Economic Research.

DOUGLAS L. MILLER is associate professor of economics at the University of California, Davis.

About the Authors

EDGAR O. OLSEN is professor of economics and public policy in the Department of Economics and the Frank Batten School of Leadership and Public Policy at the University of Virginia.

SARAH REBER is associate professor of public policy at the University of California, Los Angeles, Luskin School of Public Affairs and faculty research fellow at the National Bureau of Economic Research.

KATHERINE SWARTZ is professor of health economics and policy in the Department of Health Policy and Management at the Harvard School of Public Health.

JANE WALDFOGEL is Compton Foundation Centennial Professor for the Prevention of Children and Youth Problems at Columbia University School of Social Work and visiting professor at the London School of Economics.

BARBARA WOLFE is the Richard A. Easterlin Professor of Health Economics in the Departments of Economics and Population Health Sciences and the La Follette School of Public Affairs at the University of Wisconsin–Madison.

Chapter 1

Legacies of the War on Poverty

Martha J. Bailey and Sheldon Danziger

Many Americans live on the outskirts of hope – some because of their poverty, and some because of their color, and all too many because of both. Our task is to help replace their despair with opportunity.

This administration today, here and now, declares unconditional war on poverty in America. I urge this Congress and all Americans to join with me in that effort.

It will not be a short or easy struggle, no single weapon or strategy will suffice, but we shall not rest until that war is won. The richest Nation on earth can afford to win it. We cannot afford to lose it.

President Lyndon B. Johnson, State of the Union Address, January 8, 1964

In his first State of the Union Address, Lyndon B. Johnson declared an "unconditional war on poverty" that aimed "not only to relieve the symptom of poverty, but to cure it and, above all, to prevent it" (Johnson 1964a). Within several years, Johnson's sweeping legislative achievements transformed American schools and universities, employment and training programs, health insurance for the elderly (Medicare) and poor (Medicaid), and the nature and scope of the social safety net (for example, Food Stamps, now the Supplemental Nutrition Assistance Program [SNAP]; changes in Aid to Families with Dependent Children, now Temporary Assistance for Needy Families [TANF]; expansions of subsidized housing, and increased Social Security benefits [see table 1.1]). The 1964 Economic Opportunity Act created the Office of Economic Opportunity (OEO) to coordinate federal antipoverty initiatives and launched enduring programs such as Head Start, Job Corps, and Community Health Centers. All of these changes contributed to a more than tripling of real federal expenditures on health, education, employment and training, housing, and income transfers, as spending on these programs reached 15.1 percent of the federal budget by 1970 (Ginzberg and Solow 1974).

Less well known is that the War on Poverty is intertwined with the 1964 Civil Rights Act (CRA). The War on Poverty's "assault on discrimination" (Council of

Table 1.1 / War on Poverty's Major Legislation and Events

November 22, 1963	President Kennedy assassinated; Vice President Lyndon B. Johnson assumes the U.S. Presidency
January 8, 1964	President Johnson's State of the Union Address declares War on Poverty
February 26, 1964	The Revenue Act of 1964 (P.L. 88-272) dramatically lowers individual income tax rates and slightly lowers corporate tax rates
July 2, 1964	Civil Rights Act of 1964 (P.L. 88-352) signed into law by President Johnson
August 20, 1964	The Economic Opportunity Act of 1964 (P.L. 88-452) created Community Action Agencies to coordinate local antipoverty efforts and funds programs such as Head Start, Job Corps, Community Health Centers, Upward Bound, the Work Experience Program, Neighborhood Youth Corps, Volunteers in Service to America (VISTA), Legal Services, and federal work study programs.
August 31, 1964	The Food Stamp Act of 1964 (P.L. 88-525) creates a permanent, national program out of the food stamps pilot program begun in 1961
November 3, 1964	Lyndon Johnson wins landslide victory in Presidential Election; Democrats win two-thirds majority in both the Senate and House — the most Democratic Congress since the New Deal
April 11, 1965	The Elementary and Secondary Education Act of 1965 (P.L. 89-10) signed into law. Title I distributes funding to schools and districts with high percentages of students from low-income families
April 26, 1965	The Manpower Act of 1965 (P.L. 89-15) expanded funding under the 1962 Manpower Development and Training Act to retrain displaced workers
July 14, 1965	The Older Americans Act of 1965 (P.L. 89-73) provides for grants to help fund various support services such as caregiver support, nutritional services, and social services
July 30, 1965	Medicare and Medicaid are signed into law as part of the 1965 Amendments to the Social Security Act (P.L. 89-97)
August 6, 1965	The Voting Rights Act (P.L. 89-110) abolished literacy tests and other barriers used by state and local governments to disenfranchise voters (especially African Americans)
August 10, 1965	The Housing and Urban Development Act (P.L. 89-117) created the Department of Housing and Urban Development
November 8, 1965	The Higher Education Act of 1965 (P.L. 89-329) created federal loan programs including the Educational Opportunity Grant and Guaranteed Student Loan. It also created the college preparatory program, Talent Search.
September 30, 1966	The 1966 Amendments to the Fair Labor Standards Acts increased minimum wage from $1.25 to $1.60 by 1968 and extended coverage to public schools, nursing homes, laundries, and construction and farm workers and large farms

continued

TABLE 1.1 / Continued

October 11, 1966	The Child Nutrition Act of 1966 (P.L. 89–642) increased funding for school lunches and created a school breakfast program.
November 3, 1966	The Demonstration Cities and Metropolitan Development Act (P.L. 89-754) initiated the Model Cities Program
January 2, 1968	1967 Social Security Amendments (P.L. 90-248) dramatically increased Social Security benefits, mandated work incentive programs for AFDC recipients
April 11, 1968	Title VIII of the Civil Rights Act of 1968 (known as the Fair Housing Act), prohibited discrimination in the sale, financing, or leasing of housing

Source: Authors' compilation.

Economic Advisers 1964) leveraged federal funds to push for desegregation. Iconic depictions of forced desegregation and heroic narratives of activism shape the collective memory of the 1960s. A less-remembered aspect of the War on Poverty is the Johnson administration's decision to withhold federal money in cases where local organizations failed to desegregate. The War on Poverty's expansion of federal funding gave the Johnson administration the ability to apply pressure to local governments and private organizations to reduce racial discrimination and segregation, making compliance with the CRA a pocketbook issue.[1]

The War on Poverty initiated a new era of direct federal involvement in schools, hospitals, labor markets, and neighborhoods. This involvement engendered considerable controversy but has left a large footprint on the conceptualization, design, and implementation of antipoverty, social, and health policies; American politics; racial inequalities; and social science research. The chapters in this volume document many of the War on Poverty's lasting legacies. Programs and policies enacted during this era influenced antipoverty legislation well into the 1970s when two major antipoverty programs, Supplemental Security Income (SSI) and the Earned Income Tax Credit (EITC), were enacted. This era's programs and policies continue to define the social and health safety net today.

The War on Poverty's expansive legislative changes have been compared with those of Franklin D. Roosevelt's New Deal. But whereas the New Deal was developed in response to high unemployment and the grave economic crisis of the Great Depression, the War on Poverty was launched during a long period of widely shared prosperity. Indeed, one of Johnson's rationales in declaring War on Poverty was that the country could afford to pay for the mission. In his annual message to Congress for the release of the *Economic Report of the President* on January 20, 1964, Johnson declared,

> Americans today enjoy the highest standard of living in the history of mankind. But for nearly a fifth of our fellow citizens, this is a hollow achievement. . . . We cannot and need not wait for the gradual growth of the economy to lift this forgot-

ten fifth of our Nation above the poverty line. We know what must be done, and this Nation of abundance can surely afford to do it (Council of Economic Advisers 1964, 15).

No president since Johnson has placed fighting poverty at the top of his domestic policy agenda. And, as the chapters in this volume document, the nation's schools, universities, hospitals, labor markets and social and health safety net continue to reflect this transformational period.

Authored by economists, this volume's chapters analyze the economic legacies of the War on Poverty fifty years after its declaration—specifically, the era's policies and programs that were designed to promote more equal opportunities and increase income.

This volume makes the case that the often-heard conclusion that the War on Poverty was a "failure" is far too simplistic. Of course, poverty is still with us. Recent research by Bruce Meyer and James Sullivan (2012), however, shows that consumption-based measures of poverty, which they argue are superior for theoretical and practical reasons, have fallen by more than the official income-based measure. Several chapters document that poverty and economic hardship would have likely been much higher if the era's programs and policies had not been put in place or expanded. Another reason is that the War on Poverty was fought on many fronts, encompassed a diverse set of strategies, and affected outcomes other than income poverty rates. Its most well-documented successes are the rapid decline in elderly poverty and the provision of universal health-care coverage to the elderly. In addition, the chapters document some lesser-known long-term successes such as its powerful incentives to desegregate institutions and organizations receiving federal funding.

Other successes have recently emerged as scholars have used new developments in data collection and research methodology to reanalyze the effects of the era's programs. For instance, the effects of the War on Poverty's investments in preschool children through Head Start in the 1960s could not affect their educational attainment until many years later (Ludwig and Miller 2007). Similarly, the era's effects on racial discrimination and segregation did not unfold immediately, but gradually over decades as better access to education and health care and changing social norms contributed to greater earnings of African American workers. On the other hand, even though some of the era's employment and training programs generated earnings increases, their effects on employment and earnings were, in most cases, not large. As Medicare has extended health insurance to millions of the nation's elderly, it has also contributed to the rising costs of health care. Each chapter notes both the War on Poverty's failings and successes, many of which have been neglected or underappreciated.

Before we summarize the key findings of each chapter, we provide a brief history of the War on Poverty era, describe what the War on Poverty was, summarize the controversy over its legacies, and provide historical and economic context for interpreting its shorter and longer-term effects.

ELIMINATING POVERTY AS A CENTERPIECE OF PRESIDENT JOHNSON'S DOMESTIC AGENDA

Poverty emerged as a highly visible social problem in the late 1950s and early 1960s (O'Connor 2001). Google books n-grams (figure 1.1) shows that mentions of *poverty* were lower in 1960 than in 1940, but began to rise in the early 1960s when prominent books, including John Kenneth Galbraith's 1958 *The Affluent Society* and Michael Harrington's 1962 *The Other America*, and popular articles by journalists catapulted the "poverty problem" to national prominence. Harrington wrote that the "other America" is "an invisible land," in part, because the federal government did not publish information on the extent of poverty at that time.

Robert Lampman (1959), one of the few economists conducting research on poverty in the 1950s, prepared a study for the Joint Economic Committee of the Congress analyzing the post–World War II decline in the percentage of families with incomes below $3,000 per year, a measure used by the Council of Economic Advisers until the official poverty measure was adopted in 1965.[2] He documented that poverty had been declining since 1947, but that the rate of poverty decline had slowed after 1957. His analysis was reflected in the 1964 *Economic Report* of the President, which noted that "one fifth of our families and nearly one-fifth or our total population are poor" (Council of Economic Advisers 1964, 56).

Although there is disagreement among scholars regarding why Johnson chose the War on Poverty as a centerpiece of his domestic agenda, the facts are well known. After John F. Kennedy's assassination, Johnson was briefed on a range of issues that Kennedy had been considering. Arthur Schlesinger (1965), in his chronicle of the Kennedy administration, argues that Johnson continued what would have been Kennedy's poverty agenda. In contrast, Walter Heller, the chairman of Kennedy's Council of Economic Advisers (CEA), notes that only days before his assassination, Kennedy's thinking on the matter "had not gone beyond the vague concept of doing something that would focus specifically on the roots of poverty" (Heller 1970, 19–20).

In their first briefing, Heller recalls that Johnson immediately and unequivocally affirmed the poverty program: "That's my kind of program. I'll find money for it one way or another. If I have to, I'll take away money from things to get money for people. . . . Give it the highest priority. Push ahead full tilt" (1970, 21). Guian McKee (2011) notes that several weeks later Johnson was prepared to reject the entire antipoverty program as it was explained to him unless it were significantly expanded. Thus, in the seven weeks between Kennedy's assassination and Johnson's State of the Union Address, the War on Poverty evolved from a small, academic pilot of the CEA to an expansive program and the centerpiece of Johnson's domestic agenda.

Johnson's political or personal motivations are difficult to gauge. Using the volumes of oral histories, taped conversations, and archival documents, commentators and historians have pieced together competing, but not mutually exclusive, narratives of this era's political economy: how the War on Poverty evolved from

FIGURE 1.1 / Google Books N-Grams of Mentions of Poverty

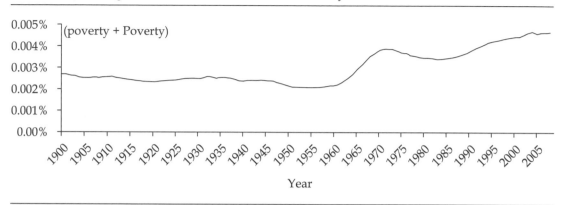

Source: Authors' tabulations using http://books.google.com/ngrams.

the academic brainchild of the CEA into a controversial and enduring legacy of his presidency (see, for example, Gettleman and Mermelstein 1966; Levitan 1969; Ginzberg and Solow 1974; Davies 1996; Gillette 1996; Alston and Ferrie 1999; O'Connor 2001; Germany 2007; Orleck and Hazirjian 2011; Caro 2012).[3]

After Johnson's State of the Union declaration, he promoted the War on Poverty agenda in a public relations tour. In April 1964, he visited unemployed coal miner Tom Fletcher, his wife, and eight children who lived in Appalachia. The Fletchers had been chosen by the White House as the face of the hardworking Americans who lived in poverty. Johnson is said to have remarked to a reporter, "I don't know if I'll pass a single law or get a single dollar appropriated, but before I'm through, no community in America will be able to ignore poverty in its midst" (Jordan and Rostow 1986, 16). Indeed, Walter Bennett's iconic *Time* magazine photo of Johnson's chat with the Fletchers on their front porch (printed on the front of this volume) achieved just that.[4]

WHAT WAS THE WAR ON POVERTY?

The War on Poverty—what it was and what it wasn't—has been defined and redefined by contemporaries, politicians, and social scientists. Some accounts define it as a single piece of legislation (for example, only the 1964 Economic Opportunity Act; Gillette 1996), and others primarily as the "welfare programs" (for example, Ronald Reagan's 1988 State of the Union Address or Charles Murray's 1984 *Losing Ground*).

Defining the War on Poverty is also complicated because of differences of opinion within the administration. Johnson is reported to have told Sargent Shriver, head of the OEO, "no doles," and to have rejected proposals both to expand welfare and to provide jobs for the long-term unemployed. Robert Haveman describes Johnson's strategy as being premised on the view that the problem was ultimately one of low labor market productivity. The poor were viewed as being in that state because they did not work enough, or because [they] did not work hard enough, or because their meager skills and qualifications were insufficient to raise them out of poverty even if they did work hard. This condition was in turn attributed to several factors — the lagging state of the economy, the characteristics of the poor, and discrimination against them by those who controlled access to jobs or goods and services. . . . The remedy required overt policy measures by the federal government designed to improve the performance of the economy, the productivity characteristics of the poor, and the attitudes (or at least the behavior) of those who hired or sold to the poor. (1987, 14–15)

Nonetheless, within a few years, economists — including James Tobin, a member of Kennedy's CEA, and Robert Lampman (1971), the poverty staff expert for Heller's CEA — were advocating a negative income tax as a feasible policy to eliminate income poverty.[5] According to Lampman,

the elimination of income poverty is usefully thought of as a one-time operation in pursuit of a goal unique to this generation. That goal should be achieved before 1980, at which time the next generation will have set new economic and social goals, perhaps including a new distributional goal for themselves. (1971, 53)

This optimistic view assumed that poverty could be eliminated not only because government transfers could raise family incomes but also because it was expected that robust economic growth would continue to raise the employment and earnings of the poor along with those of other workers. This view was sensible at the time, as economic growth had lifted the earnings at the lower end of the skill distribution since the end of World War II.

This volume defines the War on Poverty as Johnson did: the full legislative agenda laid out in the 1964 State of the Union and in the eleven goals contained in chapter 2 of the *1964 Economic Report of the President*, titled "Strategy against Poverty" (Council of Economic Advisers 1964, 73–77). These goals include maintaining high employment, accelerating economic growth, fighting discrimination, improving regional economies, rehabilitating urban and rural communities, improving labor markets, expanding educational opportunities, enlarging opportunities for youth, improving the Nation's health, promoting adult education and training, and assisting the aged and disabled. Henry Aaron summarized the administration's broad view of the War on Poverty as

part or all of such traditional programs as social security (old age, survivors and disability insurance), public assistance, veterans' benefits, public housing, urban renewal, Medicare, and Medicaid. It also included programs operating under the Manpower Development and Training Act and aid to poor school districts under the Elementary and Secondary Education Act of 1965. . . . Indeed, only a small part of total expenditures under the War on Poverty represented commitments by OEO. (1978, 27)

Many aspects of this agenda have been neglected by previous evaluations. The War on Poverty was more than a disparate set of programs. One of its unifying elements was *prevention* of economic hardship. An example is Medicare. Although Medicare is targeted to all of the elderly, not just the elderly poor,[6] Johnson stressed its capacity to prevent poverty. His 1964 State of the Union noted the need to "provide hospital insurance for our older citizens . . . to protect him in his old age . . . against the devastating hardship of prolonged or repeated illness." Johnson went on to say that "every American will benefit by the extension of social security to cover the hospital costs of their aged parents." That is, Medicare not only prevented financial ruin among the elderly — it also protected their adult children from having to pay for the costs of their parents' illness.

The War on Poverty's human capital programs, from Head Start to subsidizing access to higher education, and workforce development programs sought to increase workers' opportunities and increase their lifetime employment and earnings. Increased access to health care among the poor (Medicaid) sought to reduce the incidence of health problems and the related costs of attaining higher education, thereby also contributing to increased lifetime earnings. Rehabilitating neighborhoods and expanding income support and subsidized housing for poor families aimed to facilitate human capital investments among children and raise their longer-term earnings potential. Expanding income support for the elderly both raised their living standards and reduced the burden for their care on their adult children. These programs aimed to prevent poverty in both the short and the longer term.

Some scholars of the civil rights movement might argue that federal efforts on racial discrimination were distinct from the War on Poverty. But the 1964 State of the Union and *Economic Report* were also explicit about the "assault on discrimination." Johnson's State of the Union explicitly made this connection: "Let me make one principle of this administration abundantly clear: All of these increased opportunities — in employment, in education, in housing, and in every field — must be open to Americans of every color."

Echoing his lofty rhetoric calling for the elimination of poverty, he called for the abolition of "not some, but *all* racial discrimination" [emphasis added]. The Economic Report noted that fighting discrimination would "open additional exits from poverty" and that ending discrimination would require "business and labor, other private organizations and individuals, and all levels of government" to share in its removal. The report justifies its focus on ending racial discrimination both in terms of efficiency and equity goals:

> The economic costs of discrimination to the total society are also large. By discrimination in employment the Nation denies itself the output of which the talents and training of the nonwhite population are already capable. By discrimination in education and environment, the Nation denies itself the potential talents of one-ninth of its citizens. But the basic case against discrimination is not economic. It is that discrimination affronts human dignity. (Council of Economic Advisers 1964, 74)

After decades of failed attempts to pass effective civil rights legislation (Caro 2012), Johnson's political skills in persuading Congress to enact the 1964 Civil Rights Act altered the legal protections afforded to African Americans and other minorities in the labor market, in access to public facilities and government resources including health care, higher education, and housing.

On June 5, 1965, Johnson's commencement address at Howard University emphasized the challenges to achieving economic equality for African American families "buried under a blanket of history and circumstance." David Carter notes Johnson's frequent use of this metaphor: "It was like you couldn't pick up the blanket off a Negro at one corner, you had to pick it all up. . . . It had to be housing and it had to be jobs and . . . everything you could think of" (2009, 6).

In the Howard University address, Johnson spoke of civil rights as opening the "gates of opportunity" but insisted that more could be done so that "all our citizens . . . have the *ability* [emphasis added] to walk through those gates." Calling this "the next and the more profound stage of the battle for civil rights," Johnson championed the cause of "not just legal equity but human ability, not just equality as a right and a theory but equality as a fact and equality as a result." This logic represented a turn in Johnson's expression of what constituted equality—a shift from classical liberalism's focus on individual opportunity to his growing concern that the unequal "life chances" of millions of Americans rendered the promise of equal opportunity largely meaningless.

Johnson's commitment to this rhetoric is evident in his use of the federal purse to encourage racial integration. Key to federal power in this regard was its ability to withhold funds in cases where local organizations failed to desegregate. Douglas Almond, Kenneth Chay, and Michael Greenstone (forthcoming) show this policy had teeth. The threat that hospitals could lose Medicare reimbursements if they failed to comply with Title VI of the CRA catalyzed the desegregation of Southern hospitals. This, in turn, contributed to large reductions in black infant mortality rates. Elizabeth Cascio, Nora Gordon, Ethan Lewis, and Sarah Reber (2010) show that this policy affected southern schools as well. Districts with more federal money at stake under the 1965 Elementary and Secondary Education Act engaged in more school desegregation.

The Office of Economic Opportunity and other federal offices monitored compliance with the Civil Rights Act and threatened to withhold funding in response to violations. As the War on Poverty infused federal spending into communities across the country, these dollars encouraged reductions in de jure and de facto segregation in the delivery and distribution of services and resources. The War on Poverty's ideals of equal opportunity and equal access—whether racial or socioeconomic—were reinforced by the large financial incentives created by federal dollars for its programs.

Altogether, the War on Poverty was a grand policy experiment. An important conclusion of the volume is that the *combined* influence of its programs and policies was greater than the impact of any individual program. Many accounts fail to credit the War on Poverty with the broad expansion of the nation's human capital, health, housing, and income support programs. Many accounts fail to recognize its connections to civil rights compliance and improvements in opportunities for minorities.

Even though the scope of this volume's treatment of the War on Poverty is broad, it still cannot do justice to the myriad ways the era affected the economy, social relations, and politics. Authored by economists, the volume's chapters evaluate the War on Poverty programs and policies that sought to promote economic opportunities, improve outcomes, and prevent poverty—those related to improving educational attainment, raising employment, earnings, and family incomes; improving the quality of housing; and promoting access to health care and health outcomes.

A LEGACY OF CONTROVERSY

The controversial legacy of the War on Poverty poses a challenge to any evaluation. In the early years, political and public support for the program was significant. In 1965, OEO Director Sargent Shriver told Congress that "the most important and exciting thing about the War on Poverty" was "that all America is joining in . . . religious groups, professional groups, labor groups, civic and patriot groups are all rallying to the call" (Gettleman and Mermelstein 1967, 207). Similarly, the *New York Times* featured the "group of leaders" in "every city and community" who "believe this job can be done and who are helping."[7] However, this enthusiasm for fighting poverty faded, particularly when public attention turned away from the War on Poverty to the Vietnam War and urban race riots. The longer-term legacies of the War on Poverty have been challenged by partisan and racial politics, disillusionment on the part of both the right and the left, and the backlash against federal authority.

From the outset, the use of federal funds to promote more equal opportunities for the poor and particularly African Americans generated strong resistance from state and local government officials in all regions of the country. Communities wanted federal money, but many objected to federal demands for equal access to services (for instance, access for African Americans) and for citizen involvement in the operation programs (for instance, potential beneficiaries of the programs).

The result was a number of widely publicized showdowns, as Shriver challenged high-profile politicians. For example, in 1965, the OEO authorized a grant to Louisiana to start an antipoverty program. When Governor John McKeithen announced the names of his program's appointees, opponents wrote to Washington that they were "rabid segregationists" (Haddad 1965, 48; Germany 2007, 49). Although Shriver did not have the power to select the appointees, he had the authority to withhold funds. In protest, McKeithen appealed to Congress, the president, and the vice president, and finally met Shriver in Washington. Ultimately, McKeithen lost this showdown and selected a new set of appointees. Only then did OEO money flow into Louisiana. Supporters on the left were gratified by Shriver's fearless exercise of power for the cause of greater racial integration.

The federal government's efforts were not always this successful. Another symbolic political battle relates to the Child Development Group (CDG) of Mississippi, which obtained a grant to set up a Head Start program in rural Mississippi. After a promising start and a media bonanza for the administration, the CDG became one of OEO's most controversial and divisive grants. According to Carter, Mississippi's Governor Paul Johnson wrote the OEO an angry letter describing CDG as little more than a front for "extremists and agitators" seeking "to subvert legal authority in Mississippi and to create division and dissension between the races" (2009, 37). Carter also notes that CDG infuriated politicians and other white Mississippians because it threatened their economic control and offered a blueprint for desegregation in Mississippi's public schools. Carter quotes Tom Levin, one of the CDG's planners, as saying, "We were not disturbed by [the opposition of] Senator [John] Stennis. He showed good judgment in considering us a danger to the status quo in Mississippi. We *were* a danger" (40).

Nonetheless, Stennis was ultimately successful when, as chair of the Senate Appropriations Committee, he threatened to hold the president's other legislation hostage, including funding for the Vietnam War. "Acquiesing," the administration reduced CDG's funding and changed the controversial Head Start organization. Containing this political backlash on the right, thus, angered CDG supporters on the left.

The result is that the War on Poverty has been labeled a failure by both the right and the left of the political spectrum. Critics from the left argue that not enough money was spent on the poor and that the Johnson administration did too little to change the institutional practices of firms and labor markets. Ira Katznelson contends that the administration

> stopped well short of attempts to reorganize and modify the marketplace. It entirely left alone the organization of work, the patterns of investment, and the role of the business class. It did not call into question either the larger contours and rationality of the American political economy or the tools, a version of Keynesianism, that had been elaborated over the course of a quarter-century to manage the macroeconomic issues of growth, employment, and inflation. If at the heart of the Great Society was a war on poverty, this was quite a timid call to arms, with the enemy identified circumspectly.
>
> The most compelling characteristic of the Great Society was that it was a program of mainstream economists and technicians who conceded from the start the framework of ideas and practices of the larger political economy. It sought to correct inequities and problems on the margin of a thriving system of production and consumption. (1989, 198–99)

In contrast, critics from the right contend that the War on Poverty cultivated a "culture of dependency" by expanding entitlements that discouraged work, personal savings, and marriage.[8] They emphasize that the official poverty rate remains high even though substantial federal funds are spent each year on programs for low-income families. President Reagan invoked these ideas in his 1988 State of the Union address:

My friends, some years ago, the federal government declared war on poverty, and poverty won. Today, the federal government has 59 major welfare programs and spends more than $100 billion a year on them. What has all this money done?

Too often it has only made poverty harder to escape. Federal welfare programs have created a massive social problem. With the best of intentions, government created a poverty trap that wreaks havoc on the very support system the poor need most to lift themselves out of poverty — the family. Dependency has become the one enduring heirloom, passed from one generation to the next, of too many fragmented families.

Academic evaluations were no more generous. Eli Ginzberg and Robert Solow concluded in their ten-year review that

of the Great Society programs, the war on poverty is the most open to criticism. The promises were extreme; the specific remedial actions were untried and untested; the finances were grossly inadequate; the political restructuring was so vulnerable that it had to be radically reformed within a few years after the program was launched. (1974, 219)

James Patterson speculates that "perhaps no government program in modern American history promised so much more than it delivered" (2000, 147). Unlike the New Deal, the public remembers the War on Poverty as an expensive and unsuccessful battle. Patterson concludes that "more than any other program of Johnson's so-called Great Society, the war on poverty accentuated doubts about the capacity of social science to plan, and government to deliver, ambitious programs for social betterment" (147–48).

The persistence of high poverty rates according to the official poverty measure, as shown in figure 1.2, has fueled these critiques. Poverty rates were falling both before and after Johnson's declaration of War on Poverty. But, since the mid-1970s, poverty rates for all persons have fluctuated in a narrow range. In 2011, in the wake of the Great Recession, 46 million Americans, or 15.0 percent, lived in poverty, as did one in five children. The share of Americans living in poverty today is lower than the 19 percent of 1964, but higher than the 11.1 percent reached in 1973.

An important political legacy of the War on Poverty is the perception that federal antipoverty programs inhibit progress against poverty, rather than encourage it. The collective memory of the War on Poverty programs has also been colored by discontent with the Johnson administration. Johnson dropped out of the 1968 presidential campaign, primarily due to widespread discontent with the Vietnam War. Shortly after taking office in 1969, President Richard Nixon, with the help of his OEO director, Donald Rumsfeld, disbanded the OEO and transferred many of its popular programs to other agencies. Popular programs like Head Start, Medicare, the Civil and Voting Rights Acts, and federal funding for K-12 and higher education were rebranded as distinct from the War on Poverty. This volume reclaims Johnson's definition of the War on Poverty and reevaluates its legacies in longer-term perspective using a broad set of programs and outcome measures.

FIGURE 1.2 / U.S. Poverty Rates

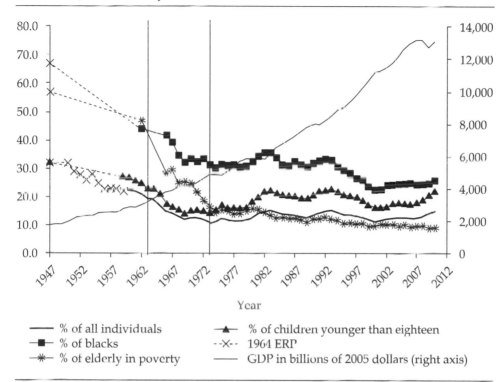

Year

- ——— % of all individuals
- —■— % of blacks
- —*— % of elderly in poverty
- —▲— % of children younger than eighteen
- --×-- 1964 ERP
- ——— GDP in billions of 2005 dollars (right axis)

Source: Authors' calculations based on U.S. Census Bureau (2012a, 2012b). Pre-1960 estimates are taken from the 1964 *Economic Report of the President*, chapter 2, table 3.
Note: Before 1959 (or the first solid line), estimates for poverty rates are the share of individuals in the group in households earning less than $3,000 per year in 1960 dollars, roughly Mollie Orshansky's poverty line for a family of four. These numbers are not directly comparable to modern poverty lines. Ross, Danziger, and Smolensky (1987) estimate overall earnings poverty rate at 40.5 percent using 1950 census.

CHALLENGES TO PRIOR EVALUATIONS

One reason for the War on Poverty's controversial political legacy is the difficulty of measuring success. The most simplistic evaluations of the War on Poverty compare the official poverty rate today with the official poverty rate in 1964 and attribute changes in the poverty rate to the War on Poverty's programs and policies. As shown in figure 1.2, this comparison yields disappointing results. Researchers have long noted the inadequacy of the official rate. For instance, the official poverty measure is based only on money income before taxes and thus misses important changes in federal in-kind programs, such as food stamps or housing assistance, and changes in the tax code, such as the earned income tax credit.[9]

Recent research demonstrates that these concerns are important. Meyer and Sullivan (2012) compute a consumption-based measure of poverty, which includes gains in material resources accruing from changes in the tax code and War on Poverty programs or their outgrowths, such as the food stamps, housing benefits, in-kind transfers and the Earned Income Tax Credit. This measure shows a 26 percentage point decline from 1960 to 2010, just over two-thirds of the drop occurring before 1980. This leads the authors to conclude that antipoverty programs have been much more successful than previously believed.

Another challenge to evaluating the War on Poverty's effects on poverty relates to fundamental shifts in the economy, in the demographic composition of the population, and in social norms and in institutions over the past fifty years. Many of these factors have been poverty-increasing, independent of any effects of antipoverty programs (Cancian and Danziger 2009).

One important factor has been the slowdown and periodic reversal in earnings growth over the past four decades at the bottom end of the skill distribution. After the early 1970s, the rising tide of economic growth no longer lifted all boats. Figure 1.3 illustrates this trend by depicting the growth in the real hourly wages of full-time, full-year men from 1949 to 2009 for different percentiles in the wage earnings distribution (see data appendix for details on these computations). Each line depicts the change in earnings for the relevant period. In the decade from 1949 to 1959, real hourly wages increased by roughly 7 percent at the 10th percentile but by 13 percent at the 90th percentile. In the first decade of the War on Poverty, the series depicted by the line labeled 1963 to 1973, hourly wages increased even faster at the 10th percentile and growth at the 90th percentile remained steady. Thus, from 1949 to 1973, real wages grew rapidly at both the top and bottom of the wage distribution.

After the early 1970s, however, wage growth slowed dramatically.[10] For workers in the bottom half of the distribution, hourly wages fell from 1973 to 1993 by as much as 4 percent per decade at the 10th percentile. Over the same period, hourly wage growth for those at the 75th and 90th percentiles slowed to 1 to 2 percent per decade. Although earnings for workers across the wage distribution rose by 5 to 8 percent in the economic boom of the 1990s, they remained below the levels achieved in the early 1970s. The first decade of the twenty-first century again shows almost no wage gains and slight losses in the lower end of the income distribution.[11]

The fact that each of the lines is positively sloped with respect to percentile in the wage distribution indicates that wage inequality rose. Wages at the top percentiles increased more rapidly than wages at the bottom. In addition, that the lines for the 1970s and 1980s are significantly below those for the 1950s and 1960s highlights the slowdown in wage growth in the decades after the War on Poverty began. These trends worked counter to the optimism of Tobin, Lampman (1971), and other CEA economists, who expected that economic growth would continue to be widely shared by all workers, including the less skilled.

After the early 1970s, economic growth was no longer raising the wages of less-skilled workers as it had in the 1960s, and the rapid decline in poverty rates came

FIGURE 1.3 / Changes in Hourly Wage Earnings Among Full-Time Men at Various
Percentiles in the Distribution

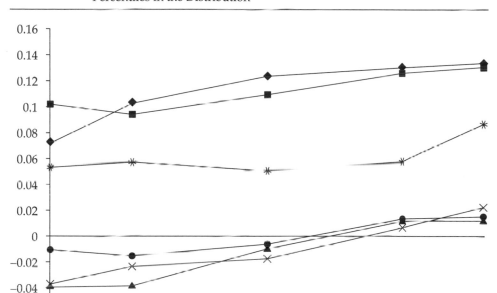

Percentile of Wage Distribution

—◆— 1949–1959 Census   —✕— 1983–1993
—■— 1963–1973   —✳— 1993–2003
—▲— 1973–1983   —●— 2003–2009 ACS

Source: All calculations from the March Current Population Surveys (1963–2003) except for the 1949 to 1959 series, which is from the decennial census, and the 2003 to 2009 series, which is from the American Community Survey.
Note: See text and data appendix for detailed notes on the construction of series

to an end. Since the 1970s, economic growth has tended to benefit the most-educated and highest earners. Both the slowing rate of overall earnings growth and the periodic contraction of wages for the lowest earners tended to increase poverty rates, all else equal.

Countervailing demographic and institutional changes also worked against attempts to reduce poverty and to increase children's economic opportunities. Slow earnings growth in the lower end of the skill distribution has coincided with the growth in male incarceration rates; the rise in nonmarital childbearing; and the growth of female-headed households.

After remaining fairly stable from 1925 to 1975, male incarceration rates more than quadrupled from 1975 to 2004. Steven Raphael and Michael Stoll (2009) con-

FIGURE 1.4 / Nonmarital Births as a Percentage of All Births

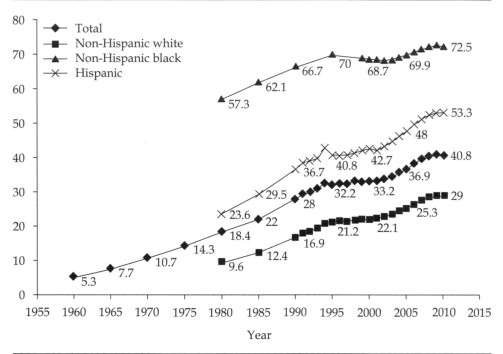

Source: Authors' calculations drawn from various publications of the National Center for Health Statistics. See data appendix for details.

clude that the causes of these trends are changes in public policies relating to sentencing and punishment—not changes in underlying criminal behavior. These changes began almost a decade after the War on Poverty and have contributed to reductions in the employment and earnings of the increasing numbers of ex-offenders, because many employers are reluctant to hire them (Holzer 2009). This trend tends to increase poverty, as removing workers from the labor market reduces their human capital and removing breadwinners from poor families reduces family resources.

Figure 1.4 shows that nonmarital childbearing increased almost linearly from 1960 to 2010—including the five years before the War on Poverty began. Although the rates of nonmarital childbearing are higher among African American women, the trends have been similar across racial-ethnic groups. The causes of these trends are multifaceted. But, it is difficult to argue that they were caused or even jump-started by the War on Poverty (Murray 1984, 2012). Analyses by Robert Moffitt (1998) and David Ellwood and Christopher Jencks (2004) conclude that only a small fraction of the overall increase is explained by changes in the generosity of welfare programs.

Together, increased incarceration and nonmarital childbearing, along with the

TABLE 1.2 / Characteristics of the Non-Elderly Poor

| | 1960 Census | | 2010 Census | | 2011 ACS | |
	Poor persons	All persons	Poor persons	All persons	Poor persons	All persons
Age less than eighteen	0.510	0.403	0.383	0.282	0.379	0.279
Male	0.468	0.490	0.459	0.496	0.459	0.497
Female	0.532	0.510	0.541	0.504	0.541	0.503
Black	0.288	0.108	0.222	0.129	0.219	0.129
Hispanic	0.064	0.034	0.278	0.179	0.285	0.182
White	0.635	0.849	0.427	0.614	0.420	0.609
Native-born	0.965	0.954	0.831	0.855	0.829	0.854
Immigrant	0.035	0.046	0.169	0.145	0.171	0.146
Head married	0.767	0.879	0.324	0.628	0.322	0.622
Head single with children	0.149	0.066	0.386	0.189	0.388	0.193
Head single no children	0.084	0.056	0.291	0.184	0.291	0.185
Head education less than high school	0.801	0.572	0.274	0.120	0.271	0.117
Head worked in previous year	0.301	0.442	0.306	0.565	0.304	0.563

Source: Authors' calculations based on 1960 Census 1% Sample, 2010 ACS Sample, and 2011 ACS Sample, and Ruggles et al. (2010).
Note: The numbers represent the fraction of individuals with particular characteristics among the non-elderly poor or all non-elderly. Age, ethnicity, and immigrant status are assigned based on individual characteristics. Family composition, education, and employment are assigned based on characteristics of the family head. For the primary family in each household, family head is the head of household. For secondary families, the oldest adult is considered the family head. For secondary families with no adult members, family head is assumed to be the head of household. Individuals are considered non-elderly if they are sixty-four or younger. Excludes institutional inmates.

rise in divorce rates and the growth in women's earnings power, have increased the share of all children living in female-headed households. Sara McLanahan (2004) concludes that these forces have resulted in "diverging destinies" for poor children, as growing income inequality and changing family structure have reduced children's current economic resources and future opportunities.

These changes (and others) have combined to change both the composition of the population and the face of America's poor. Table 1.2 shows that today's non-elderly poor, compared with 1960, are increasingly Latino, foreign born, and single-household heads with children. In 1960, more than 50 percent of the non-elderly poor were children, whereas that number fell to 38 percent in 2010 and 2011. In 1960, 64 percent of the non-elderly poor were white, whereas today only 42 percent are. Similarly, the share of non-elderly poor who are black also fell. In contrast, the share of the non-elderly poor who are Latino or foreign born rose dramatically. In 1960, 77 percent of the non-elderly poor were married and only 15 percent were single with children. In 2010 and 2011, only 32 percent of the non-elderly poor were married and 39 percent were single heads with children. Finally, the percentage of non-elderly poor who had less than a high school degree decreased from 80 to 27 percent from 1960 to 2011.

An important objective of this volume is therefore to understand the extent to which the poverty rates—and other dimensions of Americans' material hardship—have been reduced by War on Poverty policies and programs in a context where economic, demographic, and other countervailing forces contributed to higher poverty rates.

A FIFTY-YEAR RETROSPECTIVE

This volume reviews the legacies of the War on Poverty's major human capital, income support, housing, and medical care policies and programs. Each chapter seeks to understand the extent to which the War on Poverty's investments have paid off or have fallen short. Each chapter also seeks to understand how the War on Poverty changed the well-being of individuals and changed how institutions operate.

The volume's critical reappraisal takes advantage of the longer-term perspective afforded by fifty years of hindsight. The human capital and health programs of the War on Poverty represent a long-term investment which aimed "not only to relieve the symptom of poverty but to cure it, and above all to prevent it." The early retrospectives, such as those by Ginzberg and Solow (1974), Haveman (1977), and Aaron (1978), could not assess the era's long-term effects.

The reappraisal also benefits from the availability of newly released data and improvements in research design. These developments have allowed researchers to better account for the positive and negative effects of economic, demographic, and social forces and, consequently, to provide more precise estimates of some previously unmeasured effects of War on Poverty programs. Each chapter highlights these studies and discusses how social scientists' understanding of the era has evolved since the early 1970s.

The volume is organized into three sections, each of which addresses one major area of War on Poverty programs and policies. We briefly review each chapter and highlight both how much the War on Poverty has accomplished and also how much remains to be done if we are to fulfill the expansive goals that President Johnson set out in 1964.

PART I: INCREASING HUMAN CAPITAL, EMPLOYMENT, AND EARNINGS

If children of poor families can be given skills and motivation, they will not become poor adults. Too many young people are today condemned to grossly inadequate schools and instruction. Many communities lack resources for developing adequate schools or attracting teachers of high quality. . . .

The school must play a larger role in the development of poor youngsters if they are to have, in fact, "equal opportunity." This often means that schooling must start on a preschool basis and include a broad range of more intensive services (Council of Economic Advisers 1964, 75–76).

The four chapters in part I focus on the primary goal of the War on Poverty — expanding opportunities to raise educational attainment and job skills to reduce poverty through increased employment and earnings. This section begins with Chloe Gibbs, Jens Ludwig, and Douglas Miller's chapter 2 review of the record of Head Start, a program that has provided early education and health services to low-income preschoolers since the summer of 1965. Although the program was popular with the public from the outset, the authors document how researchers have struggled to resolve persistent questions about the program's effects on participants. They note that even though Head Start's impacts on test scores erode in the short term, the program has persistent, longer-term effects for participants. However, they caution against evaluating Head Start solely on the basis of students' test scores, because the program also affects noncognitive skills, such as motivation and attitudes, that contribute to longer-term educational achievement and earnings growth. For example, Jens Ludwig and Douglas Miller (2007) find that a 50 to 100 percent increase in Head Start funding is associated with an increase in schooling attainment of about one-half year and a 15 percent increase in the likelihood that participants attend some college. The authors acknowledge that the Head Start program could be improved, but conclude that it can "rightfully be considered a success for much of the past fifty years."

Chapter 3, by Elizabeth Cascio and Sarah Reber, evaluates the effects of Title I of the 1965 Elementary and Secondary Education Act (ESEA), which sharply increased federal funding for K-12 education. Not only were Title I funds explicitly directed toward poorer districts, receipt also required school districts to desegregate their schools to some extent. Using newly collected data, the authors demonstrate that Title I dramatically changed the relationship between poverty and school funding and reduced the gaps in per pupil school spending between poorer and richer states. They also evaluate the relationship between increased Title I funding and school desegregation and report that, by 1966, Title I had prompted many southern school districts to take their first steps toward desegregation. Nonetheless, in the early years, only a small percentage of black students moved to previously all-white schools.

President Nixon ended enforcement of the fund-withholding provisions of the Civil Rights Act, but desegregation efforts were continued by the courts. Several recent studies have found that increased federal funding and school integration are both associated with improved educational and labor market outcomes among blacks (Guryan 2004; Ashenfelter, Collins, and Yoon 2006; Reber 2010; Johnson 2011). Cascio and Reber conclude that the "good news is that gaps — at least between richer and poorer states — in both inputs and outputs have declined dramatically since the War on Poverty began. The bad news is that they are both still quite large."

Chapter 4, by Bridget Terry Long, examines the War on Poverty's policies and programs to make higher education more accessible for those who could not afford it. The Johnson administration dramatically increased federal spending on student aid and transformed the postsecondary financial aid system. New programs included Educational Opportunity Grants, a needs-based program that was the precursor to the Pell grant; the Guaranteed Student Loan Program, which allow students to apply for federally guaranteed private loans; an expansion of federally subsidized loans; and the work study program. Recognizing that financial aid might not be enough to promote access of the disadvantaged to college, War on Poverty programs such as Upward Bound aimed to enhance academic preparation for college among lower income and minority students. These programs continue to operate today.

Long documents that Pell grants have grown substantially since the early 1970s—about 40 percent of all college students receive them today. But she also documents how four-year college costs have increased more rapidly than expected over the last thirty years. Additionally, because the maximum Pell grant has not kept up with either general inflation or the costs of higher education, students have increasingly relied on federally subsidized public and private loans to fill the growing gap between college costs and grants. The increased net cost of college attendance for students from low-income families has been one factor that has prevented them from increasing their college going as rapidly as students from high-income families. Thus, even though the War on Poverty programs have greatly increased access for lower income and minority students over the past fifty years, large disparities in college attendance and completion by income and race-ethnicity remain.

The War on Poverty also sought to increase employment and earnings by expanding job training programs for out-of-school youth and adults. Workforce development was a core component of the *1964 Economic Report*, which presciently noted that "in an economy characterized by continual technological advance, many adults will not be able to earn incomes above the poverty line without new skills and training" (Council of Economic Advisers 1964, 76). Chapter 5, by Harry J. Holzer, examines the evolution of workforce development programs and the extent to which they have raised the employment and earnings of the disadvantaged. He documents the rapid increase in federal spending on employment and training programs in the post–War on Poverty decade. However, after 1980, inflation-adjusted federal spending on workforce development programs declined dramatically.

The nature of these programs has also evolved considerably in the last fifty years, and an extensive evaluation literature has documented their effects. Holzer notes that most studies conclude that even though the benefits of many programs exceed their costs, few have generated large enough increases in educational attainment, employment and earnings to have a significant effect on poverty. He also notes how extensive changes in the labor market in recent decades—labor-saving technological changes, globalization, rising incarceration rates—have made it much more difficult for programs for the disadvantaged to help participants find jobs that pay enough for them to escape poverty.

Holzer concludes that one size does not fit all in terms of program effectiveness.

Programs that are effective for women have often not worked for men, and those that have been effective for adults and youth with relatively strong basic skills and work experience are often not effective for the hardest to employ. He also notes that sectoral programs, which combine skill certification in jobs for which there is high employer demand with additional support services, have shown promise. Nevertheless, because these programs may not meet the needs of the most disadvantaged workers, he concludes with suggestions for promising workforce development programs.

PART II: RAISING INCOMES AND LIVING STANDARDS

The War on Poverty's core strategy for eliminating poverty emphasized increasing human capital to raise the labor market productivity of the poor. One reason that poverty was high, according to Johnson's economic advisers, was that the poor's skills were insufficient to generate higher earnings, even if they worked hard. To complement the human capital and job training programs, Johnson pledged in two addresses to Congress "to assure all citizens of decent living standards regardless of economic reverses or the vicissitudes of human life and health" (1964a). In a later address, he mentioned some of the programs that are the focus of the chapters in part II: "programs to protect those who are especially vulnerable to the ravages of poverty . . . a food stamp program for the needy, coverage for millions not now protected by a minimum wage, new and expanded unemployment benefits for men out of work, a Housing and Community Development bill for those seeking decent homes" (1964b).

Even though Johnson's stated goal was to provide a "hand up" and not a "hand out," some members of his CEA and administrators within the OEO soon emphasized increasing income transfers for the poor. In particular, the rapid growth in caseloads and benefits under Aid to Families with Dependent Children (AFDC) became the focus of intense debate about antipoverty policies. The three papers in part II focus on programs designed to raise the incomes, consumption, living standards, and housing conditions of the poor.

Chapter 6, by Jane Waldfogel, summarizes the evolution of the cash and near-cash safety net for families with children. She begins by reviewing the expansion of Food Stamps (renamed the Supplemental Nutrition Assistance Program in 2008) and the 1966 Child Nutrition Act. She also discusses major cash assistance programs (AFDC and SSI) and the introduction in 1975 and subsequent evolution of the Earned Income Tax Credit (EITC) and child-care subsidies.

Waldfogel emphasizes that the War on Poverty's most enduring imprints on the nation's safety net are its expansion of food and nutrition programs for low-income families with children. She notes that, in comparison with the cash welfare programs, these programs have proven fairly resilient to political pressures and backlash. They have also achieved a solid track record in terms of reducing poverty and food insecurity, improving nutrition, and yielding benefits for child health and development, which may in turn lead to future reductions in poverty.

She also notes that the legacy of the War on Poverty in terms of cash welfare is more problematic. One year into the War on Poverty, Johnson and his key administrators, although favoring opportunities over handouts, were already discussing the need for a guaranteed minimum income for low-income families with children. For low-income families with disabled children, the SSI program meets this goal. For other low-income families, the Johnson-era proposals never came to fruition. Waldfogel notes that the United States is exceptional in this regard with respect to other industrialized countries. She concludes that child poverty, according to the official poverty statistics is lower today than it was fifty years ago (20 percent versus 27 percent) and racial gaps are smaller (the African American poverty rate is twice that of whites today, versus three times as high in 1959), but winning the war on poverty remains an unfulfilled vision.

One of the most successful legacies of the War on Poverty era is the dramatic decline in the official poverty rate of the elderly. In the mid-1960s, the poverty rate for persons over sixty-five was roughly twice that for adults between eighteen and sixty-four. Today, the poverty rate among the elderly is lower than the rate for adults. In chapter 7, Kathleen McGarry reviews the evolution of the social safety net for the elderly and documents how new legislation and expansions of Social Security benefits contributed to this development. These include the enactment of the Older Americans Act of 1965, several congressional actions that substantially increased Social Security benefit levels and then indexed them to inflation, and the passage in 1974 of the federal Supplemental Security Income (SSI) program that provides the elderly poor and the blind and disabled with a guaranteed annual income. SSI replaced less-generous state Old Age Assistance programs and greatly expanded the access of the poor elderly, particularly in southern states, to public benefits.

Despite the rapid decline in poverty among all groups of elderly persons, McGarry documents great remaining disparities in poverty rates among the elderly, particularly widows and African Americans. She also notes that the low-income elderly spend a substantial share of their income on medical expenses not covered by Medicare and Medicaid. The supplemental poverty measure (SPM), unlike the official poverty measure, subtracts these out-of-pocket medical expenditures from income, thereby raising their SPM poverty rate to roughly the same level as that of the non-elderly. Nonetheless, McGarry concludes that the War on Poverty has been a great success for the elderly.

Another legacy of the War on Poverty is its impact on housing. In chapter 8, Edgar O. Olsen and Jens Ludwig note that the War on Poverty's housing initiatives were designed to increase the stock of low-income housing, improve its quality, and reduce the economic and racial segregation of low-income families. About half of all public housing units were authorized during or shortly after the Johnson administration. Notably, a 1965 amendment to the Housing Act of 1937 for the first time allowed public housing authorities to pay a portion of the rent of the poor in private units that met minimum housing standards—a program that evolved into what is now called the Section 8 Housing Voucher Program.

A lasting, and underappreciated legacy of the War on Poverty, according to Olsen and Ludwig, is a substantial increase in the number of households receiving housing assistance. As is true for Food Stamps and the EITC, housing assistance is not counted in the official poverty measure, but it is counted in the SPM. Another legacy is the shift in policy away from the construction of public housing units toward the use of housing vouchers, which have improved the efficiency of housing assistance by lowering costs per participant and allowing a greater number of families to be served with a given budget.

Another important legacy of the era's housing policies is its interaction with the provisions of the Civil Rights Act, which contributed to reductions in racial residential segregation. Aside from these successes, however, they note that the effects of housing policies on factors that were expected to result from improved housing quality and reduced residential segregation, like better educational and employment outcomes, have been understudied and remain unknown.

PART III: IMPROVING ACCESS TO MEDICAL CARE AND HEALTH

The poor receive inadequate medical care, from birth to old age. Additionally, poverty is perpetuated by poor health, malnutrition, and chronic disabilities: Many aged persons are confronted by medical needs beyond their financial means. Passage of the program to provide hospital insurance for the aged under the social security system is an urgent immediate step (Council of Economic Advisers 1964, 76).

The two chapters in part III address the War on Poverty goal that has consumed an ever-increasing share of the federal budget over the past fifty years: increasing access to medical care and improving the nation's health. If the War on Poverty's legacy is measured in terms of spending or coverage, Medicare and Medicaid stand out. For example, in 2011, about one-third of all Americans were covered by either Medicare or Medicaid—this includes almost everyone sixty-five or older and almost two-thirds of children. Chapter 9 focuses on the effects of health programs for non-elderly adults and children, and chapter 10 addresses their effects on the elderly. Both chapters document that even though the poor today are still less likely to have access to medical care and are more likely to have health problems than the affluent, these disparities are much narrower than they were before the War on Poverty was declared.

Chapter 9, by Barbara Wolfe, describes the legacy of the War on Poverty with respect to access to medical care and improved health among non-elderly adults and children. This era's reforms significantly expanded the provision of medical services (the supply side) and also increased the ability of households to pay for these services (the demand side); they continue to define the medical safety net today.

On the supply side, neighborhood health centers, known today as community health centers (CHCs) or federally qualified health centers (FQHCs), were first funded under the 1964 Economic Opportunity Act to increase the convenience and availability of subsidized medical care for underserved populations. Today, these centers serve about 20 million patients and are slated to double their capacity to 40 million under the 2010 Patient Protection and Affordable Care Act (ACA).

On the demand side, Medicaid, which is funded jointly by the states and the federal government, was and has remained the primary program to extend health insurance to poor families and provide long-term or nursing home care to seniors. Today, Medicaid serves around 60 million people, including children, pregnant women, people with disabilities and chronic health problems, and low-income seniors. Combined with recent initiatives, such as the 1997 Child Health Insurance Program (CHIP) that extended health insurance coverage to low-income children who do not qualify for Medicaid, the percentage of children who are uninsured has fallen relative to the percentage of adults who are uninsured. In 2011, 9.4 percent of all children were uninsured, compared with 21 percent of adults between thirty-five and forty-four.

These programs, Wolfe concludes, have contributed to large reductions in infant mortality and increased life expectancy, in part because the Johnson administration demanded that, to receive federal funds, hospitals desegregate. Nonetheless, large disparities remain in health outcomes between the poor and the nonpoor. Wolfe notes that in 2010, the poor remain more than twice as likely to be uninsured as the nonpoor, 29 versus 13 percent. Her chapter concludes by drawing lessons from the War on Poverty era for the implementation of the 2010 ACA.

Chapter 10, by Katherine Swartz, documents the legacy of the War on Poverty's health programs for the elderly. Primary among these is Medicare, which has provided health insurance coverage to all individuals sixty-five and older since 1966. Part A (hospital insurance) is financed primarily by the payroll tax, and Part B (physician services) by monthly premiums paid by the elderly and general federal revenues. For the elderly poor, Medicaid covers part B payments and plays an important role in funding long-term care services, both in nursing homes and in the homes of the elderly.

Both programs redefined the health and financial risks facing the (poor and nonpoor) elderly in the 1960s, and they continue to do so today. Both decrease the risk of financial ruin for the elderly due to the high costs of medical care, and both decrease the risk that the elderly would not be able to afford the medical care they needed. As a result, all of the elderly now have health insurance, versus only about half in the mid-1960s, and health insurance for the elderly is no longer linked to employment. Thus, Medicare has facilitated retirement without the loss of health insurance. More controversial is that the higher-income and better-educated elderly are more likely than others to receive medical procedures that improve the quality of their life. As rising health-care costs have strained federal coffers, the share of Medicare benefits going to the high-income elderly have made the financing of Medicare increasingly contentious.

Swartz concludes that Medicare created large benefits for the country as a whole. The program was a significant factor in the racial integration of hospitals. Its funding fostered the development of medical treatment options, some of which have increased life expectancy and improved the quality of life for the elderly and non-elderly. Medicare, as the largest single payer of health care, has also facilitated the implementation of new initiatives for delivering medical care including improvements in quality and record keeping and reductions in waste. But these benefits have come at a high budgetary cost. An important lesson from the War on Poverty era is that the increased coverage for medical treatments may have the unintended consequences of increasing medical costs for all Americans, not just the elderly. Swartz concludes with a discussion of options for slowing the growth of medical costs and restructuring the financing of Medicare and Medicaid.

CONCLUSION

This volume offers a fifty-year retrospective on many of the legacies of the War on Poverty, noting many remarkable and underappreciated successes. The chapters also note policy missteps, implementation failures, and the often unanticipated consequences of federal initiatives. They offer lessons for reforming existing programs and suggest new antipoverty initiatives.

Perhaps the greatest failure of the War on Poverty planners was their inability to predict fundamental changes in the economy that lowered employment and distributed the gains from economic growth unevenly. Since the 1970s, unemployment rates have rarely fallen below 5 percent and earnings growth has been slow at the bottom of the skill distribution. If economic growth had continued to lift the incomes of less-skilled workers at the same rate as in the two decades before the War on Poverty began, poverty rates would be much lower today (Danziger and Gottschalk 1995; Danziger 2007). Understanding these broader economic changes is important for understanding the War on Poverty's legacies. Many of the era's programs and policies significantly reduced poverty and increased opportunities, even if they were not large enough to offset the increases in poverty due to other economic and demographic changes. Another success relates to civil rights. By making funding contingent on compliance with the Civil Rights Act, the Johnson administration used the power of the federal purse to foster racial integration and reduce racial inequalities in opportunities in schools, hospitals, the labor market and housing.

These successes do not constitute a defense of the status quo. As the chapters highlight, many programs could be better targeted, made more efficient, and be better implemented. A good deal of learning about antipoverty policies and programs has occurred since Johnson launched his grand experiment. Fifty years after the War on Poverty's declaration, the war has not been won, but poverty rates are lower today than they would have been had the War on Poverty never been declared. Nonetheless, poverty and racial inequalities remain pressing social problems and Johnson's vision of the "elimination of poverty" remains unfulfilled.

DATA APPENDIX

Processing of the March Current Population Survey Data   The Current Population Survey (CPS) datasets for the earnings analyses are available at http://economics .mit.edu/faculty/dautor/data/autkatkear08 (accessed August 15, 2012). David Autor, Lawrence Katz, and Melissa Kearney (2008) used the March CPS for 1964 to 2007—covering earnings years 1963 to 2006—for workers age sixteen to sixty-four with up to thirty-nine years of potential experience whose class of work in their longest job during the earnings year was either private or government employment. As in their analysis, we limit our sample to full-time, full-year men, defined as those who work at least thirty-five hours per week (using the full-time worker flag) and forty-plus weeks in the prior year. Full-time hourly earnings for wage-salary workers are calculated as the annual earnings divided by the product of weeks worked and usual hours worked per week. Allocated earnings observations are excluded after (sample year) 1966 using family earnings allocation flags (1964 to 1975) or individual earnings allocation flags (1976 forward), except where allocation flags are unavailable. Workers earning below $1.675 per hour in 1982 dollars are dropped. Hourly wages exceeding 1/1400th of the top-coded value of total labor earnings are recoded to be equal to this cutoff.

Following Autor, Katz, and Kearney, we use the following weights. Full-time hourly earnings are weighted by the product of the CPS sampling weight, weeks worked, and usual hours worked per week in the prior year.

Following Autor, Katz, and Kearney, we adjust as follows for top-coding. Before the March 1988 CPS, all wage and salary income was reported in a single variable, which was top-coded at values between $50,000 and $99,999 in years 1964 to 1987. For these cases, we multiply the top-coded earnings value by 1.5. Commencing in 1989, wage and salary incomes were collected in two separate earnings variables, corresponding to primary and secondary labor earnings. After adjusting for top-coding, we sum these values to calculate total wage and salary earnings. Starting in 1988, top-codes are handled as follows. For the primary earnings variable, top-coded values are reported at the top-code maximum up to 1995. We multiply these values by 1.5. Starting in 1996, top-coded primary earnings values are assigned the mean of all top-coded earners. In these cases, we reassign the top-coded value and, again, multiply by 1.5. For the secondary earnings value, the top-coded maximum is set at $90,000, $95,000, or $99,999 from 1988 to 1995, falls to $25,000 for 1996 through 2002, and rises to $35,000 in 2003 through 2006. We again use the top-coded value multiplied by 1.5. Earnings numbers are deflated using the personal consumption expenditure (PCE) deflator to 2011 dollars.

In 1964 through 1975, weeks worked and usual hours worked per week in the prior year are not available. We follow Autor, Katz, and Kearney, who used the data from 1976 to 1978 to impute these variables. Between 1964 and 1975, the variable weeks worked last year is available only in intervals of weeks. They calculated the mean weeks worked last year by race and sex from 1976 to 1978 for each interval and imputed those means for the years from 1964 to 1975. For hours, first they created hours' intervals using hours worked last week for 1964 to 1975 and 1976 to 1978 data. Then, using data for 1976 to 1978, they regressed usual hours worked per week on dummies of hours' intervals, and dummies of full-time workers, labor force status, and their interactions. Finally, they imputed the usual hours of 1964–1975 using the coefficients obtained from the 1976 to 1978 data, the hours intervals generated from hours worked last week and the same dummies as used in the regressions.

Processing of the Census and American Community Survey Data   We use the Census Integrated Public Use Microdata Series (IPUMS) 1 percent extracts for 1950, 1960, and 1970, 5 percent extracts for 1980, 1990, and 2000, and 2001–2009 American Community Survey (ACS) data available at http://www.ipums.org (accessed August 15, 2012). Our sample includes respondents age sixteen through sixty-four who were not in armed forces and did not live in group quarters. For the analyses of earnings, we exclude the self-employed and unpaid family workers. The analyses are limited to full-time, full-year workers, defined as those working at least thirty-five hours per week (using hours worked last week for 1950 through 1970, usual hours worked per week for 1980 through 2010) and forty-plus weeks in the prior year. As in the CPS, our labor supply measure is the product of weeks worked and usual hours worked per week in the prior year. Workers with missing hours or weeks are dropped when either of these variables is missing. Weeks worked in the prior years are available in 1950, 1980, 1990, and 2000 through 2007. Usual hours worked per week in the prior years are available in 1980, 1990, and 2000 through 2010.

For years when weeks or hours are not available, we impute labor supply using the mean of workers of the same sex, race (white, black, and other), occupation, education (the highest grade of school completed is less than twelve, the highest grade of school completed is twelve or with high school diploma or equivalent, some college, four years of college and more), and worked weeks interval (available through all years) group in years when weeks and hours are available. For cells that cannot be matched with 1980 data due to the missing weeks' intervals in that year, we assign the mean for the sex-race-education-occupation group. We use the 1990 Census Bureau occupational codes. When doing the imputations, we use the broad occupational categories implicit in the 1990 scheme: managerial and professional (000–200); technical, sales, and administrative (201–400); service (401–470); farming, forestry, and fishing (471–500); precision production, craft, and repairers (501–700); operatives and laborers (701–900); Nonoccupational responses (900–999). Weeks in 1960 and 1970 are imputed using the 1980 data, and weeks in 2008 through 2010 are imputed using the data in 2007. Hours in 1950, 1960, and 1970 are imputed using the data in 1980.

Hourly wages are calculated as total wage and salary income divided by annual hours of work. We drop the bottom 1 percent of hourly earners and multiply hourly wages of top-coded earners by 1.5. We limit the maximum hourly wage (via truncation) to 1.5 times the maximum annual income amount divided by 1,750 (thirty-five hours per week for fifty hours per year). All calculations are weighted by the product of census person weights and calculated or imputed annual hours of labor supply. Wages are deflated to 2011 dollars using the PCE deflator.

Figure 1.3. Data for 2010: Martin et al. 2012. Births: Final data for 2010. *National Vital Statistics Reports* 61(1): table I-4. http://www.cdc.gov/nchs/data/nvsr/nvsr60/nvsr60_07.pdf (accessed October 12, 2012).

2009: Martin et al. 2011. Births: Final data for 2009 *National Vital Statistics Reports* 60(1). http://www.cdc.gov/nchs/data/nvsr/nvsr60/nvsr60_01.pdf (accessed October 12, 2012).

2008: Martin et al. 2010. Births: Final data for 2008. *National Vital Statistics Reports* 59(1). http://www.cdc.gov/nchs/data/nvsr/nvsr59/nvsr59_01.pdf (accessed October 12, 2012).

2007: Martin, Hamilton, Sutton et al. 2010. Births: Final data for 2007. *National Vital Statistics Reports* 58(24): table 18 http://www.cdc.gov/nchs/data/nvsr/nvsr58/nvsr58_24.pdf (accessed October 12, 2012).

2006: Martin, Hamilton, Sutton et al. 2009. Births: Final data for 2006. *National Vital Statistics Reports* 56(6): table 18. http://www.cdc.gov/nchs/data/nvsr/nvsr57/nvsr57_07.pdf (accessed October 12, 2012).

2005: Hamilton, Martin, and Ventura 2007. Births: Final data for 2005. *National Vital Statistics Reports* 56(6): table 18. http://www.cdc.gov/nchs/data/nvsr/nvsr56/nvsr56_06.pdf (accessed October 12, 2012).

2004: Martin, Hamilton, Sutton et al. 2006. Births: Final data for 2004. *National Vital Statistics Reports* 55(1): table 18. http://www.cdc.gov/nchs/data/nvsr/nvsr55/nvsr55_01.pdf (accessed October 12, 2012).

2003: Martin, Hamilton, Sutton et al. 2005. Births: Final data for 2003. *National Vital Statistics Reports* 54(2): tables 13, 14, 17. http://www.cdc.gov/nchs/data/nvsr/nvsr54/nvsr54_02.pdf (accessed October 12, 2012).

2002: Martin et al. 2003. Births: Final data for 2002. *National Vital Statistics Reports* 52(10): table 17. http://www.cdc.gov/nchs/data/nvsr/nvsr52/nvsr52_10.pdf (accessed October 12, 2012).

2001: Martin et al. 2002. Births: Final data for 2001. *National Vital Statistics Reports* 51(2): table 17. http://www.cdc.gov/nchs/data/nvsr/nvsr51/nvsr51_02.pdf (accessed October 12, 2012).

2000: Martin et al. 2002. Births: Final data for 2000. *National Vital Statistics Reports* 50(5): table 17. http://www.cdc.gov/nchs/data/nvsr/nvsr50/nvsr50_05.pdf (accessed October 12, 2012).

1999: Ventura et al. 2001. Births: Final data for 1999. *National Vital Statistics Reports* 49(1): table 17. http://www.cdc.gov/nchs/data/nvsr/nvsr49/nvsr49_01.pdf (accessed October 12, 2012).

1960 through 1998: Ventura and Bachrach 2000; *National Vital Statistics Reports* 48(16): table 4. http://www.cdc.gov/nchs/data/nvsr/nvsr48/nvs48_16.pdf (accessed October 12, 2012).

The authors thank William Collins, Harry Holzer, Hilary Hoynes, Robert Margo, Eugene Smolensky, Gavin Wright, and two anonymous reviewers for very helpful comments on a previous draft and Johannes Norling, Xiaoqing Song, and Austin Davis for research assistance. This project was made possible by funds provided to the National Poverty Center at the University of Michigan by the Office of the Assistant Secretary for Planning and Evaluation, U.S. Department of Health and Human Services; the Ford Foundation; the Russell Sage Foundation; and the University of Michigan's Office of the Vice President for Research; College of Letters, Sciences, and Arts; and Department of Economics.

NOTES

1. The effectiveness of federal policy in the context of employment remains more elusive. In the case of blacks' labor market earnings, John Donohue and James Heckman conclude that "the precise mechanism through which Federal pressure was translated into black economic gains is not yet clear" (1991, 1607) — especially given the relatively small budget and scale of the Equal Employment Opportunity Commission (EEOC) and the Office of Federal Contract Compliance (OFCC).

2. The poverty thresholds were originally developed in 1963 and 1964 by Mollie Orshansky, an economist in the Social Security Administration (see U.S. Census Bureau 2012b). In May of 1965, the OEO adopted Orshansky's poverty lines as the official poverty measure and analysts constructed poverty rates for 1959 using the 1960 census data (for a more detailed history, see Fisher 1992).

3. Several hypotheses suggest the reasons Johnson adopted poverty as his domestic agenda. One is that the implementation of the War on Poverty reflects his long-suppressed humanitarian agenda. Robert Caro, Johnson's biographer, notes that "Throughout Lyndon Johnson's life, there had been hints of what he might do with great power, should he ever succeed in attaining it . . . hints of compassion for the downtrodden, and of a passion to raise them up; hints that he might use power not only to manipulate others but to help others — to help, moreover, those who most needed help" (2002, xxi).

   Another hypothesis is that Johnson perceived the War on Poverty as a bold political maneuver to emerge from Kennedy's shadow and build a new longer-term electoral consensus, much as Roosevelt had tried to use New Deal funds (Wright 1974; Couch and Shugart 1998; Wallis 1987, 1998, 2001; Fishback, Kantor, and Wallis 2003; Fishback and Wallis 2012). Supporting this view is Johnson's record of political Machiavellianism. According to Caro, "Johnson's ambition was uncommon — in the degree to which it was unencumbered by even the slightest excess weight of ideology, of philosophy, of principles, of beliefs" (1982, 275).

   Yet another hypothesis is that the burst of social legislation passed because Southern members of Congress relented. Lee Alston and Joseph Ferrie (1993, 1999) note that the mechanization of cotton harvesting should have reduced the incentives of the southerners in Congress to oppose federal social policies. "The difference in the 1960s was that rather than blocking legislation that threatened their interests, as [southern members of Congress] had since the New Deal, they now sought to alter legislation in ways that encouraged migration out of the South by farm workers rendered superfluous by mechanization. The Great Society programs of the Johnson administration were crafted by southerners... in order to reduce the burden on local elites that unemployed farm workers would have imposed" (Alston and Ferrie 2007, 503).

Assessing the importance of these competing (but not mutually exclusive) accounts is difficult because ample documentary evidence and oral history interviews provide some support for them all. Johnson, a masterful politician, made promises to everyone and would "cajole and plead and threaten and lie" (Caro 2002, xxiii). The War on Poverty thus reflects not only his difficult-to-discern motivation, but also the changing constraints in Congress and the political realities of his presidency (Bailey and Duquette 2012).

4. This publicity of white, Appalachian poverty contrasts sharply with the War on Poverty's later racialization. As Hugh Heclo notes, "Social programs originally justified in terms of advancing individual opportunity soon were perceived to be, and in part became, means of group advancement for blacks. Before any War on Poverty programs were in place . . . the Watts riot of August 1965 had begun the process of alienating white support from antipoverty efforts" (1984, 408).

5. James Tobin, "It Can Be Done? Conquering Poverty in the U.S. by 1976," *New Republic*, June 3, 1967, pp. 14–18.

6. About 30 percent of all of the elderly were poor in the early 1960s.

7. James Reston, "The Problem of Pessimism in the Poverty Program," *New York Times*, January 10, 1965, p. E12.

8. Many empirical studies by economists have found that War on Poverty programs have had some negative effects on work, savings and marriage. However, the magnitudes of these effects in the short term tend to be smaller than the programs' antipoverty effects (Danziger, Haveman, and Plotnick 1981; Ben-Shalom, Moffitt, and Scholz 2012).

9. According to the Census Bureau's supplemental poverty measure, which counts non-cash government benefits and tax refunds as income, these programs significantly reduce poverty. However, the supplemental poverty measure also raises the poverty line and subtracts work-related child care and transportation expenses and out-of-pocket medical costs from income. As a result, the supplemental poverty rate is slightly higher overall than the official rate in any year (Short 2011).

10. Poverty is measured based on total family income from all sources. It has been well documented (for example, Danziger and Gottschalk 1995), however, that slow growth and rising inequality in male earnings in the 1970s and 1980s were poverty-increasing. In contrast, increased earnings of women continued to be poverty-reducing over these years.

11. David Autor, Lawrence Katz, and Melissa Kearney (2008) show that weekly earnings of a similar sample of full-time men grew by only 10 percent at the 10th percentile but by over 60 percent at the 90th percentile. By contrast, our series show a smaller increase in hourly wages at the 90th percentile. Autor et al. also show that the increased earnings inequality among women was even more dramatic. Our wage series also correspond closely to Chunhui Juhn, Kevin Murphy, and Brooks Pierce (1993) who document that the real wages of workers at the 10th percentile fell by roughly 5 percent from 1963 to 1988.

REFERENCES

Aaron, Henry. 1978. *Politics and the Professors: The Great Society in Perspective*. Washington, D.C.: Brookings Institution Press.

Almond, Douglas, Jr., Kenneth Y. Chay, and Michael Greenstone. forthcoming. "Civil Rights, the War on Poverty, and Black-White Convergence in Infant Mortality in the Rural South and Mississippi." *American Economic Review*.

Alston, Lee J., and Joseph P. Ferrie. 1993. "Paternalism in Agricultural Labor Contracts in the U.S. South: Implications for the Growth of the Welfare State." *American Economic Review* 83(4): 852–76.

———. 1999. *Southern Paternalism and the American Welfare State: Economics, Politics, and the Institutions in the South, 1865–1965*. Cambridge: Cambridge University Press.

———. 2007. "Shaping Welfare Policy: The Role of the South." In *Government and the American Economy*, edited by Price Fishback et al. Chicago: University of Chicago Press.

Ashenfelter, Orley, William J. Collins, and Albert Yoon. 2006. "Evaluating the Role of Brown v. Board of Education in School Equalization, Desegregation, and the Income of African Americans." *American Law and Economics Review* 8(2): 213–48.

Autor, David H., Lawrence F. Katz, and Melissa S. Kearney. 2008. "Trends in U.S. Wage Inequality: Revising the Revisionists." *Review of Economics and Statistics* 90(2): 300–23.

Bailey, Martha J., and Nicolas J. Duquette. 2012. "How Johnson Fought the War on Poverty: Evidence from the Community Action Program" University of Michigan Working Paper, available at www-personal.umich.edu/~baileymj/Bailey-Duquette.pdf.

Ben-Shalom, Y., Robert Moffitt, and Jon Karl Scholz. 2012. "An Assessment of the Effect of Antipoverty Programs in the United States." In *Oxford Handbook of the Economics of Poverty*, edited by P. Jefferson. Oxford: Oxford University Press.

Cancian, Maria, and Sheldon Danziger. 2009. *Changing Poverty, Changing Policies*. New York: Russell Sage Foundation.

Caro, Robert A. 1982. *The Path to Power*. New York: Knopf.

———. 2002. *Master of the Senate*. New York: Knopf.

———. 2012. *The Passage of Power*. New York: Alfred A. Knopf.

Carter, David. 2009. *The Music Has Gone Out of the Movement: Civil Rights and the Johnson Administration, 1965–1968*. Chapel Hill: University of North Carolina Press.

Cascio, Elizabeth, Nora Gordon, Ethan Lewis, and Sarah Reber. 2010. "Paying for Progress: Conditional Grants and the Desegregation of Southern Schools." *Quarterly Journal of Economics* 125(1): 445–82.

Couch, Jim F., and William F. Shugart. 1998. *The Political Economy of the New Deal*. New York: Edward Elgar.

Council of Economic Advisers. 1964. *Economic Report of the President*. Washington: U.S. Government Printing Office. Available at: http://www.presidency.ucsb.edu/economic_reports/1964.pdf (accessed October 15, 2012).

Danziger, Sheldon. 2007. "Fighting Poverty Revisited: What Did Researchers Know 40 Years Ago? What Do we Know Today?" *Focus: Institute for Research on Poverty, University of Wisconsin* 25(1): 3–11.

Danziger, Sheldon, and Peter Gottschalk. 1995. *America Unequal*. Cambridge, Mass.: Harvard University Press and Russell Sage Foundation.

Danziger, Sheldon, Robert Haveman, and Robert Plotnick. 1981. "How Income Transfer Programs Affect Work, Savings, and the Income Distribution." *Journal of Economic Literature* 19 (September): 975–1028.

Davies, Gareth. 1996. *From Opportunity to Entitlement: The Transformation and Decline of Great Society Liberalism.* Lawrence: University Press of Kansas.

Donohue, John J., and James Heckman. 1991. "Continuous Versus Episodic Change: The Impact of Civil Rights Policy on the Economic Status of Blacks." *Journal of Economic Literature* 29 (December): 1603–43.

Ellwood, David T., and Christopher Jencks. 2004. "The Uneven Spread of Single Parent Families: What Do We Know? Where Do We Look for Answers?" In *Social Inequality*, edited by Kathryn Neckerman. Cambridge, Mass.: Harvard University.

Fisher, Gordon M. 1992. "The Development and History of the Poverty Thresholds." *Social Security Bulletin* 55(4): 3–14.

Fishback, Price, Shawn Kantor, and John Wallis. 2003. "Can the New Deal's Three R's Be Rehabilitated? A Program-by-Program, County-by-County Analysis," *Explorations in Economic History* 40(3): 278–307.

Fishback, Price, and John Wallis. 2012. "What Was New About the New Deal?" In *The Great Depression of the 1930s: Lessons for Today*, edited by Nicolas Crafts and Peter Fearon. Oxford: Oxford University Press.

Galbraith, John Kenneth. 1958. *The Affluent Society.* New York: New American Library.

Germany, Kent B. 2007. *New Orleans After the Promises: Poverty, Citizenship, and the Search for the Great Society.* Athens: University of Georgia Press.

Gettleman, Marvin E., and David Mermelstein. 1966. "Sargent Shriver to the House Subcommittee on the War on Poverty, April 12, 1965." In *The Great Society Reader: The Failure of American Liberalism.* New York: Random House.

Gillette, Michael L. 1996. *Launching the War on Poverty: An Oral History.* New York: Twayne Publishers.

Ginzberg, Eli, and Robert M. Solow. 1974. *The Great Society: Lessons for the Future.* New York: Basic Books.

Guryan, Jonathan. 2004. "Desegregation and Black Dropout Rates." *American Economic Review* 94(4): 919–43.

Haddad, William. 1965. "Mr. Shriver and the Savage Politics of Poverty." *Harpers* 231 (December): 43–46.

Hamilton, B. E., Martin, J. A., and Ventura, S. J. 2007. "Births: Final Data for 2005." *National Vital Statistics Reports* 56(6), table 18. Hyattsville, Md.: National Center for Health Statistics. Available at: http://www.cdc.gov/nchs/data/nvsr/nvsr56/nvsr56_06.pdf (accessed October 12, 2012).

Harrington, Michael. 1962. *The Other America: Poverty in the United States.* New York: Macmillan.

Haveman, Robert, ed. 1977. *A Decade of Federal Antipoverty Programs: Achievements, Failures, and Lessons.* New York: Academic Press

———. 1987. *Poverty Policy and Poverty Research: The Great Society and the Social Sciences.* Madison: University of Wisconsin Press.

Heclo, Hugh. 1984. "Poverty Politics." In *Confronting Poverty*, edited by Sheldon H. Danziger, Gary D. Sandefur, and Daniel H. Weinberg. Cambridge, Mass.. Harvard University Press.

Heller, Walter F. 1970. "Oral History Interview 1, February 20." Austin, Tex.: Lyndon B. Johnson Library.

Holzer, Harry J. 2009. "Collateral Costs: Effects of Incarceration on Employment and Earnings Among Young Workers." In *Do Prisons Make Us Safer? The Benefits and Costs of the Prison Boom*, edited by Steven Raphael and Michael A. Stoll. New York: Russell Sage Foundation.

Johnson, Lyndon B. 1964a. "Annual Message to Congress on the State of the Union." January 8, 1964. Austin, Tex.: Lyndon B. Johnson Library. Available at: http://www.lbjlib.utexas.edu/johnson/archives.hom/speeches.hom/640108.asp (accessed October 15, 2012).

———. 1964b "Special Message to Congress Proposing a War on the Sources of Poverty." March 16, 1964. Santa Barbara: University of California, American Presidency Project. Available at: http://www.presidency.ucsb.edu/ws/index.php?pid=26109 (accessed October 15, 2012).

———. 1965. "Commencement Address at Howard University: 'To Fulfill These Rights.'" June 4, 1965. Austin, Tex.: Lyndon B. Johnson Library. Available at: http://www.lbjlib.utexas.edu/johnson/archives.hom/speeches.hom/650604.asp (accessed October 15, 2012).

Johnson, Rucker C. 2011. "Long-Run Impacts of School Desegregation and School Quality on Adult Attainments." Working paper 16664. Cambridge, Mass.: National Bureau of Economic Research.

Jordan, Barbara C., and Elspeth D. Rostow. 1986. *The Great Society: A Twenty-Year Critique*. Austin, Tex.: Lyndon B. Johnson School of Public Affairs.

Juhn, Chinhui, Kevin Murphy, and Brooks Pierce. 1993. "Wage Inequality and the Rise in Returns to Skill." *Journal of Political Economy* 101(3): 410–42.

Katznelson. Ira. 1989. "Was the Great Society a Lost Opportunity?" In *The Rise and Fall of the New Deal Order: 1930–1980*, edited by Steve Fraser and Gary Gerstle. Princeton, N.J.: Princeton University Press.

Lampman, Robert. 1959. "The Low Income Population and Economic Growth." U.S. Congress, Joint Economic Committee study paper no. 12. Washington: Government Printing Office.

———. 1971. *Ends and Means of Reducing Income Poverty*. Chicago: Markham.

Levitan, Sar A. 1969. *The Great Society's Poor Law: A New Approach to Poverty*. Baltimore, Md.: Johns Hopkins University Press.

Ludwig, Jens, and Douglas L. Miller. 2007. "Does Head Start Improve Children's Life Chances? Evidence from a Regression Discontinuity Design." *Quarterly Journal of Economics* 122(1): 159–208.

Martin, J. A., Hamilton, B. E., Sutton, P. D., et al. 2005. "Births: Final Data for 2003." *National Vital Statistics Reports* 54(2), tables 13, 14, and 17. Hyattsville, Md.: National Center for Health Statistics. Available at: http://www.cdc.gov/nchs/data/nvsr/nvsr54/nvsr54_02.pdf (accessed October 12, 2012).

———. 2006. "Births: Final Data for 2004." *National Vital Statistics Reports* 55(1), table 18.

Hyattsville, Md.: National Center for Health Statistics. Available at: http://www.cdc .gov/nchs/data/nvsr/nvsr55/nvsr55_01.pdf (accessed October 12, 2012).

———. 2009. "Births: Final Data for 2006." *National Vital Statistics Reports* 56(6), table 18. Hyattsville, Md.: National Center for Health Statistics. Available at: http://www.cdc .gov/nchs/data/nvsr/nvsr57/nvsr57_07.pdf (accessed October 12, 2012).

———. 2010. "Births: Final Data for 2007." *National Vital Statistics Reports* 58(24), table 18. Hyattsville, Md.: National Center for Health Statistics. Available at: http://www.cdc .gov/nchs/data/nvsr/nvsr58/nvsr58_24.pdf (accessed October 12, 2012).

Martin, J. A., Hamilton, B. E., Sutton, P. D., Ventura, S. J., Mathews, T. J., and Osterman, M. J. K. 2010. "Births: Final Data for 2008." *National Vital Statistics Reports* 59(1). Hyatts-ville, Md.: National Center for Health Statistics. Available at: http://www.cdc.gov/ nchs/data/nvsr/nvsr59/nvsr59_01.pdf (accessed October 12, 2012).

Martin, J. A., Hamilton, B. E., Sutton, P. D., Ventura, S. J., Menacker, F., and Munson, M. L. 2003. "Births: Final Data for 2002." *National Vital Statistics Reports* 52(10), table 17. Hyatts-ville, Md.: National Center for Health Statistics. Available at: http://www.cdc.gov/ nchs/data/nvsr/nvsr52/nvsr52_10.pdf (accessed October 12, 2012).

Martin, J. A., Hamilton, B. E., Ventura, S. J., Menacker, F., and Park, M. M. 2002. "Births: Final Data for 2000." *National Vital Statistics Reports* 50(5), table 17. Hyattsville, Md.: Na-tional Center for Health Statistics. Available at: http://www.cdc.gov/nchs/data/nvsr/ nvsr50/nvsr50_05.pdf (accessed October 12, 2012).

Martin, J. A., Hamilton, B. E., Ventura, S. J., Menacker, F., Park, M. M., and Sutton, P. D. 2002. "Births: Final Data for 2001." *National Vital Statistics Reports* 51(2), table 17. Hyatts-ville, Md.: National Center for Health Statistics. Available at: http://www.cdc.gov/ nchs/data/nvsr/nvsr51/nvsr51_02.pdf (accessed October 12, 2012).

Martin, J. A., Hamilton, B. E., Ventura, S. J., Osterman, M. J. K., Kirmeyer, S., Mathews, T. J., and Wilson, E. C. 2011. "Births: Final Data for 2009." *National Vital Statistics Reports* 60(1). Hyattsville, Md.: National Center for Health Statistics. Available at: http://www.cdc .gov/nchs/data/nvsr/nvsr60/nvsr60_01.pdf (accessed October 12, 2012).

Martin J. A., Hamilton B. E., Ventura S. J., Osterman M. J. K., Wilson E. C., and Mathews, T. J. 2012. "Births: Final Data for 2010." *National Vital Statistics Reports* 61(1), table I-4. Hyattsville, Md.: National Center for Health Statistics. Available at: http://www.cdc .gov/nchs/data/nvsr/nvsr60/nvsr60_07.pdf (accessed October 12, 2012).

McKee, Guian A. 2011. "'This Government Is with Us': Lyndon Johnson and the Grassroots War on Poverty." In *The War on Poverty: A New Grassroots History 1864–1980*, edited by Annelise Orleck and Lisa Gayle Hazirjian. Athens: University of Georgia Press.

McLanahan, Sara. 2004. "Diverging Destinies: How Children Fare Under the Second Demo-graphic Transition." *Demography* 41(4): 607–27.

Meyer, Bruce, and James X. Sullivan. 2012. "Winning the War: Poverty from the Great Soci-ety to the Great Recession." In *Brookings Papers on Economic Activity Fall 2012*, edited by David H. Romer and Justin Wolfers. Washington, D.C.: Brookings Institution.

Moffitt, Robert. 1998. "The Effect of Welfare on Marriage and Fertility: What Do We Know and What Do We Need to Know? In *Welfare, the Family, and Reproductive Behavior*, edited by Robert Moffitt. Washington, D.C.: National Academies Press.

Murray, Charles. 1984. *Losing Ground: American Social Policy, 1950–1980*. New York: Basic Books.

———. 2012. *Coming Apart: The State of White America, 1960–2010.* New York: Crown Forum.

O'Connor, Alice. 2001. *Poverty Knowledge: Social Science, Social Policy, and the Poor in the Twentieth-Century U.S. History.* Princeton, N.J.: Princeton University Press.

Orleck, Annelise, and Lisa Gayle Hazirjian. 2011. *The War on Poverty: A New Grassroots History, 1864–1980.* Athens: University of Georgia Press.

Patterson, James T. 2000. *America's Struggle Against Poverty in the Twentieth Century.* Cambridge, Mass.: Harvard University Press.

Raphael, Steven, and Michael Stoll. 2009. "Why Are So Many Americans in Prison?" In *Do Prisons Make Us Safer? The Benefits and Costs of the Prison Boom*, edited by Steven Raphael and Michael Stoll. New York: Russell Sage Foundation.

Reagan, Ronald. 1988. "Address Before a Joint Session of Congress on the State of the Union." January 25, 1998. Santa Barbara, Calif.: American Presidency Project. Available at: http://www.presidency.ucsb.edu/ws/index.php?pid=36035 (accessed April 1, 2013).

Reber, Sarah J. 2010. "Desegregation and Educational Attainment for Blacks." *Journal of Human Resources* 45(4): 893–914.

Ross, Christine, Sheldon Danziger, and Eugene Smolensky. 1987. "The Level and Trend in Poverty, 1939–1979." *Demography* 24(4): 587–600.

Ruggles, Steven, J. Trent Alexander, Katie Genadek, Ronald Goeken, Matthew B. Schroeder, and Matthew Sobek. 2010. *Integrated Public Use Microdata Series: Version 5.0* [Machine-readable database]. Minneapolis: University of Minnesota.

Short, Kathleen. 2011. "The Research Supplemental Poverty Measure: 2010." *Current Population Reports*, series P60, no. 241. Washington: U.S. Census Bureau. Available at: http://www.census.gov/hhes/povmeas/methodology/supplemental/research/Short_Research_SPM2010.pdf (accessed October 12, 2012).

Schlesinger, Arthur, Jr. 1965. *A Thousand Days: John F. Kennedy in the White House.* Boston, Mass.: Houghton Mifflin.

U.S. Census Bureau. 2012a. "Historical Tables, People." Table 2, "Poverty Status, by Family Relationship, Race, and Hispanic Origin: 1959–2011." Washington: U.S. Department of Commerce. Available at: http://www.census.gov/hhes/www/poverty/data/historical/people.html (accessed April 17, 2013).

———. 2012b. "Historical Tables, People." Table 3, "Poverty Status, by Age, Race, and Hispanic Origin: 1959–2011." Washington: U.S. Department of Commerce. Available at: http://www.census.gov/hhes/www/poverty/data/historical/people.html (accessed April 17, 2013).

Ventura, S. J., and Bachrach, C. A. 2000. "Nonmarital Childbearing in the United States, 1940–1999." *National Vital Statistics Reports* 48(16), table 4. Hyattsville, Md.: National Center for Health Statistics. Available at: http://www.cdc.gov/nchs/data/nvsr48/nvs48_16.pdf (accessed October 12, 2012).

Ventura, S. J., Martin, J. A., Curtin, S. C., Menacker, F., and Hamilton, B. E. 2001. "Births: Final Data for 1999." *National Vital Statistics Reports* 49(1), table 17. Hyattsville, Md.: National Center for Health Statistics. Available at: http://www.cdc.gov/nchs/data/nvsr/nvsr49/nvsr49_01.pdf (accessed October 12, 2012).

Wallis, John J. 1987. "Employment, Politics, and Economic Recovery during the Great Depression." *Review of Economics and Statistics* 69(3): 516–20.

———. 1998. "The Political Economy of New Deal Spending Revisited, Again: With and Without Nevada." *Explorations in Economic History* 35: 140–70.

———. 2001. "The Political Economy of New Deal Spending, Yet Again: A Reply." *Explorations in Economic History* 38: 305–14.

Wright, Gavin. 1974. "The Political Economy of New Deal Spending." *Review of Economics and Statistics* 56(1): 30–38.

Part I

Increasing Human Capital, Employment, and Earnings

Chapter 2

Head Start Origins and Impacts

Chloe Gibbs, Jens Ludwig, and Douglas L. Miller

Head Start is an early childhood education, health, and parenting intervention started in 1965 as part of the War on Poverty by the Office of Economic Opportunity (OEO), and remains one of the federal government's primary tools aimed at reducing disparities in children's outcomes before they enroll in K-12 education. The importance of early childhood education, emphasized at the inception of the War on Poverty, has only grown over time with our improved understanding of the developmental plasticity of children during the earliest years of life (National Research Council 2000). Head Start is one of the more popular and enduring elements of the War on Poverty, currently serving around 900,000 mostly low-income children per year with total federal spending of more than $7 billion (Haskins and Barnett 2010). Public opinion polls in 2003 suggest that the vast majority of Americans (92 percent) support the existence of a program like Head Start, and among those knowledgeable about Head Start specifically—80 percent—have favorable feelings about the program (Allen and Okamoto 2004; ORC International 2003). As then-New York City Mayor John Lindsay argued in 1968, "Head Start has been one of the few real successes of OEO" (Moynihan 1969, 184).

Yet from the beginning, Head Start has also been plagued by concerns about whether the program generates any lasting benefits to participating children. The first national study of Head Start was published in 1969, claiming that whatever impacts Head Start had on children faded out by second or third grade. Although the methodology of that non-experimental study was widely criticized, in 1998 the federal government finally authorized a randomized clinical trial of Head Start of the sort that generates gold-standard evidence of intervention impacts in medicine. The National Head Start Impact Study (NHSIS) showed positive impacts on cognitive skill assessments measured at the end of the program year, but differences were no longer statistically significant in the first grade. These findings have led many observers to conclude that Head Start is fundamentally deficient and needs to be redesigned or even folded into other preschool programs. For example, Joe Klein of *Time* magazine argued that the evidence is "indisputable" that

"Head Start simply does not work," and that continued funding is "criminal, every bit as outrageous as tax breaks for oil companies" ("Time to ax public programs that don't yield results," July 7, 2011). W. Steven Barnett argues that Head Start yields "poor results" and might need to "focus more resources on the classroom to recruit and retain better teachers" (2011, 977). In response to the findings, the Obama administration advanced proposals to measure classroom quality of Head Start, and require low-quality programs to compete again for—and possibly lose—funding.

This chapter describes the goals and evolution of the Head Start program since its inception, and argues that despite fifty years of research on the program considerable debate remains about whether the program generates long-term improvements in the life chances of low-income children. As the research designs and data available to study Head Start have improved, we have seen accumulating evidence that for children participating in Head Start several decades ago, the program has had important long-term impacts on outcomes like schooling attainment and earnings despite fade-out of the program's initial impacts on achievement test scores. A similar pattern has been observed for other early childhood interventions as well. For more recent cohorts of Head Start children, for whom only short-run impacts can be measured, we see similar signs of short-term test score impacts that then dissipate. One common hypothesis is that Head Start and other early interventions have impacts on nonacademic or "social-cognitive" skills that mediate long-term improvements in adult outcomes. Unfortunately, too little is currently known about how this process works to determine whether the children participating in Head Start today will experience the same long-term benefits experienced by previous program participants. Current claims that Head Start does not work may be too pessimistic, or at the very least premature.

A (BRIEF) HISTORY OF HEAD START

Head Start was rolled out early in the War on Poverty by OEO, but was not an explicit part of the Economic Opportunity Act of 1964 (for excellent and more complete histories of the program, see Vinovskis 2005; Zigler and Muenchow 1992). Its origins stemmed in part from the difficulty that OEO had spending allocations for its Community Action Programs (CAP) fund, which was designed to help encourage "the maximum feasible participation" of poor families in the local organizations that were funded. The search for alternative ways to spend CAP funds led to the idea of an intervention targeted at low-income, preschool-age (three to five years old) children (Zigler and Muenchow 1992). President Johnson announced Project Head Start in his January 1965 State of the Union address. Key administration figures in the launching and early development of the program were Sargent Shriver (director of the OEO), Julius Richmond (director of the Head Start program), and Jule Sugarman (associate director of the program).

The program began just months later as an eight-week summer program in 1965, serving 560,000 children. It was subsequently expanded to the entire year,

FIGURE 2.1 / Growth in Head Start

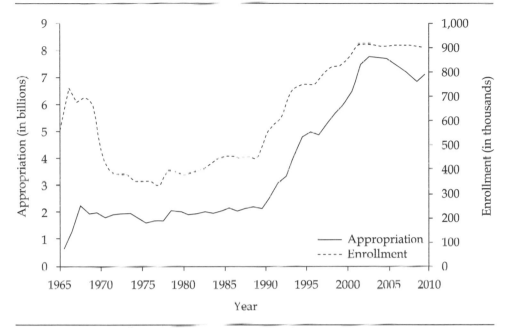

Source: Authors' compilation based on Administration for Children and Families (2011).
Note: Appropriations are in 2009 constant dollars.

serving 20,000 children in the initial year and 160,000 in 1966 (Vinovskis 2005). Although summer programs made up the majority of enrollment in Head Start's early years, these programs were phased out in the 1970s. Figure 2.1 shows the growth in number of children served by Head Start over time, and also plots the program's appropriation in constant 2009 dollars in the same years. When summer programs were phased out in the early 1970s, enrollment numbers dropped, reflecting the program's new focus on serving year-round participants. In the mid-1970s, Head Start served approximately 350,000 children, a number that had grown to more than 900,000 in the 2009 program year. Current enrollment levels are equal to about one-half the total number of three- and four-year-olds living below the poverty line (Haskins and Barnett 2010).

Other than the programmatic shift from summer to year-round provision in the early 1970s, the program was also marked by an expansion in 1990, resulting in substantial increases in both the number of children served and congressional appropriations. In 1990, Congress passed the Head Start Expansion and Quality Improvement Act, and in 1994 authorized the creation of a new companion program, Early Head Start, intended to serve low-income families with children younger than Head Start age (birth to three years old). The 1990 legislation reauthorized Head Start and also allocated funds to strengthening and enhancing program quality (U.S. General Accounting Office 1997).

One feature of Head Start that may seem puzzling from today's perspective is that the program is supported by federal government funding distributed directly to local Head Start providers. Why did the federal government choose to work with thousands of local providers across the country rather than allocate funds to a much smaller number of state governments instead, which could then take on the job of working with local providers and also help coordinate Head Start with state K-12 education activities? This decision is less puzzling when one recalls that a key goal of Head Start and OEO activities more generally was to help the nation's most economically disadvantaged people, including African Americans, many of whom were living in southern states where civil rights were not actively and adequately protected in the 1960s. Direct federal funding to local providers was an important way to circumvent state policymakers and ensure that poor blacks would share in the benefits of Head Start.

Although Head Start is today often thought of as an early childhood education program, given the living conditions at the time of so many poor children—particularly low-income, black children—Head Start was intentionally designed from the beginning as a "whole child" program. Its multiple components included medical and dental services, nutrition, education, parental involvement, and even parent employment, consistent with the goals of the larger CAP effort.

The initial motivation for implementing Head Start as a whole child intervention can be understood by considering how economically disadvantaged the program population was when Head Start began. For example, among Head Start participants in 1966–1967, 29 percent had family incomes below $2,000 per year ($14,000 per year in 2012 dollars), and 67 percent had incomes below $4,000 per year ($28,000) (Westinghouse Learning Corporation 1969, appendix A). By contrast, in the United States as a whole only about 6 percent of four-year-olds lived in families with less than $2,000 in annual income and fewer than one in five were in families with annual incomes below $4,000. Approximately half of Head Start children were black (about 11 percent of the total U.S. population at the time), one-quarter were white, and another 10 percent were classified as Mexican American (Westinghouse Learning Corporation 1969).

The motivation to focus Head Start on the whole child is even more apparent when considering the severe health disadvantages among children during the earliest years of the program. An Office of Child Development (1972) analysis showed that among full-year Head Start participants in 1969, nearly one-third had not received the full diphtheria, pertussis, and tetanus (DPT) vaccination, and nearly two in five had not been fully vaccinated against polio (more than one-third of whom had not received any polio vaccine). In response to these needs, Head Start provided health services such as vaccinations and blood tests for health problems such as anemia. Head Start also provided dental examinations; among 1969 full-year participants, at least 70 percent received a dental exam. Of those, about half had at least one cavity, with a median number, excluding zeros, of seven teeth affected (Office of Child Development 1972).

The health conditions of young children in the United States have improved considerably since the time Head Start was established. Figure 2.2 shows that in

FIGURE 2.2   /   Childhood Mortality

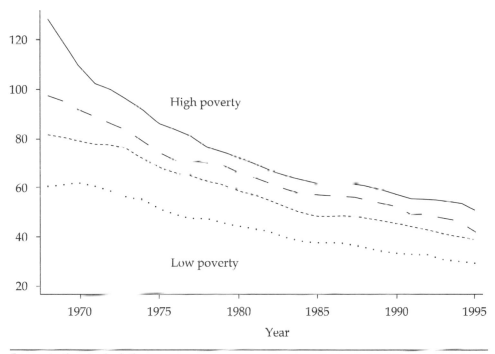

Source: Authors' calculations.
Note: Average mortality per 100,000 for children age one to four in counties defined by 1960 poverty rates of 35 to 100 percent (solid line), 20 to 35 percent (long dashed line), 10 to 20 percent (short dashed line), and 0 to 10 percent (dotted line). Three-year moving averages. Actual values for end years.

1968, the mortality rate for children ages one through four living in the poorest one-quarter of counties in the United States was fully 129 per 100,000, more than twice the rate among children in the least-poor quartile of counties in 1968 (sixty-one per 100,000) and nearly twice as high as the mortality rate in the poorest counties today. Figure 2.2 also makes it clear that much of the decline in child mortality and convergence by county poverty rates occurred before 1980. The largest declines occurred among black children, who historically have had higher mortality rates than white children living in the same county poverty categories, and in the South. Child mortality rates have tended to be higher in the South than in the rest of the country, but differences at the time Head Start began were not large, holding county poverty constant.[1]

Another important change over the course of Head Start's existence is the overall level of preschool enrollment among young children in the United States and the preschool alternatives to Head Start. In 1964, very few children were enrolled in nursery school settings, and the majority of those attended private rather than public schools. In this year, when data were first collected on three- and four-year old school enrollment, 9 percent of white children and 11 percent of black children

FIGURE 2.3 / Three- and Four-Year-Old Population in School

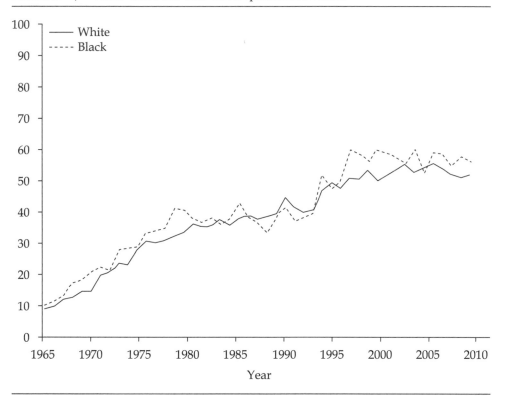

Source: Authors' compilation based on U.S. Census Bureau (2011).
Note: Numbers in percentages.

were enrolled in school. Figure 2.3 illustrates the increases over time in enrollment by race. In 2010, fully 52 percent of white children and 56 percent of black children in this age group were enrolled in school with most of this increase explained by increases in preschool, or nursery school, participation.[2] More than 4.8 million children were enrolled in nursery school in 2010, 2.8 million in public programs, and the remaining 2 million in private offerings. Much of the growth in preschool or nursery school enrollments occurred in public- rather than private-sector settings, as evidenced in figure 2.4.

Besides growing considerably in total enrollment and funding over the past fifty years, the Head Start program itself has changed in a number of ways. The program population has changed somewhat; although one-quarter of Head Start children are white (about the same as in the earliest years of the program), around one-third are black (down from the 1960s) and a growing share—now more than one-third—are Hispanic (Hulsey et al. 2011). As is true for all children in the United States, the share of Head Start participants living with two parents has been declining over time as well (Hulsey et al. 2011).

FIGURE 2.4 / Students in Nursery School in Public Settings

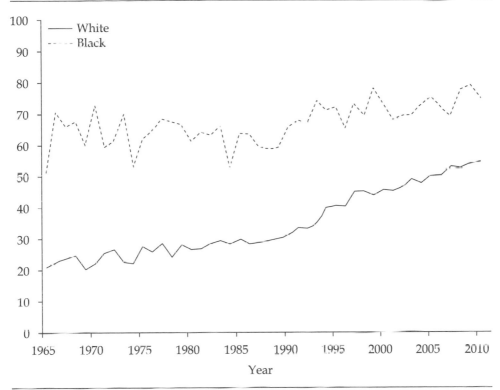

Source: Authors' compilation based on U.S. Census Bureau (2011).
Note: Numbers in percentages.

In 1969, the Nixon administration transferred Head Start from OEO to what was then the Department of Health, Education, and Welfare, and the program now sits in the Department of Health and Human Services (HHS). The program continues to focus on multiple aspects of children's well-being, but increasing attention has been paid to strengthening the academic mission of the program, and indeed periodic proposals have been made to shift Head Start from HHS to the Department of Education.[3] The program's origins as part of CAP meant that in the beginning, many Head Start teachers were the parents of Head Start children. Over time, and especially since 2000, the program has become more professionalized, which has led to increased schooling levels of Head Start teachers and efforts to improve program quality and develop a system of performance standards. For example, the share of Head Start teachers with an associate's degree or more increased from 57 percent in 2000 to 82 percent in 2009, and the share of Head Start teachers with a bachelor's degree or more increased from 39 to 49 percent (Hulsey et al. 2011). Nonetheless concerns remain about the fact that around half of Head Start teachers still do not have a bachelor's degree, and about the variability in program quality observed across Head Start centers (see, for example, Ramey and Ramey 2010). Whether Head Start in its current form is capable of generating lasting benefits to low-income children, and whether the program can be modified to enhance its effectiveness, are the questions we take up in the remainder of this chapter.

WHAT WE KNOW (AND DON'T KNOW) ABOUT HEAD START'S EFFECTIVENESS

Since the time Head Start was launched, disparities in children's outcomes during the earliest years of life have narrowed considerably. Data from the mid-1960s showed that black-white gaps in achievement test scores were fully 1.50 standard deviations measured in first grade (Coleman et al. 1966). More recent studies suggest that early black-white gaps are on the order of 0.80 to 1.00 standard deviations measured during the preschool years (Jencks and Phillips 1998). Data from the more recent Early Childhood Longitudinal Study, Kindergarten Class of 1998–1999 (ECLS-K) show smaller gaps still, but that may be due to the narrow focus of the ECLS-K assessments (Rock and Stenner 2005; Murnane et al. 2006). To what degree can any of these changes be attributed to Head Start? Put differently, what do we know about whether Head Start works?

A growing body of quasi-experimental research, which we describe, provides credible evidence that Head Start generated lasting benefits for children in the first few decades of the program's existence. In what follows we sample from the early evaluation literature and then review newer studies that apply stronger quasi-experimental research designs retrospectively to data on children who were in Head Start many years ago. We then discuss results from the recent randomized experiment that—given the rapid fade-out of Head Start impacts on achievement test scores—many people have interpreted to be disappointing. The results may not, however, be out of line with Head Start's short-term impacts on earlier cohorts of participants, or the effects of other early childhood programs that have also had similarly sized initial impacts. That evidence demonstrates the pattern of both test score fade-out and long-term beneficial impacts for participants.

Early Evaluations

The history of Head Start program evaluation reveals several recurrent themes that emerged in the very early years of the program, and in some cases before its inception, that persist to this day. First is the discussion of Head Start as a primarily academic or cognitive intervention versus one that focuses on the whole child. In particular, Head Start evaluations typically rely on cognitive measures to the exclusion of non-IQ impacts, and do not include long-term measures of program impact. The issue of fade-out of program effects in the primary grades of formal schooling, and possible explanations for these patterns, has also pervaded the research and policy discussions about the program. Finally, in considering the impact of Head Start, we need to be aware of the comparison condition in the absence of Head Start participation—sometimes this is family or nonrelative care in a home setting, sometimes other preschool or center-based care, and sometimes a mixture of the two.

In 1969, the first national evaluation of Head Start, conducted by Westinghouse Learning Corporation (WLC) and Ohio University, was released. The WLC study relied on a matched comparison group of nearly 2,000 nonparticipating children to assess the impact of Head Start on approximately 2,000 participating children in a nationally representative sample of Head Start centers. Given the low preschool enrollment rates of the era, the comparison situation is primarily in-home care. The sampled programs included summer and year-round operations. The study concluded that summer programs did not improve students' cognitive or affective skill development, and year-round participants had marginal—and limited in practical meaningfulness—cognitive advantages. These cognitive effects manifested themselves in school readiness assessments in first grade. No effects were found for Head Start participants in the second and third grades, a fact often interpreted as impermanency of Head Start effects (see, for example, Robert Semple Jr., "Head Start Pupils Found No Better Off Than Others," *New York Times*, April 13, 1969, p. 1).[4]

The WLC report was widely criticized, including for its focus on cognitive outcomes to the exclusion of other outcome domains and for the attribution of fade-out of impacts to Head Start rather than to the possible role played by subsequent primary school quality (Smith and Bissell 1970). Moreover, because the WLC study compared outcomes of children in first, second, and third grades by Head Start status retrospectively reported, what looks like fade-out could simply be improvements over time in program quality, or other differences across different cohorts of children (Smith and Bissell 1970; Barnow and Cain 1977). Reanalyses of the WLC data suggested potential impacts from some year-round programs, particularly centers serving black children in urban settings (Smith and Bissell 1970), and at least short-term cognitive impacts on minority children as well as white children from mother-headed households (Barnow and Cain 1977).

Quasi-Experimental Evidence on Long-Term Impacts

Long-term effects of Head Start can be identified only for those children who participated in the program a long time ago (see Ludwig and Phillips 2007a, on which this section draws heavily). The main challenge in identifying the long-term effects on earlier cohorts comes from the problem of trying to figure out what the outcomes of Head Start participants would have been had they not enrolled in the program. Simply comparing the long-term outcomes of children who did participate with those who did not may provide misleading answers. For example, Head

Start recipients come from more disadvantaged families than other children. If researchers are unable to adequately control for all aspects of family disadvantage, then simple comparisons of Head Start recipients with other children may understate the program's effectiveness. The opposite bias may result if instead the more motivated and effective parents are the ones who are able to get their children into, or are selected by program administrators for, scarce Head Start slots.

Eliana Garces, Duncan Thomas, and Janet Currie (2002) study the long-term effects of Head Start by using longitudinal data from the Panel Study of Income Dynamics to compare the experiences of siblings who did and did not participate in the program. Their research design is a substantial improvement over previous research, by accounting for unobserved family-level factors that are shared by all children within the same household and might differ systematically between families that do versus do not enroll their children in Head Start. However, this research design is in principle still vulnerable to potential bias from changes in family circumstances that cause families to enroll one child but not the child's sibling in Head Start, or unobserved child-specific attributes that lead some children to become enrolled in the program. Put differently, some uncertainty remains with these studies about why some children within a family but not others participate in Head Start. For example, sibling comparisons might overstate or understate Head Start's impacts if parents enroll their more or less able children in the program. This study design might also understate Head Start's impacts if there are positive spillover effects of participating in the program on other members of the family, since in this case the control group—siblings who do not enroll in Head Start themselves—will be partially treated—in other words, benefit to some degree from having a sibling participate in Head Start.

With these caveats in mind, Garces and her colleagues (2002) report that—for cohorts born around 1970—non-Hispanic white children who were in Head Start are about 22 percentage points more likely to complete high school than their siblings in some other form of preschool, and about 19 percentage points more likely to attend some college. These impact estimates are equal to around one-quarter (high school) and one-half (college) of the average schooling attainment levels of their non–Head Start siblings. For blacks, the estimated impact on schooling attainment is small and not statistically significant, but for this group Head Start relative to other preschool experiences is estimated to reduce the chances of being arrested and charged with a crime by around 12 percentage points, which is a very large effect.

David Deming (2009) applied the same sibling-difference design to data from the children of the National Longitudinal Survey of Youth (CNLSY), which follows a national sample of children who would have participated in Head Start between 1984 and 1990. CNLSY children were administered the Peabody Picture Vocabulary Test (PPVT) sometime between the ages of three and five, and then again sometime after age ten. Children were also administered the Peabody Individual Achievement Test Math (PIAT-M) and Reading Recognition (PIAT-RR) subtests every survey year for those age five through fourteen.

Deming (2009) also shows that, compared with siblings who did not participate in any other form of preschool, those enrolled in Head Start had higher average PIAT scores (averaging the math and reading tests together) of 0.15 standard deviations measured at ages five and six, of 0.13 measured at age seven through ten, and of 0.06 measured at age eleven through fourteen. Initial impacts on the PIAT tests are larger for blacks than for whites or Hispanics, but show suggestive signs of fading out more rapidly for blacks than for nonblacks. Despite the fade-out in test scores for the overall study sample, Deming's findings suggest that Head Start has lasting beneficial impacts on an index of long-term outcomes—high school graduation, college-going, idleness, crime, teen parenthood, and health, all measured after age eighteen—equal to 0.23 standard deviations.

Jens Ludwig and Douglas Miller (2007) use a different research design that exploits a discontinuity in Head Start funding across counties generated by the way that the program was launched in 1965. Specifically, OEO provided technical grant-writing assistance for Head Start funding to the 300 counties with the highest 1960 poverty rates in the country, but not to other counties. The result is that Head Start participation and funding rates are 50 to 100 percent higher in the counties with poverty rates that just barely put them into the group of the 300 poorest counties compared to those counties with poverty rates just below this threshold. As long as other determinants of child outcomes vary smoothly by the 1960 poverty rate across these counties, any discontinuities (or jumps) in outcomes for those children who grew up in counties just above versus below the county poverty-rate cutoff for grant-writing assistance can be attributed as effects of the extra Head Start funding. Using this regression discontinuity design, Ludwig and Miller find that a 50 to 100 percent increase in Head Start funding is associated with an increase in schooling attainment of about one-half year, and an increase in the likelihood of attending some college of about 15 percent of the control mean. Importantly, the estimated effects of extra Head Start funding on schooling are found for both blacks and whites.

Ludwig and Miller (2007) also find that this increase in funding does not lead to statistically significant increases in student achievement test scores in eighth grade in either math or reading as measured in the National Education Longitudinal Survey of 1988 (NELS), although they cannot rule out impacts smaller than around 0.20 standard deviations; nor do they have adequate sample sizes to examine impacts on test scores separately for blacks and whites. Their estimates are calculated for children who would have participated in Head Start during the 1960s or 1970s, and cannot be calculated for more recent birth cohorts because the Head Start funding discontinuity across counties at the heart of this research design seems to have dissipated over time.

Taken together, these impact estimates suggest that Head Start as it operated in the 1960s through 1980s seems to have generated substantial long-run benefits, despite fade-out in initial achievement test impacts. Follow-up calculations (Currie 2001; Ludwig and Miller 2007; Frisvold 2007) suggest that the benefit-cost ratio is very likely to exceed 1, and might be as high—or perhaps even higher—as those estimated for some of the benefit-cost figures cited for smaller model programs.[5] For example, Deming's (2009) study finds that Head Start's impact on his standardized index of long-term outcomes is about 80 percent as large as those from the Perry Preschool Project and the Carolina Abecedarian Project, even though the per-participant costs of those programs are many multiples those of Head Start.

The National Head Start Impact Study

The impacts of Head Start on children depend on the difference in the quality of the program versus the quality of the environments that low-income children would have experienced otherwise. Over time, the Head Start program has improved in quality, but so have the alternatives to Head Start for poor children.[6] It is not clear which environment is improving more rapidly, which also means we cannot necessarily forecast the effects of today's Head Start from studies of the program in the past.

Fortunately, the federal government sponsored a randomized experimental study of Head Start, the National Head Start Impact Study, or NHSIS (see Puma et al. 2005, 2010). Starting in 2002, nearly 4,700 three- and four-year-old children whose parents applied for Head Start were randomly assigned to a treatment group, eligible to participate in Head Start, or a control group that was not offered Head Start, but could participate in other local preschool programs if slots were available. The eighty-four Head Start centers participating in the experiment were selected to be representative of all programs in operation across the country that had waiting lists.[7] The experiment seems to have been done fairly well; randomization was implemented properly, careful assessments were made of a wide variety of children's cognitive and noncognitive outcomes, and parents were studied as well as their children.

One common source of confusion about this experiment stems from the fact that the main results, particularly those in the executive summaries that accompany the 300- or 400-page technical reports, are intention-to-treat (ITT) estimates that compare the average outcomes of all children assigned to the Head Start "treatment group" with all children assigned to the control group — that is, with offering children the chance to participate in Head Start through the NHSIS experiment. These ITT estimates will not equal the effects of actually participating in Head Start — the effects of treatment on the treated (TOT) — because not all children assigned to the program group participate in Head Start, and some of those assigned to the control group get into Head Start on their own. Specifically, around 86 percent of four-year-olds assigned to the experimental treatment group enrolled in Head Start, and 18 percent of those assigned to the control group did (Puma et al. 2005, 3–7).[8] If we assume that the average quality of the Head Start centers attended by those in the treatment group is about the same as for these "control group crossovers," and that randomization to the treatment group had no effect on the treatment group other than by affecting Head Start enrollment likelihoods, then the TOT effect will be around 1.50 times as large as the ITT (Bloom 1984; Angrist, Imbens, and Rubin 1996).

In table 2.1, we show the ITT impacts on each of the cognitive outcome domains

Table 2.1 / Effect Sizes from the National Head Start Impact Study

Outcome	Three-Year-Olds		Four-Year-Olds	
	ITT	TOT	ITT	TOT
Woodock-Johnson letter identification	.235* (.074)	.346* (.109)	.215* (.099)	.319* (.147)
Letter naming	.196* (.080)	.288* (.117)	.243* (.085)	.359* (.126)
McCarthy draw-a-design	.134* (.051)	.197* (.075)	.111 (.067)	.164 (.100)
Woodcock-Johnson spelling	.090 (.066)	.132 (.096)	.161* (.065)	.239* (.097)
PPVT vocabulary	.120* (.052)	.170* (.077)	.051 (.052)	.075 (.076)
Color naming	.098* (.043)	.144* (.064)	.108 (.071)	.159 (.107)
Parent-reported literacy skills	.340* (.066)	.499* (.097)	.293* (.075)	.435* (.112)
Oral comprehension	.025 (.062)	.036 (.091)	-.058 (.052)	-.086 (.077)
Woodcock-Johnson applied problems	.124 (.083)	182 (.122)	.100 (.070)	.147 (.103)

Source: Recreated with permission from Ludwig and Phillips (2007a, table 1; 2007b, table 1).
Note: First and third columns reproduce ITT impact estimates for all cognitive outcomes reported in Westat's executive summary of the first-year findings report from the National Head Start Impact Study, reported as effect sizes, that is, program impacts divided by the control group standard deviation (Puma et al. 2005). Standard errors are shown in parentheses also in effect-size terms; these were not included in the Westat report but were generously shared by Ronna Cook of Westat. Second and fourth columns are our estimates for the effects of treatment on the treated (TOT) derived using the approach of Bloom (1984), which divides the ITT point estimates and standard errors by the treatment-control difference in Head Start enrollment rates. For three-year-olds the adjustment is to divide ITT by (.894 − .213) = .681, for four-year-olds adjustment is to divide ITT by (.856 − .181) = .675 (see Puma et al. 2005, 3–7, exhibit 3.3).
*$p \leq .05$

reported in the executive summary for the first-year findings of the experiment (Puma et al. 2005),[9] as well as the TOT effects that come from rescaling the ITT effects by the difference in the treatment and control groups' Head Start enrollment rates. If the Head Start programs that treatment-group children attend are better than those the control group attends, this TOT estimate will somewhat overstate the effects of participating in Head Start. Point estimates and standard errors have been divided by the control group standard deviation for the relevant outcome measure so that they can be compared to other studies reporting results as "effect sizes."

Table 2.1 shows that, at least for cognitive skills, all of the Head Start impact estimates point in the direction consistent with beneficial program impacts, although many point estimates are not statistically significant and in general are somewhat larger for three-year-olds than four-year-olds. For vocabulary, pre-reading, and pre-writing skills, Head Start's effects (TOT impacts) range from 0.15 to 0.35 standard deviations. Parent-reported literacy skills show larger impacts, equal to 0.5 and 0.4 standard deviations for three- and four-year-olds, respectively. Impacts on the Woodcock-Johnson applied math problems test are equal to 0.18 and 0.15 standard deviations, respectively, but are not statistically significant. Jens Ludwig and Deborah Phillips (2007a) note that if one pooled the three- and four-year-old cohorts in the NHSIS and analyzed them together, rather than separately, Head Start impacts would be statistically significant for every outcome shown in table 2.1 except for oral comprehension.

HOW WORRISOME IS FADE-OUT OF HEAD START TEST SCORE IMPACTS?

How concerned should we be about the fade-out of Head Start's test score impacts found in the recent randomized experimental study of the program? Does this evidence suggest, as critics have argued, that Head Start has failed?

Fade-Out and Long-Term Impacts for Other Childhood Interventions

Many people have assumed that the rate of test score fade-out in the NHSIS implies that the program will have no long-term lasting benefits. The premise behind this conclusion is that measured cognitive skills such as IQ or reading and math achievement test scores are the key mechanism through which Head Start helps improve children's long-term life outcomes.

Notably, other heralded early childhood programs, including the Perry Preschool Project and Abecedarian, demonstrate a similar pattern of attenuation of test score differences between treatment and control groups combined with sizable long-term effects on behavioral outcomes later in adolescence and adulthood (Anderson 2008; Campbell et al. 2002; Schweinhart et al. 2005). Alan Krueger and Diane Whitmore (2001) show a similar pattern for the effects of class-size reduction during grades K-3 in Tennessee's Project STAR (Student-Teacher Achievement Ratio) experiment.

The recent study by Raj Chetty and his colleagues (2011) on the long-term effects of kindergarten quality, including small class size, provides a striking example of how early fade-out can be a very inaccurate predictor of long-run impacts. The authors document that there is strong test score fade-out—test score impacts seem to go away immediately after kindergarten—but long-term impacts on adult earnings are still evident. Further, these impacts are best predicted by the short-term test score impacts, and are poorly predicted by the medium-term test score (non-) impacts. That is, looking at (say) third-grade children who experienced higher versus lower quality kindergarten, we would have predicted no difference in long-term earnings based on the similarity in their achievement test scores measured in third grade. We actually see, in the long-term earnings data, gains to higher quality kindergarten settings of the sort we would predict from end-of-kindergarten test score impacts despite rapid fade-out of these early advantages.

Fade-Out and the Experience of Early Cohorts

The NHSIS finding of early test score gains, and the presence of fade-out, also applied to early cohorts of Head Start participants. For these cohorts, we have evi-

TABLE 2.2 / Cognitive Outcomes for Head Start Participants

Cohort and group	Age				
	5.5	6	7	8.5	12.5
Pre-1990 Head Start cohort (Deming)					
All	0.145			0.133	0.055
White (including Hispanic)	−0.057			0.111	0.156
Black	0.287			0.127	0.031
2002 Head Start four-year-old cohort (NHSIS)					
All	0.021	−0.025	0.058		
White	0.261	0.177	0.231		
Black	0.093	−0.115	0.009		
Hispanic	0.214	−0.058	−0.013		

Source: Authors' compilation based on Deming (2009) and Puma et al. (2010).
Note: Impact estimates for cognitive outcomes are reported as effect sites.

dence of long-term benefits despite fade-out of test score impacts. Although we cannot provide direct evidence about whether children who were in Head Start in recent years experience similar long-term benefits, we can at least see how the size of Head Start's short-term impacts on test scores have changed over time—assuming that the size of short-term test score impacts are proportional to long-term benefits.

The initial impacts of Head Start found in the NHSIS for recent cohorts of program participants are about the same size as those estimated for children who participated in the program in the 1960s through 1980s. For those cohorts of Head Start participants, the program seems to have produced long-term benefits large enough to outweigh program costs—despite fade-out of initial test score impacts (Garces, Thomas, and Currie 2002; Ludwig and Miller 2007; Deming 2009).

The surprise from the NHSIS is not that Head Start's initial impacts on children are too small, nor that they attenuate over time, but rather that they seem to attenuate more rapidly compared with the rate of fade-out observed for previous cohorts of program participants. For cohorts of children who were in Head Start in the 1960s through 1980s, the program's impacts on test scores seemed to persist at least through early elementary school (Currie and Thomas 1995; Deming 2009). In contrast, for the NHSIS study sample of children who were three to four years old in 2002 the initial Head Start impacts on test scores are no longer significant one year after children leave the program.

This pattern is illustrated in table 2.2, which compares Head Start impacts by age for the four-year-old cohort in the NHSIS with the estimated Head Start impacts by age from Deming (2009), who as noted studied children who would have been in Head Start no later than around 1990. Head Start impacts measured around age five are fairly similar for the recent cohort of children studied in the NHSIS and the earlier cohorts of children examined by Deming. But the table shows that the impacts attenuate quite rapidly in the NHSIS, and by the end of first grade are very small in magnitude. In contrast, in Deming's study, impacts are of about the same size at ages seven to ten as at ages five and six.

Although it is not clear that the rate of fade-out in the NHSIS for recent cohorts of Head Start children is statistically distinguishable from that for earlier cohorts, the NHSIS does seem to show more rapid fade-out than what we see from other studies of early childhood programs. A meta-analysis of sixty-five early childhood interventions (Leak et al. 2012) estimates an average effect size on cognition at completion of program (that is, short-run impacts) equal to 0.30 standard deviations. The same study estimated slow average fade-out, taking about ten years to fade to zero. These numbers come from a pooling of studies and effect-size estimates. Their fixed-effect estimates of fade-out are close to zero, and rule out fade-out faster than 0.05 standard deviations per year. Leak and colleagues were unable to analyze long-run impacts of early childhood programs with their data.

Table 2.2 also presents the results separately by race-ethnicity, pooling together Hispanics and whites for the earlier cohorts. In Deming's study, results are larger initially for blacks than nonblacks, but fade out more rapidly for blacks than nonblacks. In the NHSIS, Head Start's impacts seem to fade out less rapidly for blacks than nonblacks. This could be a fluke finding, but it may also be a useful diagnostic for understanding the differences across cohorts.

Explaining Short-Run Fade-Out and Long-Run Benefits

Several reasons are possible for fade-out of initial program effects. One is that Head Start may be an ineffective intervention, as some people have claimed. But given the evidence cited, that Head Start seems to have generated lasting benefits to earlier cohorts of participants, and that the short-term test score impacts evidenced in the NHSIS for recent cohorts of children are of about the same size as for earlier cohorts, we are not yet convinced that this is the answer. We see several possible explanations that are consistent with long-run benefits. First is the possibility that the positive impacts of Head Start operate through channels other than test scores, such as through social-cognitive channels. Second is the possibility that gains from Head Start are eroded due to poor elementary school environments. Finally, fade-out could be explained by spillovers of Head Start to nonparticipants, so that their test scores catch up to those of their Head Start counterparts. The data we have available to test these hypotheses are limited, but keeping this in mind, do not provide much support for the first or second hypotheses. No data are available that we know of to test the third hypothesis.

Social-Emotional Skills One candidate explanation for why Head Start's impacts on test scores fade out, yet still realize long-run benefits, is that the test scores are not the only important channel through which participants derive long-term benefits from the program. By process of elimination, researchers typically assume the mediator driving long-term behavioral impacts must be nonacademic (that is, social-emotional and behavioral or social-cognitive) skills such as self-regulation, persistence, and future orientation. For example, Greg Duncan and his colleagues (2007) have shown that early childhood measures of attention skills are important in predicting future test scores. This pathway is all the more plausible given the whole-child intervention nature of the Head Start program. To the best of our knowledge, none of the studies that follow Head Start participants from early childhood into adulthood have good measures of these social-emotional and behavioral skills.

The NHSIS does include some measures of social-emotional and behavioral skills but finds few impacts. In the NHSIS, the closest measure to attention skills—the social-emotional-behavioral measure implicated in the Duncan study as an important predictor of later outcomes—is a variable for hyperactive behavior. For this outcome, we see a Head Start impact of –0.26 standard deviations for three-year-olds (that is, in the direction of a protective effect), but no effect for four-year-olds. Few of the other social-emotional outcomes measured in the NHSIS showed signs of statistically significant program impacts.

How worried should we be about a lack of detectable impacts on social-emotional outcomes in the NHSIS? It could be that Head Start truly had no impact on any social-emotional skills for children in the NHSIS. The lack of detectable impacts could instead reflect the fact that social-emotional outcomes are more difficult to measure than reading and math scores; when observing young children, one can see that while reading skills are similar from day to day, attention and temperament may be quite variable. It could also be that the NHSIS simply did not measure the social-emotional outcomes that are most important for mediating impacts on long-term outcomes.

If Head Start impacts on social-emotional skills help prop up lasting achievement test gains and are the key mediators for long-term impacts on schooling attainment and other adult life outcomes, then the possibility of smaller Head Start impacts on social-emotional skills for recent versus earlier cohorts of participating children could explain why test scores might be fading out more quickly for recent cohorts of children. Even if we knew that Head Start had small impacts on social-emotional outcomes for recent cohorts, this hypothesis for increasingly rapid fade-out of Head Start test score impacts would still be difficult to test directly because of the lack of data on social-emotional and behavioral skills for previous cohorts of Head Start participants.

Elementary School Environment   A different candidate explanation for why Head Start's impacts on test scores fade out focuses on the quality of the elementary schools that children attend after leaving Head Start. For example, Janet Currie and Duncan Thomas (2000) link black children's test score fade-out to lower school quality of black Head Start participants over nonparticipants. This suggests that low-quality elementary schools squander the benefits of Head Start. However, Ludwig and Miller (2007) find long-term benefits even for a group of children—African Americans living in the poorest parts of the Deep South in the 1960s—who were attending public schools of an average quality that would, by any fair assessment, be termed appalling. It is hard to imagine that very many poor children in contemporary America attend schools that are actually worse than those that states like Mississippi provided to blacks living in the Delta forty or fifty years ago. However, we cannot make definitive conclusions based on this cohort, because we do not know what their rate of fade-out was for test score impacts.

For low elementary school quality to explain fade-out of Head Start's test score impacts, and in particular explain any acceleration over time in fade-out of such impacts, elementary school quality would need to be declining over time. However, the available data do not seem consistent with that explanation. For example, Bobby Rampey, Gloria Dion, and Patricia Donahue document trends in average reading scores on the National Assessment of Educational Progress (NAEP) for nine-year-old children over the period from 1971 to 2008 (2009, figure 4). They show that overall reading scores are increasing over time, indicating improved schooling quality. The black-white gap in average reading scores also seems to be narrowing. They also show a similar pattern for math scores (Rampey, Dion, and Donahue 2009, figure 10). In contrast, the NHSIS results show a more rapid fade-out than for earlier Head Start cohorts, the opposite of what we would expect if school quality was improving over time and particularly so for disadvantaged children.

Fade-Out Versus Catch-Up   This pattern of increased elementary school quality, particularly for relatively more disadvantaged students, such as minorities, suggests an alternative hypothesis for how changing elementary school conditions might matter. Perhaps elementary schools are becoming increasingly effective at remediating academic deficits among children who enter kindergarten or first grade behind their peers. That is, what looks like fade-out among Head Start children is actually catch-up by low-skilled nonparticipants. It might be that elementary school teachers focus more and more on helping students who did not participate in Head Start to catch up. If individualized teacher attention is developmentally productive, then Head Start generates social returns (in the form of reducing the number of students for whom the teacher needs to do remediation) that may exceed the private returns. Part of the benefits of Head Start come in the form of improved outcomes for non–Head Start children, and so would be invisible in a study that compares the average outcomes of Head Start and non–Head Start children. In this model, the best way to address what looks like Head Start fade-out might be to actually expand Head Start enrollment.

Empirically distinguishing between the fade-out and catch-up hypotheses is challenging in part because children's achievement test scores change a great deal as children age during their earliest years of life. Note that children in both the Head Start treatment and control groups in the NHSIS are experiencing considerable increases in overall achievement levels over time. By definition, the rate of increase is slower for the treatment than control groups, given that the initial Head Start impact attenuates over time, but from this fact alone we cannot conclude whether poor school quality is suppressing the trajectories of Head Start children or whether remedial efforts by teachers are accelerating the trajectories of non–Head Start children.[10]

WHAT NEXT FOR HEAD START?

Head Start remains one of the more enduring and popular programs arising from the War on Poverty. Although researchers and policymakers have been concerned about fade-out of Head Start impacts on achievement test scores from the very beginning of the program, in retrospect we now know that earlier cohorts of children seem to have experienced long-term improvements in their life outcomes as a result of Head Start participation—despite fade-out of test score impacts.

The fade-out of test score impacts in the recent Head Start randomized experimental study (the NHSIS) raises concerns about whether recent cohorts of Head Start children should be expected to obtain long-term benefits from the program. We believe that the question is still open. The initial (before fade-out) test score impacts for recent cohorts of Head Start children are of about the same size as what we saw for earlier cohorts of children. For those earlier cohorts, there is strong evidence of long-term benefits. What might have changed over time is the rate at which these test score impacts fade out. Whether this is worrisome is itself unclear, because the early childhood field includes other examples of programs (such as the kindergarten quality study of Chetty et al. 2011) that have test score fade-out as rapid as what we see in the NHSIS yet still produce improvements in the long-term life chances of participants. Given this uncertainty, the fade-out of test score impacts documented in the NHSIS is not sufficient evidence at this point to rule out the possibility of long-run benefits.

Uncertainty is not an excuse for inaction. If there are ways to make Head Start better, we should consider them. We discuss three proposals: make Head Start more academic in orientation and deemphasize the whole child focus, invest more money into intensifying the Head Start experience for program participants, and think about shifting resources away from Head Start toward alternative early childhood interventions that a growing number of people believe outperform Head Start on a dollar-per-dollar basis, particularly the newer state-run universal pre-K programs. Although we understand and appreciate the logic behind each one of these proposals, each of them also has some risk, and in our view the available empirical evidence is such that we cannot know whether acting on any of these proposals will on balance make the lives of low-income children better or worse.

Making Head Start More Academic

Given the widespread assumption that rapid fade-out of test score impacts is a problem for Head Start, policy analysts and policymakers have proposed numerous changes to the program. For example, Ron Haskins and Steven Barnett (2010) have argued that Head Start should have its primary focus, "on learning and teaching in the classroom"—that is, we should make Head Start more academic. But the possibility that effects on social-emotional and behavioral skills are an important mediator through which early childhood programs improve long-term life outcomes raises the possibility that making Head Start more academic could exacerbate the problem of Head Start fade-out and erode the program's overall effectiveness.

The possibility that nonacademic skills might be an important mediator for long-term program impacts on children is also relevant to recent proposals by the Obama administration to use data-driven accountability reforms to weed out the least effective programs. The success of these proposals will depend in part on our ability to identify programs that have high value-added for children. We are concerned that a blind emphasis on academic criteria in the selection process may result in inappropriate elimination of programs that are effective at instilling important nonacademic skills.

Increasing Per-Child Resource Intensity

Another common type of proposal for modifying Head Start is to increase the intensity of the program. Many observers have noted that Head Start teachers still have less education on average than either K-12 public school teachers or those who have worked in model programs like Perry Preschool or Abecedarian, that class sizes in Head Start tend to be larger than in model programs, and that a large share of Head Start children participate in only half-day rather than full-day programming. Would it make sense to increase the intensity of Head Start?

We think the answer right now is at best maybe, given evidence that expanding access to Head Start to more children could at present be a higher value-added use of additional funding than intensifying the program. As noted, Deming (2009) finds that at least for previous cohorts of children, Head Start's long-term impacts on adult outcomes are on the order of 80 percent as big as what we see for much more expensive early childhood programs like Perry Preschool and Abecedarian. Ludwig and Phillips (2010) noted that the National Day Care study found that cutting class sizes in half increased test scores, but only by 20 percent, whereas studies of Perry Preschool found that children who participated for two years did better than those who did for only one year, but did not benefit twice as much. The one exception may be shifting from half-day to full-day programs, which Chloe Gibbs (2012) finds to be an extremely cost-effective approach at least in kindergarten settings. In general, increasing the share of low-income children who receive early childhood experiences of at least the intensity level of today's Head Start could be a more helpful way to deploy any additional early childhood funding that is available.

Expanding access to Head Start could also increase the persistence of Head Start's test score impacts if the explanation for test score fade-out in the NHSIS is catch-up by control group members. We think one candidate explanation for catch-up is that children who were not in Head Start or similar programs may wind up requiring remediation that either lowers the academic targeting of classroom instruction or diverts teacher time from working with other children in the classroom. Expanding preschool coverage would help address this problem to the extent it exists.

Pre-Kindergarten

Recently attention has been focused on expanding state pre-K programs as an alternative to Head Start resources, or as a model for reforming Head Start. Steven Barnett (2011), for example, believes that room for improvement in Head Start is substantial in part because he believes that much larger test score impacts have been found with other early childhood programs that do not cost much more than Head Start, particularly newer, state-sponsored universal pre-K programs.

However, the evidence currently available has not yet convinced us that universal pre-K programs are substantially more effective than Head Start at improving children's outcomes (see, for example, Gormley and Gayer 2005; Wong et al. 2008). Although these recent studies use an age-based regression discontinuity design that improves on previous studies, they are still vulnerable to bias from differences between the treatment and control groups that are being compared (for details, see Gibbs, Ludwig, and Miller 2011). Moreover, this research design precludes the ability to examine the key concern with the present Head Start findings—whether impacts fade out over the medium- and long-term. Consequently, we believe that at present it is not clear that this is a superior alternative to Head Start.

CONCLUDING THOUGHTS

Although Head Start has been one of the most popular and enduring elements of the War on Poverty, concerns about fade-out of program impacts on children's scores on IQ and achievement tests have surrounded the program from the beginning. A common assumption had been that such measures are the key mediators through which early childhood interventions translate into long-term benefits for participating children. Researchers have recognized the challenges of isolating the causal effects of Head Start on children, given the possibility that participants and nonparticipants may differ in important ways that are difficult to adequately measure in available datasets, but findings of fade-out of test score impacts have been a source of concern for decades.

Over time, the research community has learned that early childhood interventions can generate lasting benefits to program participants despite fade-out of test score impacts, and indeed that Head Start itself generated long-term gains for participants during the first several decades of the program's existence. The long-term impacts on earlier cohorts of Head Start participants seem to be nearly as large as what we see from model early childhood programs like Perry Preschool and Abecedarian that have much higher costs per participant (Deming 2009). Although these findings of long-term benefits for earlier cohorts of Head Start children do not come from randomized experiments, which are usually considered the gold standard for evidence about program impacts, the accumulation of evidence from different datasets and high-quality quasi-experimental or natural experiment research designs has convinced us that the program as it operated at least from the 1960s through the 1980s worked and easily passed a benefit-cost test.

What is less clear is whether Head Start remains an effective way to improve the long-term life chances of poor children. The impact of the program on children comes from the difference in the developmental quality of Head Start versus what children would experience otherwise. By most indications, the Head Start program has on average improved over time, but so have the alternative environments experienced by low-income children. So for Head Start, evidence of past success is no guarantee of current success. The short-term impacts of Head Start on recent cohorts of participating children, from the first randomized experimental test of the program, are of about the same size as effects for previous cohorts of children for whom we have direct evidence of long-term Head Start benefits. What seems to be different about the recent experimental findings is the rate at which these test score impacts fade over time—although other early childhood studies have found that even rapid fade-out of test score impacts can be consistent with long-term benefits in adulthood.

Nonacademic skills (variously called social-emotional and behavioral skills, or social-cognitive skills) are one possible set of key mediating pathways that link early childhood programs to long-term gains. But not enough is known about this process at present to know what the short-term results available from the Head Start experiment imply about whether today's program participants will experience benefits into adolescence and adulthood. That the Head Start experiment found few detectable impacts on those social-emotional and behavioral outcomes measured is not definitive proof about the program's long-term impacts; the experiment might have inadequately measured those skills most important for long-term success. But all else equal, surely everyone would rather see impacts on the available measures than not. Learning more about the pathways through which early childhood interventions generate long-term improvements in children's life chances, and what the most important early markers are of those processes, remains a high priority for research in this area.

Also unclear at present is whether there are more effective ways to deploy Head Start's budget to help reduce poverty in America. Proposals to make Head Start more academic in its orientation could make the program worse, not better, if nonacademic skills are the most important mediator that generates long-term benefits for children. Efforts to make Head Start programs more accountable need to also pay attention to nonacademic skills in their attempts to measure the effectiveness of local program providers. Proposals to shift more and more early childhood funding to the growing number of state-sponsored universal pre-K programs rather than Head Start also carries with it some risks, in our view, given the limitations with the available evidence about those pre-K alternatives. Understanding more about whether there are ways to strengthen Head Start, or whether other program models are superior, is also an important priority for future research.

Despite the uncertainty surrounding the absolute or relative effectiveness of

Head Start for current cohorts of low-income children, our assessment of the evidence suggests that the millions of children who participated in Head Start for the first several decades of the program had better adult outcomes on average as a result of their participation. While there might be room for improvement with the current program model, Head Start can rightfully be considered a success for much of the past fifty years.

Jens Ludwig received financial support from visiting scholar awards from the Russell Sage Foundation and LIEPP at Sciences Po, Doug Miller received financial support as a visiting research scholar from the Center for Health and Wellbeing at Princeton University, and Chloe Gibbs received support from a National Academy of Education / Spencer Foundation dissertation fellowship in education, and a fellowship from the U.S. Department of Education Institute of Education Sciences pre-doctoral interdisciplinary training program in the education sciences at the University of Chicago. Thanks to Laura Brinkman for research assistance and to Martha Bailey, Sheldon Danziger, David Deming, Katherine Magnuson, Jacob Vigdor, two anonymous referees, and seminar participants at the American Economic Association meetings, the Brookings Institution, MDRC, and the Society for Research on Educational Effectiveness conference for helpful discussions. All opinions and any errors are of course our own.

NOTES

1. Using mortality micro records and the one percent sample from the 1960 census, we calculate that in the Deep South states (Alabama, Georgia, Louisiana, Mississippi, and South Carolina) black mortality for children ages one to four in 1960 was 227 per 100,000. For whites in the Deep South, the corresponding number was ninety-six per 100,000. Outside the South (in the non-Confederate states), the 1960 mortality rates were 166 per 100,000 for black children and ninety-two per 100,000 for white children

2. The Census Bureau's Current Population Survey first added questions about nursery school enrollment in 1964.

3. Much of our discussion of changes in Head Start comes from the California Head Start Association (http://caheadstart.org/HeadStartHistory.pdf). In 1972, Head Start was mandated to have at least 10 percent of its program population be children with disabilities. In 1974, the first performance standards were issued. In 1986, the federal government began to exert some pressure on local programs to serve children for only one year, to increase the number of separate three- and four-year-olds who could be served. The 1994 Head Start reauthorization included a revision of the performance standards and a major focus on program quality, with additional changes to the performance standards in 1997. The 1998 reauthorization of Head Start changed the program's focus from development of social competence to school readiness, added educational performance standards, and required at least one teacher in each Head Start classroom to have an associate's degree.

4. However, the later grades correspond to earlier cohorts of Head Start exposure; the lack of a longitudinal design in the study means that it could not separate fade-out from differing effects by cohort.

5. Because a key goal of Head Start is distributional (expansion of life chances for disadvantaged children), focusing on benefit-cost ratios may omit important aspects of a full social welfare analysis of the program.

6. During its early years, Head Start did not score well on commonly used indicators of early childhood program quality, such as teacher educational attainment. This was based in part on Head Start's origin as part of the Community Assistance Program of the War on Poverty with its emphasis on involvement of the poor in the design and implementation of new social programs (Vinovskis 2005), including roles as classroom teachers and aides. For poor children in the 1960s through 1980s, the evaluation studies described imply that the environments Head Start children would have experienced if not enrolled in the program were even less developmentally productive than Head Start. Over time, the quality of the Head Start program has improved, but arguably so have the alternatives to Head Start for poor children: parent educational attainments and real incomes have increased since the 1960s and alternative forms of center-based early education, such as state-funded preschool programs, have been introduced.

7. The design of the NHSIS raises a subtle point about external validity: by randomly assigning income-eligible children to the treatment and control conditions, the Head Start experiment uncovers the effects of making Head Start available to all eligible children. If, in practice, Head Start centers focus on enrolling the most disadvantaged of the eligible children that apply, and if the impacts of Head Start are more pronounced for more disadvantaged children, then the experimental impact estimates may understate the effect of Head Start on the average program participant in the nation at large.

8. The figures for three-year-olds assigned to the treatment and control groups are 89 percent and 21 percent, respectively.

9. Although the published Westat report did not show standard errors for impact estimates, Ronna Cook at Westat has very generously made these available to us.

10. A different way to test for catch-up versus fade-out is to try to directly examine the degree to which teachers try to "smooth" outcomes between Head Start and other children. Unfortunately, most existing datasets are not good at capturing classroom process measures like the amount of time teachers spend with individual students. Another potential way to test for catch-up would be to identify a setting where comparable groups of nonparticipants were exposed to varying fractions of Head Start peers. Ideally, this variation in number of Head Start peers would be experimentally (or quasi-experimentally) controlled, to avoid confounding the spillover effects of background characteristics of participants. We are unaware of studies that use either of these approaches.

REFERENCES

Administration for Children and Families. 2011. *Head Start Program Fact Sheet, Fiscal Year 2010*. Washington: U.S. Department of Health and Human Services. Available at: http:// eclkc.ohs.acf.hhs.gov/hslc/mr/factsheets (accessed May 28, 2012).

Allen, Ben, and Jill Okamoto. 2004. "American Public and Head Start Directors' Perceptions Toward Head Start." Alexandria, Va.: National Head Start Association, Research and Evaluation Department. Available at: http://www.nhsa.org/research/full_research _studies (accessed January 15, 2013).

Anderson, Michael L. 2008. "Multiple Inference and Gender Differences in the Effects of Early Intervention: A Reevaluation of the Abecedarian, Perry Preschool, and Early Training Projects." *Journal of the American Statistical Association* 103(404): 1481–95.

Angrist, Joshua D., Guido W. Imbens, and Donald B. Rubin. 1996. "Identification of Causal Effects Using Instrumental Variables." *Journal of the American Statistical Association* 91(343): 468–72.

Barnett, W. Steven. 2011. "Effectiveness of Early Educational Intervention." *Science* 333 (August 19): 975–78.

Barnow, Burt S., and Glen G. Cain. 1977. "A Reanalysis of the Effect of Head Start on Cognitive Development: Methodology and Empirical Findings." *Journal of Human Resources* 12(2): 177–97.

Bloom, Howard S. 1984. "Accounting for No-Shows in Experimental Evaluation Designs." *Evaluation Review* 8(2): 225–46.

Campbell, Frances A., Craig T. Ramey, Elizabeth Pungello, Joseph Sparling, and Shari Miller-Johnson. 2002. "Early Childhood Education: Young Adult Outcomes from the Abecedarian Project." *Applied Developmental Science* 6(1): 42–57.

Chetty, Raj, John N. Friedman, Nathaniel Hilger, Emmanuel Saez, Diane Whitmore Schanzenbach, and Danny Yagan. 2011. "How Does Your Kindergarten Classroom Affect Your Earnings? Evidence from Project STAR." *Quarterly Journal of Economics* 126(4): 1593–660.

Coleman, James S., Ernest Q. Campbell, Carol J. Hobson, James McPartland, Alexander M. Mood, Frederic D. Weinfeld, and Robert L. York. 1966. "Equality of Educational Opportunity." Washington: U.S. Department of Health, Education, and Welfare.

Currie, Janet. 2001. "Early Childhood Education Programs." *Journal of Economic Perspectives* 15(2): 213–38.

Currie, Janet, and Duncan Thomas. 1995. "Does Head Start Make a Difference?" *American Economic Review* 85(3): 341–64.

——. 2000. "School Quality and the Longer-Term Effects of Head Start." *Journal of Human Resources* 35(4): 755–74.

Deming, David. 2009. "Early Childhood Intervention and Life-Cycle Skill Development: Evidence from Head Start." *American Economic Journal: Applied Economics* 1(3): 111–34.

Duncan, Greg J., Amy J. Claessens, Katherine Magnuson, Aletha C. Huston, Pamela Klebanov, Linda Pagani, Leon Feinstein, Mimi Engel, Jeanne Brooks-Gunn. 2007. "School Readiness and Later Achievement." *Developmental Psychology* 43(6): 1428–446.

Frisvold, David. 2007. "Head Start Participation and Childhood Obesity." Paper presented at the Allied Social Science Association Meetings. Chicago (January 6, 2007).

Garces, Eliana, Duncan Thomas, and Janet Currie. 2002. "Longer Term Effects of Head Start." *American Economic Review* 92(4): 999–1012.

Gibbs, Chloe. 2012. "Experimental and Quasi-Experimental Evidence on the Impact of Full-Day Kindergarten." Ph.D. diss., University of Chicago.

Gibbs, Chloe, Jens Ludwig, and Douglas L. Miller. 2011. "Does Head Start Do Any Lasting Good?" *NBER* working paper 17452. Cambridge, Mass.: National Bureau of Economic Research.

Gormley, William T., and Ted Gayer. 2005. "Promoting School Readiness in Oklahoma: An Evaluation of Tulsa's Pre-K Program." *Journal of Human Resources* 40(3): 533–58.

Haskins, Ron, and W. Steven Barnett. 2010. "New Directions for America's Early Childhood Policies." In *Investing in Young Children: New Directions in Federal Preschool and Early Childhood Policy*, edited by Ron Haskins and W. Steven Barnett. Washington, D.C.: Brookings Institution Press.

Hulsey, Lara K., Nikki Aikens, Ashley Kopack, Jerry West, Emily Moiduddin, and Louisa Tarullo. 2011. "Head Start Children, Families, and Programs: Present and Past Data from FACES." *OPRE* report 2011–33a. Washington: U.S. Department of Health and Human Services.

Jencks, Christopher, and Meredith Phillips. 1998. "The Black-White Test Score Gap: An Introduction." *The Black-White Test Score Gap*, edited by Christopher Jencks and Meredith Phillips. Washington, D.C.: Brookings Institution Press.

Krueger, Alan B., and Diane M. Whitmore. 2001. "The Effect of Attending a Small Class in the Early Grades on College-Test Taking and Middle School Test Results: Evidence from Project STAR." *The Economic Journal* 111 (January): 1–28.

Leak, Jimmy, Greg J. Duncan, Weilin Li, Katherine Magnuson, Holly Schindler, and Hirokazu Yoshikawa. 2012. "Early Childhood Education Program Impacts: Variation and Persistence by Starting Age and Program Duration." Working paper. Irvine: University of California.

Ludwig, Jens, and Douglas L. Miller. 2007. "Does Head Start Improve Children's Life Chances? Evidence from a Regression-Discontinuity Design." *Quarterly Journal of Economics* 122(1): 159–208.

Ludwig, Jens, and Deborah A. Phillips. 2007a. "The Benefits and Costs of Head Start." *NBER* working paper 12973. Cambridge, Mass.: National Bureau of Economic Research.

———. 2007b. "The Benefits and Costs of Head Start." *Social Policy Report* 21(3): 3–13.

———. 2010. "Leave No (Young Child) Behind: Prioritizing Access in Early Childhood Education." In *Investing in Young Children: New Directions in Federal Preschool and Early Childhood Policy*, edited by Ron Haskins and W. Steven Barnett. Washington, D.C.: Brookings Institution and the National Institute for Early Education Research.

Moynihan, Daniel P. 1969. *Maximum Feasible Misunderstanding: Community Action in the War on Poverty*. New York: Free Press.

Murnane, Richard J., John B. Willett, Kristen L. Bub, and Kathleen McCartney. 2006. "Understanding Trends in the Black-White Mathematics Achievement Gap During the First Years of School." *Brookings-Wharton Papers on Urban Affairs*. Washington, D.C.: Brookings Institution Press.

National Research Council. 2000. *From Neurons to Neighborhoods: The Science of Early Childhood Development*. Washington, D.C.: The National Academies Press.

Office of Child Development. 1972. "Project Head Start 1969–1970: A Descriptive Report of Programs and Participants." Washington: U.S. Department of Health, Education, and Welfare.

ORC International. 2003. "Public Attitudes Towards the 'Head Start' Program: Summary of Survey Findings." Presentation to the National Head Start Association. Alexandria, Va. (August 7, 2003). Available at: http://www.nhsa.org/research/full_research_studies (accessed January 15, 2013).

Puma, Michael, Stephen Bell, Ronna Cook, and Camilla Heid. 2010. *Head Start Impact Study: Final Report.* Washington: U.S. Department of Health and Human Services. Available at: http://www.acf.hhs.gov/programs/opre/hs/impact_study/reports/impact_study/hs_impact_study_final.pdf (accessed April 4, 2013).

Puma, Michael, Stephen Bell, Ronna Cook, Camilla Heid, and Michael Lopez. 2005. *Head Start Impact Study: First Year Findings.* Washington: U.S. Department of Health and Human Services. Available at: http://www.acf.hhs.gov/sites/default/files/opre/first_yr_finds.pdf (accessed April 4, 2013).

Ramey, Craig T., and Sharon Landesman Ramey. 2010. "Head Start: Strategies to Improve Outcomes for Children Living in Poverty." In *Investing in Young Children: New Directions in Federal Preschool and Early Childhood Policy,* edited by Ron Haskins and W. Steven Barnett. Washington, D.C.: Brookings Institution Press.

Rampey, Bobby D., Gloria S. Dion, and Patricia L. Donahue. 2009. *NAEP 2008 Trends in Academic Progress.* NCES 2009-479. Washington: U.S. Department of Education.

Rock, Donald A., and A. Jackson Stenner. 2005. "Assessment Issues in the Testing of Children at School Entry." *The Future of Children* 15(1): 15–34.

Schweinhart, Lawrence J., Jeanne Montie, Zongping Xiang, W. Steven Barnett, Clive R. Belfield, and Milagros Nores. 2005. *Lifetime Effects: The High/Scope Perry Preschool Study Through Age 40.* Ypsilanti, Mich.: High/Scope Press.

Smith, Marshall S., and Joan S. Bissell. 1970. "Report Analysis: The Impact of Head Start." *Harvard Educational Review* 40(1): 51–104.

U.S. Census Bureau. 2011. *Current Population Survey, October Supplement, 1955–2010.* Washington, D.C.: Government Printing Office. Available at: http://www.census.gov/hhes/school/data/cps/index.html (accessed May 28, 2012).

U.S. General Accounting Office. 1997. *Head Start: Research Provides Little Information on Impact of Current Program.* HEHS-97-59. Washington, D.C.: Government Printing Office.

Vinovskis, Maris A. 2005. *The Birth of Head Start: Preschool Education Policies in the Kennedy and Johnson Administrations.* Chicago: University of Chicago Press.

Westinghouse Learning Corporation. 1969. *The Impact of Head Start: An Evaluation of the Effects of Head Start on Children's Cognitive and Affective Development.* Executive Summary. Ohio University Report to the Office of Economic Opportunity. Washington, D.C.: Clearinghouse for Federal Scientific and Technical Information.

Wong, Vivian C., Thomas D. Cook, W. Steven Barnett, and Kwanghee Jung. 2008. "An Effectiveness-Based Evaluation of Five State Pre-Kindergarten Programs." *Journal of Policy Analysis and Management* 27(1): 122–54.

Zigler, Edward, and Susan Muenchow. 1992. *Head Start: The Inside Story of America's Most Successful Educational Experiment.* New York: Basic Books.

Chapter 3

The K-12 Education Battle

Elizabeth Cascio and Sarah Reber

In a special congressional address on January 12, 1965, President Johnson declared a "national goal of Full Educational Opportunity." In so doing, he expanded the battlefield in the War on Poverty to include education at all levels, offering as a new weapon a large infusion of federal funds to support programs for the poor. Three months later, his proposal for K-12 education was signed into law. Title I of the Elementary and Secondary Education Act of 1965 (ESEA) authorized $1 billion in new federal funding ($7 billion in 2009 dollars) for supplemental academic programs for poor "educationally deprived" children. The program doubled the existing federal commitment to K-12 education and explicitly directed more federal aid to poorer school districts for the first time in history.

Despite the fact that Title I remains the largest federal program for elementary and secondary education today, it was deemed a failure even by many supporters within several years of its inception. Early comparisons of Title I program participants to similar nonparticipants suggested Title I program participation was not closing the achievement gap (Glass et al. 1970), and a highly publicized report by the NAACP (National Association for the Advancement of Colored People) Legal Defense and Education Fund (Martin and McClure 1969) revealed that Title I funds were widely used in unintended ways, such as to provide educational services for ineligible kids, services that were supposed to be paid for from state or local funds, or tax relief. The 1966 Coleman Report also cast doubt on the program's very premise, arguing that a school's resources were much less important for student performance than family background and neighborhoods were (Coleman et al. 1966). Further nonexperimental evaluations of Title I over the decades to follow and research on the relationship between school spending and student performance in the post-ESEA era seem to support this conclusion, but much of this literature suffers from serious methodological issues.

This chapter assesses the legacy of the ESEA, focusing on Title I. We begin by describing how Title I represented an historic shift in federal education policy and how the program operates. Although Title I funds were designated for special programs to raise the academic achievement of poor children, inadequate or ineffective federal monitoring has meant that they have not always met this mandate, having instead been used to supplant existing state and local funds for education or to support educational services for other students, as Ruby Martin and Phyllis McClure suggested (1969). Title I is, however, more than just a "funding stream" (Cohen and Moffitt 2009) even if it is not a well-defined compensatory educational intervention. In the context of a federal system, the threat of withdrawal of funds is an important policy lever for the federal government to encourage school districts to implement other reforms. For example, Title I funds in the program's earliest years came to the de jure racially segregated districts of the southern states conditional on desegregation under Title VI of the 1964 Civil Rights Act. More recently, the No Child Left Behind Act has required states to adopt accountability standards or risk losing Title I funds.

The legacy of Title I thus likely extends beyond its impacts on participants in nominally designated Title I programs. In addition to reviewing the Title I evaluation literature, we therefore review literature on the impacts of Title I — direct and indirect (via school desegregation) — on educational spending and on educational outcomes in the population at large. To complement these studies using district-level data, we also present new evidence of how Title I's introduction may have affected spending and attainment gaps across richer and poorer states. Federal policy is uniquely positioned to address across-state inequality, and narrowing of gaps in school spending across states was in fact one of Title I's goals. Although the gaps across richer and poorer states in both school spending and educational attainment were so large before the ESEA that it would have been difficult for any single program to close them, they have narrowed considerably over the past sixty years, and there is suggestive evidence that Title I contributed to these trends, particularly in the case of school spending. We conclude with a speculative discussion of other ways in which education in America today looks different because of Title I.

HISTORICAL BACKGROUND

"Poverty has many roots but the tap root is ignorance."

Lyndon B. Johnson, January 12, 1965

In his special address to Congress in January 1965, President Johnson outlined the central role of education in the cycle of poverty: those with low levels of completed education were much more likely to live in poverty, and poverty itself was concentrated in "particular urban neighborhoods or rural areas" where school districts had "inadequate financial resources" to "address the largest educational needs." The statistics he cited on school resource differentials across regions were stark: the suburbs of big cities spent 50 percent more per student on education than the cities themselves did, and the five highest-income states spent more than twice as much on education per pupil as the five lowest-income states. Differences in educational attainment across these two groups of states were also stark. We calculate that as of 1960, a native-born white between the ages of twenty-six and thirty born in one of the five highest-income states was nearly 20 percentage points more likely to have graduated from high school than his or her counterpart in one of the five lowest-income states (71.0 percent versus 52.3 percent). For native-born African Americans and other nonwhites, the differential was even larger, at nearly 27 percentage points (53.4 percent versus 26.6 percent).[1]

The central provision of the 1965 ESEA—Title I—was designed to alleviate inequities in school spending, in the hopes of increasing educational attainment among the poor and breaking the cycle of poverty. The ESEA (Public Law 891–0), signed into law April 11, 1965, was "an Act to strengthen and improve educational quality and educational opportunities in the Nation's elementary and secondary schools." Title I authorized financial assistance for school districts (local educational agencies, or LEAs) with "concentrations of low-income families" to "improve their educational programs by various means . . . which contribute particularly to meeting the special educational needs of educationally deprived children." The ESEA had other provisions—for textbooks, library books, and other instructional materials (Title II), for supplementary school centers and services (Title III), for improvement of educational research and training by institutions of higher education (Table IV), and for improvement of the functioning of state educational agencies (SEAs) (Title V). But Title I received an appropriation more than three times larger than those for Titles II, III, IV, and V combined, and distribution of Title I funds was based explicitly on area child poverty rates. We focus on Title I from here forward.

Title I was an historic shift in federal policy on several grounds (for historical accounts of the origins of the ESEA, see, for example, Davies 2007; Graham 1984; Kaestle 2001). First, federal programs for elementary and secondary education historically had not been compensatory. That is, the federal government had not directed more funds to poorer school districts.[2] Second, federal programs for elementary and secondary education had not been so large.[3] Third, federal programs had not exerted federal control over schools. In conjunction with Title VI of the 1964 Civil Rights Act (CRA), the introduction of Title I exerted federal control over schools in one very important way: receipt of funds was contingent on nondiscrimination. The Johnson administration enforced this provision in the South, requiring the first steps toward desegregation of the region's de jure segregated schools for compliance. These changes marked the beginning of the end of school segregation in the South (see, for example, Cascio et al. 2008, 2010; Orfield 1969; Rosenberg 1991), which we consider to be part of Title I's legacy.[4] Another legacy is the precedent of contingent federal education funding. More recently, receipt of Title I funds has been made contingent on adoption of school accountability programs under the No Child Left Behind Act of 2001 (NCLB) and will likely be made contingent upon efforts to improve teaching under the NCLB's reauthorization.

THE TITLE I PROGRAM

As mentioned, the enabling legislation distributed Title I funds on the basis of area child poverty, with the intent of improving educational spending on and opportunities for poor children. However, the legislation made for a potentially weak program in two regards. First, although compensatory, the funding formula penalized the low-spending states where poor children were concentrated. Second, the legislation provided few safeguards against unintended use of Title I funds.

The Funding Formula

The initial Title I appropriation was distributed primarily based on counts of poor children from the 1960 census,[5] and grants per eligible child were smaller in states with lower average state and local spending on schools.[6] Because spending was lower on average in poorer states, this feature of the formula meant that the grant per eligible child was smaller in poorer states, and the program was less compensatory than it would have been had each state received the same amount per eligible child. Still, the program was large enough—and the relationship between poverty and per-pupil Title I grants strong enough—that its introduction marked the beginning of compensatory federal education aid in the United States.

We show this in figures 3.1 and 3.2 using state-level data on educational revenues from the federal government and poverty rates. These figures plot per-pupil federal revenue for K-12 education on the vertical axis against the 1960 state child poverty rate, that is, the share of the state's students who were eligible for Title I.[7] Figure 3.1 shows this relationship for the 1963–1964 school year, before Title I was implemented. Figure 3.2 shows the same relationship for the 1969–1970 school year, after Title I had been in effect for a few years. In 1963–1964, school districts in higher-poverty states did not receive more per-pupil federal funding on average; the slope of the fitted line in figure 3.1 is small and statistically insignificant. By 1969–1970, school districts in higher-poverty states received substantially more federal funding compared to those in lower-poverty states; the slope of the fitted line in figure 3.2 is $1,213 (in real 2009 dollars), indicating that a 10 percentage point increase in the poverty rate was associated with an increase in per-pupil federal revenue of about $121. The change in slope can be fully accounted for by the introduction of Title I.[8]

Although Title I formula amounts were larger both in absolute terms and relative to existing spending levels in poorer states and school districts,[9] the program was small relative to existing school spending gaps associated with poverty. This is suggested by figure 3.3, which plots trends in real per-pupil school spending and federal revenue received by local school districts from 1953 forward. The figure shows that federal education aid has historically been quite small relative to overall spending on elementary and secondary education. This has especially been

FIGURE 3.1 / Child Poverty and Per-Pupil Federal Revenue, Before Title I, 1963–1964 School Year

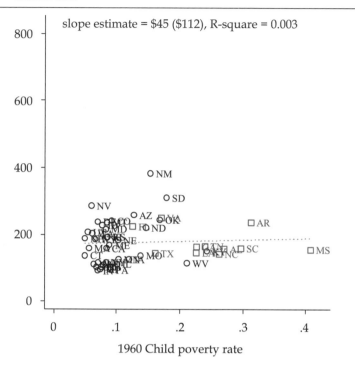

Source: Authors' calculations based on U.S. Congress (1965); Minnesota Population Center (2011); U.S. Department of Health, Education, and Welfare (1965, 1967).
Note: Per-pupil federal revenue for K-12 education is expressed in real 2009 dollars. The slope estimate gives the slope coefficient (standard error) on the fitted line. Slope coefficients are the predicted difference in per-pupil federal revenue for K-12 education between a state with only poor children and a state with no poor children. Regressions give each state equal weight.

the case more recently, but was also true at Title I's inception, when it reached only 10.2 percent of overall K-12 spending.[10] More directly, consider the statistic Johnson gave in his January 1965 address: the five richest states spent more than twice as much per pupil on education as the five poorest states. Using data from the 1963–1964 school year, we calculate that this spending differential amounted to (at least) $1,850 per student (in real 2009 dollars). By contrast, the analogous difference in Title I funding was only $194 per pupil—one-tenth of this figure.

Thus, instead of infusing lots of funds into those "particular urban neighborhoods" and "rural areas" with the highest concentrations of poverty, the Title I funding formula allocated a poor child the same amount of funding regardless of whether he lived in a richer or poorer community in a given state, and poor children in poorer states tended to receive less. This formula was likely a strategy that

FIGURE 3.2 / Child Poverty and Per-Pupil Federal Revenue, After Title I, 1969–1970 School Year

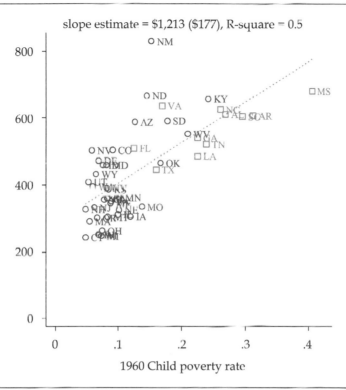

slope estimate = $1,213 ($177), R-square = 0.5

Source: Authors' calculations based on U.S. Congress (1965); Minnesota Population Center (2011); U.S. Department of Health, Education, and Welfare (1970b, 1973a).
Note: Per-pupil federal revenue for K-12 education is expressed in real 2009 dollars. The slope estimate gives the slope coefficient (standard error) on the fitted line. Slope coefficients are the predicted difference in per-pupil federal revenue for K-12 education between a state with only poor children and a state with no poor children. Regressions give each state equal weight.

fostered passage of the ESEA—it allocated funds to nearly every legislative district in the country (Cohen and Moffitt 2009)—but is one reason why Title I may have proven less effective than hoped.

Statutory Intent

Congress intended Title I funds be used for supplemental academic programs for "educationally deprived" poor children, and required districts to submit plans to state education agencies (SEAs) for how they would use the funds. On the books, most Title I programs have been implemented as "pull out" programs, whereby eligible students are taken out of their regular classrooms to participate; the re-

FIGURE 3.3 / Trends in Per-Pupil School Spending and Federal Revenue

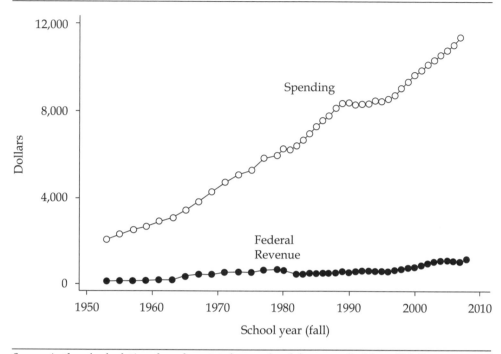

Source: Authors' calculations based on state by year level data compiled from U.S. Department of Health, Education, and Welfare (1956, 1957, 1960a, 1960b, 1964–1968, 1969b, 1970a, 1970b, 1973a, 1973b, 1974, 1975, 1976a, 1976b, 1979); U.S. Department of Education (1978, 1980, 1981–1983, 1986–1989, 1991a, 1991b, 1992–1995, 1997, 1999–2012).
Note: 2009 dollars. Means are unweighted.

mainder have been implemented at the class level, in preschool, after school, or during the summer.

It has been difficult, however, to ensure that Title I funds are used in practice as they are on paper. This was particularly the case at the program's origins. Aside from the described contingencies on Title I receipt, the program respected state and local control—yet another strategy that likely fostered the ESEA's passage, and yet another reason the program may have been less effective than hoped. In part, this was true by default: the program was large relative to the federal staff available to administer it. It was also true by design: although LEAs were required to submit proposals to SEAs to receive Title I funds, they in principle could design programs to best suit their needs. To the extent that school districts are better than the federal government at developing programs for their students, such discretion might have promoted effective use of the funds, as emphasized in the economic theory of fiscal federalism (Oates 1972). On the other hand, it could mean that Title I funds have not been spent on supplemental programs for poor children as intended.

Martin and McClure (1969) provide many examples of such spending in Title I's earliest years. These included investments in capital – buildings, swimming pools, audiovisual equipment – and expenditures on band and football uniforms. They also describe how school districts moved state and local revenues away from the poorer schools where Title I grants were spent, in which case the programs provided by Title I were not "supplemental," or reduced the revenue they raised when they received Title I dollars. In the latter case, Title I funds were not spent on education at all – a phenomenon referred to as *crowd-out* in economics.

Regulations that took effect in the early 1970s attempted to improve the targeting of Title I funds and to reduce crowd-out. For example, *maintenance of effort* (MOE) provisions require local and state governments to maintain revenues at some (high) fraction of the previous year's levels, and *comparability* requires that state and local funds be equalized across schools within districts, so that Title I funds are purely supplemental for the schools that receive them. Nevertheless, MOE provisions still allow for substantial crowd-out, particularly if the counterfactual is one of increasing revenue (Gordon 2004), and evidence is substantial even today that the comparability requirement is violated in practice (Roza 2010; Heuer and Stullich 2011).

Thus, Title I funds need not be spent on supplemental educational programs for poor children. This suggests that an exclusive focus on the Title I evaluation literature potentially misses some of the program's more important effects – on overall school spending, on the population at large, and, given the contingent nature of Title I funding receipt, on the adoption of other school policies.

EFFECTS OF PROGRAM PARTICIPATION: STUDENTS AND SCHOOLS

Annual evaluations of Title I are required by federal law and focus on the effects of individual student participation in nominal Title I programs on reading and math achievement. To date, these studies have used observational data; no randomized controlled trials have been conducted. These evaluations have produced little evidence that Title I reduces the achievement gap by socioeconomic status, a result that has been the source of much criticism of the program. This achievement gap is impressive. For example, using parental education as a measure of socioeconomic status, Sean Reardon and Joseph Robinson (2007) estimate that gaps in math scores between the children of parents with only a high school degree and children of parents with only a college degree range from about 0.50 to 0.67 standard deviations at age thirteen and from about 0.60 to 0.75 standard deviations at age seventeen; gaps in reading scores are only slightly smaller.

Title I evaluations have fallen into three broad categories. The first – the approach commonly used by states and school districts – compares performance of participants on a nationally norm-referenced test before and after program participation (for example, at the beginning and the end of the academic year).[11] Title I is deemed successful if participants move up in the national achievement distribution. However, this approach can give reliable estimates of the effect of Title I on participating students only if participants would have remained in the same place in the achievement distribution in the absence of the program. In their meta-analysis of Title I evaluations, Geoffrey Borman and Jerome D'Agostino (1996) point out several reasons that this assumption may not hold: regression to the mean (participants would have moved up in the distribution even in the absence of the program), the importance of the test cycle (larger impacts when students are tested fall-spring rather than annually due to relatively large "summer setback" for the educationally disadvantaged), and manipulation of the testing environment to favor the second (or post) test. Each of these factors would tend to overstate the effects of program participation despite negative selection of Title I eligible students.

At the heart of these criticisms is the fact that this approach implicitly compares Title I eligible students to all non-eligible students nationally, despite their likely lack of comparability. The other two categories of evaluation have addressed the question of how to choose a comparison group in two different ways. The second category has compared the achievement of participants before and after program participation to the change in achievement of some subset of nonparticipants over the same period of time — a difference-in-differences approach. Three such federally mandated evaluations have been conducted. The earliest compared Title I participating students in the late 1960s to nonparticipating students in Title I eligible schools, those with sufficient concentrations of poverty within their districts to host Title I programs (Glass et al. 1970). The *Sustaining Effects* study compared Title I participants to students deemed most in need of compensatory education (by their teachers) at Title I ineligible schools (Carter 1984). In the most recent *Prospects* study (Puma et al. 1997), the comparison group consisted of nonparticipating students in both Title I eligible and ineligible schools. In the third category of evaluation, two studies use a regression-discontinuity technique, comparing the test scores of (all) students in schools that are barely eligible for Title I designation given their poverty rate to those of students in schools that are barely ineligible (van der Klaauw 2008; Matsudaira, Hosek, and Walsh 2012).

Despite differences in empirical approach, the Title I evaluation literature is unified in producing discouraging results. Borman and D'Agostino's (1996) meta-analysis, which draws on studies of the first and second variety, suggests effect sizes of 0.10 to 0.12 standard deviations for math and reading test performance — hardly enough to close the achievement gap by socioeconomic status. Their analysis also implies that studies of the second variety produce significantly smaller effects, consistent with expectations.[12] The regression-discontinuity studies in the third category find no significant effect of a school's Title I designation on its overall test performance. However, those studies also find no evidence that Title I schools have more resources, suggesting that school districts crowded out the significantly higher federal aid flowing to Title I schools.

The findings of the regression-discontinuity studies point to a possible reason why studies of the first and second variety yield small effect sizes: we might expect little impact to the extent that school districts diverted state or local funds to Title I ineligible schools on receipt of Title I funds. For example, students in the ineligible schools, who served as comparison students in the *Sustaining Effects* and *Prospects* studies, may be indirectly "treated" by and benefit from Title I. Put differently, the standard approaches to evaluating Title I are likely to understate its effects on poor students if Title I funds are misallocated within districts. This suggests the benefits of taking a more aggregate approach to analyzing Title I — using the school district or the state, rather than the student or the school, as the unit of analysis — and considering non-eligible children as potential Title I beneficiaries.

EFFECTS ON SCHOOL SPENDING AND EDUCATIONAL OUTCOMES

Setting aside how Title I funds are allocated across students and schools within districts, how much has Title I raised spending on education at the school district level? That is, how much has it narrowed gaps in school spending between richer and poorer school districts?[13] In a world where school districts do not have discretion over how to spend Title I grants and cannot alter their decisions about how much revenue to raise locally, this question would be moot: Title I would increase school spending dollar-for-grant dollar, and hence relatively more in poorer districts because they received larger Title I grants. The question thus becomes one of how much school districts crowded out Title I through tax reductions, and how much states crowded out Title I by allocating less tax revenue to education or making its distribution less compensatory. Such offsetting behavior naturally has implications for how much the program might narrow the gap in educational attainment between richer and poorer school districts. Further, if school districts must undertake additional action, such as school desegregation, to receive their Title I funds, that additional action might also affect school spending and educational outcomes.

Direct Effects

In economics parlance, Title I is a restricted block grant from the federal government to school districts. Such a grant sets a floor on school spending for the district: it must spend at least as much as the grant on educational services. But for school spending levels beyond this, a school district has some discretion. In particular, it can spend the grant either on education or on other goods and services (via tax reduction), just like any other source of income. In this case, we would expect spending on education to increase potentially much less than dollar-for-grant dollar — this is crowd-out. The spending decision of a state government is more difficult to model, in light of the large number of policy functions at the state level. However, one might expect that Title I frees up states to devote less state tax revenue to education or to distribute aid in a less compensatory manner, partially offsetting the compensatory distribution of federal aid.

A numerical example might be of some help. Suppose that a school district is allocated a $100 per-pupil Title I grant. If it receives $10 less per pupil from the state as a result, the total income of the population in the school district effectively increases by $90 per pupil. The voters may allocate that $90 between education and other goods and services. If typically voters would spend 20 cents of each additional dollar of income on education, we would expect spending on education out of this $90 in exactly the same ratio. Thus, spending on education by the district should go up by $18 per pupil—not by the $90 per pupil in additional income in the district or the $100 per-pupil Title I grant. In this example, the $100 grant has bought $18 in spending on education, $10 in tax relief for state taxpayers (or alternative state-provided services), and $72 in tax relief for local taxpayers.

Three studies to date have estimated the education spending responses to Title I using district-level data. Two of these studies imply a much larger increase in spending response to Title I than in the numerical example. For example, Martin Feldstein (1978) used the variation in Title I grant amounts across similar school districts in different states in 1970 and found that spending increased by about 70 cents for each additional dollar of Title I revenue, suggesting little crowd-out. Elizabeth Cascio, Nora Gordon, and Sarah Reber (forthcoming) exploit the precise timing of Title I's introduction in 1965 using annual data and variation across school districts in child poverty rates and find that the introduction of Title I increased school spending by about 50 cents on the dollar in the South. By contrast, Gordon (2004) analyzes on more recent data, from the early 1990s, for the entire country. Using the abrupt change in a district's Title I grant over time associated with the 1990 census update of child poverty counts, she finds that increases in Title I funding were completely offset by reductions in other sources of revenue within three years, so that spending did not increase as a result of the Title I grant in the long run.

Thus the literature yields a wide range of estimates. However, the estimated spending increases are larger in the two studies that use data closer to Title I's origins, suggesting that Title I may have succeeded in narrowing spending gaps between poorer and richer school districts in its earliest years.[14] Cascio, Gordon, and Reber (forthcoming) also examine whether the Title I–induced increases in spending affected county high school graduation rates between 1960 and 1970—that is, whether Title I also succeeded in narrowing poverty gaps in educational attainment. They find that it did, though not necessarily through improvements in attainment among Title I eligible students. They find evidence that, at least in the short run, Title I related increases in spending helped whites, but not blacks. They argue that, following decades-long practice in the South, Title I funds could easily have been diverted toward whites, particularly in the program's earliest years, when black and white schools in the region were still largely separate. However, they lack the data to show this within-district misallocation directly.

Indirect Effects: School Desegregation

The improvements in educational attainment for whites but not blacks found by Cascio, Gordon, and Reber (forthcoming) were not a desired policy outcome. However, even if Title I related spending did not directly help blacks in the earliest years, the program likely benefited them indirectly. Combined with the CRA, Title I funding provided an important "carrot" — and potentially cover — for a longer-term and fundamental transformation of southern education that ultimately increased spending on black students and black educational attainment: school desegregation.

The direct effects of Title I and the CRA on school desegregation in the South were not large, and, notably, Johnson did not use the threat of withdrawal of federal funds to promote desegregation outside the South. But Title I and CRA arguably helped to set in motion the complete breakdown of the dual educational system in the South. In 1965 and 1966, the Johnson administration required southern school districts only to move a small percentage of black students to white schools to comply with the nondiscrimination requirements of the CRA.[15] Cascio and her colleagues (2010) find that the financial incentive worked: otherwise similar districts with more Title I funds on the line were more likely to desegregate just enough to receive them. These requirements became more stringent, particularly by 1968, but ended abruptly when Nixon took office in January 1969, in fulfilling his campaign promise to the South to end enforcement of the CRA's fund-withholding provisions (Orfield 2000). Even so, by this time, support from the elected branches of government had strengthened the resolve of the courts, which until that point had been ineffective in desegregating schools, and the existence of desegregation guidelines for CRA compliance had focused the courts on more stringent requirements in the districts they supervised (Orfield 1969). The CRA enforcement efforts under Johnson also reduced the load on the federal courts, allowing them to focus on the toughest cases (Cascio et al. 2010).

Thus, by the time Nixon stopped enforcement of the CRA's fund-withholding provisions, courts were well empowered to continue the desegregation effort, and did so effectively, in the most resistant southern districts as well as outside of the South. Although the impact of school desegregation on educational resources at the school district level is theoretically ambiguous,[16] the existing evidence suggests that, on net, it increased school spending. In a study of Louisiana during the 1960s and early 1970s, Reber (2011) finds larger increases in per-pupil school expenditures for school districts with higher initial black enrollment shares as schools desegregated, arguing that the additional funding was necessary to "level up" spending in desegregated schools to that formerly experienced only in the white schools.[17] In a study using data over a longer period for the entire country, Rucker Johnson (2011) finds evidence of increases in a district's per-pupil school spending after a court order for school desegregation was handed down, with larger effects in districts with higher black enrollment shares. Several studies find that school desegregation improved educational outcomes for blacks and suggest that the mechanism was most likely this additional school spending (Guryan 2004; Ashenfelter, Collins, and Yoon 2006; Reber 2010; Johnson 2011).[18]

NEW EVIDENCE AT THE STATE LEVEL

The literature reviewed thus far suggests that, even if Title I funds have often not been used to support supplemental programs for poor students, the program may have succeeded in narrowing gaps in school spending and educational attainment between higher- and lower-poverty school districts, particularly in the 1960s and 1970s. These studies have focused on poverty gaps within states. Yet, a significant fraction of the variation in spending and attainment across school districts exists across states; for example, William Evans, Sheila Murray, and Robert Schwab (1997) estimate that inequality in school spending between states accounts for half or more of overall spending inequality at the district level. Furthermore, although Title I was clearly too small of a program to eliminate cross-state spending inequality associated with income or poverty, reducing poverty-related differentials across states in spending—and educational outcomes—was an explicit goal of the program, as described earlier.

Nevertheless, the questions of whether Title I narrowed state-level poverty gaps in school spending and educational attainment have not been addressed in the literature to date. In the next section, we present new evidence on these fronts, drawing on state-level panel data on school spending we collected from Department of Health, Education, and Welfare and Department of Education publications and data on educational attainment (high school graduation and college-going rates of young adults) we extracted from the American Community Survey (ACS) and the census (Ruggles et al. 2010).

Education Spending

As President Johnson described when pitching the ESEA to Congress in January 1965, the relationship between state poverty rates and state education spending on the eve of the ESEA was strong. We show this in figure 3.4, which plots the (natural log of) state average per-pupil spending for the 1963–1964 school year, two years before Title I was implemented, against the 1960 state child poverty rate. The slope of the fitted line is strongly negative (and statistically significant): per-pupil spending was considerably lower in higher-poverty states. We use the log of spending, rather than the level, because it facilitates comparisons of the slope coefficients over time in light of the dramatic increases in average spending shown in figure 3.3. That is, instead of the slope coefficients being expressed in dollar terms, they are expressed in percent terms. A 10 percentage point increase in the 1960 child poverty rate was thus associated with a 23 percent reduction in per-pupil spending on average. The points are also clustered fairly close to the line, suggesting that, before the ESEA, poverty accounted for a significant fraction of across-

FIGURE 3.4 / Child Poverty and Per-Pupil School Spending, 1963–1964 School Year

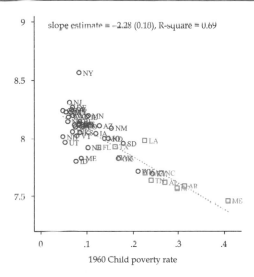

Source: Author's calculations based on U.S. Congress (1965); Minnesota Population Center (2011); U.S. Department of Health, Education, and Welfare (1965).
Note: The slope estimate gives the slope coefficient (standard error) on the fitted line. Slope coefficients are the predicted difference in log per-pupil spending on K-12 education between a state with only poor children and a state with no poor children. Regressions give each state equal weight.

FIGURE 3.5 / Child Poverty and Per-Pupil School Spending, 2006–2007 School Year

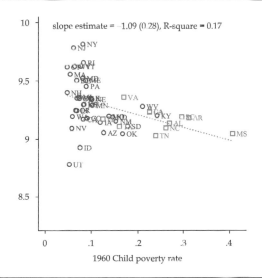

Source: Author's calculations based on U.S. Congress (1965); Minnesota Population Center (2011); U.S. Department of Education (2011).
Note: The slope estimate gives the slope coefficient (standard error) on the fitted line. Slope coefficients are the predicted difference in log per-pupil spending on K-12 education between a state with only poor children and a state with no poor children. Regressions give each state equal weight.

state spending inequality.[19] Figure 3.4 also shows that though southern states (the square markers) were significantly lower spending on average, there was no South effect; their lower spending was in line with their significantly higher poverty rates.[20] This suggests that poverty, not some other region-specific factor, like institutionalized segregation, accounts for low school spending in the South.

As described, the architects of the ESEA viewed the negative relationship between poverty and education spending as an important barrier to expanding educational opportunities and reducing poverty. By directing more federal aid to poorer states (figures 3.1 and 3.2), has Title I succeeded in weakening this relationship? As a first pass at this question, figure 3.5 is analogous to figure 3.4, but considers spending during the 2006–2007 school year—well after Title I was implemented. In this more recent year, the relationship between 1960 child poverty and log per-pupil spending is still negative and statistically significant but less than half as steep: a 10 percentage point increase in the child poverty rate was associated with an 11 percent reduction in per-pupil spending. In addition, the points are much more spread out around the fitted line, suggesting that in more recent years, variation in school spending across states has become less related to variation in poverty and more related to other factors.[21]

It would be foolhardy to interpret the change in slope shown in figures 3.4 and 3.5 as being caused by Title I; it could have been brought about by any number of forces, including increasing demand for and returns to education, changing costs for teachers and educational supplies, or state school finance equalization. Although we cannot rule out the importance of other factors, we provide more compelling evidence of a contribution of Title I in figure 3.6. Figure 3.6 shows how the slope of the fitted line depicted in figures 3.4 and 3.5 changed over time.[22] For example, the slope in figure 3.4 for 1963 is –2.3; in figure 3.6, that value is plotted for 1963—the last dot before Title I implementation in 1965 (indicated with a dashed vertical line). Likewise, the slope in figure 3.5 is –1.1, the value plotted for 2006 in figure 3.6. The other points show that same slope for other years, so we can see how the relationship between poverty and spending has changed over time, especially around the time Title I was implemented. There is a clear break in trend in 1965, suggesting that Title I contributed to a weakening of the relationship between poverty and school spending at the state level. If one assumes that, in the absence of Title I, the pre-1965 trend in the relationship between poverty and spending would have continued, one would conclude that Title I narrowed the spending gap between higher-poverty and lower-poverty states for a decade or so, but that gap ultimately returned to trend.

Despite the sharp reduction in the expected spending gap between poorer and richer states in 1965, it remained substantial then and continues to remain substantial today. Although the strong relationship between school spending and poverty prior to 1965 meant that the federal government had the scope to equalize spending across states by distributing aid on the basis of poverty, closing the gap would have required a much larger program. We alluded to this earlier, but can do some more direct calculations on the basis of our estimates. These imply that the introduction of Title I would have reduced the gap in spending between higher-poverty

FIGURE 3.6 / Child Poverty and Per-Pupil School Spending Over Time

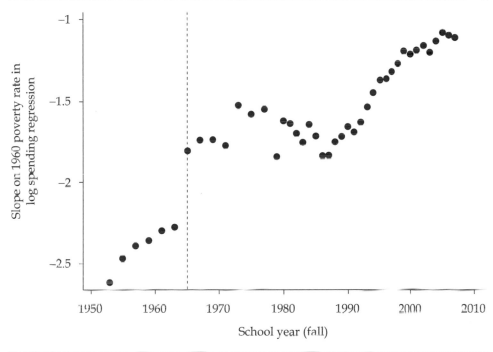

Source: Author's calculations based on U.S. Congress (1965); Minnesota Population Center (2011); U.S. Department of Education (1981, 1989, 1994, 2001, 2011; U.S. Department of Health, Education, and Welfare (1956, 1957, 1960a, 1960b, 1964–1966, 1968, 1970b, 1973b, 1974, 1976b, 1979).
Note: The figure plots slope coefficients on lines fit to year-by-year scatterplots of log per-pupil spending on K-12 education (*y*-axis) on the 1960 child poverty rate (*x*-axis). These slope coefficients give the predicted difference in log per-pupil school spending between a state with only poor children and a state with no poor children. Regressions give each state equal weight. The dashed vertical line is placed at 1965, the year Title I was introduced.

and lower-poverty states by only about 15 percent, assuming no state or local crowd-out of federal funding.[23] Thus, all else constant, the Title I program would have had to have been nearly seven times as large as it was to close the then existing poverty gap in per-pupil current school spending across states. This would have required almost $50 billion (2009 dollars) at Title I's inception, and even more if some of the funds would have been crowded out by states and school districts. Even today, Title I is only a $14 billion program.

Educational Attainment

School spending per student has long been lower in poorer states, but the relationship between poverty and spending has weakened over the past sixty years.

Though we caution against making causal inferences, our analysis of spending suggests that the introduction of Title I most likely contributed to these trends, particularly in the short to medium run. We now examine whether this narrowing of the poverty gap in school expenditure across states was accompanied by a narrowing of poverty gaps in educational outcomes.

To do this, we use the 1960 to 2000 decennial censuses and the 2010 American Community Survey (Ruggles et al. 2010) to look at the completed education for individuals who were twenty-six to thirty years old at the time of interview. We assign individuals to birth cohorts and focus our attention on six five-year birth cohorts. The first two of these cohorts (those born between 1929 and 1933 and between 1939 and 1943) had no exposure to Title I, the third (born between 1949 and 1953) had limited exposure, as teenagers, and the remaining cohorts (born between 1959 and 1963, 1969 and 1973, and 1979 and 1983) were schooled entirely in the post-ESEA period. We cannot break out our analysis separately by the poverty status of individuals in childhood, because that is not reported in the census or ACS. To the extent that whites and nonwhites have different poverty rates on average, however, separating the analysis by race can give us some sense of whether there has been convergence by childhood poverty status. Understanding trends in racial gaps in educational outcomes is also of independent interest.

Figure 3.7 shows national trends in educational attainment for each five-year birth cohort, separately for whites and nonwhites.[24] Educational attainment was low for the earlier cohorts, especially among nonwhites. For example, the open circle plotted for 1929 (with a value of 0.35) indicates that only 35 percent of non-whites born between 1929 and 1933 completed high school. Sixty-four percent of whites in those same birth cohorts completed high school. If Title I had effects on educational attainment, and no other factors also affected trends in educational attainment, we might expect to see no change in attainment across the cohorts not exposed to Title I while in school, improvement across the partially exposed cohorts, and no change across the fully exposed cohorts. That is, we would expect to see the steepest upward trend in educational attainment between 1939 and 1959. In contrast, high school graduation rates were already on the rise as Title I went into effect, especially for nonwhites. The time pattern of college attendance trends is more consistent with an effect of Title I. Here, the trend was steeper across the cohorts partially exposed to Title I (from 1939 to 1959), relative to the trend for the never exposed and the fully exposed, consistent with a potential role for Title I. However, these gains do not appear to be any larger for nonwhites than for whites.

In results not shown, we also examined whether educational attainment for people born (and presumably educated) in poorer states, relative to those born in richer states, showed any convergence, mirroring our analysis of school spending in figure 3.6. As noted, the educational attainment gaps between young adults born in higher- and lower-poverty states were indeed substantial in 1960 (the 1929 to 1933 cohort), before the ESEA was passed. Those gaps have narrowed considerably, but all in all the improvements do not coincide well with the introduction of Title I. For example, for nonwhites and whites alike, the relationship between poverty and high school completion was weaker for the 1939 to 1943 cohort—which was not exposed to Title I—and continued to weaken steadily across the remain-

FIGURE 3.7 / Trends in High School Graduation and College Attendance

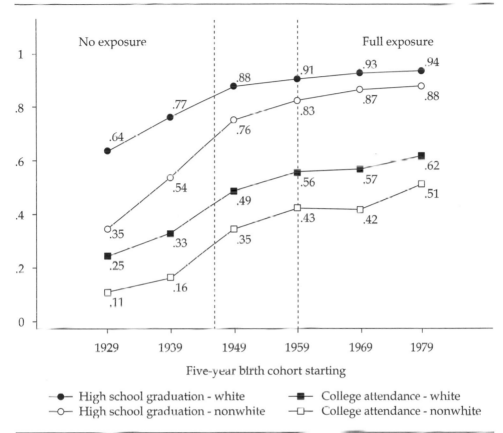

Five-year birth cohort starting

—●— High school graduation - white　　　—■— College attendance - white
—○— High school graduation - nonwhite　—□— College attendance - nonwhite

Source: Authors' calculations based on Ruggles et al. (2010).
Note: Age twenty-six to thirty. Data were collapsed to the (five-year) birth cohort by birth state by race level using person weights provided in the census and American Community Survey. Means weighted by cell size.

ing cohorts under observation. Thus the relationship between state-level rates of poverty and high school completion across cohorts with different levels of exposure to Title I provides no evidence of a trend break. The evidence is somewhat more compelling for college attendance rates: poverty-related attainment gaps increased between the 1929 to 1933 and 1939 to 1943 cohorts, but sharply reversed for cohorts exposed to Title I. Although, like the trends shown in figure 3.7, this pattern is consistent with a role for Title I, it would be surprising if Title I had improved college attendance rates without improving high school graduation rates.

All in all, we view the data and our methodology as providing at best tentative evidence of an effect of Title I on gaps in educational attainment across richer and poorer states. On the one hand, the suggestion that Title I–induced spending did not dramatically affect educational attainment would appear to be consistent with the weak relationship between school spending and educational outcomes in observational data in the modern era (Hanushek 1986, 1997). On the other hand, school spending has been found to be an important determinant of educational attainment for cohorts educated before the War on Poverty (see, for example, Ashenfelter, Collins, and Yoon 2006; Card and Krueger 1992a, 1992b), and is thought to have been an important mechanism by which school desegregation increased black educational attainment, as earlier noted. Title I was not a large program relative to existing poverty gaps in school spending or the overall trend in school spending, so its effects on educational attainment may be difficult to detect. Understanding the long-term effects of Title I on educational outcomes is a challenging but important area for future research.

SUMMARY AND CONCLUDING REMARKS

The War on Poverty fundamentally changed the role of the federal government in public education. Until the mid-1960s, K-12 education was funded almost exclusively by local and state governments, the distribution of federal aid was in no way related to poverty, and local control over public schools was a cherished and closely guarded ideal. Title I of the 1965 ESEA doubled federal spending on K-12 education, shifted the distribution of overall federal education aid sharply toward poorer school districts and states, and curtailed local control over schools—in some respects. Federal oversight over how Title I grants were spent was minimal: state governments and school districts could easily offset the Title I grants through tax reductions, and Title I funds could readily be spent on children who were not themselves "educationally deprived." However, the federal government would release the earliest Title I grants to southern school districts only if they met certain benchmarks for school desegregation, breaking local control where it had for decades resulted in egregious violations of blacks' civil rights.

Our assessment of Title I's legacy has drawn from these observations. We have taken our discussion beyond what would traditionally be construed as Title I research—the vast literature evaluating the effects of nominal Title I program participation on test scores—to the much smaller literatures on the effects of Title I on school spending, on the effects of Title I–induced spending on educational outcomes in the overall population, and on the effects of school desegregation on school spending and educational attainment. We have also presented a new analysis of how Title I affected the gaps in school spending and educational outcomes across states. Poverty-related gaps in spending have narrowed substantially since 1965, and Title I appears to have contributed to that trend. But the program was not nearly large enough to close such gaps. Educational attainment has increased dramatically across cohorts, and the gap in educational attainment between those born in richer and poorer states has shrunk. But Title I's contribution to these trends was likely small.

Title I's legacy is also broader than its grants per se, as the program has had effects on the formation of other education policies at both federal and state levels (on the legacy of the ESEA for federal education policy, see also Davies 2007). Such policies include school desegregation, which we have discussed extensively. They also include state school finance reforms. For example, the concern about crowd-out and misuse of Title I funds may have led not only to more regulation of the use of Title I funds, but also to extensive regulation in the use of state funds. When funding comes with so many (perhaps well-meaning) strings attached, educators and budget-makers may spend more time thinking about funding streams than about how to best educate children (Roza 2010; Cohen and Moffitt 2009). Finally, NCLB tied Title I receipt to state policies on student testing and accountability. Even though the federal requirements were weak, the policy appears to have had a positive effect on student achievement (Dee and Jacob 2011), and it has arguably shifted the terms of the education reform discussion.

The goal of eliminating disparities in both educational inputs such as spending and outputs such as achievement and educational attainment was ambitious. The good news is that gaps—at least between richer and poorer states—in both inputs and outputs have declined dramatically since the War on Poverty began. The bad news is that they are both still quite large.

NOTES

1. We made these calculations from the 1960 decennial census (Ruggles et al. 2010). To arrive at these figures, we ranked states by per-capita income in 1965, which we linearly interpolated from 1960 and 1970 figures. The five lowest-income states were Mississippi, Arkansas, South Carolina, Alabama, and Louisiana. The five highest-income states were Connecticut, New Jersey, California, Nevada, and New York.

2. The two main federal programs for K-12 education before the ESEA were Aid to Federally Impacted Areas—funds to offset the impacts that military installations had on local schools—and funding under the National Defense Education Act of 1958, which was intended to strengthen math and science education in light of the launch of the Soviet satellite *Sputnik*.

3. There were many objections to increased federal contributions for education. These included concerns that they would lead to increased federal control over schools, that more federal involvement in education would be socialistic, and the long-standing debate over whether federal funds should be directed to Catholic schools or to private schools. Kaestle (2001) also credits a lack of presidential leadership.

4. The Johnson administration did not enforce Title VI in the de facto racially segregated school districts outside the South, despite clear evidence, in Chicago, for example, that school attendance zones were often drawn to limit interracial contact (Orfield 1969; Davies 2007). School desegregation outside the South largely occurred in the 1970s, through court intervention. Court intervention was also important in desegregating southern school districts after Nixon stopped enforcing the fund-withholding provisions of the CRA (for more discussion of the role of the courts and the political branches in school desegregation, see Reber 2005; Cascio et al. 2008, 2010; Rosenberg 1991; Davies 2007).

5. The initial Title I formula determined the number of eligible students in a county primarily based on two categories of eligible students: counts of five- to seventeen-year-

olds living in low-income families in the county as of the 1960 census; and children in higher-income families in the county that received Aid to Families with Dependent Children (AFDC) assistance in 1962. Other categories were added over the rest of the 1960s, but most of a county's eligibility was determined on the basis of the 1960 census-based child poverty counts alone. Formula amounts for school districts (within counties) were then established by state education agencies based on available data on child poverty at the district level (Bailey and Mosher 1968).

6. Initially, the state-specific per eligible child grant was equal to one-half the average per-pupil current expenditure in the state, lagged two years and net of federal transfers. In 1967, the state factors in low-spending states were leveled up to the national average (U.S. Department of Health, Education, and Welfare 1969a).

7. Technically, this is the ratio of five- to seventeen-year-olds in low-income families (income less than $2,000) to all five- to seventeen-year-olds in the state in 1960. This is an approximation of the poverty rate used for the distribution of Title I funds. To obtain data for the numerator of the child poverty rate, we aggregated census tabulations at the county level from U.S. Congress (1965) to the state level. To obtain data for the denominator, we aggregated census tabulations at the county level published by the Minnesota Population Center (2011) to the state level.

8. We obtained state-by-year level data on federal revenue per pupil and current spending per pupil in average daily attendance on a biennial basis through 1979 from publications of the Department of Health, Education, and Welfare (various years), and thereafter for all available years from the Digest of Education Statistics (various years). Current expenditure excludes spending on capital and debt maintenance, but is measured more accurately and consistently over time. All dollar figures are given in real 2009 terms, and years refer to the fall of the school year. The sample includes all states in the continental United States, excluding Washington, D.C. Throughout, our analysis gives each state equal weight, but our substantive conclusions are unchanged if we weight by contemporaneous enrollment, by enrollment at a given point in time (such as 1963), or by the number of five- to seventeen-year-olds in the state in 1960.

9. For example, the 1965 per-pupil Title I formula amount in Mississippi represented more than 20 percent of its per-pupil spending in 1963 (in real terms). This is consistent with figures reported by Cascio, Gordon, and Reber (forthcoming) at the school district level for nine former Confederate states, which were poorer and spent less than the country as a whole.

10. However, in some low-spending, high-poverty states, such as those in the South, Title I represented a much larger share of spending in 1965.

11. Results of these evaluations were summarized by the Title I Evaluation Reporting System (TIERS) starting in the late 1970s.

12. Geoffrey Borman and Jerome D'Agostino (1996) also report smaller effects for reading, at higher grades, and for studies that used an annual (for example, fall-fall) testing cycle. They also report increasing effects over time, which they attribute to improved regulation.

13. When we refer to richer or poorer, we mean lower child poverty and higher child poverty, not higher spending and lower spending. Indeed, as a result of both Title I and state redistributive efforts, poorer districts might have ultimately become relatively high spending.

14. Nevertheless, the overall trend has been one of increasing inequality within states. For example, David Card and Abigail Payne (2002) report that the within-state spending gap between richer and poorer districts has grown since the 1970s.

15. The threat of withdrawn federal funding was not an empty one: more than 20 percent of southern school districts had their federal funds deferred or terminated by 1966 for failure to meet these desegregation guidelines (Cascio et al. 2010).

16. On the one hand, dissatisfaction with schools and white flight could have eroded the tax base and local support in districts undergoing desegregation. On the other hand, spending in blacks' schools had historically been lower, so additional revenue would be necessary to prevent whites from seeing a decline in school quality.

17. Before desegregation, the black-white gap in school resources tended to be larger in districts with higher black enrollment shares (Margo 1990). Districts with higher black enrollment shares thereby needed a larger increase in funds to maintain spending on whites at pre-desegregation levels as black and white schools combined.

18. Educational resources are likewise thought to be important determinants of educational attainment for cohorts educated before the War on Poverty (see, for example, Card and Krueger 1992a, 1992b; Ashenfelter, Collins, and Yoon 2006). Research based on the educational experiences of more recent cohorts suggests that spending buys less in the way of educational achievement (for reviews, see Hanushek 1986, 1997).

19. The R square for the least-squares regression is 0.69, indicating that variation in the state poverty rate alone can account for 69 percent of the variation in average log per-pupil spending at the state level.

20. We define the South as the former Confederacy rather than the southern census region due to its different history with school desegregation. Southern states were so much poorer than the rest of the country that it is difficult to determine whether the lower average spending in southern states is due to their high poverty rates or is some region effect caused by other factors. However, if we estimate the fitted line separately for the two sets of states, we get very similar results.

21. The R square from this regression is 0.17, down from 0.69 during the 1963–1964 school year. A full analysis of the determinants of variation in school spending across states is beyond the scope of this chapter, but in results not reported, we find evidence of a declining role for the state poverty rate and an increasing role for average income in explaining variation in average spending since the late 1980s.

22. We use the 1960 child poverty rate implicit in the Title I formula for all years. We have also used the contemporaneous poverty rate (for all people, since child poverty is not readily available in all years), interpolated between census years. Poverty did fall significantly during this period, but the correlation of state-level poverty rates over time is high; for example, the 1960 child poverty rate and the 1999 poverty rate have a correlation coefficient of 0.72. The pattern of the coefficients is quite similar if we use contemporaneous poverty instead of 1960 child poverty.

23. In level terms, a 10 percentage point increase in the 1960 child poverty rate was associated with a reduction in spending of $625 per pupil in 1963 but only a $91 increase in per-pupil Title I funding in 1969 (real 2009 dollars).

24. We assume that an individual has graduated from high school if he or she reports completing twelve years of education or having a high school degree. We assume that an

individual attended college if he or she reports any education beyond twelve years or having attended some college or more.

REFERENCES

Ashenfelter, Orley, William Collins, and Albert Yoon. 2006. "Evaluating the Role of Brown V. Board of Education in School Equalization, Desegregation, and the Income of African Americans." *American Law and Economics Review* 8(2): 213–48.

Bailey, Stephen K., and Edith K. Mosher. 1968. *ESEA: The Office of Education Administers a Law.* Syracuse, N.Y.: Syracuse University Press.

Borman, Geoffrey D., and Jerome V. D'Agostino. 1996. "Title I and Student Achievement: A Meta-Analysis of Federal Evaluation Results." *Educational Evaluation and Policy Analysis* 18(4): 309–26.

Card, David, and Alan B. Krueger. 1992a. "Does School Quality Matter? Returns to Education and the Characteristics of Public Schools in the United States." *The Journal of Political Economy* 100(1): 1–40.

——. 1992b. "School Quality and Black-White Relative Earnings: A Direct Assessment." *Quarterly Journal of Economics* 107(1): 151–200.

Card, David, and A. Abigail Payne. 2002. "School Finance Reform, the Distribution of School Spending, and the Distribution of Student Test Scores." *Journal of Public Economics* 83(1): 49–82.

Carter, Launor F. 1984. "The Sustaining Effects Study of Compensatory and Elementary Education." *Educational Researcher* 13(7): 41–43.

Cascio, Elizabeth, Nora Gordon, Ethan Lewis, and Sarah Reber. 2008. "From Brown to Busing." *Journal of Urban Economics* 64(2): 296–325.

——. 2010. "Paying for Progress: Conditional Grants and the Desegregation of Southern Public Schools." *Quarterly Journal of Economics* 125(1): 445–82.

Cascio, Elizabeth, Nora Gordon, and Sarah Reber. forthcoming. "Local Responses to Federal Grants: Evidence from the Introduction of Title I in the South." *American Economic Journal: Economic Policy.*

Cohen, David K., and Susan L. Moffitt. 2009. *The Ordeal of Equality: Did Federal Regulation Fix the Schools?* Cambridge, Mass.: Harvard University Press.

Coleman, James S. et al. 1966. *Equality of Educational Opportunity.* Washington: U.S. Department of Health, Education, and Welfare.

Davies, Gareth. 2007. *See Government Grow: Education Politics from Johnson to Reagan.* Lawrence: University Press of Kansas.

Dee, Thomas, and Brian Jacob. 2011. "The Impact of No Child Left Behind on Student Achievement." *Journal of Policy Analysis and Management* 30(3): 418–46.

Evans, William N., Sheila Murray, and Robert Schwab. 1997. "School Houses, Court Houses, and State Houses after *Serrano.*" *Journal of Policy Analysis and Management* 16(1): 10–31.

Feldstein, Martin S. 1978. "The Effect of a Differential Add-on Grant: Title I and Local Education Spending." *Journal of Human Resources* 13(4): 443–58.

Glass, Gene V. et al. 1970. *Data Analysis of the 1968–9 Survey of Compensatory Education (Title I).* Washington: U.S. Department of Health, Education, and Welfare.

Gordon, Nora. 2004. "Do Federal Grants Boost School Spending? Evidence from Title I." *Journal of Public Economics* 88(9–10): 177–92.

Graham, Hugh Davis. 1984. *The Uncertain Triumph: Federal Education Policy in the Kennedy and Johnson Years*. Chapel Hill: University of North Carolina Press.

Guryan, Jonathan. 2004. "Desegregation and Black Dropout Rates." *American Economic Review* 94(4): 919–43.

Hanushek, Eric A. 1986. "The Economics of Schooling: Production and Efficiency in Public Schools." *Journal of Economic Literature* 49(3): 114–77.

———. 1997. "Assessing the Effects of School Resources on Student Performance: An Update." *Educational Evaluation and Policy Analysis* 19(2): 141–64.

Heuer, Ruth, and Stephanie Stullich. 2011. *Comparability of State and Local Expenditures Among Schools Within Districts: A Report From the Study of School-Level Expenditures*. Washington: U.S. Department of Education.

Johnson, Rucker C. 2011. "Long-Run Impacts of School Desegregation and School Quality on Adult Attainments." *NBER* working paper no. 16664. Cambridge, Mass.: National Bureau of Economic Research.

Kaestle, Carl. 2001. "Federal Aid to Education Since World War II: Purposes and Politics." In *The Future of the Federal Role in Education*, edited by Jack Jennings. Washington, D.C.: Center for Education Policy.

Margo, Robert A. 1990. *Race and Schooling in the South, 1880–1950: An Economic History*. Chicago: University of Chicago Press.

Martin, Ruby, and Phyllis McClure. 1969. *Title I of ESEA: Is it Helping Poor Children?* Washington, D.C.: National Association for the Advancement of Colored People and Washington Research Project.

Matsudaira, Jordan, Adrienne Hosek, and Elias Walsh. 2012. "An Integrated Assessment of the Effects of Title I on School Behavior, Resources, and Student Achievement." *Economics of Education Review* 31(3): 1–14.

Minnesota Population Center. 2011. *National Historical Geographic Information System. Version 2.0*. Minneapolis: University of Minnesota.

Oates, Wallace E. 1972. *Fiscal Federalism*. New York: Harcourt, Brace, Jovanovich.

Orfield, Gary. 1969. *The Reconstruction of Southern Education: The Schools and the 1964 Civil Rights Act*. New York: Wiley-Interscience.

———. 2000. "The 1964 Civil Rights Act and American Education." In *Legacies of the 1964 Civil Rights Act*, edited by Bernard Groffman. Charlottesville: University of Virginia Press.

Puma, Michael J., Nancy Karweit, Cristofer Price, Anne Ricciuti, William Thompson, and Michael Vaden-Kiernan. 1997. *Prospects: Student Outcomes. Final Report*. Washington: U.S. Department of Education, Planning and Evaluation Service.

Reardon, Sean F., and Joseph P. Robinson. 2007. "Patterns and Trends in Racial/Ethnic and Socioeconomic Academic Achievement Gaps." In *Handbook of Research in Education Finance and Policy*, edited by Helen A. Ladd and Edward B. Fiske. London: Routledge.

Reber, Sarah J. 2005. "Court-Ordered Desegregation: Successes and Failures in Integration Since Brown vs. Board of Education." *Journal of Human Resources* 40(3): 559–90.

———. 2010. "Desegregation and Educational Attainment for Blacks." *Journal of Human Resources* 45(4): 893–914.

———. 2011. "From Separate and Unequal to Integrated and Equal? School Desegregation and School Finance in Louisiana." *Review of Economics and Statistics* 93(2): 416–35.

Rosenberg, Gerald N. 1991. *The Hollow Hope: Can Courts Bring about Social Change?* Chicago: University of Chicago Press.

Roza, Marguerite. 2010. *Educational Economics: Where Do School Funds Go?* Washington, D.C.: Urban Institute Press.

Ruggles, Steven, J. Trent Alexander, Katie Genadek, Ronald Goeken, Matthew B. Schroeder, and Matthew Sobek. 2010. *Integrated Public Use Microdata Series: Version 5.0 [Machine-readable database]*. Minneapolis: University of Minnesota.

U.S. Congress. Senate Committee on Labor and Public Welfare. Subcommittee on Education. 1965. "Maximum Basic Grants—Elementary and Secondary Education Act of 1965 (Public Law 818–74, Title II, and Public Law 891–0, Title I." Washington, D.C.: Government Printing Office.

U.S. Department of Education. 1978. *Digest of Education Statistics, 1977–78*. Washington: U.S. Government Printing Office.

———. 1980. *Digest of Education Statistics 1980*. Washington: U.S. Government Printing Office.

———. 1981. *Statistics of Public Elementary and Secondary School Systems Fall 1979*. Washington: U.S. Government Printing Office.

———. 1982. *Digest of Education Statistics 1982*. Washington: U.S. Government Printing Office.

———. 1983. *Digest of Education Statistics 1983–84*. Washington: U.S. Government Printing Office.

———. 1986. *Digest of Education Statistics 1985–86*. Washington: U.S. Government Printing Office.

———. 1987. *Digest of Education Statistics 1987*. Washington: U.S. Government Printing Office.

———. 1988. *Digest of Education Statistics 1988*. Washington: U.S. Government Printing Office.

———. 1989. *Digest of Education Statistics 1989*. Washington: U.S. Government Printing Office.

———. 1991a. *Digest of Education Statistics 1990*. Washington: U.S. Government Printing Office.

———. 1991b. *Digest of Education Statistics 1991*. Washington: U.S. Government Printing Office.

———. 1992. *Digest of Education Statistics 1992*. Washington: U.S. Government Printing Office.

———. 1993. *Digest of Education Statistics 1993*. Washington: U.S. Government Printing Office.

———. 1994. *Digest of Education Statistics 1994*. Washington: U.S. Government Printing Office.

———. 1995. *Digest of Education Statistics 1995*. Washington: U.S. Government Printing Office.

———. 1997. *Digest of Education Statistics 1997*. Washington: U.S. Government Printing Office.

———. 1999. *Digest of Education Statistics 1998*. Washington: U.S. Government Printing Office.

———. 2000. *Digest of Education Statistics 1999*. Washington: U.S. Government Printing Office.

———. 2001. *Digest of Education Statistics 2000*. Washington: U.S. Government Printing Office.

———. 2002. *Digest of Education Statistics 2001*. Washington: U.S. Government Printing Office.

———. 2003. *Digest of Education Statistics 2002*. Washington: U.S. Government Printing Office.

———. 2004. *Digest of Education Statistics 2003*. Washington: U.S. Government Printing Office.

———. 2005. *Digest of Education Statistics 2004*. Washington: U.S. Government Printing Office.

———. 2006. *Digest of Education Statistics 2005*. Washington: U.S. Government Printing Office.

———. 2007. *Digest of Education Statistics 2006*. Washington: U.S. Government Printing Office.

———. 2008. *Digest of Education Statistics 2007*. Washington: U.S. Government Printing Office.

———. 2009. *Digest of Education Statistics 2008*. Washington: U.S. Government Printing Office.

———. 2010. *Digest of Education Statistics 2009*. Washington: U.S. Government Printing Office.

———. 2011. *Digest of Education Statistics 2010*. Washington: U.S. Government Printing Office.

———. 2012. *Digest of Education Statistics 2011*. Washington: U.S. Government Printing Office.

U.S. Department of Health, Education, and Welfare. 1956. *Summary of 1953–54 Statistics of State School Systems* (Circular No. 480). Washington: U.S. Government Printing Office.

———. 1957. *Statistical Summary of State School Systems 1955–56* (Circular No. 543). Washington: U.S. Government Printing Office.

———. 1960a. *Statistics of State School Systems 1959–60* (Circular No. 691). Washington: U.S. Government Printing Office.

———. 1960b. *Statistical Summary of State School Systems 1957–58* (Circular No. 623). Washington: U.S. Government Printing Office.

———. 1964. *Statistics of State School Systems 1961–62* (Circular No. 751). Washington: U.S. Government Printing Office.

———. 1965. *Statistical Summary of State School Systems, 1963–64* (Circular No. 789). Washington: U.S. Government Printing Office.

———. 1966. *Fall 1965 Statistics of Public Elementary and Secondary Day Schools*. Washington: U.S. Government Printing Office.

———. 1967. *Digest of Educational Statistics 1967 Edition*. Washington: U.S. Government Printing Office.

———. 1968. *Statistics of Public Elementary and Secondary Day Schools, Fall 1967*. Washington: U.S. Government Printing Office.

———. 1969a. *History of Title I ESEA*. Washington: Government Printing Office.

———. 1969b. *Digest of Educational Statistics 1969*. Washington: U.S. Government Printing Office.

———. 1970a. *Digest of Educational Statistics: 1970 Edition*. Washington: U.S. Government Printing Office.

———. 1970b. *Statistics of Public Elementary and Secondary Day Schools, Fall 1969*. Washington: U.S. Government Printing Office.

———. 1973a. *Digest of Educational Statistics: 1972 Edition*. Washington: U.S. Government Printing Office.

———. 1973b. *Statistics of Public Elementary and Secondary Day Schools Fall 1971*. Washington: U.S. Government Printing Office.

———. 1974. *Statistics of Public Elementary and Secondary Day Schools, Fall 1973*. Washington: U.S. Government Printing Office.

———. 1975. *Digest of Educational Statistics: 1974 Edition*. Washington: U.S. Government Printing Office.

———. 1976a. *Digest of Education Statistics: 1975 Edition*. Washington: U.S. Government Printing Office.

———. 1976b. *Statistics of Public Elementary and Secondary Day Schools Fall 1975*. Washington: U.S. Government Printing Office.

———. 1979. *Statistics of Public Elementary and Secondary Day Schools 1977–1978 School Year (Final)*. Washington: U.S. Government Printing Office.

van der Klaauw, Wilbert. 2008. "Breaking the Link Between Poverty and Low Student Achievement: An Evaluation of Title I." *Journal of Econometrics* 142(2): 731–56.

Chapter 4

Supporting Access to Higher Education

Bridget Terry Long

With the Economic Opportunity Act of 1964 (EOA) and the Higher Education Act of 1965 (HEA 1965), President Johnson began an unprecedented period of support to help students pay for higher education. Unlike previous policies, which targeted only a limited set of students, the War on Poverty introduced and funded broad-based postsecondary programs meant to help any student prepared academically for college. With a combination of financial aid and college preparatory programs, these programs were the first major step to making mass higher education possible for all Americans.

With respect to higher education, the War on Poverty introduced several financial aid policies. First was the Educational Opportunity Grant (EOG), a need-based program that gave low-income students aid that did not need to be repaid. EOG, as the precursor to the Pell Grant created several years later, is the foundation of federal financial aid. HEA 1965 also created the Guaranteed Student Loan Program, which offered students federally guaranteed private loans. In addition to expanding the National Defense Student Loans (NDSL), a direct student loan program later called the Perkins Loan, this period also marks the birth of widespread student loans. The Federal Work Study program, created as part of EOA and moved to the Office of Education in HEA 1965, was the third type of financial aid emphasized by the War on Poverty. All continue to operate.

President Johnson also aimed to improve opportunities for low-income students by investing in college preparation programs geared toward first-generation and other disadvantaged high school students. EOA and the Office of Economic Opportunity created Upward Bound, which combined with Talent Search (created in HEA 1965) and Student Support Services (added in 1968), make up what are known as the TRIO programs. Designed to help motivate and prepare high school students, these programs provide tutoring, mentoring, information on college opportunities, and assistance completing applications.

The effect of these programs is that they established an active federal role in supporting college access, one that still exists. From this point on, the federal government would take a lead role in sharing the direct costs of college with students. The growing role of the federal government in higher education is evident from the increase in expenditures. As shown in table 4.1, from school year 1963–1964 to school year 1970–1971, federal spending on student aid to help finance postsecondary education increased by a multiple of eleven after taking into account inflation (College Board 2011). The higher education programs of the War on Poverty were also significant in that they focused on the broader population. They increasingly included new groups of potential students, attempting to make higher education available all. This was justified in part as promoting national competitiveness, but included new emphasis on educational inequities and helping low-income students. These programs also established the basic framework for financial aid, though the relative balance between programs and which types of students are eligible for aid has changed somewhat. Finally, the related legislation acknowledged that financial aid is not enough to support college access. For college to be accessible, one must also acknowledge the importance of academic preparation and information, and it is significant that the War on Poverty introduced these types of supports.

This chapter discusses how these higher education policies changed the postsecondary landscape and have evolved over time. The repercussions of these programs are evident fifty years later. The combination of grants and loans are still the backbone of the financial aid system, though the purchasing power of grants and the relative balance between grants and loans has shifted. Although a primary focus is on a student's ability to pay, middle-class students have increasingly been included as beneficiaries of federal aid programs due to dramatic increases in tuition. Over the past several decades, the importance of program and policy design has been acknowledged, and some of the early features of the War on Poverty EOG, such as the delivery mechanism and need analysis, were revised in subsequent HEAs; debate continues about how to best to design the successors of the EOG to better help low-income students. Moreover, as loan levels have increased, and many students now work significant hours, some have called into question what role loans and work study should play. That even more needs to be done with regards to the goals of the TRIO programs, however, is agreed.

SETTING THE STAGE

Although the War on Poverty was a significant step forward, it was not the first federal initiative to address issues of college access and affordability. In the 1940s, several measures provided support to veterans. During the 1950s, aid was extended to any student entering certain fields. Still, as evidenced by enrollment trends before the War on Poverty, college attendance remained limited to a fraction of the population, and gaps in enrollment by income, race, and gender were significant.

TABLE 4.1 / Student Aid to Finance Postsecondary Expenses

	1963–1964	1970–1971	1971–1972	1972–1973	1973–1974	1983–1984	1993–1994	2003–2004	2010–2011
Total federal aid	$1,643	$18,092	$21,126	$24,324	$26,154	$28,832	$42,598	$87,724	$169,061
Total federal grants	$836	$10,426	$11,499	$15,241	$17,354	$10,774	$12,228	$20,711	$49,065
EOG or SEOG	—	$920	$950	$1,094	$1,035	$770	$881	$901	$758
EEOG or Pell Grants	—	—	—	—	$234	$6,104	$8,537	$15,065	$34,762
Veterans and military grants	$772	$6,627	$7,389	$10,359	$11,523	$3,153	$2,412	$4,221	$12,152
Other grant programs	$64	$2,879	$3,160	$3,788	$4,562	$746	$399	$524	$1,394
Total federal loans	$807	$6,547	$7,920	$7,701	$7,343	$16,566	$29,205	$58,842	$103,995
NDSL or Perkins loans	$807	$1,344	$1,671	$2,070	$2,131	$1,488	$1,387	$1,942	$971
Subsidized Stafford	$0	$4,968	$5,975	$5,335	$4,908	$13,873	$18,715	$26,127	$39,692
Unsubsidized Stafford and other loans	$0	$234	$273	$297	$304	$1,205	$9,103	$30,772	$63,332
Federal work study	—	$1,120	$1,707	$1,382	$1,457	$1,491	$1,165	$1,312	$1,171
Education tax benefits	—	—	—	—	—	—	—	$6,860	$14,830
State grants	$398	$1,319	$1,441	$1,639	$1,791	$2,413	$3,585	$7,103	$9,207
Institutional grants	$1,910	$4,700	$5,040	$5,100	$4,970	$4,970	$13,360	$23,480	$38,110
Private and employer grants	—	—	—	—	—	—	$4,260	$9,130	$10,840
Total federal, state, institutional, and private aid	$3,951	$24,112	$27,606	$31,063	$32,915	$36,215	$63,803	$140,257	$235,089

Source: Author's compilation of data from College Board (2011).

Note: Constant 2010 dollars in millions. Components may not sum to totals because of rounding. Other grant programs include Social Security Student Benefit Program, LEAP, SMART grants, Academic Competitiveness grants, and other federal grants. Unsubsidized Stafford and other loans includes PLUS, SLS, and other federal loans. Other aid includes state grant programs, institutional grants, private and employer grants, and nonfederal loans. Federal loan dollars reflect disbursements beginning 1995–1996. Before 1995–1996 the data reflect gross loan commitments. These amounts are approximately 11 percent higher than disbursements. The Ford Direct Student Loan Program (FDSLP) began in 1992–1993. From that year, Federal Family Education Loan (FFEL) and FDSL volumes are reported separately. Private and employer grants are estimated based on NPSAS data and surveys conducted by the National Scholarship Providers Association. Data for these programs were not estimated before 1993–1994, even though funds were available from these sources. Where precise data are not available, the division of aid between undergraduate and graduate students is based on the NPSAS.

Early Higher Education Policy Before the War on Poverty

The GI Bill of 1944 is the most significant precursor to the War on Poverty higher education programs. Unlike grants to states or institutions to support innovation, the GI Bill (Servicemen's Readjustment Act of 1944) focused on individuals, in this case veterans, supporting college attendance for up to one year and three additional years for a limited number of veterans with special aptitudes (Cervantes et al. 2005). As noted by Dongbin Kim and John Rury, "hundreds of thousands of former GIs poured onto the nation's campuses, taking advantage of a little heralded program to provide tuition and other benefits to veterans of the recently concluded World War II" (2007, 302). The authors mark this as "the beginning of a remarkable period of expansion in higher education."

The 1947 President's Commission on Higher Education, known as the Truman Commission, was formed to examine the possibility of expanding the role of the federal government with the aim of "making higher education equally available to all young people . . . to the extent that their capacity warrants a further social investment in their training" (5). The commission suggested an expansive and inclusive system and estimated that nearly half of young people could benefit from postsecondary study (Kim and Rury 2007, 302). They suggested the creation of financial aid for academically qualified students. Although Congress did not fund the initiative, the recommendation for more broad-based support for higher education later proved an inspiration for the War on Poverty programs (Cervantes et al. 2005). The commission also grappled with issues of racial integration, which divided the panel (Kim and Rury 2007).

Nearly a decade later, President Eisenhower signed the National Defense Education Act of 1958 (NDEA), which targeted aid only to students pursuing degrees in science, math, and modern foreign language. Although this program was intended to be only temporary, similar to future programs, it used a need-based formula to provide low-interest loans (Cervantes et al. 2005).

Higher Education Trends in the 1960s

Although higher education had been the focus of several previous policies, college enrollment in the early 1960s clearly did not reflect the inclusion of all students. Because previous financial support was directed only to specific groups (veterans) or fields (science and math), a college education remained largely out of reach for most students. According to the 1960 U.S. Census, among persons age twenty-five and older, men had a median of 10.3 years of education and women 10.9 years. Differences in educational outcomes by race were also large. The median educational attainment of white men was 10.7 years and only 7.9 years for black men.

Many Americans had not even completed a high school degree by 1960. Among the population age twenty-five and older, only 20 percent of black men and women had completed four or more years of high school, versus 43 percent of white men

TABLE 4.2 / Median Family Income 1965 and Average College Tuition 1964–1965

	Whites	Blacks
Median family income	$7,251	$3,993
Public institutions		
Total tuition and R&B		
Universities	14.5%	26.3%
Other four-year	12.0%	21.7%
Two-year	8.8%	16.0%
Tuition and required fees		
Universities	4.1%	7.5%
Other four-year	3.1%	5.6%
Two-year	1.4%	2.5%
Private institutions		
Total tuition and R&B		
Universities	30.4%	55.1%
Other four-year	25.0%	45.3%
Two-year	20.1%	36.4%
Tuition and required fees		
Universities	17.9%	32.5%
Other four-year	14.1%	25.6%
Two-year	9.7%	17.6%

Source: Author's calculations based on U.S. Bureau of the Census (1977, 1987a, 1987b, 1991); National Center for Education Statistics 2008.
Note: The figures for black families include other races. These figures are not precisely comparable with data for later years. The tuition data are for the entire academic year and are average total charges for full-time attendance. Tuition and fees were weighted by the number of full-time-equivalent undergraduates to calculate the national average. Room and board were based on full-time students. Tuition and required fees are in-state charges for public institutions. Detail may not sum to totals because of rounding.

and women. College completion was at much lower levels. Eight percent and 3 percent of white and black individuals age twenty-five and older, respectively, had completed four or more years of college by 1960 (U.S. Census Bureau 2013). Around the time of the War on Poverty, differences in enrollment by race were pronounced. Among high school graduates who were eighteen to twenty-four years old in 1967, 34.5 percent of white students but only 23.3 percent of black students were enrolled in degree-granting institutions (National Center for Education Statistics 2008).

Financial concerns were one barrier to college access both overall and for minority students specifically. A comparison of family incomes and college tuition levels in 1965 illustrates how expensive higher education was for the average family. As shown in table 4.2, for white families at the median, the total cost of a public four-year university for tuition and room and board for one student was about 14.5 percent of annual income; for a private university, the figure was 30 percent. Affordability was an even greater concern for black families, given that their incomes were only a little over half that of white families. A public four-year university would have cost the median black family 26 percent of annual income and a private university 55 percent.

Inequities in the higher education system by race were also highlighted by the Truman Commission, which noted the system to be largely white. However, its members did not agree on what to do about African American students (Kim and Rury 2007, 320). By 1960, although high school graduation rates had improved for African American and Hispanic youth, their graduation and college entry rates still fell significantly behind white students. "While higher education had expanded substantially by 1960, white males continued to predominate on the campuses, perhaps even more than before the war. It was in the 1960s, the decade of civil rights and widespread agitation over issues of equity and social justice, when things began to change" (Kim and Rury 2007, 326–27).

Given affordability concerns even for whites, it is not surprising that college attendance varied by parental income level. Although contemporaneous data is not available, data from 1975 suggests that students from the top 20 percent of the family income distribution were 30 percentage points more likely to attend college the October immediately after high school than students from the bottom 20 percent. About one-third of low-income students enrolled versus about half of middle-income and two-thirds high-income students attended. As such, during the early years of the War on Poverty, leaders had concerns about gaps in college access by income level.

THE PROGRAMS AND THEIR SIGNIFICANCE

The higher education policies of the War on Poverty largely grew out of a task force created by President Johnson in 1964 to study the role of the federal government in aid. Led by John W. Gardner, who became secretary of Health, Education, and Welfare in 1965, the task force focused on increasing college access for needy students. This focus was motivated partly by a study that found one in six students who took the National Merit Scholarship test in high school did not attend college. The task force recommended grants to able needy students, more extensive use of loans and loan guarantees, and customized aid packages determined by a student's financial need (Cervantes et al. 2005). With the Civil Rights Act of 1964, the task force and resulting legislation ignored concerns about race and integration, which had plagued earlier efforts to expand financial aid (for example, the Truman Commission). Instead, similar to the Elementary and Secondary Education Act (ESEA), the administration emphasized concerns about national growth and economic prosperity and framed the policies as an attempt to improve the outcomes of all poor, low-income students.

The War on Poverty higher education programs were incorporated in both the Economic Opportunity Act of 1964 and the Higher Education Act of 1965. These acts established the foundation of the federal financial aid system that exists today, as promoting access to higher education become a major goal of the federal government.

Legislation and Major Initiatives

The Economic Opportunity Act of 1964 introduced many programs designed to promote health, education, and general welfare, including Head Start, Job Corps, and the Federal Work Study program.[1] The Federal Work Study program is geared toward low-income students and subsidizes their wages for work done in a college-sponsored job. Due to his involvement in the National Youth Administration, a New Deal project that provided education and jobs to youth ages sixteen to twenty-five, Johnson was a great supporter of this program (Cervantes et al. 2005). EOA also introduced community action demonstration projects, including Upward Bound, a college preparation program that began with seventeen pilot projects during the summer of 1965 (Groutt 2003).

The Higher Education Act of 1965 did more to imprint the War on Poverty on higher education by consolidating work study under the Office of Education and created several new programs.[2] Title IV of HEA 1965 focuses on the financial aid programs and the other parts strengthen community service programs (Title I), give assistance to libraries (Title II), support the development of mainly African American institutions but include two-year and technical colleges (Title III), and established Teacher Corps (Title V).

Part A of Title IV introduced the Educational Opportunity Grant (EOG), a need-based grant focused on low-income students showing academic potential. In an attempt to avoid making some of the population feel that the federal government had overstepped bounds, EOG funds were originally appropriated to states, which then allocated funding to postsecondary institutions to decide how to distribute the money to students based on their own need analysis. Therefore, one student could get very different EOGs at different colleges and universities based on differences in institutional need analysis. Future revisions to the policy (discussed later) changed this distribution and need-analysis model.

Part B of Title IV created the Guaranteed Student Loan program. Unlike previous federal loan programs that lent directly to a small group of students, such as veterans, this program allowed the federal government to guarantee private loans. This set up solved a problem at the time: low-income students could not provide collateral to secure loans and so lacked liquidity to pay for college. With the federal guarantee, banks were willing to participate. Although the program was conceived to provide financial support to middle-income students too, the federal government provided low-income students (those with family incomes below $15,000) with a subsidy that paid for the interest on the loan while the student was in college.

Parts C of Title IV moved the Work Study program from Office of Economic Opportunity (OEO) to the Office of Education. Part D extended the National Defense Student Loans, which were originally enacted as part of the National

Defense Education Act of 1958. This is a direct loan program in which the government provides funds to students in the form of loans. The 1965 legislation provided full loan forgiveness for graduates who worked in an underserved area for seven years.

In terms of the college preparatory programs, HEA 1965 added Talent Search and Student Support Services was added as part of the 1968 Reauthorization. The HEA 1968 also transferred Upward Bound from the Office of Economic Opportunity to the Office of Education (Groutt 2003). Together, these three TRIO programs assist first-generation and other disadvantaged youth to prepare for and attend college. The services provided include tutoring, mentoring, information or college opportunities, and assistance completing applications.

Putting the War on Poverty in Perspective

The collection of financial aid policies and college preparatory programs created by the War on Poverty was a significant departure from prior higher education policies. This framework for financial aid persists today and is a major legacy of the War on Poverty. In addition, these programs represent several significant changes in the role of the higher education and the policies that govern it. The War on Poverty did much to change the status quo of educational patterns and shaped greatly the financial aid system that exists today. I discuss four major aspects of the legacy of these War on Poverty programs and policies.

Establishing the Significant Federal Role in Higher Education　Although the federal government had invested in postsecondary training for individuals before the War on Poverty, 1965 marks an unprecedented increase in federal expenditures for college student support. Table 4.1 tracks federal expenditures on student financial aid, along with those from states, institutions, and private sources, from 1963–1964 to 2010–2011. Shortly before the War on Poverty, total federal aid was only $1.6 billion in 2010 dollars, and this was mostly due to aid to veterans through grants and the National Defense Student Loans. By 1970–1971, federal expenditures exceeded $18 billion (2010 dollars) through a combination of grants ($10.4 billion), loans ($6.6 billion), and work study ($1.1 billion). This increase was previously unheard of. By 2010–2011, total federal aid amounted to more than $169 billion.

Previously, the federal government had avoided involvement in this area to avoid criticism that they were acting like "big brother" and due to opposition to racial integration and the support of religious schools among some groups (Cervantes et al. 2005). The War on Poverty overrode these concerns based on two strong arguments for federal involvement. The first was a carryover from earlier decades: national competitiveness. Given the Cold War and increasing globalization, policymakers pointed to education as a key factor in sustaining economic prosperity. The second emphasized the development of human capital as the best way to reduce poverty. In terms of higher education, increasing educational attainment and reducing large gaps in college attendance by income and race were paramount goals. Although unequal access to higher education was not a new concern, the War on Poverty signifies a turning point when the federal government actually put into practice programs and policies that had previously been debated and recommended but not funded.

Economic justifications for federal intervention easily supported the unequal educational patterns of the time. Without government involvement, low educational attainment among many groups suggested that large numbers of academically prepared students were not attending college. Earlier tasks forces had estimated that half of high school graduates would benefit from college attendance, far greater than enrollment rates at the time. Moreover, with the growth of the civil rights movement and the passage of the Civil Rights Act in 1964, attention focused on the large gaps in attendance by race.

One failure in the market was the lack of liquidity, or access to capital. Without collateral or a financial track record, talented, low-income students could not secure loans. Such a market failure justified the various federal interventions.

The War on Poverty higher education legislation reflects the delicate balancing act of dramatically increasing the federal role while relying on partners to lessen the appearance of the federal overreach.[3] This compromise is evident in the design of some programs. For example, the EOG was not distributed directly from the federal government to students; the funds were given to states, then to the institutions that awarded it to students. Additionally, funds for the Guaranteed Student Loan Program came from private banks, with the federal government guaranteeing loan repayment and providing subsidies to the banks. Significant changes came later with the Reauthorization of the Higher Education Act in 1972.

The Movement Toward Mass Higher Education and Focus on Individuals   A second important distinction of the War on Poverty programs is how they supported any low-income student who was academically prepared for college. Rather than focusing only on gifted students, Johnson is quoted as saying, "The important role of the federal government is somehow to do something for the people who are down and out, and that's where its major energy in education ought to go." Other research confirms that "Title IV represented the first generally available aid program for postsecondary students" (Cervantes et al. 2005, 20).

As mentioned, the higher education task force created by Johnson noted that among students who took the National Merit Scholarship test and had families who could contribute only $300 or less to their educations, about 75 percent of men and 55 percent of women noted that they would have attended college if more money had been available (Cervantes et al. 2005). The increasing documentation of lost potential justified the federal expansion, as did the realization that the changing labor market was increasing the demand for college graduates.

Although most financial support from states is in the form of appropriations to colleges and universities for operating expenses, which in turn subsidizes the price for in-state students, the federal approach to financial aid has been to give the funds directly to students. Rather than an across-the-board subsidy, much federal aid is customized to the specific financial circumstances of the individual student. The focus on supporting the individual student set the norm for future changes in financial aid programs and is still part of need-based programs today.

Establishing the American Landscape of Aid Programs   What may be the greatest contribution of the War on Poverty to higher education is the establishment of the basic aid landscape—a mixture of grant, loan, and work study programs—that continues today. Until this point, aid programs were small, piecemeal, and geared toward limited goals without much thought to coordination across programs or long-term levels of support. In contrast, the mixture of grant, loan, and work study programs created during the War on Poverty continue to be the predominant forms of financial assistance, though the exact design and relative size of each program has changed over time.

The War on Poverty established grants as the foundation of the aid system: the combination of EOG and grants to veterans quickly became the bulk of student support, constituting 63 percent of total federal aid during the 1972–1973 school year. However, although much of the War on Poverty rhetoric focused on addressing the needs of low-income students, the EOG was originally smaller than other federal college grant programs. As mentioned, its original design, which relied on colleges to determine need, was problematic. By allowing colleges and universities to allocate the federal funds to students based on their institutional assessment of need, two students with the same financial resources and facing the same costs could be awarded very different EOG amounts. The system of federal grants quickly evolved with the Reauthorization of the Higher Education Act in 1972 (HEA 1972),[4] which addressed some of the need-analysis problems of EOG and greatly expanded need-based grants. This was partly spurred by a 1969 report by Assistant Secretary of Health, Education, and Welfare Alice Rivlin, which found that income was still the primary determinant of college enrollment (Mumper 1996).

HEA 1972 built from the EOG to create the Basic Educational Opportunity Grant (BEOG), which was renamed the Pell grant in 1980. BEOG provides direct assistance to students and uses a centralized need assessment defined by the federal government. As such, BEOG had the same basic tenets of EOG, but policymakers corrected some of its design problems. After 1972, EOG became known as the Supplemental Educational Opportunity Grant (SEOG). As shown in table 4.1, BEOG began small in 1973, awarding $234 million in aid, but together with SEOG, these programs quickly formed the core of federal financial support for needy students. In the 2010–2011 school year, 9.1 million students, 43 percent of all students, received the Pell grant, and 1.3 million received the SEOG. Together these programs awarded more than $35.5 billion (Baum and Payea 2011).

One weakness that originated with EOG and remains a part of successor grant programs is that they are not entitlement programs. For this reason, Congress must appropriate money to the program each year. Failure of action has meant that the value of Pell grant has not kept up with inflation and has trailed rapid increases in college costs. For example, in constant 2005 dollars, the maximum Pell grant in 1975–1976 was $5,064; it was only $4,050 by 2005, a 20 percent decrease after accounting for inflation (Baum and Payea 2006). Recently, federal grant aid has increased due to a combination of increasing the maximum Pell grant along with changing economic conditions, but there are concerns about the sustainability of this growth (Baum and Payea 2011).

Meanwhile, loans have grown in importance. The Guaranteed Student Loan Program eventually became the Stafford Loan Program. Where the federal role focused originally on the public nature of educational investments, with large support for grants that do not have to be repaid, over time the focus shifted more to emphasizing the individual returns and private nature of the return to college, and the loan programs grew considerably.[5]

Figure 4.1 graphs the growth of financial aid from school year 1963 1964 to school year 1991 1992. There was a leap in federal expenditures from 1964 to 1970, and this was predominately in the form of grants. However, grant expenditures peaked in 1976, and loans had passed grants in terms of expenditures by the early 1980s.

The role of loans increased even more after 1992 with the Reauthorization of the Higher Education Act (HEA 1992) which created the Stafford Unsubsidized Loan Program, which joined the Stafford Subsidized Loan Program (the Guaranteed Student Loan Program had been renamed in 1988). This act made federal loans available to all students although the interest subsidies were available only to low-income students. As shown in table 4.1, during the 1993–1994 school year, loan expenditures increased dramatically the first year after this policy change. HEA 1992 also created a direct lending pilot, in which 300 institutions could get loan funds directly from the federal government, foregoing the involvement of private lenders and guarantee agencies (Cervantes et al. 2005). The direct lending pilot, together with the National Defense Student Loan Program, which was renamed the Perkins Loan Program in 1986, the federal government greatly increased its involvement in direct lending. Today, loans remain the dominant form of aid, counter to the original intent of the War on Poverty. This is due not only to changes in the importance of different types of aid, but also a shifting focus in the target population of federal aid.

The expansion of loan availability to all students highlights the growing attention middle-income students have received in financial aid policy. Although the War on Poverty focused most of its attention on low-income students, as college costs increased, the concerns of the middle class became more prominent. As summarized by then President Bush in 1992 with respect to HEA 1992, "This act that I'm signing today gives a hand up to lower income students who need help the most. But it also reaches out into the middle-income families, the ones who skipped a vacation and drove the old clunker so that their kids could go to college" (Bush 1992).

Therefore, low-income students remain a priority, but the beneficiaries of financial aid have broadened beyond President Johnson's conceptualization.

Several policy developments illustrate the change in focus. In 1992, along with the opening of loans to all students, federal financial need calculations began to

FIGURE 4.1 / Student Aid Used to Finance Postsecondary Education Expenses

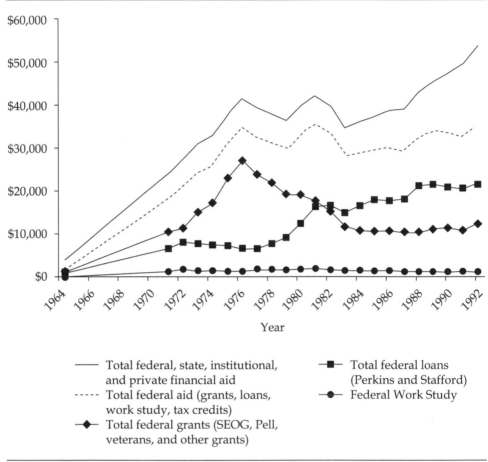

Year

— Total federal, state, institutional,
and private financial aid
---- Total federal aid (grants, loans,
work study, tax credits)
—◆— Total federal grants (SEOG, Pell,
veterans, and other grants)

—■— Total federal loans
(Perkins and Stafford)
—●— Federal Work Study

Source: Author's compilation based on College Board (2011).
Note: Constant 2010 dollars in millions. Fiscal years are shown: 1964 equals the 1963–1964 academic school year. Other grant programs include Social Security Student Benefit Program, LEAP, SMART grants, Academic Competitiveness grants, and other federal grants. Unsubsidized Stafford and other loans includes PLUS, SLS, and other federal loans. Other aid includes state grant programs, institutional grants, private and employer grants, and nonfederal loans.

exclude home equity, thereby allowing many more middle-class families to qualify for need-based support (Schenet 1993). The emphasis on helping middle-class families continued in 1997, when higher education tax credits were introduced. At the time, families had to have tax liability to receive the tax credit, and few families with incomes under $30,000 qualified. As a result, most beneficiaries had family incomes over $50,000 (Long 2004). These tax credits are now refundable, thereby making them available to lower-income families.

The same is true of the tax benefits associated with college savings plans. Jennifer Ma (2004) finds that the median income among users of these plans was $100,000, far higher than the median income and median wealth among all families. Undoubtedly, college is a difficult expense for most families to manage. However, the shift of financial aid policy in the context of limited resources has diverted attention from the problems of low-income students who were the focus during the War on Poverty.

The War on Poverty also created the Work Study program, which has remained small from creation to the present (see figure 4.1). Still, the program acknowledges that some students need employment to help pay for college expenses. Students have increasingly sought employment to help with college costs. According to Judith Scott-Clayton (2012), among full-time undergraduates age eighteen to twenty-two, student employment nearly doubled from 1970 to 2000. However, only about one in five working undergraduates receives support from the Work Study Program.

The Important Roles of Preparation and Information The fourth major contribution of the War on Poverty is the acknowledgement of the importance of support for academic preparation and the provision of information in making college access possible. The TRIO programs represent the first major effort to address these issues related to the transition from high school to college. Affordability is a barrier, but academic preparation can also be one. Students often do not finish high school or do so below grade-level competency (Bettinger and Long 2009), which affects their ability to access and succeed in higher education. Gaps are also significant in test scores by race and income (Jencks and Phillips 1998), which contribute to access inequality. Lack of information is another important impediment. College attendance is the culmination of a series of steps and benchmarks, and the process is too complex and difficult for many families, especially low-income families, to decipher and navigate. Thomas Kane and Chris Avery (2004) showed that low-income high school students possess little understanding of how to handle this admissions process or knowledge about actual college tuition levels. Other research has also found a significant lack of information among prospective college students in general (Ikenberry and Hartle 1998; Horn, Chen, and Chapman 2003). Although more could be done to address academic and informational barriers, early attention to these barriers is another contribution of the War on Poverty.

In 2004, about 52,000 students participated in 727 regular Upward Bound projects around the country (Myers et al. 2004). At least two-thirds of each project's participants must be both low-income and potential first-generation college students. Students typically enter the program while in ninth or tenth grade and may participate through the summer following twelfth grade; most remain in Upward Bound for about twenty-one months. Projects provide students with a variety of services, including instruction, tutoring and counseling. In addition to regularly scheduled meetings throughout the school year, there is an intensive instructional program that meets daily for about six weeks during the summer. Most projects are hosted by four-year colleges (Myers et al. 2004).

THE EFFECTS OF THE WAR ON POVERTY ON COLLEGE ACCESS AND SUCCESS

The War on Poverty created an impressive set of financial aid policies, but the true measure of their impact is what effects they have had on increasing college access. Without the subsidies, it seems highly unlikely that the nation's poor would have been able to capitalize on higher education opportunities. However, affordability is but one issue, and policy design matters for effectiveness. Moreover, as the programs have evolved into the current system of aid, certain tenets of the War on Poverty have lost prominence. This section examines the long-term effects of the War on Poverty on college access and postsecondary attainment.

Trends in Spending and Enrollment

Where table 4.1 and figure 4.1 show federal expenditures for financial aid increased, figure 4.2 displays the average amount of inflation-adjusted aid a full-time equivalent (FTE) student has received. Although these figures include aid from states and institutions, most funding is from the federal government. In 1973–1974, as the Pell grant (then called the BEOG) became the predominant grant program, the average grant aid per FTE was $3,497 in 2010 dollars; by 2010–2011, total grant aid per FTE had increased to $6,566. However, there have also been periods of reductions and stagnation. For instance, during the 1980s, grant aid amounts fell, and it was not until 1997 that the mean grant aid per FTE passed the level of aid in 1973. In contrast, the average amount in federal loans per FTE has increased steadily. Although students received only $1,108 in federal loans per FTE in 1971–1972 (2010 dollars), they received $6,368 per FTE by 2010–2011, a multiple of nearly six. Federal loans passed grants in aid per FTE in the mid-1990s (Baum and Payea 2011).

Overall, since the War on Poverty created the original federal financial aid programs, support to students has reduced substantially the price of higher education for families with total aid (federal grants, loans, and work study) amounting to $13,005 per FTE in 2010 (Baum and Payea 2011). However, college prices have increased far greater than the rate of financial aid growth during most years. From 1976–1977 to 2010–2011, the average total cost (tuition, fees, and room and board) of a four-year institution grew from $8,402 to $18,133 (2010 constant dollars). As a result, the net cost to families remains a substantial challenge to low-income families, and much of the support from the growth in government support has been in the form of cost deferment (with loans) rather than cost forgiveness (with grants).

Enrollment rates have also increased since the War on Poverty. In 1967, 33.7 percent of high school graduates age eighteen to twenty-four enrolled at degree-granting institutions; in 2007, 46.1 percent did so (National Center for Education Statistics 2008, table 212). Measured another way, 50.7 percent of young people

FIGURE 4.2 / Average Aid Per Full-Time Equivalent (FTE) Student

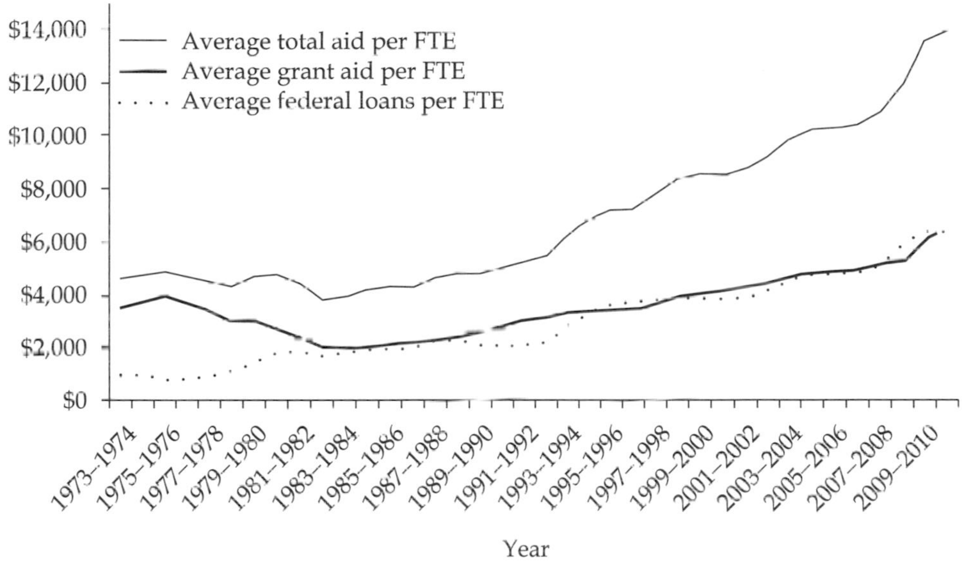

Source: Author's compilation based on College Board (2011).
Note: Constant 2010 dollars. The figures reported here reflect total student aid amounts divided across all students, including nonrecipients. Total aid includes federal work study and education tax benefits. Loan numbers do not include private nonfederal loans. For years 1995–1996 and earlier, net commitments are estimated.

had enrolled in college the October immediately following high school graduation in 1975, versus 68.1 percent in 2010. These numbers suggest that the goals of the War on Poverty were at least partially realized in the decades afterward, though it is debatable what proportion of the credit is due to financial aid programs and what to the increasing return to higher education.

However, beyond aiming to increase college enrollment, the War on Poverty attempted both to improve the opportunities available to low-income students to bring them out of poverty and to reduce gaps in college access by race and income. There is less evidence to suggest these goals have been met. Although the percentage of low-income students who attend college has increased over time, as shown in figure 4.3, the percentage of high school graduates enrolled in college the October immediately after high school continues to vary widely by family income level. By 2010, 82.2 percent of students from high-income families attended college, versus only 52.3 percent of those from low-income families. The gap between the high- and low-income families has not lessened during the last thirty-five years (29.7 percentage points in 1975 and 29.9 percentage points in 2010), and at times, it has grown. For instance, in 1995, students from high-income families were 41 4 percentage points more likely to enroll in college than their counterparts from low-income families (U.S. Census Bureau 2011).[6] Therefore, despite some progress in

FIGURE 4.3 / High School Graduates in College the October Immediately Following High School Completion Within Six Months

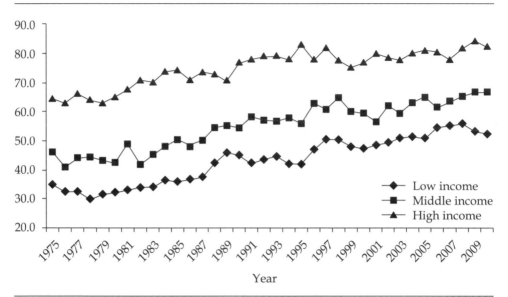

Source: Author's compilation based on U.S. Census Bureau (2010).
Note: Low income refers to the bottom 20 percent of all family incomes, *high income* refers to the top 20 percent of all family incomes, and *middle income* refers to the 60 percent in between. The low-income figures are a three-year moving average due to small sample size. For 1975 and 2010, a two-year moving average is used. Includes high school completers age sixteen to twenty-four, who account for about 98 percent of all high school graduates in a given year.

terms of increasing the proportion of low-income students who enter higher education overall, low-income students still face greater barriers to college access than other groups, and the programs and policies created by and since the War on Poverty have not been successful in decreasing inequality in college attendance rates by income.

Similar gaps in enrollment by race are also evident. As shown in figure 4.4, the college enrollment rates of eighteen- to twenty-four-year-olds differ by race. Despite an upward trend for the three groups from 1955 to 2010, white students still attend college at rates higher than those for black and Hispanic students, and the size of the gap persists. Focusing on eighteen to twenty-four-year-old high school graduates attending degree-granting institutions, the data suggest recent progress in closing the gaps between black and white students, but that those between Hispanic and white students have been widening. For example, in 1967, the black-white college enrollment gap was 13.9 percentage points; in 2009, it was 7.3 points. For Hispanics, the gap increased from 13.8 percentage points in 1972 to 17.5 points in 2009 (National Center for Education Statistics 2010). Trends in the white-Hispanic gap may reflect changes in the flow of Latino immigrants from different countries with varying amounts of social capital.

FIGURE 4.4 / Percentage of Those Age Eighteen to Twenty-Four in College

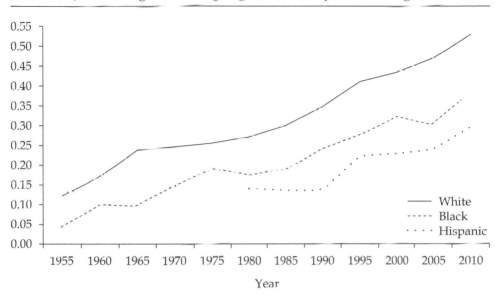

Source: Author's compilation based on U.S. Bureau of the Census (1980, 2000); U.S. Census Bureau (2010, table A-6).
Note: Calculations by author using population estimates and college enrollment figures. Population estimates are for the resident population plus armed forces overseas age eighteen to twenty-four. College enrollment figures are for the civilian non-institutionalized population of eighteen- to twenty-four-year-olds. Data for black in 1955 and 1960 are for black and other races. Starting in 2003 respondents could identify more than one race. From 2003 onward, data represent those respondents who indicated only one race category. Hispanics may be of any race.

Following college enrollment trends, baccalaureate degrees by background also reflect major racial-ethnic gaps. Only 36 percent of low-income students who were college-qualified completed a bachelor's degree within eight years, versus 81 percent of high-income students (Adelman 2006).[7] Stark differences also exist by race. Graduation rates at four-year institutions among first-time, full-time, degree-seeking undergraduates were highest for Asian–Pacific Islander students (65 percent) followed by white, non-Hispanic students (58 percent) for cohorts entering in fall of 1998. Black and Hispanic students in this cohort graduated at much lower rates, 40 percent and 46 percent, respectively (Knapp, Kelly-Reid, and Whitmore 2006).

The remaining inequality in college access and completion are not that surprising. Even if financial aid programs are effective, substantial costs remain. Bridget Long and Erin Riley (2007) document the unmet financial need faced by many, particularly students from low-income backgrounds and students of color. After accounting for the family's contribution, the Expected Family Contribution (EFC), and the receipt of all grants, dependent students in the 2003–2004 school year faced an average unmet need of $7,195. For full-time, full-year students, unmet need was even greater ($8,323).[8] Increasingly, students have acquired loans to make up this remaining difference. However, even after taking into account government and institutional loans, unmet need is still significant. Long and Riley (2007) found that dependent students faced $5,911 in unmet need after all loans and grants, versus $4,503 for independent students. Among full-time, full-year students, the amount of unmet need was again higher even after taking into account loans: $6,726 for dependent students and $7,049 for independent students. Given substantial unmet need, questions about the effectiveness of the system of financial aid often focus on whether current amounts are adequate. In other words, calls for reform have focused on increasing the level of financial aid awards. Although billions of dollars are spent each year on financial aid, these unmet need figures suggest that current funding is inadequate.

Have the Grant Programs Worked?

Many studies have examined the impact of grant aid on student enrollment. The general conclusion is that money does matter, but policy design is an important determinant of a program's effectiveness, and easy-to-understand programs have the largest impact. Unfortunately, many studies are critical of the complexity of the main War on Poverty program: the BEOG, now Pell Grant. The Pell Grant in particular has been challenging to study because it is difficult to identify a comparison group of similar nonrecipients, given the national nature of the program. However, the research literature on other state and institutional grant programs confirms the rationale of the War on Poverty that giving grants could spur an increase in college enrollment.

To determine the effectiveness of the BEOG/Pell Grant, researchers have used a before and after comparison technique of differences-in-differences by comparing the enrollment rates of low-income students for a period before and after 1972 (Kane 1996). The income groups that were not eligible for the Pell grant serve as the control group. To avoid the influence of the Vietnam draft on men's enrollment decisions, Kane studies women only and finds that enrollment grew 2.6 percentage points more slowly for the lowest-income quartile, the expected beneficiaries of the Pell grant, contrary to predictions. Only public two-year college enrollment seemed to grow more quickly for low-income youth. Studies by Charles Manski and David Wise (1983) and Lee Hansen (1983) also found no disproportionate growth in college enrollment or completion of a bachelor's degree by low-income students after the introduction of Pell.

It is possible that the Pell grant might have had an impact only on college choice rather than attendance. Alternatively, Larry Leslie and Paul Brinkman (1987) suggest that the aid may have worked well enough to maintain the distribution of students during the 1970s and 1980s. If true, this suggests that enrollment rates among low-income students would have fallen even more had Pell not been created. However, the most convincing explanations for the lack of a response among low-income students to the Pell Grant focus on problems with the program itself. Researchers and practitioners suggest that low program visibility, the complexity of the application process, and intimidating audit procedures contributed to limiting the aid program's impact.

Interestingly, the impact of the Pell Grant was greater for older, nontraditional students. Neil Seftor and Sarah Turner (2002) examine how changes in the means-tested federal Pell Grant program affected enrollment decisions of potential students in their twenties and thirties. They report sizable effects of the introduction of the Pell Grant on college enrollment decisions for older students. They also underscore concerns about the complexity of the Pell Grant, suggesting that because older workers have more experience with processes such as tax and government support forms, they may be more adept and less daunted by complex aid application processes.

Research on other grant programs lends credibility to the notion that the Pell Grant could be more effective if it were simplified and increased in visibility. Susan Dynarski (2002) examines the impact of eliminating a federal financial aid source. The Social Security Student Benefit (SSSB) program gave eighteen- to twenty-two-year-old children of dead, disabled, or retired Social Security beneficiaries monthly support while they were enrolled full-time in college. At its peak, it provided grants totaling $3.3 billion annually to one of ten students. In contrast to the Pell Grant, awareness among potential beneficiaries was high due to notification from the government and the extremely simple application process. In 1982, Congress discontinued the program. Dynarski estimates that doing so reduced college access and attainment by noting a difference of over 25 percent between the treatment and control groups. This translates into $1,000 (1997 dollars) of grant aid increasing education attainment by 0.20 years and the probability of attending college by 5 percentage points.

The Georgia HOPE (Helping Outstanding Pupils Educationally) Scholarship, created in 1993, is also simple in design and much effort was made to publicize the program and train high school guidance counselors on how to help students access it. Dynarski (2000), using a natural experiment, compares enrollment rates in Georgia to other southern states before and after the program. She finds that Georgia's program has had a surprisingly large impact on the college-attendance rate of middle- and high-income youth—each $1,000 in aid (in 1998 dollars) increased the college attendance rate by 3.7 to 4.2 percentage points. Also, there was a much larger impact on college choice. Chris Cornwell, David Mustard, and Deepa Sridhar (2006) also examine Georgia Hope using different data and estimate that the scholarship increased the overall freshmen enrollment rate by 6.9 percentage points, with the gains concentrated in four-year schools.

As shown by these studies and others (see, for example, Long 2007), grants can increase college enrollment. However, though the existence of aid programs was once thought enough to enable enrollment, the visibility and design of the aid also matters. This has also been found in the examinations of other social programs. Janet Currie (2004) finds that the take-up rates on social programs increase when eligible participants are automatically enrolled and administrative barriers are reduced. Therefore, researchers have advocated for simplification of federal need-based grants. An intervention that greatly simplified the financial aid application process among individuals likely to be eligible for the Pell grant found strong effects. Families who were randomly assigned help with the Free Application for Federal Student Aid (FAFSA), the application necessary to qualify for federal aid like the Pell Grant, were much more likely to enroll in college, receive financial aid, and persist after three years in comparison with families that did not receive help with the FAFSA (Bettinger et al. 2012). This suggests that though the War on Poverty correctly predicted the important role of grants in college access, more careful attention to policy design, including the application process, is warranted to improve the effectiveness of programs.

Lessons from the War on Poverty: Other Types of Financial Aid

Has access to loans affected college decisions? The increasing use of student loans suggests their growing importance, perhaps due to unmet financial need. However, growing reliance on loans rather than grants has implications for college access and persistence. Unfortunately, little is also known about how the availability of loans affects college access. Dynarski (2003) studies whether the availability of government loans affects schooling decisions. Identifying the effect of loans is empirically challenging, because eligibility for federal loans is correlated with observed and unobserved determinants of schooling. Dynarski exploits variation in loan eligibility after the Higher Education Amendments of 1992, which removed home equity from the set of assets that are taxed by the federal financial aid formula. She concludes that loan eligibility had a positive effect on college attendance and appears to have shifted students toward four-year private colleges. On the other hand, Elizabeth Savoca (1991) examines whether the shift in the composition of aid away from grants toward loans adversely affected college enrollments in the 1970s and 1980s. She finds that the probability of attending college falls when loans replace grants, dollar for dollar, in the financial aid package.

The burden of the debt has also been a popular topic of debate. Sandy Baum (2003) reports that half of those surveyed reported feeling burdened by their student debt payments. To gauge whether loan levels are worrisome, one should examine indicators of a student's ability to pay back the debt. Debt burden, calculated as the percentage of monthly income a student must dedicate to loan payments, provides one measure of whether rising loan amounts are problematic for students. In 2004, the American Council on Education (ACE) concluded that the median debt burden of 7 percent was manageable and stable for students graduating with bachelor degrees in the 1990s (2004). However, the report also found that one-third of borrowers face debt burdens above 8 percent, a level considered unmanageable by financial aid researchers.[9] In addition, although debt levels may have largely been manageable for most students in previous decades, the situation has probably changed for current students. Higher cumulative debts combined with recent changes in federal loan programs suggest today's college students face even higher debt burdens, and these are likely to continue increasing in the future.

Debt burden is also troublesome for students who do not complete a college degree (Long and Ansel 2007).

Student loans could also have unintended negative consequences on students' choice of major, deterring students from public service fields, such as teaching and social work, to higher-paying fields. According to recent studies, 23 percent of graduates from public institutions and 38 percent of graduates from private colleges and universities would face unmanageable debt burdens if they entered teaching based on average starting salaries (Swarthout 2006). Loans could also have an impact on life decisions after college such as buying a house, getting married, or having children. The evidence is mixed (Baum and Saunders 1998; Baum and O'Malley 2006), but research by Nellie Mae over the past fifteen years suggests that attitudes toward education debt are becoming more negative.

During the War on Poverty, loans were not meant to be the dominant form of financial aid, but now that their role has increased substantially, much more research is needed to more fully understand their effects. Unfortunately, as noted, little research documents the full effects of loans on student behavior and decisions. On the other hand, many studies highlight a list of concerns, including that some groups are reluctant to use them and excessive student debt may have long-term negative repercussions. Therefore, the increased complexity of loans in terms of both short- and long-term outcomes should be considered when determining policy. While loans may seem like a cheaper policy option for the government because they must be repaid by students, once taking into account the indirect negative effects loans can have, they may actually be more expensive in the long run than other policy options, like grant programs.

The impact of the Federal Work Study program has also received little attention. More broadly, the effects of student employment on educational outcomes have been mixed. Some studies find small negative effects from working; others find a small, positive correlation between academic outcomes and low levels of on-campus work. The one quasi-experimental study on the effects of the Work Study compares eligible and ineligible students at colleges in West Virginia. Exploiting differences in the amount of Work Study funding institutions receive, Scott-Clayton (2011) does not find significant effects of the program on academic outcomes, though the effects appear to be large and negative for women and positive for men.

Beyond Financial Aid

As noted, the War on Poverty attempted to address more than just the financial barriers to college access. With the creation of Upward Bound, the government also aimed to provide first-generation and other disadvantaged high school students with college preparation programs. Upward Bound provides tutoring, mentoring, information on college opportunities, and assistance completing applications, and evaluations of the program suggest these services may have positive effects for some students. The U.S. Department of Education employed Mathematica Policy Research (MPR) to evaluate the program using data from surveys (a baseline survey conducted from 1992 to 1994 and follow-up surveys in 1994 and 1995, 1996 and 1997, and 1998 to 2000), high school and postsecondary transcripts, and reports on participation from Upward Bound project staff. The research design of these studies is experimental, and the results suggest that, for the average student, Upward Bound increased the number of high school math credits earned but did not affect other measures. Upward Bound may have also increased enrollment at four-year institutions, particularly for students with lower educational expectations, but "the evidence is not conclusive" (Myers et al. 2004, xvii). The evidence is more definitive in establishing that students with lower expectations who participated in Upward Bound did earn more credits at four-year colleges. The number of credits completed on average doubled from eleven to twenty-two credits, suggesting that Upward Bound may increase educational attainment for some students. However, students with higher expectations did not experience similar gains, and there was no overall effect on enrollment or total credits earned (Myers et al. 2004). It is difficult to discern which of the many components of Upward Bound have been most effective, but both reports suggest that Upward Bound would have had larger effects had students remained in the program for longer periods, given that many left after during the first year of participation (Myers and Schirm 1999; Myers et al. 2004; Long 2010).

CONCLUSIONS AND IMPLICATIONS

Fifty years later, the effects of the War on Poverty are evident in the programs that established a significant role for the federal government in higher education and put into practice the goal of making higher education available to all. The programs also established the basic framework for financial aid that persists today despite changes in the relative balance between programs and which types of students are eligible for aid. Finally, with the creation of the TRIO programs, the War on Poverty acknowledged that financial aid is not enough to support college access, and that academic preparation and information have important roles.

The legacy of the War on Poverty is positive, but one cannot conclude that it was completely successful. Despite substantial increases in access to higher education over the last several decades, postsecondary attendance continues to be stratified by family income and race. This may be related to the large amounts of unmet financial need students have. Moreover, questions about how to improve the design of grants and concerns about the complicated effects of loans remain. Information and academic preparation also remain as barriers for many low-income students. As such, a great deal remains to be done to realize the goal of making higher education truly possible for all students.

Given the critical role higher education plays in both individual economic success and the public good, increasing college access should continue to be a major goal of the government. To improve policy, based on the research literature, the first implication is that information and simplicity are important. The mere existence of an aid program is not enough to encourage enrollment: the visibility and design of the program also matter. In several cases, researchers have failed to document large, general responses to the introduction of financial aid programs (for example, the Pell grant). On the other hand, the research suggests aid programs can be very successful when they are well publicized, and they are relatively easy for students to understand and apply.

Second, not all aid is equal. Although grants have been shown to be effective, if designed properly, in influencing student decisions, research suggests that loans are less effective in increasing enrollment than grants. The direct cost to the government for providing loans is less than that of grants because loans must be repaid by students, but it is still not clear whether loans are a more cost-effective policy option. When the increased complexity of loans and their potential negative impacts on short- and long-term outcomes are taken into account, the full costs of loans are much higher than just the direct costs. Debt burden can negatively affect academic, career, and family decisions, and it is unclear whether recent efforts to reduce the interest rate on government loans as well as extend the federal loan forgiveness program will do much to mitigate these indirect effects.

Still, many questions about the role of our current financial aid and college access programs and what new supports might be necessary to improve college access and success are unanswered. First, more needs to be understood about the effects of the loan and work study programs, including the long-term effects of loans and debt burden. Moreover, additional research is needed on the specific design elements necessary to make a policy successful. Related to this is the role of information and marketing. How students perceive a policy is vital, but more concrete recommendations are necessary on how to reach students. This is a concern particularly for low-income students, who do not have the same access to high-speed Internet resources or guidance counselors in schools. Little is also known about how the responses of students vary by race and age.

The role of schools, colleges, and universities should also not be underestimated, but more research is needed to understand how these institutions interact with aid policy. They could be partners in informing students about their options and in meeting financial needs. On the other hand, although research on the behavior of colleges does not document major tuition responses to federal financial aid, these institutions could also react in ways to reduce the impact of policies. Family and community support are also thought to be essential in efforts to increase college access. These types of support may be especially important for initiatives designed to raise education aspirations and increase information about aid and the application process, and so partnerships should be created to include families and communities. Otherwise, ignoring these important elements could undermine the effectiveness of a policy.

NOTES

1. Public Law No. 88-452, 78 Stat. 500 (1964).
2. Public Law No. 89-329, 79 Stat. 1219 (1965).

3. Similar concerns also influenced ESEA, which created programs geared towards primary and secondary education.
4. Higher Education Amendments of 1972 (P.L.92-318).
5. For a brief time, subsidized loans were made available to virtually all students in 1978 with the Middle Income Student Assistance Act (MISAA), and the number of guaranteed students loans grew from 1 million in 1978 to 3.1 million in 1982 (Mumper 1996). However, due to escalating costs, Congress reinstated an income ceiling on subsidized loans in 1981. Still, MISAA was the beginning of the creation of several new federal loan programs, including the Parent Loans for Undergraduate Students (PLUS) program in 1980 (Cervantes et al. 2005).
6. Low income refers to the bottom 20 percent of all family incomes, high income refers to the top 20 percent, and middle income refers to the 60 percent in between. The low-income figures are a three-year moving average due to small sample size. For 1975 and 2010, a two-year moving average is used: data for 1975 reflect an average of 1975 and 1976, and data for 2010 reflect an average of 2009 and 2010. Includes high school completers ages sixteen to twenty-four, who account for about 98 percent of all high school graduates in a given year.
7. Students were judged to be college qualified if they met any of five criteria that would place them among the top 75 percent of four-year college students for that criterion. The minimum values for "qualified" were: a class rank of the 46th percentile, an academic grade point average (GPA) of 2.7, an SAT combined score of 820, an ACT (American College Testing) composite score of 19, or a NELS-88 test score of the 56th percentile (Berkner and Chavez 1997)
8. Note that the information on private and outside financial aid is self-reported and may not capture all aid. Credit card debt is not included in these calculations.
9. Guidelines regarding the percentage of pretax income devoted to student loans are meant to ensure borrowers can meet other expenses such as car payments, rent or mortgage, and additional expenses. The 8 percent rule was derived from credit-underwriting standards that limit monthly mortgage payments to 25 to 29 percent of borrower's income and total monthly debt payments to 36 to 41 percent of income (Scherschel 1998).

REFERENCES

Adelman, Clifford. 2006. Internal analysis from the National Educational Longitudinal Study of 1988. Unpublished document. U.S. Department of Education, Office of Vocational and Adult Education.

American Council on Education. 2004. *Debt Burden: Repaying Student Debt*. Washington, D.C.: American Council on Education Center for Policy Analysis.

Baum, Sandy. 2003. "The Role of Student Loans in College Access." *National Dialogue on Student Financial Aid* research report 5. New York: The College Board.

Baum, Sandy, and Marie O'Malley. 2006. *College on Credit: How Borrowers Perceive Their Education Debt: Results of the 2002 National Student Loan Survey*. Braintree, Mass.: Nellie Mae Corporation.

Baum, Sandy, and Kathleen Payea. 2006. *Trends in Student Aid*. New York: The College Board.

————. 2011. *Trends in Student Aid*. New York: The College Board.

Baum, Sandy, and Diane Saunders. 1998. "Life After Debt: Results of the National Student Loan Survey." *Journal of tudent Financial Aid* 28(3): 7–23.

Berkner, Lutz, and Lisa Chavez. 1997. *Access to Postsecondary Education for the 1992 High School Graduates*. Washington, D.C.: National Center for Education Statistics.

Bettinger, Eric, and Bridget Terry Long. 2009. "Addressing the Needs of Under-Prepared College Students: Does College Remediation Work?" *Journal of Human Resources* 443(3): 736–71.

Bettinger, Eric, Bridget Terry Long, Philip Oreopoulos, and Lisa Sanbonmatsu. 2012. "The Role of Application Assistance and Information in College Decisions: Results from the H&R Block FAFSA Experiment." *Quarterly Journal of Economics* 127(3): 1–38.

Bush, George H.W. 1992. "Remarks on Signing the Higher Education Amendments of 1992 in Annandale, VA." *The American Presidency Project*. Available at: http:/www.presidency.ucsb.edu/ws/index.php?pid=21260andst1=higher+education (accessed May 18, 2012).

Cervantes, Angelica, Marlena Creusere, Robin McMillion, Carla McQueen, Matt Short, Matt Steiner, and Jeff Webster. 2005. *Opening the Doors to Higher Education: Perspectives on the Higher Education Act 40 Years Later*. Round Rock: Texas Guaranteed Student Loan Corporation.

College Board. 2011. *Trends in Student Aid*. Washington, D.C.: The College Board. Available at: http://trends.collegeboard.org/sites/default/files/Student_Aid_2011.pdf (accessed April 5, 2013).

Cornwell, Chris, David Mustard, and Deepa Sridhar. 2006. "The Enrollment Effects of Merit-Based Financial Aid: Evidence from Georgia's HOPE Scholarship." *Journal of Labor Economics* 244(4): 761–86.

Currie, Janet. 2004. "The Take Up of Social Benefits." NBER Working Paper No. 10488.

Dynarski, Susan. 2000. "Hope for Whom? Financial Aid for the Middle Class and Its Impact on College Attendance." *National Tax Journal* 53(3): 629–62.

————. 2002. "The Behavioral and Distributional Implications of Subsidies for College." *American Economic Review* 92(2): 279–85.

————. 2003. "Loans, Liquidity, and Schooling Decisions." Unpublished manuscript. Harvard University.

Groutt, John. 2003. "Milestones of TRIO History, Part I." *Opportunity Outlook* 21–27. Washington, D.C.: Journal of the Council for Opportunity in Education.

Hansen, W. Lee. 1983. "Impact of Student Financial Aid on Access." In *The Crisis in Higher Education*, edited by Joseph Froomkin. New York: Academy of Political Science.

Horn, Laura J., Xianglei Chen, and Chris Chapman. 2003. "Getting Ready to Pay for College: What Students and Their Parents Know About the Cost of College Tuition and What They Are Doing to Find Out." NCES 2003-030. Washington: U.S. Department of Education.

Ikenberry, Stanley O., and Terry W. Hartle. 1998. *Too Little Knowledge Is a Dangerous Thing: What the Public Thinks About Paying for College*. Washington, D.C.: American Council on Education.

Jencks, Christopher, and Meredith Phillips. 1998. *The Black-White Test Score Gap*. Washington, D.C.: Brookings Institution Press.

Kane, Thomas J. 1996. "Lessons from the Largest School Voucher Program Ever: Two Decades of Experience with Pell Grants." In *Who Chooses? Who Loses? Culture, Institutions, and the Unequal Effects of School Choice,* edited by Bruce Fuller, Richard Elmore, and Gary Orfield. New York: Teachers College Press.

Kane, Thomas, and Chris Avery. 2004. "Student Perceptions of College Opportunities: The Boston COACH Program." In *College Decisions: The New Economics of Choosing, Attending and Completing College,* edited by Caroline Hoxby. Chicago: University of Chicago Press.

Kim, Dongbin, and John L. Rury. 2007. "The Changing Profile of College Access: The Truman Commission and Enrollment Patterns in the Postwar Era." *History of Education Quarterly* 47(3): 302–27.

Knapp, Laura G., Janice E. Kelly-Reid, and Roy W. Whitmore. 2006. "Enrollment in Postsecondary Institutions, Fall 2004; Graduation Rates, 1998 and 2001 Cohorts; and Financial Statistics, Fiscal Year 2004." NCES 2006–155. Washington: U.S. Department of Education.

Leslie, Larry, and Paul Brinkman. 1987. "Student Price Response in Higher Education." *Journal of Higher Education* 58(2): 181–204.

Long, Bridget Terry. 2004. "The Impact of Federal Tax Credits for Higher Education Expenses." In *College Choices: The Economics of Which College, When College, and How to Pay for It,* edited by Caroline M. Hoxby. Chicago: University of Chicago Press and the National Bureau of Economic Research.

———. 2007. "The Contributions of Economics to the Study of College Access and Success." *Teachers College Record* 109(10): 2367–443.

———. 2010. "High School Dropout Prevention and College Preparatory Programs." In *Targeting Investments in Children: Fighting Poverty When Resources Are Limited,* edited by Phillip B. Levine and David J. Zimmerman. Chicago: University of Chicago Press, Robin Hood Foundation, and the National Bureau of Economic Research.

Long, Bridget Terry, and Dana Ansel. 2007. "As Student Debt Increases, Colleges Owe More in Performance." *Connection: The Journal of the New England Board of Higher Education,* XXI(Winter): 23–24.

Long, Bridget Terry, and Erin K. Riley. 2007. "Financial Aid: A Broken Bridge to College Access?" *Harvard Educational Review* 77(1): 39–43.

Ma, Jennifer. 2004. "Education Saving Incentives and Household Saving: Evidence from the 2000 TIAA-CREF Survey of Participant Finances." In *College Choices: The Economics of Which College, When College, and How to Pay for It,* edited by Caroline M. Hoxby. Chicago: University of Chicago Press and the National Bureau of Economic Research.

Manski, Charles, and David Wise. 1983. *College Choice in America.* Cambridge, MA: Harvard University Press.

Mumper, Michael. 1996. *Removing College Price Barriers: What Government Has Done and Why It Doesn't Work.* Albany: State University of New York Press.

Myers, David, Robert Olsen, Neil Seftor, Julie Young, and Christina Tuttle. 2004. "The Impacts of Regular Upward Bound: Results from the Third Follow-Up Data Collection." Report PR04–30. Washington, D.C.: Mathematica Policy Research.

Myers, David, and Allen Schirm. 1999. "The Impacts for Upward Bound: Final Report for Phase I of the National Evaluation." Report PR99–51. Washington, D.C.: Mathematica Policy Research.

National Center for Education Statistics. 2008. *Digest of Education Statistics 2007.* NCES 2008-022. Washington: U.S. Department of Education.

———. 2010. *Digest of Education Statistics 2009*. NCES 2010-013. Washington: U.S. Department of Education.

President's Commission on Higher Education 1947. *Higher Education for American Democracy: A Report of the President's Commission for Higher Education*, vol. 1, chap. 2. New York: Harper and Brothers.

Savoca, Elizabeth. 1991. "The Effect of Changes in the Composition of Financial Aid on College Enrollments." *Eastern Economic Journal* 17(1): 109–21.

Schenet, Margot A. 1993. "Recent Changes in Federal Student Aid." *CRS report* 94-10. Washington, D.C.: Congressional Research Service.

Scherschel, Patricia M. 1998. *Student Indebtedness: Are Borrowers Pushing the Limits?* USA Group Foundation.

Scott-Clayton, Judith. 2011. "The Causal Effect of Federal Work-Study Participation: Quasi-Experimental Evidence from West Virginia." *Educational Evaluation and Policy Analysis* 33(4): 506–27.

———. 2012. "What Explains Trends in Labor Supply Among U.S. Undergraduates?" *National Tax Journal* 65(1): 181–201.

Seftor, Neil, and Sarah Turner. 2002. "Back to School: Federal Student Aid Policy and Adult College Enrollment." *Journal of Human Resources* 37(2): 336–52.

Swarthout, Luke. 2006. *Paying Back, Not Giving Back. Student Debt's Negative Impact on Public Service Career Opportunities*. Los Angeles: State Public Interest Group Higher Education Project.

U.S. Bureau of the Census. 1977. "Money Income in 1975 of Families and Persons in the United States." *Current Population Report* series P60, no. 105. Washington: U.S. Department of Commerce. Available at: http://www2.census.gov/prod2/popscan/p60-105.pdf (accessed April 16, 2013).

———. 1980. "National Population Estimates by Age, Sex, and Race: 1900 to 1979." PE-11. Washington: U.S. Department of Commerce. Available at: http://www.census.gov/popest/data/national/asrh/pre-1980/PE-11.html (accessed April 16, 2013).

———. 1987a. "Money Income and Poverty Status of Families and Persons in the United States: 1986." *Current Population Report* series P60, no. 157. Washington: U.S. Department of Commerce. Available at: http://www2.census.gov/prod2/popscan/p60-157.pdf (accessed April 16, 2013).

———. 1987b. "Money Income of Households, Families, and Persons in the United States: 1987." *Current Population Report* series P60, no. 162. Washington: U.S. Department of Commerce. Available at: http://www2.census.gov/prod2/popscan/p60-162.pdf (accessed April 16, 2013).

———. 1991. "Money Income of Households, Families, and Persons in the United States: 1990." *Current Population Report* series P60, no. 174. Washington: U.S. Department of Commerce. Available at: http://www2.census.gov/prod2/popscan/p60-174.pdf (accessed April 16, 2013).

———. 2000. "U.S. Population Estimates by Age, Sex, Race, and Hispanic Origin." Washington: U.S. Department of Commerce. Available at: http://www.census.gov/population/estimates/nation/natdoc.txt (accessed April 16, 2013).

U.S. Census Bureau. 2010. "Current Population Survey (CPS), October Supplement, 1975–2010." Washington: U.S. Department of Commerce.

———. 2011. "National Population Estimates by Age, Sex, and Race: 1900 to 1979." Washington: U.S. Department of Commerce. Available at: http://www.census.gov/popest/data/national/asrh/pre-1980/PE-11.html (accessed April 5, 2013).

——— . 2013. "Current Population Survey Data on Educational Attainment." Washington: U.S. Department of Commerce. Available at: http://www.census.gov/hhes/socdemo/education/data/cps (accessed April 5, 2013).

Chapter 5

Workforce Development Programs

Harry J. Holzer

In early 1964, when President Lyndon B. Johnson first announced the War on Poverty, employment and training programs for the poor barely existed in the United States at the federal level. The only federal manpower program of the era, the Manpower Development and Training Act (MDTA), was launched in 1962 with relatively little funding or fanfare. Its main purpose was to counteract a bout of "structural unemployment" that many at the time feared would arise as a result of ongoing automation in the economy and worker displacements by technology.

As a result of the War on Poverty, the primary focus of MDTA shifted from the employment problems of the displaced to those of minorities and the poor. Funding for MDTA expanded, and a new set of programs was undertaken—including the Job Corps, which still exists, and many other programs, which do not.

Since the Johnson administration, employment and training programs and policies have undergone several major shifts. MDTA was replaced by the Comprehensive Employment and Training Act (CETA) in 1973. CETA, in turn, was replaced by the Job Training Partnership Act (JTPA) in 1982, which was then replaced by the Workforce Investment Act (WIA) in 1998.

Funding for employment and training programs for the poor reached an all-time high under CETA in 1979 and 1980. But doubts about the cost-effectiveness of these programs had already emerged, and funding levels soon began to decline under President Reagan; both the doubts and the funding declines have continued ever since. By the time the Obama administration entered office, funding for WIA and related programs had greatly diminished and is now easily surpassed by expenditures for the poor on higher education, notably Pell grants. Federal funding of job training for the poor in WIA and elsewhere has almost (but not quite) disappeared. Congressional interest in reauthorizing WIA, which technically expired in 2005, has remained fairly low.

Although federal funding for employment and training efforts has waxed and waned, a great deal of experimentation and evaluation has occurred, much of it at the state and local levels. These efforts give us a much greater sense of what does and does not work in this arena, which could be used to better structure such policies in the future.

In addition, inequality in earnings between skilled and unskilled workers has grown dramatically since the 1970s, and the supply of worker skills lags behind the growth in labor market demand for them, especially among the disadvantaged. Accordingly, there is a need to increase education and labor market skills among the disadvantaged, and understanding the role of employment and training programs—or what is now called workforce development—in doing so should remain a high priority.

In this chapter, I review the trends in employment and training policy for the poor since the War on Poverty was launched, beginning with a description of new programs and new approaches begun under President Johnson from 1964 through early 1969.

BEGINNINGS: EMPLOYMENT AND TRAINING PROGRAMS

As noted earlier, passage and implementation of MDTA were motivated by a fear of growing structural unemployment that might be associated with ongoing automation in the economy. As the 1960s wore on, and unemployment for the overall population consistently declined, these fears diminished. President Johnson's announcement of the War on Poverty and subsequent implementation of the program helped expand funding for MDTA and refocus it on a different structural problem: the low skill levels and employment of the poor, especially among young people and African Americans. Several major events in the mid-1960s—such as ongoing legislative battles over civil rights and voting rights, along with major outbreaks of violence in urban areas—all contributed to a growing sense of urgency on the need to improve skills and employment levels among these populations.

The economic vision on which the War on Poverty, and especially job training programs, was based can be found in chapter 2 of the 1964 *Economic Report of the President*. Johnson's economic advisers argued that the best way to increase overall employment, including among the poor, was through macroeconomic policy, particularly tax cuts to spur aggregate demand. They also believed that ongoing productivity growth would raise wages for all workers. At the same time, they recognized that employment among minorities was limited by discrimination, and so they strongly argued for passage of the Civil Rights Act, which was passed and signed into law that summer. They also recognized the problems of education and skill deficiencies among the poor, citing the vicious circle that limits human capital investments among them. Calling for preschool and other educational programs for poor children, they also called for job training programs for both youth and poor adults. Training programs for adults, along with job placement services and information on job openings, would also address the displacement of both poor and nonpoor workers from their jobs due to technological change, enabling them to find new ones of equal or better quality.

Not all members of the Johnson administration were so sanguine about the ability of education and training programs alone, with modest levels of funding, to address these problems. Secretary of Labor Willard Wirtz and Assistant Secretary of Labor Daniel Patrick Moynihan argued for a broader effort focused not only on job training but also on job creation for the poor. Their view, reflected in the 1965 Moynihan report *The Negro Family: The Case for National Action* and elsewhere, was that even in a relatively healthy economy, the low skills and weak job market contacts of the poor (plus discrimination) might prevent them from finding enough private-sector jobs to fill on their own. They thus perceived problems for the poor on both the supply (workers) and demand (employers-jobs) sides of the labor market.

Of course, Moynihan worried especially about poor black men, whose employment rates had been declining and whose participation in crime and urban violence was already growing, and black families were increasingly headed by single mothers. He believed that a much more robust effort on jobs for these men was necessary to combat these developments. But President Johnson rejected the Moynihan-Wirth arguments in favor of a more fiscally conservative and modest approach, consistent with the views of his economic advisers.

How, then, were these views reflected in the job training programs they created? Besides refocusing and expanding MDTA, one significant new program was launched during the War on Poverty period: the Job Corps, which was inspired to some extent by the Civilian Conservation Corps (CCC) of the New Deal. The Job Corps nonetheless had a different focus: it targeted low-income youth rather than a broader unemployed population, and it was primarily designed to build skills, (including softer skills such as "character"), that would raise employability among these youth.[1]

A unique characteristic of the Job Corps is that it is a residential program, designed to take troubled youth out of unhealthy home and neighborhood environments. The original Job Corps sites were either former CCC camps in rural areas or former military sites in urban areas; these were run by the Departments of Agriculture and the Interior in the former case and by the Office of Economic Opportunity in the latter. Private firms were also contracted at the urban sites to teach more vocational skills than those in rural areas, with the latter reserved for youth viewed as harder to employ and not yet ready for direct training (Levitan 1969; Gillette 2010).

Although Johnson rejected proposals for significant job creation for the poor, a modest job creation effort was included: the Neighborhood Youth Corps (NYC), which provided summer jobs to low-income youth and was run through the Labor Department. Over the next few years, other programs were added that targeted both youth and adult populations and helped generate more jobs for the poor. Given a growing concern over low employment rates and weak work incentives for the growing welfare population, known at the time as Aid to Families with Dependent Children (AFDC), the Work Incentives program (WIN) was added to generate more such employment, though its funding and enforcement was always modest. In 1968, Job Opportunities in the Business Sector (JOBS) became the first federally funded effort to subsidize employment of low-income people in the private sector, though again at quite modest levels.

By the end of the Johnson administration in January 1969, annual funding for these efforts had expanded to about $2 billion (in current dollars), though this sum might be considered quite modest relative to need.[2] In retrospect, it is also striking that many of these efforts were undertaken with very little formal analysis and virtually no evidence of what constitutes cost-effective practices in improving skills and employment among the poor (Ginzberg and Solow 1974).

Still, the goal of raising such skills and employment, and committing significant resources to this effort, had been established. The understanding that one size does not fit all among the disadvantaged, and that different programs should be targeted to different subpopulations (like welfare recipients or less employable youth), also seem to have taken hold, as did the notion that government programs might need to expand job opportunities as well as skills among the poor.

THE RISE AND FALL OF EMPLOYMENT AND TRAINING PROGRAMS

During the 1970s, federal resources for employment and training of the poor were increased. CETA was signed into law by President Nixon in 1973, replacing MDTA; its funding was greatly expanded in subsequent years, especially under President Carter in the late 1970s. Public service employment (PSE) for the poor, as well as worker training and a focus on low-income youth, were all implemented at fairly large levels. But enthusiasm for these efforts diminished, especially after Ronald Reagan became president in 1981. Perceived flaws in CETA were addressed with several legislative changes. These occurred first through the passage in 1982 and subsequent implementation of JTPA, which eliminated all funding for public service jobs, and then with passage of WIA in 1998 and its implementation under President Clinton. Federal funding for these efforts shrank after 1980.

These policy changes, however, also reflected important changes in labor market outcomes that began in the 1970s and continued in the 1980s and beyond. Some of these changes are apparent in figures 5.1 through 5.6, computed from Decennial Census of Population (U.S. Bureau of the Census 1950–2010) or March Current Population Survey (CPS) data (U.S. Bureau of Census 1964–2007), where trends over time in real hourly earnings and labor force participation appear for U.S. workers by gender and by education or race. Explanations of these trends abound in the economics literature (see, for instance, Holzer and Hlavac 2012) and are briefly summarized here, as are their implications for poverty trends and policy.

First, the high rates of real earnings growth that all groups in the U.S. economy enjoyed after World War II, and which the president's economic advisers expected to last, slowed dramatically in the 1970s, reflecting the economic stagflation and declining productivity growth that resulted from two major oil shocks. Second, although productivity growth would gradually recover in the 1980s and especially the 1990s, the earnings increases it generated in the later periods were much more unevenly distributed than before, and earnings inequality between and within education groups grew dramatically.[3] Third, women experienced larger gains in

FIGURE 5.1 / Mean Hourly Wages for Men

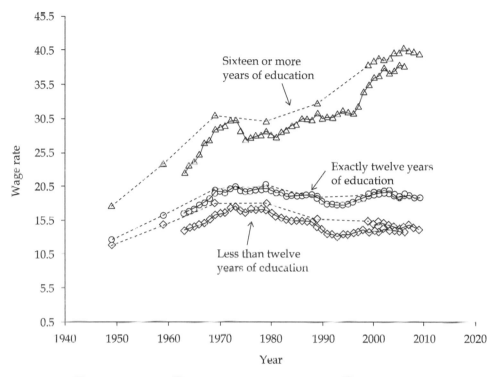

Source: Author's calculations based on U.S. Bureau of the Census (1950–2010).
Note: The dashed line in this and all other figures represent computations from the IPUMS files of the Decennial Census of Population, while solid lines reflect computations based on the March Current Population Surveys between 1964 and 2007. Details of the computations are available in a data appendix from the author and volume editors.

labor force activity and earnings than men as gender discrimination declined (Blau and Kahn 1997), female work experience and education levels grew, and the structure of the economy shifted from manufacturing industries to services. Rising earnings and labor force activity were especially pronounced among highly educated women. Fourth, gaps in hourly earnings between whites and blacks diminished somewhat after passage of the Civil Rights Act of 1964 and the implementation of affirmative action programs thereafter (Heckman and Payner 1989; Heckman and Donohue 1991; Holzer and Neumark 2000);[4] but this progress stalled after 1980 as industrial jobs disappeared and racial gaps in education grew more important (Bound and Freeman 1992).[5] Employment declines for black men were especially pronounced over the entire period.

As a result of all of these economic and labor market changes, low-income workers with relatively weak education and skills enjoyed less earnings growth after

FIGURE 5.2 / Labor Force Participation for Men, Education

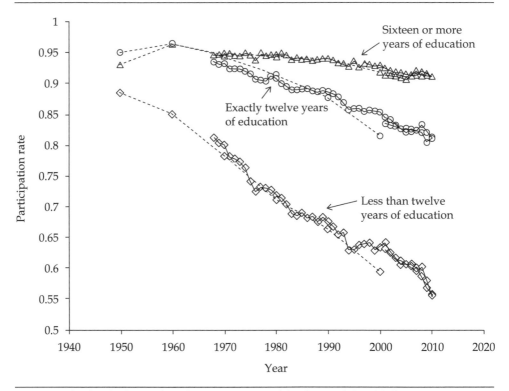

Source: Author's calculations based on U.S. Bureau of the Census (1950–2010).

1970 than before, and declines in the measured poverty rate stalled. Less-educated men tended to work substantially less over time as their real wages stagnated or declined. Among black men, not only did employment rates drop substantially, their marriage rates declined as well, even as crime, incarceration, and childbearing outside marriage all grew. Indeed, the trends that so concerned Pat Moynihan in 1965 grew much worse, in part because of changes in the structure of the labor market (in terms of occupations, industries, and relative wages that are described more fully below) that neither he nor anyone else could have foreseen.[6]

These economic developments had strong implications for antipoverty policy. The growing importance of education and academic "achievement" in determining earnings levels in America would lead to a reduced focus on job training as an appropriate remedy for the skill deficiencies of the poor. Policies that strengthened work incentives among the poor, rather than skill training and job creation, would also grow more important over time.

Figure 5.3 / Labor Force Participation for Men, Race

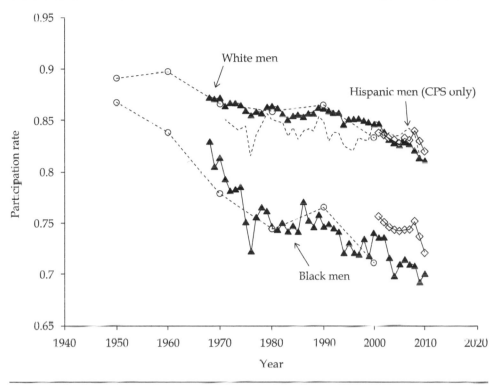

Source: Author's calculations based on U.S. Bureau of the Census (1950–2010).

CETA: High-Water Mark

The incorporation and subsequent expansion of PSE into CETA began as a countercyclical measure.[7] The years 1974 and 1975, in which CETA was first implemented, coincided with what was at that time the most serious recession since the 1930s. PSE was viewed as a useful tool in combating high unemployment rates, which reached nearly 10 percent in 1975.

As the economy recovered from this recession, the focus of PSE shifted from countercyclical efforts to an attempt to create jobs for the disadvantaged and especially minorities. By 1978, PSE was funding year-round jobs for nearly 1 million adults and youth, and summer jobs for another 1 million youth (Gottschalk 1998). Funds were allocated either to state-local agencies or to nonprofit organizations to generate new jobs for the poor.

In addition, the Carter administration used tax credits to private employers to

FIGURE 5.4 / Mean Hourly Wages for Women

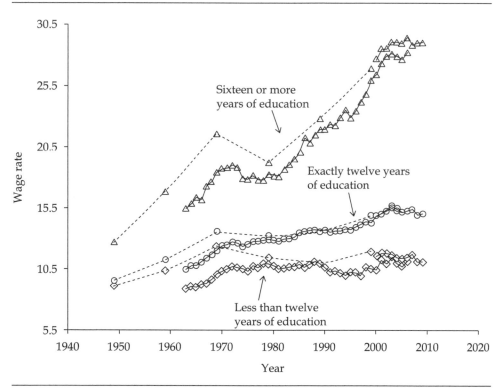

Source: Author's calculations based on U.S. Bureau of the Census (1950–2010).

expand job opportunities. The New Jobs Tax Credit in 1977 and 1978 was a broad marginal tax credit for companies expanding their payrolls above some base level. The Targeted Jobs Tax Credit (TJTC) that same year generated tax credits for employers hiring certain categories of disadvantaged workers.[8] Job training for disadvantaged adults under CETA was also expanded, and now included approaches such as classroom training, on-the-job training (OJT), and subsidized work.

Disadvantaged youth received particular attention in the late 1970s when awareness of high youth unemployment rates was growing. In 1977, in addition to expanded Job Corps funding, the Carter administration passed the Youth Employment Demonstration Projects Act (YEDPA), which funded pilot projects and evaluation efforts. One notable job creation program was the Youth Incentive Entitlement Pilot Project (YIEPP). This program guaranteed public sector jobs at the minimum wage, part-time during the school year and full-time in the summer, to urban youth who remained in school.

CETA also began a longer-term process of decentralizing and devolving responsibility for the development and implementation of employment and training programs to states and localities. Unlike MDTA, in which all funds were spent by

FIGURE 5.5 / Labor Force Participation for Women, Education

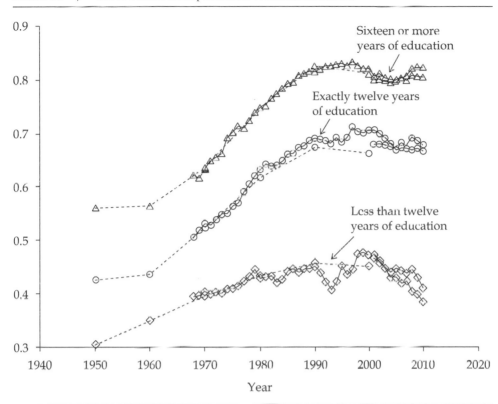

Source: Author's calculations based on U.S. Bureau of the Census (1950–2010).

federal authorities, most funds under CETA were distributed to state agencies, which had considerable discretion over their distribution across localities and types of training or job creation.

Funding for CETA in program year 1979 reached over $18 billion, the high-water mark for federal expenditures on employment and training.

JTPA and WIA: Devolving Programs and Shrinking Funding

Beginning in 1981, the Reagan administration reduced funding for many domestic discretionary programs, CETA in particular. PSE funding was eliminated, and funds for job training shrank as well.

What accounted for this sudden change in funding and interest? Part of the story is political. A much more conservative administration, along with a newly

FIGURE 5.6 / Labor Force Participation for Women, Race

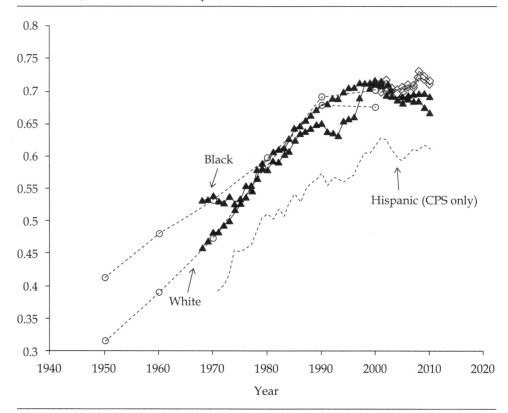

Source: Author's calculations based on U.S. Bureau of the Census (1950–2010).

Republican Senate, brought a more skeptical eye to publicly funded programs in general and to efforts for the poor in particular. But skepticism about cost-effectiveness extended beyond the Reagan administration, as accounts of wasteful spending under CETA and especially PSE appeared frequently in the media (Ellwood and Welty 2000). Economists argued that public employment likely generated fiscal substitution, in which local governments and nonprofits at least partly use public funding to replace their own funds instead of generating new jobs. Concern also grew that these programs might substitute public for private-sector employment that would otherwise exist (Haveman and Palmer 1982; Ellwood and Welty 2000). As a result, net new job creation by PSE was likely to be smaller than the gross numbers of jobs funded. And the extent to which such employment created goods and services valued by the public, as well as useful work experience and skills for the disadvantaged, was debated as well.

In addition, skepticism about the value and cost-effectiveness of job training for the disadvantaged emerged. Beginning in the late 1970s, economists began to use newer methods of program evaluation to estimate the public and private benefits of such training, relative to their costs. I discuss these findings in greater detail, but early estimates of these impacts seemed fairly modest, and these reinforced questions about the overall effectiveness of these programs.

A Changing Economy and Policy Focus   The skepticism about the value of employment and training programs was reinforced by a growing awareness in the 1980s and 1990s of dramatic changes in the economy and the labor market—such as growing earnings inequality and the associated increase in the value and importance of education.

Beginning with the 1983 publication of *A Nation at Risk*, by the National Commission on Excellence in Education, policymakers increasingly focused on how to improve the quantity and quality of education received, especially among the disadvantaged. As awareness of increased earnings inequality grew in the 1980s, policy focused more on educational opportunities than on training for the disadvantaged. A view often implicit in this focus was that publicly funded job training was a weak substitute for the obtaining of better education credentials.

This focus and these views continue to this day. Most economists argue that the labor market rewards to education credentials have grown because the demand for those skills, driven mostly by new technologies and globalization, has outpaced the growth in their supply (for example, Goldin and Katz 2008; Autor, Katz, and Kearney 2008). Interestingly, the concerns about new technology and "automation" expressed by President Johnson's advisers thus reappeared, but in a quite different and more serious form. In addition to job displacements and the need for workers to be modestly retrained, technical change that was skill-biased led to longer-term shifts in demand from less- to more-educated workers, especially among men. Large changes in their relative wages, and therefore in their employment and labor force participation rates would result (Juhn 1992), well beyond the modest short-term unemployment of displaced individuals that President Johnson's advisers foresaw.

Social scientists also discovered that a large achievement gap, between minority-poor Americans and others, accounts for substantial portions of subsequent differences in education and earnings between these groups.[9] These developments led most policymakers to focus more on improving academic skill than on occupational training. Furthermore, recent research on growing labor market polarization shows that the middle of the job market is shrinking as both the top and bottom continue to grow, reinforcing the shift away from occupational training for middle-wage jobs, though some economists (myself included) have disputed that implication.[10]

Other critics on both the political left and right have disputed the near-exclusive focus on achievement and education as the best way to improve labor market outcomes for the poor as well as the middle class. On the left, revisionist economists argue that gradual changes in the supply and demand for skills cannot account for dramatic changes in outcomes that occur in short time frames, and in the growth of extremely high inequality observed between the top 1 percent of workers and everyone else (for example, Card and Dinardo 2007; Mishel, Bernstein, and

Sherholz 2010). They argue instead that the quality of jobs, not workers, has declined, because institutions like unions and minimum-wage laws have weakened. They advocate for strengthening these institutions, rather than increasing education or job training for the poor (for evidence on how job quality affects the earnings of the poor and has changed over time, see Andersson, Holzer, and Lane 2005; Holzer et al. 2011). However, mainstream economists generally believe that unions and minimum wages have more difficulty raising wages without causing job loss in the more competitive and global product and labor markets that now exist.

On the right, other critics (for example, Mead 2004; Haskins 2005) have argued that the earnings of the poor could be better raised by providing incentives or requiring them to work more, especially in strong economic periods when low-wage jobs seem relatively available for the poor, rather than through relatively ineffective skill-building efforts. These arguments ultimately led to the passage of the 1996 welfare reform, along with expansions of the Earned Income Tax Credit (EITC) and other efforts, such as child-care funding, to "make work pay" for the poor. This combination of forces, plus a very strong economy in the mid- to late 1990s, led to a dramatic increase in labor force activity among poor women, though some—up to a third—of this increase diminished after 2000 (Lower-Basch and Greenberg 2008) and more declined after 2007 at least temporarily due to the Great Recession.

Changing Programs: JTPA and WIA   Growing skepticism about the value of publicly funded employment and training, along with criticisms of CETA, led to the passage of JTPA in 1982 and ultimately WIA in 1998. Both bills, and especially the latter, continued several trends that began in the early 1980s:

- a decline in federal funding, and the elimination of PSE funding;
- a decline in longer-term training and a growing focus on the provision of employment services, including job search assistance;
- a more universal approach to employment services, with more limited focus on the disadvantaged;[11]
- an emphasis on employers as well as workers as those to be served by employment services;
- a decentralized administrative structure, with most funds devolved to local boards comprised primarily of business owners which determined how they were spent;
- a greater focus on worker choice among competing service providers; and
- a resurgence of interest in dislocated workers as well as in the disadvantaged.

The primary funding streams of Title I of WIA, for adults, youth, and dislocated workers respectively, now represent less than $3 billion in total funding (in a $16 trillion economy), and about $5 billion when we include the Job Corps and other targeted efforts. Relative to 1979, this represents a cut of roughly 75 percent in real dollars, and considerably more relative to the growing population or gross domestic product (GDP).

These funds are dispersed to state and primarily local workforce investment boards (WIBs) which then allocate the money. By statute, the WIBs are dominated by local business owners, with the goal of generating employment services and training that are relevant to their demands.

All Department of Labor activities are provided in some three thousand *One Stop* offices. *Core* services, which mostly constitute job search assistance, are available to any job seekers. Some can also get *intensive* services, such as career counseling and testing. Training is made available to only a limited subset of the latter group, and including both disadvantaged and nondisadvantaged workers. Training is usually short term and funded through vouchers known as individual training accounts (ITAs) where workers can choose from lists of local providers with limited guidance from One Stop staff.

WIA also funds the Job Corps, which continues to serve youth in residential centers, as well as smaller programs for specific groups, including seniors, migrant workers, and Native Americans. Funding for Adult Basic Education appears in Title II of WIA and for the administration of One Stop offices and the Employment Service in Title III.

Importantly, federal funds for employment and training can be found in the budgets of several other agencies—notably in Temporary Assistance for Needy Families (TANF), vocational education under the Carl T. Perkins Act, and vocational rehabilitation services. The Government Accountability Office has estimated that as many as forty-seven federal programs fund employment and training services; it suggests that consolidating some programs would be efficient (2011).

On the other hand, most programs are very small and focus on specific populations, such as Native Americans, migrant farmworkers, veterans, or disabled workers. Total funding is about $16 billion per year, which is still just 0.1 percent of GDP—considerably less than in most other industrial countries (O'Leary, Straits, and Wandner 2004). In contrast, total spending on means-tested programs, including in-kind programs like Medicaid and tax credits but excluding Social Security, reached over 4 percent of GDP before the Great Recession (Scholz, Moffit, and Cowan 2009) and considerably more afterward.

Beyond WIA: New Developments

Most federal funding today for employment and training activities are included in the higher education budget, administered through the Department of Education, rather than that for job training or workforce activities, through the Department of Labor. Community colleges are now the locus of most job training activities for the poor. In addition, substantial workforce activities occur at the state and local levels with their own funding or private foundation support.

The clearest indication of the funding shifts from job training to higher education can be found in the dramatic increases in federal funding for Pell grants from $10 billion in fiscal year (FY) 2000 to $35 billion in FY2011 (Baum 2012). Pell grants are vouchers that pay college tuition and related expenses for qualifying low-income people (see chapter 3, this volume). Spending on Pell grants dwarfs total spending on WIA, and is roughly double the combined spending on all federal workforce programs. Furthermore, about 60 percent of students funded by Pell grants are in vocational programs that can be considered forms of job training. On the other hand, completion rates for students in these programs are very low, raising questions about Pell grants alone as a new form of job training. Improving the quality of remediation services and the information available about careers and labor market opportunities for Pell recipients might improve these outcomes (Holzer and Nightingale 2009; Holzer 2011).[12]

At the state and local levels, new workforce initiatives have been developed in the past decade that are mostly independent of federal programs or funding (Edelman et al. 2011; Center for Best Practices 2009).[13] In particular, many states developed workforce systems — based heavily on partnerships between community colleges, workforce boards, and industry associations — which were sectoral and designed to improve the responsiveness of the workforce system to local labor market trends. The sectoral approach involves training targeted to specific sectors of the economy, and even specific employers, where labor demand is strong and well-paying jobs are available for workers with some postsecondary occupational education or training. Sectoral programs can be integrated with economic development activities at the metropolitan or state levels, contributing to their growing popularity with state governments and the business community (for discussions of sectoral approaches, see Conway, Blair, and Helmer 2012; Maguire et al. 2010).

According to the National Governors' Association Center for Best Practices (2009), about thirty states have developed workforce systems that were at least partly sectoral. Dozens of cities and regions within these states have also built local systems, funded by foundations through the National Fund for Workforce Solutions (www.nfwsolutions.org). A focus on career pathway development, which usually involves combinations of community college training and work experience as disadvantaged workers move up the occupational ladder, can be found in these efforts (for example, Spence 2007). Many states have also developed incumbent worker training programs which support on-the-job training activities by employers for new hires at the entry level or being promoted from that level (Hollenbeck 2008).

Not all of these efforts target the disadvantaged, because tension is not uncommon between industry and employer desires for highly skilled workers who are not disadvantaged (and for whom they do not have to pay) and those of funders and intermediaries, who view disadvantaged workers as well as these employers as their clients.[14] Nevertheless, where employers have some difficulty hiring and retaining skilled workers on their own, their reluctance can be overcome — especially when trusted intermediaries or training providers with good track records vouch for the abilities of the job candidates.

Another problem is that many disadvantaged and disconnected adults and youth, often referred to as the hard-to-employ, have poor basic skills and work-readiness, and therefore will not benefit much from these programs. In the aftermath of welfare reform for single mothers, the fraction of these women who have left the welfare rolls but are not employed, sometimes for lengthy periods, has grown (for a discussion of former welfare mothers who are "disconnected" from both welfare and work, see Blank 2008; for evidence on welfare mothers with multiple barriers to employment, see Danziger and Seefeldt 2002).

Furthermore, the enormous growth of incarceration rates among young black men—one in three ultimately spending time in prison, and two in three among high school dropouts—has led to large numbers of such men in the general population with criminal records, who are also frequently in arrears on their child support payments. These problems, in turn, have rendered many of them hard to employ, given that criminal records greatly reduce employer demand for them, and child support debts reduce their willingness to work in the formal economy (for evidence on the effects of incarceration and child support problems on black male employment rates, see Pager 2003; for more discussion specifically of how incarceration impairs employability, see Holzer, Offner, and Sorensen 2006; Raphael 2008). Efforts to provide employment opportunities for this population include *transitional* jobs, which provide paid work experience in a supportive environment for six to twelve months, along with other *reentry* and *fatherhood* efforts. The Department of Health and Human Services (HHS) and the Department of Justice (DOJ) often take the lead in these efforts, and with much experimentation at the state level as well. Finally, the American Recovery and Reinvestment Act (ARRA), the Obama economic stimulus program, spent an additional $4 billion on training programs administered through the Department of Labor. These often involved career pathway programs in fields such as health care and green jobs. Emergency funding for subsidized jobs in the private sector, both for low-income students, especially in summer, and adults, was added to the TANF budget in ARRA as well (Pavetti, Schott, and Lower-Basch 2011). But these were one-time efforts that largely disappeared as ARRA expired.

In sum, the decline in federal support for employment and training activities has been accompanied by a rise in Pell grant funding and attention to community colleges. The federal government, the states, and major foundations have initiated much innovative activity in the past decade, but it has been fragmentary, spread across federal agencies and funded by multiple public and private actors. States and localities have tried to tie these fragmentary pieces into coherent education and workforce systems, though we do not yet know how successful they have been.

EMPLOYMENT AND TRAINING: WHAT REALLY WORKS?

A large literature evaluates employment and training programs (for reviews, see Lalonde 1995; Friedlander, Greenberg, and Robins 1997; Heckman, Lalonde, and

Smith 1999; Karoly 2001; Holzer 2009; Lee 2009; Card, Kluve, and Weber 2010; for discussions of methodological issues, and especially the value of experimental versus certain nonexperimental approaches, such as propensity score matching along certain key variables like extensive work history, and inverse propensity score weighting, see Burtless 1995; Heckman and Smith 1995; Heckman, Lalonde, and Smith 1999; Bloom 2005).

The impacts on earnings of many programs—such as CETA, JTPA, and to a lesser extent WIA—have been studied extensively. The National JTPA Study (NJS), which involved a randomized control design at sixteen sites in the late 1980s and early 1990s (Bloom et al. 1997). Studies of CETA and WIA to date have been mostly nonexperimental, though often with credible methodologies.[15]

The results of these studies are broadly consistent. Training for the disadvantaged has generated modest positive impacts on the earnings of disadvantaged adults, with those for women often larger than those for men. Most earnings increases were attributable to increases in hours worked rather than higher wages. The JTPA impacts faded with time, and were mostly insignificant five years later. Still, most analysts find the impacts for disadvantaged workers large enough to be considered cost-effective, given the modest costs expended on mostly short-term training in these studies.[16] Nonexperimental estimates of training impacts under WIA for adult men and women are also positive, as are smaller estimates of the impacts of core and intensive services delivered at One Stop offices.[17]

A lengthy literature also exists on the impacts of (mostly mandatory) employment and training programs for welfare recipients, though estimated impacts have been quite mixed (Friedlander, Greenberg, and Robins 1997). Our national experience with welfare reform, and the dramatic decline in the welfare caseload that followed it, has reduced interest in this area, and supported the views of those who believe that financial incentives and work supports can be effective in raising employment among the poor, even if their skills are not enhanced (Blank 2002).

Given the modest benefits of training, are some approaches more effective than others? The strongest evidence supports the sectoral approaches described earlier. For example, Sheila Maguire and her colleagues (2010) found large training impacts for disadvantaged adults at three sites, for at least two years after random assignment; and a study of Year Up, which is a sectoral program specializing in IT training for youth, found estimates of roughly $4,000 per year (Roder and Elliott 2011).[18]

Important questions remain, however. Will the short-term impacts fade with time? Would we know how to replicate these efforts and bring them to scale at other sites, especially in a limited period? Are these impacts really measuring net new earnings, or merely a limited number of well-paying jobs which are rationed across workers?[19] Furthermore, even if successful and lasting, these programs seem to screen workers quite extensively before admitting them, and do not provide potential avenues for those with poor basic skills or otherwise hard to employ.

A number of local programs across the country for disadvantaged adults seem quite promising (Holzer and Martinson 2005). A mix of support services, such as child care and job placement assistance, and financial incentives, such as enhanced wage subsidies, along with outreach to employers, often complement the job training or employment services provided in these programs. However, rigorous estimation of impacts is yet not available in most cases.[20]

Specific Populations: Youth and the Hard-to-Employ

If the estimated impacts of training for adults seem modest, except at a few local programs using sectoral strategies for those with fairly strong basic skills and work experience, what do we know about the cost-effectiveness of training for other groups—such as adults considered hard to employ or youth?

It is harder to generate positive education or earnings impacts among disadvantaged youth than adults—perhaps because they are not yet ready to focus on their employment, or because of the greater skepticism among employers of their work-readiness, or both. Indeed, estimated impacts for youth in JTPA were either zero or even negative, and many other strategies have failed as well.[21]

What has worked for out-of-school youth? One of the bright spots has been an original War on Poverty program: the Job Corps. Many early studies (for example, Mallar et al. 1981) found positive impacts of the Job Corps on youth, though their methodology was questioned. In a study using randomized controls, early effects were positive and large enough to be cost-effective (despite the high costs of keeping youth in residential settings for up to a year) if they did not fade with time. Unfortunately, a later study (Schochet, Burghardt, and McConnell 2008) showed some fading of effects with time, and the impacts for the overall sample were no longer cost-effective. However, impacts for older youth (ages twenty to twenty-four) were still large enough to be cost-effective, even though some fadeout of impacts occurred for them as well.

Other programs providing training and service employment without the residential environments of Job Corps have not yet shown positive impacts.[22] Programs often vary in terms of the levels of deficiencies among the youth whom they target, as well as their overall treatments, so it can be hard to generalize about their effectiveness.

If the Job Corps appears more effective than other approaches, because its residential setting takes youth out of problematic home and neighborhood environments, are there other programs that have tried to deal with adverse neighborhood environments? The National Guard ChalleNGe program, funded through the Department of Defense, provides not only a residential setting, but also a highly structured environment based on a military model in which young high school dropouts pursue high school diplomas or GEDs (General Educational Development test). The evaluation evidence (Millenky et al. 2011) shows that, three years after random assignment, much higher percentages of students in the program earned a high school diploma or GED (72 percent) than in the control group (56 percent).

The Youth Opportunity program in the late 1990s provided grants to thirty-six small low-income neighborhoods around the country, in an effort to saturate these neighborhoods with education and employment opportunities, and thereby perhaps change the behaviors and norms of the overall neighborhood as well as those of individual program participants.[23] The outcomes among youth in these neighborhoods, compared with similar ones not receiving the grants, suggested mostly positive impacts on schooling and employment outcomes (Jackson 2008).

Career Academies have had impressive impacts for at risk teens still in school (Kemple 2008). These are specialized occupational training programs, within roughly 3,000 broader comprehensive high schools, that target particular sectors — such as IT, health care, or financial services — and provide students with targeted training and paid work experience while they take general academic classes outside the academy. As many as eight years after random assignment, students in the Career Academies had significantly higher earnings than those in the control groups. For at-risk young men, the gains were especially large — nearly 20 percent in annual earnings with little fadeout of impacts over time. Given that Career Academies ultimately had no impacts on educational achievement or attainment, it appears that the contextual training plus early work experience might be responsible for positive impacts. But it is also noteworthy that the academies did not appear to track participants away from postsecondary education, as the participants attended and completed postsecondary school at the same rate as the controls.

As for truly hard-to-employ adults, such as ex-offenders or those with multiple and serious barriers to work (such as poor skills or physical or emotional health problems), the results of various approaches have been mixed. The National Supported Work (NSW) demonstration of the 1970s showed strong positive impacts on former welfare recipients but few for other populations. More recently, transitional jobs have generated few improvements in post-program earnings, but some programs have been successful in reducing recidivism for ex-offenders or returning to welfare for long-term recipients who had left the rolls. Unfortunately, these positive impacts have rarely been replicated in other studies.[24] Even for this population, providing financial incentives and other supports can raise work activity and earnings, even when skills are not directly enhanced (Bloom and Butler 2007; for a proposal to expand the EITC for childless adults, to incent low-income men and especially noncustodial fathers to participate more regularly in the labor market, see Edelman, Greenberg, and Holzer 2009).

Direct Job Creation for the Disadvantaged

Earlier, we noted that efforts to expand employment opportunities for the hard to employ might be necessary, especially if training programs and other efforts to improve their work-readiness might not succeed — or during a downturn when employment is generally less available for the poor. Indeed, Secretary of Labor Willard Wirtz argued that position unsuccessfully during the Johnson administration, though some interest in this point of view developed later and picked up steam in the 1970s. On the other hand, large-scale implementation of public service employment became unpopular in the 1980s and after, due to concerns over its high cost and potentially limited net employment creation we discussed earlier.

For programs that provide publicly funded paid work experience for the disadvantaged, whether in the public or private sectors, what impacts have been estimated either during the programs or afterward? Do they even raise net employment levels in the short term, while the programs are in effect, or earnings afterward?

In the case of PSE, net costs per participants are high—as much as $15,000 to 20,000 per person-year. Furthermore, postprogram impacts on participants seem to be limited in most cases, except where a fairly intensive set of services and supports have been provided in addition to the job (Ellwood and Welty 2000).[25] Estimates of net employment effects, however, suggest that, when both jobs and program participants are carefully targeted, substitution offsets of job increases can be quite limited. When the workers are generating services that are not available in the private sector but which local residents seem to value, the estimated benefits of the programs can rise as well.

Estimated effects of targeted tax credits for private-sector employers—like the earlier TJTC and the more recent WOTC—suggest positive effects on employment while in effect (Katz 1998; Hamersma 2005) but little lasting effect on worker outcomes. Studies of the emergency TANF jobs programs showed about 250,000 jobs created relatively quickly during ARRA (Pavetti, Schott, and Lower-Basch 2011), including many in the private sector, at for-profit and not-for-profit firms, though we have no estimates of the extent to which these jobs were offset by substitution that limited net increases in employment.[26]

Finally, as mentioned earlier, a program for youth funded under YEDPA, the Youth Incentive Entitlement Pilot Project, guaranteed a publicly funded minimum-wage job to any youth in several cities who wanted part-time work and remained enrolled in school. Although the program was terminated before any impacts on long-term outcomes could be estimated, it generated striking improvements in employment rates of minority youth while the program was in effect. Indeed, differences in employment rates between minority and white youth were eliminated, suggesting that paid work experience can have strong positive effects in motivating youth to participate in education or training programs.

YIEPP was expensive to administer at such a large scale, and questions remain as to whether youth interest in minimum-wage jobs would be as great today as in the 1970s. At a minimum, YIEPP demonstrated that paid work experience for youth who are otherwise engaged in schooling or training can strongly motivate them to persist in the program.

CONCLUSION

The history of employment and training programs since the War on Poverty has been uneven. After an uncertain beginning under Lyndon Johnson, employment and training programs for the disadvantaged grew quite dramatically in the 1970s, but have greatly diminished in magnitude since then. The declines in public support for these programs reflect a number of factors, including doubts about their cost-effectiveness and greater attention to remedying gaps between the poor and others in education and achievement. The importance of financial incentives to work, rather than just skills training, has also been demonstrated repeatedly.

In recent years, workforce development efforts have been dwarfed by growth in funding for Pell grants and other community college efforts, even if program completion rates among Pell grantees and at these colleges remain low. Innovative activity outside WIA has occurred with support from both the federal government and private foundations, but this support has been fragmentary and uneven. The states and some localities have tried to build coherent systems with uncertain success. Additionally, during the Great Recession, the federal government supported some countercyclical job creation efforts for the poor in ARRA, though those have expired and have not been renewed.

Based on the evaluation evidence reviewed, I draw these conclusions about the efficacy of these programs and suggestions for their future:

- The small expenditures on mostly short-term training under JTPA and WIA can generate positive impacts that are cost-effective but perhaps not large enough to make a substantial difference in the earnings capacities of most trained workers.

- When considering different disadvantaged populations, one size does not fit all. Programs that seem effective for adults might not work for youth, and those for adults and youth with relatively strong basic skills and work experience might not be effective for the hard-to-employ.

- For those with decent basic skills, a combination of skill certification, sectoral targeting (especially those with strong demand and well-paying jobs), employer involvement, and a range of support services tied together by experienced intermediaries can be successful. Questions remain about whether these strong impacts last over time, especially if labor demand shifts or workers move to other sectors, and whether the most effective smaller programs can be brought to scale. States have begun to build education-workforce systems based on these models, but we have no evidence to date on their cost-effectiveness.

- For the harder to employ, the evidence is less clear. Direct job creation can generate net increases in labor demand, often at a high price, for their employment in the short term. But, if potential earnings remain low indefinitely for these populations, it might take a long-term combination of financial supports, such as the EITC and child-care financing, and other support services to help people remain attached to the labor market. A particular focus on the difficulties and circumstances of ex-offenders and noncustodial fathers, and the legal and policy barriers that often magnify the employment barriers they face, is needed.[27]

- Disadvantaged and disconnected youth are also a challenge. For those in school but at risk, high-quality career and technical education can be helpful, along with other approaches that create pathways into postsecondary education. Paid work experience helps motivate young people and is most successful when tied to skill-building efforts. Residential programs, such as Job Corps and ChalleNGe, seem successful at removing young people from harmful home and neighborhood environments but they are expensive. Systemic approaches that target these neighborhoods, such as Youth Opportunities, also show promise.

- Pell grants alone, without any effort to connect students with support services or the labor market, might be ineffective at raising postsecondary attainments for the disadvantaged. Providing appropriate services at community colleges, however, and especially those that improve links to occupational training and the job market, such as career counseling and integrated remediation, are more promising.

In light of these findings, what is the legacy of the War on Poverty for employment and training programs? Given the political and fiscal environments, how can we move ahead to achieve more of the goals envisioned by its founders?

At one level, the economic and social vision of Johnson and his economic advisers, as expressed in the 1964 *Economic Report of the President*, proved fairly accurate, and the policies based on that vision have withstood the tests of time. In particular, the importance they placed on improving education and skill outcomes among the poor, through programs ranging from early childhood to higher education, was well founded and has gained even more traction over time. Their view that job training programs for youth, like the Job Corps, as well as those for adults could complement education programs and contribute to poverty reduction has survived as well, even if the locus of training activity at community colleges has mostly shifted from the Department of Labor to the Department of Education. Their evolving sense that one size does not fit all in employment and training programs, and that the hardest to employ might need additional services and supports as well as some direct job creation, has also lasted, though the latter view has not flourished. To this day, workforce development programs for the poor funded by the various federal agencies, and at the state and local levels, mostly reflect these views.

But, at another level, the optimism of President Johnson's economists that a series of new and modestly funded programs in a growing economy could greatly reduce or even eliminate poverty proved unfounded. For instance, technical change along with globalization proved much more costly to the poor than they envisioned, as the growth of earnings among the less-educated stalled or was even reversed. For less-educated and especially black men, these forces were devastating—and resulted in falling employment, falling marriage rates, increasing births outside marriage, and rising crime and incarceration—much as Pat Moynihan feared they would. The modest employment and training programs these economists envisioned and created were overwhelmed by these developments; and, when carefully evaluated, they proved only modestly cost-effective, while the best of them were hard to replicate and bring to scale. Large-scale implementation of public service jobs also became unpopular after the 1970s and was discontinued, due to concerns over its high costs and possibly limited net effects on job creation.

As for the future of workforce policy, the prospects that WIA will be reauthorized at all over the next few years look quite limited, and further budget cuts in the daunting fiscal environment of the coming years are almost certain. Whatever occurs at the federal level, however, the efforts of states to better integrate their higher education and workforce systems, and to tie both more closely to trends in labor demand, have been promising and deserve further support. Elsewhere, I have proposed a new federal grants program—modeled in some ways on Race to the Top in the field of K-12 education—to provide incentives and support states to move in this direction (Holzer 2011). The states and local regions would combine the fragmentary supports they have received from various federal agencies and private foundations into something more systemic, and would need to generate sustainable sources of funding. Generating systems that effectively mix general and specific training, and are flexible enough to respond to unanticipated shifts over time in market demand, would be critical to their success. Evaluation work and successful results would be required for ongoing funding.

At the same time, we need to acknowledge that sectoral workforce programs and community college training will probably not meet the needs of the hardest to employ. Despite the polarized environment in Washington, bipartisan interest exists in the states to help find more successful strategies for these populations, given the enormous costs on states and localities associated with incarceration and single parenthood. Continued experimentation at the state level with federal support, and an expanded EITC, are warranted. Some direct job creation should continue to occur as we slowly recover from the Great Recession. Other efforts to induce employers to improve job quality, as well as worker skills, might be useful as well.[28]

What we have now, and where we will be going, in workforce development policy thus look quite different from where we started under President Johnson fifty years ago. But the basic insights that such policies can play an important role, and must be tailored to address the needs of diverse disadvantaged populations, remain true today.

NOTES

1. *Soft skills* (for example, Moss and Tilly 2001) often refer to the attitudes or values and social or communication skills that employers seek of workers they hire.
2. All dollar figures are in 2011 dollars. Reported spending levels in federal programs are drawn from Jonathan Simonetta (2004) until the current year, which are drawn from various charts on the website of the National Skills Coalition (http://www.national skillscoalition.org).
3. In figures not shown, real hourly earnings computed at the 10th, 25th, 50th, 75th, and 90th percentiles of the initial wage distribution show a very substantial fanning out over time, indicating growing inequality at all parts of the earnings distribution.

4. Affirmative action programs began with Executive Order 11246, issued by Lyndon Johnson in 1965, requiring federal contractors to take affirmative steps to improve the status of minorities (and later women) in employment. Federal enforcement of affirmative action requirements was strengthened considerably during the 1970s. Affirmative action by colleges and universities in admissions, rather than employment, remain very controversial to this day and are mostly undertaken voluntarily.

5. The substantially lower hourly earnings observed among Hispanics, especially in the 1980s and 1990s, reflect the large influx of less-educated Hispanic immigrants during those decades. The immigrant men have relatively high rates of labor force participation compared with other less-educated groups, whereas those of immigrant women tend to lag behind their female counterparts. The question used in the Current Population Survey to measure Hispanic versus non-Hispanic origin changed a bit in 1976, so data points before that date are not strictly comparable with those measured afterward.

6. William Wilson (1987) and Harry Holzer (2009) argue that subsequent economic forces led to labor market changes very consistent with Moynihan's observations and predictions in 1965 (for evidence that incarceration rates have been highly correlated with declining employment among less-educated black men across states and overt time, see also Holzer, Offner, and Sorensen 2006).

7. Even before CETA, a Public Employment Program (PEP) was set up under the Emergency Employment Act of 1970. PSE under CETA was an extension of these programs.

8. The TJTC has been transformed into the Work Opportunity Tax Credit (WOTC) in recent years.

9. Among the first to measure the achievement gap and show its effects on subsequent education and earnings gaps were Richard Herrnstein and Charles Murray (1994) and various chapters in Christopher Jencks and Meredith Phillips (1998).

10. For different views on job market polarization, see David Autor (2010) and Harry Holzer (2010). Autor emphasizes the large decline in middle-wage jobs, especially production and clerical work where routine tasks now are done by computers. I argue that new middle-skill jobs, which require some postsecondary education or training below a bachelor's degree, can still provide good wages for those who obtain these skills and credentials.

11. The argument for providing employment services more universally to workers rests on the notion that targeting them to the disadvantaged tends to stigmatize the service providers and make employers more skeptical of their value.

12. For instance, the Integrated Basic Education and Skills Training (I-BEST) program in Washington state has been associated with improved educational outcomes among low-income community college students, though it has not yet been rigorously evaluated. Also, providing better career counseling should improve the ability of students to gain more of the credentials that the labor market actually rewards, which many fail to do now (Jacobson and Mokher 2009).

13. Although mostly developed independently of WIA, many of these programs have relied heavily on the 15 percent or more of WIA funding streams over which governors had discretion until recently.

14. Economists generally believe that employers will not pay for general training of their workers, because these workers could leave and employers would lose their invest-

ments. In the presence of certain market failures, such as imperfect information and externalities from training, a stronger case can be made that public support for training improves labor market efficiency, as well as equity (if the training is mostly provided to disadvantaged workers). In the United States, employers provide most of their own training to professional and managerial employees (Lerman, McKernan, and Riegg 2004).

15. An experimental evaluation of WIA is now under way but no impact estimates are yet available. The best evaluation of WIA impacts to date in nonexperimental studies can be found in Kevin Hollenbeck (2006) and Carolyn Heinrich and colleagues (2009).

16. James Heckman (2008) argues that the estimated JTPA impacts are too small to be cost-effective, though he assumes high efficiency costs of taxation and high discount rates. Given that the costs of training now are quite low, and that most training is short term, Heinrich and Christopher King (2010) argue that estimated WIA impacts are large enough for such training to be cost-effective.

17. Heinrich and her colleagues find that WIA raises quarterly earnings for adults by about $800 for women and $500 to 600 for men respectively. As much as four years entry into WIA services they find little effect of fadeout. Results for dislocated workers are weaker. The results are also broadly consistent with those of Frederik Andersson and his colleagues (2012).

18. Various nonexperimental studies have found very positive outcomes that suggest large impacts in other sectoral programs, such as Project Quest in San Antonio (Osterman 2007).

19. Private training impacts may exceed social impacts in value if, for example, higher-paying jobs are rationed and the trained workers displace other workers whose alternative earnings will now be lower. That is more likely true in the short run than long run and perhaps in particular locations that depend heavily on high-wage sectors.

20. Currently, the Department of Health and Human Services is evaluating programmatic efforts to improve employment outcomes for low-income parents, including current and former welfare recipients, in its Innovative Strategies for Increasing Self-Sufficiency (ISIS) project.

21. Robert Lalonde (1995) and other reviews note the less positive estimates for youth programs under MDTA and CETA as well as JTPA. Other failed efforts for youth include JobStart, which was a nonresidential version of the Job Corps, and the Center for Employment and Training (CET) programs that targeted youth.

22. Youth Build provides work experience at low-income housing sites, along with other kinds of education and leadership training; positive impacts are suggested by nonexperimental studies (for example, Cohen and Piquero 2008). Other programs that rely on service employment, such as the Youth Service and Conservation Corps, have shown no post-program impacts (Price et al. 2011), despite earlier evidence of positive in-program effects (Jastzrab et al. 1997).

23. An alternative interpretation of the estimated positive impacts was that low-income youth who frequently fall between the cracks in other settings were now tracked and frequently referred to services when needed.

24. Experimental evidence shows that the Center for Employment Opportunity in New York (CEO), which guarantees a transitional job plus support services to released offenders from Riker's Island reduces recidivism for those who enter the program very

shortly after release; and a transitional work program for long-term welfare recipients exiting the rolls reduced recidivism back into welfare (Bloom et al. 2009). On the other hand, the Transitional Jobs Reentry Demonstration (TJRD) for ex-offenders generally failed to reduce recidivism or have any positive impacts (Jacobs 2012).

25. The New Hope program in Milwaukee (Duncan, Huston, and Weisner 2007), which guaranteed public employment for those who could not find private-sector employment and also supplemented the wages and benefits of private-sector jobs, generated strong positive outcomes on both adults and children, at least some of which survived the termination of the program. For instance, among families whose parents had one barrier to work, employment rates after eight years were 13 percentage points higher in the treatment group than the control group (60 versus 47 percent). School engagement and achievement effects were found for some groups of youth eight years later as well.

26. About half of these were summer-only jobs for low-income youth.

27. For ex-offenders, other supportive policies might include enforcement of Equal Employment Opportunity laws that limit the discretion of employers to not hire offenders into some kinds of jobs, as well as expungement of criminal records if individuals have desisted from crime for some number of years, expanded bonding to cover potential employer legal liabilities from hiring an offender, or efforts to encourage states to reconsider legal barriers on all offender employment in some growing sectors (such as elder care facilities). For noncustodial parents, supportive policies might include arrears forgiveness and reform of the processes by which default orders are set, as well as general supports for fatherhood (see Edelman, Holzer, and Offner 2006).

28. Holzer (2011) and Holzer and his colleagues (2011) argue that subsidies and technical assistance could be provided to catalyze or assist employers who take the high road in providing career ladders and other promotion possibilities to their entry-level employees.

REFERENCES

Andersson, Fredrik, Harry Holzer, and Julia Lane. 2005. *Moving Up or Moving On: How Do Workers Advance in the Low-Wage Labor Market*. New York: Russell Sage Foundation

Andersson, Fredrik, Harry Holzer, Julia Lane, David Rosenbaum, and Jeffrey Smith. 2012. "Does Federally Funded Job Training Work? Nonexperimental Estimates of WIA Training Impacts Using Longitudinal Data on Workers and Firms." Mimeo, Georgetown University, Washington, D.C.

Autor, David. 2010. "The Polarization of Job Market Opportunities in the US." Washington, D.C.: Center for American Progress.

Autor, David, Lawrence Katz, and Melissa Kearney. 2008. "The Polarization of the U.S. Labor Market." *NBER* working paper 11986. Cambridge, Mass.: National Bureau of Economic Research.

Baum, Sandy. 2012. "Background on the Pell Grant Program." Unpublished paper, George Washington University, Washington, D.C.

Blank, Rebecca. 2002. "Evaluating Welfare Reform in the United States. " *Journal of Economic Literature* 40(4): 1105–166.

————. 2008. "Helping Disconnected Single Mothers." Ann Arbor: University of Michigan, National Poverty Center.

Blau, Francine, and Lawrence Kahn. 1997. "Swimming Upstream: Trends in the Gender Wage Differential in the 1980s." *Journal of Labor Economics* 15(1): 1–42.

Bloom, Dan, and David Butler. 2007. "Overcoming Employment Barriers: Strategies to Help the Hard-to-Employ." In *Reshaping the American Workforce in a Changing Economy*, edited by Harry Holzer and Demetra Nightingale. Washington, D.C.: Urban Institute Press.

Bloom, Dan, Sarah Rich, Cindy Redcross, Erin Jacobs, Jennifer Yahner, and Nancy Pindus. 2009. "Alternative Welfare-to-Work Strategies for the Hard-to-Employ: Testing Transitional Jobs and Pre-Employment Services in Philadelphia." New York: MDRC.

Bloom, Howard, ed. 2005. *Learning More from Social Experiments: Evolving Analytical Approaches*. New York: Russell Sage Foundation.

Bloom, Howard, Larry Orr, Stephen Bell, George Cave, Fred Doolittle, Winston Lin, and Johannes Bos. 1997. "The Benefits and Costs of JTPA Title II-A Programs." *Journal of Human Resources* 32(3): 549–76.

Bound, John, and Richard Freeman. 1992. "What Went Wrong? The Erosion of Relative Earnings and Employment Among Young Black Men in the 1980s." *Quarterly Journal of Economics* 107(1): 201–32.

Burtless, Gary. 1995. "The Case for Randomized Field Trials in Economic and Policy Research." *Journal of Economic Perspectives* 9(2): 63–84.

Card, David, and Jonathan Dinardo. 2007. "The Impact of Technological Change on Low-Wage Workers: A Review. " In *Working and Poor: How Economic and Policy Changes Are Affecting Low-Wage Workers*, edited by Rebecca Blank, Sheldon Danziger, and Robert Schoeni. New York: Russell Sage Foundation.

Card, David, Jochen Kluve, and Andrea Weber. 2010. "Active Labor Market Policy Evaluations: A Meta-Analysis." *The Economic Journal* 120(548): F452–77.

Center on Best Practices. 2009. *State Sector Strategies: Regional Solutions to Worker and Employer Needs*. Washington, D.C.: National Governors' Association.

Cohen, Mark, and Alex Piquero. 2008. "Costs and Benefits of a Targeted Intervention Program for Youth Offenders: The Youth Build USA Ex-Offender Project." Unpublished manuscript, Vanderbilt University.

Conway, Maureen, Amy Blair, and Matt Helmer. 2012. *Courses to Employment: Partnering to Create Paths to Education and Careers*. Washington, D.C.: Aspen Institute.

Danziger, Sandra, and Kristin Seefeldt. 2002. "Barriers to Employment and the Hard to Serve: Implications for Services, Sanctions and Time Limits." *Focus* 2(2): 151–60.

Duncan, Greg, Alethea C. Huston, and Thomas Weisner. 2007. *New Hope for the Working Poor and Their Children*. New York: Russell Sage Foundation.

Edelman, Peter; Mark Greenberg, and Harry J. Holzer. 2009. "The Administration and Congress Should Adopt a Comprehensive Approach to Youth Education, Employment, and Connection." Washington, D.C.: Georgetown University Center on Poverty, Inequality and Public Policy.

Edelman, Peter, Harry J. Holzer, and Paul Offner. 2006. *Reconnecting Disadvantaged Young Men*. Washington, D.C.: Urban Institute Press.

Edelman, Peter, Harry J. Holzer, Eric Seleznow, Andy Van Kluenen, and Elizabeth Watson.

2011. "State Workforce Policy: The Future of Innovations in a Changing Environment." Chicago: National Skills Coalition.

Ellwood, David, and Elisabeth Welty. 2000. "Public Service Employment and Mandatory Work: A Policy Whose Time Has Come and Gone and Come Again?" In *Finding Jobs: Work and Welfare Reform*, edited by David Card and Rebecca Blank. New York: Russell Sage Foundation.

Friedlander, David, David H. Greenberg, and Philip K. Robins. 1997. "Evaluating Government Training Programs for the Economically Disadvantaged." *Journal of Economic Literature* 35(4): 1809–855.

Gillette, Michael. 2010. *Launching the War on Poverty: An Oral History*. Oxford: Oxford University Press.

Ginzberg, Eli, and Robert Solow, eds. 1974. *The Great Society: Lessons for the Future*. New York: Basic Books.

Goldin, Claudia, and Lawrence Katz. 2008. *The Race Between Education and Technology*. Cambridge, Mass.: Harvard University Press.

Gottschalk, Peter. 1998. "The Impact of Changes in Public Employment on Low-Wage Labor Markets." In *Generating Jobs: How to Increase Demand for Less-Skilled Workers*, edited by Richard Freeman and Peter Gottschalk. New York: Russell Sage Foundation.

Hamersma, Sarah. 2005. "The Work Opportunity and Welfare-to-Work Tax Credits." *Tax Policy Issues and Options* brief 15. Washington, D.C.: Urban Institute Press.

Haskins, Ron. 2005. *Work Over Welfare*. Washington, D.C.: Brookings Institution Press.

Haveman, Robert, and John Palmer. 1982. *Jobs for Disadvantaged Workers*. Washington, D.C.: Brookings Institution Press.

Heckman, James. 2008. "Schools, Skills, and Synapses." *NBER* working paper no. 14064. Cambridge, Mass.: National Bureau of Economic Research.

Heckman, James, and John Donohue. 1991. "Continuous v. Episodic Change: The Impact of Civil Rights Policy on the Economic Status of Blacks." *Journal of Economic Literature* 29(4): 1603–643.

Heckman, James, Robert Lalonde, and Jeffrey Smith. 1999. "The Economics and Econometrics of Active Labor Market Programs." In *Handbook of Labor Economics*, vol. 3A, edited by Orley Ashenfelter and David Card. Amsterdam: North Holland.

Heckman, James, and Brook Payner. 1989. "Determining the Impact of Federal Antidiscrimination Policy on the Economic Status of Blacks: A Study of South Carolina." *American Economic Review* 79(1): 138–77.

Heckman, James, and Jeffrey Smith. 1995. "Assessing the Case for Social Experiments." *Journal of Economic Perspectives* 9(2): 85–110.

Heinrich, Carolyn, and Christopher King. 2010. "How Effective Are Workforce Development Programs? Implications for U.S. Workforce Policy in 2010 and Beyond." Prepared for conference on Workforce Policy, Ray Marshall Center, University of Texas at Austin (October 19, 2010).

Heinrich, Carolyn, Peter Mueser, Kenneth Troske, Kyung-Seong Jeon, and Daver Kahvecioglu. 2009. "New Estimates of Public Employment and Training Program Net Impacts: A Nonexperimental Evaluation of the Workforce Investment Act Programs." *IZA* discussion paper 4569. Bonn: Institute for the Study of Labor.

Herrnstein, Richard, and Charles Murray. 1994. *The Bell Curve*. New York: Free Press.

Hollenbeck, Kevin. 2006. "Net Impact and Cost-Benefit Analysis of the Workforce Development System in Washington State." Technical report no. TR03-018. Kalamazoo, Mich.: W. E. Upjohn Institute for Employment Research.

———. 2008. "Is There a Role for Public Support of Incumbent Worker Training Programs?" Working paper 08-138. Kalamazoo, Mich.: W. E. Upjohn Institute for Employment Research.

Holzer, Harry J. 2009. "The Labor Market and Young Black Men: Updating Moynihan's Perspective." *Annals of the American Academy of Political and Social Science* 621 (January): 47–69.

———. 2010. "Is the Middle of the Labor Market Disappearing? Comments on the Polarization Hypothesis." Washington, D.C.: Center for American Progress.

———. 2011. "Raising Job Quality and Worker Skills in the U.S.: Creating More Effective Education and Workforce Systems in the States." Washington, D.C.: Brookings Institution Press.

Holzer, Harry J., and Marek Hlavac. 2012. "A Very Uneven Road: U.S. Labor Markets in the Past 30 Years." New York: Russell Sage Foundation.

Holzer, Harry, Julia Lane, David Rosenblum, and Fredrik Andersson. 2011. *Where Are All the Good Jobs Going? What National and Local Job Quality and Dynamics Mean for U.S. Workers.* New York: Russell Sage Foundation.

Holzer, Harry, and Karin Martinson. 2005. "Can We Improve Job Retention and Advancement Among Low-Income Working Parents?" Working Paper, National Poverty Center, University of Michigan, #05-10.

Holzer, Harry J., and David Neumark. 2000. "Assessing Affirmative Action." *Journal of Economic Literature* 38(3): 483–568.

Holzer, Harry J., and Demetra Nightingale. 2009. *Strong Students, Strong Workers: Models for Student Success Through Workforce Development and Community College Partnerships.* Washington, D.C.: Center for American Progress.

Holzer, Harry J., Paul Offner, and Elaine Sorensen. 2006. "Declining Employment Among Young Black Men: The Role of Incarceration and Child Support." *Journal of Policy Analysis and Management* 25(2): 329–50.

Jackson, Russell H. 2008. *Youth Opportunity Grant Initiative: Executive Summary.* Houston, Tex., and Washington, D.C.: Decision Information Resources and U.S. Department of Labor.

Jacobs, Erin. 2012. "Returning to Work After Prison: Final Results from the Transitional Jobs Reentry Demonstration." New York: MDRC.

Jacobson, Louis, and Christine Mokher. 2009. *Pathways to Boosting the Earnings of Low-Income Workers by Increasing Their College Attainment.* New York: The Hudson Institute.

Jastrzab, Joann, John Blomquist, Julie Masker, and Larry Orr. 1997. "Youth Corps: Promising Strategies for Young People and Their Communities." Cambridge, Mass.: Abt Associates.

Jencks, Christopher, and Meredith Phillips. 1998. *The Black-White Test Score Gap.* Washington, D.C.: Brookings Institution Press.

Juhn, Chinhui. 1992. "Decline of Male Labor Market Participation: The Role of Declining Market Opportunities." *Quarterly Journal of Economics* 107(1): 79–122.

Karoly, Lynn. 2001. "Investing in the Future: Reducing Poverty Through Human Capital

Investments." In *Understanding Poverty*, edited by Sheldon Danziger and Robert Haveman. New York: Russell Sage Foundation.

Katz, Lawrence. 1998. "Wage Subsidies for the Disadvantaged." In *Generating Jobs: How to Increase Demand for Less-Skilled Workers*, edited by Richard Freeman and Peter Gottschalk. New York: Russell Sage Foundation.

Kemple, James. 2008. "Career Academies: Long-Term Impacts on Labor Market Outcomes, Educational Attainment and Transitions to Adulthood." New York: MDRC.

Lalonde, Robert. 1995. "The Promise of Public-Sector Sponsored Training Programs." *Journal of Economic Perspectives* 9(2): 149–68.

Lee, David. 2009. "Training, Wages, and Sample Selection: Estimating Sharp Bounds on Treatment Effects." *Review of Economic Studies* 76(3): 1071–102.

Lerman, Robert, Signe-Mary McKernan, and Stephanie Riegg. 2004. "The Scope of Employer-Provided Training in the U.S.: Who, What, Where, and How Much." In *Job Training Policy in the United States*, edited by C. O'Leary et al. Kalamazoo, Mich.: W. E. Upjohn Institute for Employment Research.

Levitan, Sar. 1969. *The Great Society's Poor Law: A New Approach to Poverty*. Baltimore, Md.: Johns Hopkins University Press.

Lower-Basch, Elizabeth, and Mark Greenberg. 2008. "Single Mothers in the Era of Welfare Reform." In *The Gloves-Off Economy: Workplace Standards at the Bottom of America's Labor Market*, edited by A. Bernhardt et al. Champaign, Ill.: Labor and Employment Relations Association.

Maguire, Sheila, Joshua Freely, Carol Clymer, Maureen Conway, and Deena Schwartz. 2010. *Tuning in to Local Labor Markets: Findings from the Sectoral Employment Impact Study*. Philadelphia, Pa.: Public/Private Ventures.

Mallar, Charles, Stuart Kerachsky, Craig Thornton, and David Long. 1981. *Evaluation of the Economic Impact of the Job Corps Program*. Princeton, N.J.: Mathematica Policy Research.

Mead, Lawrence. 2004. *Government Matters: Welfare Reform in Wisconsin*. Princeton, N.J.: Princeton University Press.

Millenky, Megan, Dan Bloom, Sarah Muller-Ravett, and Joseph Broadus. 2011. *Staying the Course: Three-Year Results of the National Guard Youth ChalleNGe Evaluation*. New York: MDRC.

Mishel, Lawrence, Jared Bernstein, and Heidi Sherholz. 2010. *State of Working America*. Washington, D.C.: Economic Policy Institute.

Moss, Philip, and Chris Tilly. 2001. *Stories Employers Tell*. New York: Russell Sage Foundation.

Moynihan, Daniel Patrick. 1965. *The Negro Family: The Case for National Action*. Washington: Office of Policy Planning and Research, U.S. Department of Labor.

National Governors Association. 2009. *State Sector Strategies: Regional Solutions to Worker and Employer Needs*. Washington, D.C.: Center for Best Practices.

O'Leary, Christopher, Robert Straits, and Stephen Wandner. 2004. "U.S. Job Training: Types, Participants, and History." In *Job Training Policy in the United States*, edited by Christopher O'Leary, Robert Straits, and Stephen Wandner. Kalamazoo, Mich.: W. E. Upjohn Institute for Employment Research.

Osterman, Paul. 2007. "Employment and Training Policies: New Directions for Less-Skilled Adults." In *Reshaping the American Workforce in a Changing Economy*, edited by Harry Holzer and Demetra Nightingale. Washington, D.C.: Urban Institute Press.

Pager, Devah. 2003. "The Mark of a Criminal Record." *American Journal of Sociology* 108(5): 937–75.

Pavetti, LaDonna, Liz Schott, and Elizabeth Lower-Basch. 2011. "Creating Subsidized Employment Opportunities for Low-Income Parents." Washington, D.C.: Center on Budget and Policy Priorities.

Price, Cristofer, Julie Williams, Laura Simpson, JoAnn Jastrzab, and Carrie Markovitz. 2011. *National Evaluation of Youth Corps: Findings at Follow-Up*. Washington, D.C.: Abt Associates.

Raphael, Steven. 2008. "Boosting the Earnings and Employment of Low-Skilled Workers in the U.S.: Making Work Pay and Removing Barriers to Employment and Social Mobility." In *A Future of Good Jobs? America's Challenge in the Global Economy*, edited by Timothy Bartik and Susan Houseman. Kalamazoo Mich.: W. E. Upjohn Institute for Employment Research.

Roder, Anne, and Mark Elliott. 2011. *A Promising Start: Year Up's Initial Impacts on Earnings of Young Adults*. New York: Economic Mobility Corporation.

Schochet, Peter, John Burghardt, and Sheena McConnell. 2008. "Does Job Corps Work? Findings from the National Job Corps Impact Study." *American Economic Review* 98(5): 1864–886.

Scholz, J. Karl, Robert Moffitt, and Benjamin Cowan. 2009. "Trends in Income Support." In *Changing Poverty, Changing Policies*, edited by Maria Cancian and Sheldon Danziger. New York: Russell Sage Foundation.

Simonetta, Jonathan. 2004. "Appendix A: Job Training Data." In *Job Training Policy in the United States*, edited by Christopher O'Leary, Robert Straits, and Stephen Wandner. Kalamazoo, Mich.: W. E. Upjohn Institute for Employment Research.

Spence, Christopher. 2007. *Career Pathways: A Strategy for Transforming America's Workforce Education System to Support Economic Growth*. Barrington, R.I.: Workforce Strategy Center.

U.S. Bureau of the Census. 1950–2010. Decennial Census of Population, Integrated Public Use Micro Datasets (IPUMS).

———. 1964–2007. Current Population Surveys Microdata.

U.S. Government Accountability Office. 2011. *Multiple Employment and Training Programs: Providing Information on Colocating Services and Consolidating Administrative Structures Could Promote Efficiencies*. Washington, D.C.: Government Printing Office.

Wilson, William J. 1987. *The Truly Disadvantaged*. Chicago: University of Chicago Press.

Part II

Raising Incomes and Living Standards

Chapter 6

The Safety Net for Families with Children

Jane Waldfogel

In his 1964 State of the Union address, President Lyndon B. Johnson made a statement that still seems remarkable today: "This administration, here and now, declares unconditional war on poverty in America . . . It will not be a short or easy struggle, no single weapon or strategy will suffice, but we shall not rest until that war is won" (Johnson 1964a).

This chapter considers three of the major legacies of the War on Poverty's efforts to strengthen the safety net for low-income families with children: expanded food and nutrition programs, that is, Food Stamps–Supplemental Nutrition Assistance Program (SNAP), school breakfast and lunch, and the special supplemental feeding program for women, infants, and children (WIC); extended cash assistance programs, that is, Aid to Families with Dependent Children (AFDC)–Temporary Assistance for Needy Families (TANF) and Supplemental Security Income (SSI) for the nonelderly; and new income support programs tied to employment or employment-related activities, in particular, the Earned Income Tax Credit (EITC) and child-care subsidies.

For each program, the chapter discusses the context at the start of the War on Poverty and action taken during the decade following the declaration of the War on Poverty; a brief overview of the subsequent legislative history and status, including trends in, and current levels of, expenditures and numbers of recipients; the adequacy of the program with regard to reach, level, and type of benefits; and effectiveness at meeting stated program goals.

Because the War on Poverty aimed not only to reduce poverty and hardship but also to improve children's life chances, the chapter also reviews empirical evidence, where available, on how these programs affect child health and development. A large body of research documents that children from low-income families have poorer health and developmental outcomes than their more advantaged peers (for example, Duncan and Brooks-Gunn 1997). However, these differences in outcomes are not necessarily due to the causal effects of income, and may instead at least partly reflect the influence of other factors that are correlated with income (for example, Mayer 1997). We therefore cannot be certain whether and how much child outcomes could be improved by raising the incomes of low-income families. This chapter places particular emphasis on studies that use rigorous research methods to address this question.

The safety net programs considered in this chapter must be understood in the context of the American welfare state and its distinctive approach to the provision of help to the poor. Compared with other advanced industrialized nations, the United States has taken a more residual approach, expecting individuals to look first to family, community, and employer resources before turning to government assistance. In addition, welfare programs in the United States have been plagued by several common concerns. Americans have always been sensitive to the notion that welfare programs may induce dependency. Unconditional cash and near-cash assistance programs have also been viewed as undermining work incentives and, if provided to unmarried families with children, creating incentives for nonmarital childbearing or family break-up (Murray 1984). For much of the history of these programs, these concerns have been amplified by the disproportionate representation of African American families among the low-income population, leading to racialized attitudes toward welfare that have further eroded public support (Gilens 1999). More recently, concerns about immigration have also undermined public support and led to sharp restrictions on immigrants' eligibility for many programs (Fix, Capps, and Kaushal 2009). Finally, a common theme has been concern about the rising cost of these programs, even though the United States spends a substantially lower share of its gross domestic product on safety net programs than most other advanced industrialized countries do (Waldfogel 2008). The chapter considers the success of the safety net programs in light of this context as well as the extent to which these concerns have eroded political and public support for the programs.

FOOD AND NUTRITION PROGRAMS

A major legacy of the War on Poverty is the introduction or expansion of food and nutrition programs through the 1964 Food Stamp Act and the 1966 Child Nutrition Act. For the most part, these programs either did not exist before the War on Poverty or existed in only small-scale or pilot programs. Instead, what little food assistance was available was provided primarily by community-based groups in the form of programs such as food pantries and soup kitchens.

It is easy to forget that hunger and inadequate nutrition were major issues in the United States at the time of the War on Poverty. These problems were particularly acute among poor African Americans in the South, as documented by physician Raymond Wheeler, who joined with psychiatrist Robert Coles and others to bring the problems of malnutrition to the nation's attention. Wheeler's influential *Hunger Report* documented the dire conditions that existed in poor areas in the South in the 1960s:

We saw children whose nutritional and medical conditions we can only describe as shocking—even to a group of physicians whose work involves daily confrontation with disease and suffering. In child after child we saw: evidence of vitamin and mineral deficiencies . . . in boys and girls in every county we visited, obvious evidence of severe malnutrition, with injury to body's tissues—its muscles, bones and skin as well as an associated psychological state of fatigue, listlessness, and exhaustion. . . . We saw homes with children who are lucky to eat one meal a day. . . . We saw children who don't get to drink milk, don't get to eat fruit, green vegetables, or meat. (1967, 4)

But national data indicated that the inadequate nutrition was not confined to the South. The 1965–1966 Household Food Consumption Survey found that one-fifth of Americans had a poor diet, with that share nearly doubling, to 36 percent, among low-income households (USDA 1969). In addition, a study of Selective Service rejectees (cited in Johnson 1964c) brought further attention to the problem of ill health and malnutrition among low-income Americans and provided additional impetus to address the problem.

Food Stamps–SNAP

Food Stamps, now the Supplemental Nutrition Assistance Program (SNAP), provide help to low-income individuals and families to purchase food. The program is not limited to families with children but I focus on that population here.

Although programs that distributed surplus food commodities date back to the 1930s and 1940s, Food Stamps as we know them today did not exist until the War on Poverty. A pilot program of food coupons operated in about half the counties in the United States but was discontinued in 1943. President John Kennedy reinstated the program on a pilot basis in 1961, but it operated in only eight areas (USDA 2012a).

Johnson pledged in his 1964 State of the Union address to establish "a broader food stamp program" (1964a). The 1964 Food Stamp Act fulfilled this pledge by establishing the national Food Stamp Program. Food Stamps provide low-income individuals and families with benefits that they can use to purchase food. Originally, benefits were provided in the form of stamps or coupons, which families had to purchase. Subsequent legislation eliminated the purchase requirement, effective 1979. To reduce stigma and administrative costs and increase ease of use, states gradually shifted to providing benefits through electronic benefit transfer (EBT) cards. As of 2008, when the program was renamed SNAP, all benefits are provided by EBT (USDA 2012b).

The number of Food Stamp recipients grew rapidly during the War on Poverty—from a half million persons in 1965, to 1 million in 1966, and to 2 million in 1967 (USDA 2012b). By 1974, when the program reached all counties, participation had reached nearly 13 million, and by 1994, a record high of 27.5 million (Scholz,

Moffitt, and Cowan 2009; Ben-Shalom et al. 2011; see also table 6.A1). Participation fell sharply after the welfare reforms of 1996, which excluded most legal immigrants from receiving Food Stamps and also established time limits for able-bodied nonworking adults without dependents. The drop in participation may also have reflected the misperception among low-income families that Food Stamp eligibility was tied to welfare eligibility (Scholz, Moffitt, and Cowan 2009).[1] Food Stamp–SNAP caseloads have risen since 2000, as later reforms reinstated eligibility for some legal immigrants, streamlined application procedures, and changed the rules to allow recipients to own a car (Scholz, Moffitt, and Cowan 2009). The program experienced an especially steep increase in participation in the late 2000s during and after the Great Recession. By January 2011, 46.5 million Americans—15 percent of the population—were receiving Food Stamps–SNAP (FRAC 2012).

Food Stamps–SNAP play an important role in reducing poverty. This has not always been evident, because Food Stamps are a *near-cash* benefit and are not taken into account in the official poverty measure; this problem has been recognized since the War on Poverty and its aftermath (see, for example, Lampman 1973; Smeeding 1975). But the role of Food Stamps–SNAP in reducing poverty is readily apparent with the new supplemental poverty measure (SPM), which does take into account near-cash benefits such as Food Stamps–SNAP. Census estimates using the SPM suggest that in 2010, the child poverty rate would be 3 percentage points higher, 21.2 percent instead of 18.2 percent, if Food Stamps–SNAP were not counted as income (Short 2011). In addition, Food Stamps reduce the depth of poverty among the population with incomes below the poverty line. Analysts measure the depth of poverty using the concept of the poverty gap—the money a family would need to have its income rise to the poverty line. By providing resources to families with incomes below the poverty line, Food Stamps reduce the poverty gap. John Scholz, Robert Moffitt, and Benjamin Cowan (2009) estimate that in 2004, means-tested transfers closed 36 percent of the poverty gap, Food Stamps alone reducing the poverty gap by 6 percent.

Food Stamps are intended not just to reduce poverty but also to reduce hunger and improve nutrition. Whether they achieve the latter goals depends on whether recipients use the benefits to purchase more food and better food, rather than just to offset the cost of food they would have bought in any case. Unfortunately, we lack consistent data on hunger and nutrition over time. A national survey in the mid-1960s found that 21 percent of all Americans had poor diets, consuming less than two-thirds of the recommended level of at least one of seven specified nutrients; that share rose to 36 percent among low-income households. Fifty percent of all Americans (and 37 percent of low-income households) had good diets, meeting standards for all seven nutrients. The remainder had diets falling somewhere in between (USDA 1969). By the time of the next national survey, in 1977 and 1978, analysts noted a weaker connection between income and food consumption than previously: the share of households with good diets rose to 55 percent overall and to 50 percent among low-income families (USDA 1985). In addition, just 3 percent of all households, and 9 percent of poor households, reported that they did not have enough food (Swan 1983). Another national survey was conducted in the late 1980s but was limited by low response rates (USDA 1994).

Since 1995, what analysts refer to as *food security* has been consistently measured using data from a food security supplement to the Current Population Survey (CPS). Food security is defined in terms of problems or limitations with regard to access to food, with particular attention to individuals who are food insecure — that is, experience reduced quality, variety, or desirability of diet, but show little or no indication of reduced food intake — or who experience very low food security — that is, are characterized by multiple indications of disrupted eating patterns and reduced food intake (USDA 2012f). The CPS food security data show 10 to 12 percent of Americans experiencing food insecurity and 3 to 5 percent experiencing very low food security (indicative of hunger) in most years, those shares rising during the Great Recession in 2009 to 15 percent and 6 percent respectively (USDA 2012f). In 2010, rates of food insecurity and very low food security were 14.5 percent and 5.4 percent, respectively, for all households, and 40 percent and 16.5 percent for households below the poverty line (Coleman-Jensen et al. 2011).

Reviewing the econometric evidence, Janet Currie (2003, 2006) concludes that Food Stamps do lead to reduced food insecurity and that they also improve nutrition as well as other aspects of child health and development. Some of the most compelling evidence comes from studies of the War on Poverty Food Stamp expansions. Hilary Hoynes and Diane Schanzenbach (2009) show that as counties introduced Food Stamps, families reduced their out-of-pocket spending on food while increasing food expenditures; however, they also find that the roll-out of Food Stamps somewhat reduced single mothers' labor supply, since Food Stamps are an income transfer and are not conditioned on work (Hoynes and Schanzenbach 2012). Also taking advantage of the difference in the timing of the introduction of the program across counties, Douglas Almond and his colleagues find that women living in counties with Food Stamp programs three months before birth delivered higher birth-weight babies, particularly at the lower end of the birth-weight spectrum (Almond, Hoynes, and Schanzenbach 2011). Meanwhile Hilary Hoynes and colleagues (2012) find that individuals who had access to Food Stamps in childhood are healthier as adults — that is, less likely to experience obesity, high blood pressure, and diabetes — and, among women, more likely to be economically self-sufficient.

Studies using more recent data also find positive effects on child health and development. Using administrative data from Illinois, Bong Joo Lee and Lucy Mackey-Bilaver (2007) find that children whose families received Food Stamps or WIC were less likely to be victims of abuse or neglect and less likely to be diagnosed with anemia, failure-to-thrive, or nutritional deficiency. Edward Frongillo and his colleagues (2006) find that children whose families moved onto Food Stamps between kindergarten and third grade had slightly greater gains in reading and math than those moving off Food Stamps.

Overall, then, the Food Stamp program must be judged a success in reducing poverty, combating hunger and food insecurity, and improving nutrition and related outcomes for low-income children and families. There is, however, room for improvement. The program still does not reach all eligible families because administrative barriers, lack of coordination, and stigma deter some recipients from enrolling (Berg 2010; Currie 2006). As of 2010, an estimated 25 percent of eligible individuals and 35 percent of eligible working poor individuals did not participate (USDA 2012g). The program might also do more to promote good nutrition. The program places very few limits on what recipients can buy. Proposals to restrict recipient choice, by banning the purchase of soda, for example, are controversial, however (Patrick McGeehan, "U.S. Rejects Mayor's Plan to Ban Use of Food Stamps to Buy Soda," *New York Times*, August 19, 2011). Critics have also argued that the program may contribute to obesity, although research controlling for selection into the program does not find this to be the case (Kaushal 2007). Nevertheless, it might be worth experimenting with reforms to provide the benefits on a more regular basis throughout the month to see whether the availability helps families establish a more balanced diet.

School Breakfast and Lunch

The school breakfast and lunch programs provide free or reduced cost meals for low-income children in schools and child-care settings. They offset food costs for families and may also have direct effects on children's food security and nutrition, as well as their school attendance and achievement.

School nutrition programs date back to the 1940s but were greatly expanded during the War on Poverty. The case for them was made as follows: "Poverty is perpetuated by poor health, malnutrition, and chronic disabilities. New and expanded school health and school lunch programs will improve both health and education" (Johnson 1964c, 76).

The 1966 Child Nutrition Act increased funding for school lunches and introduced a small school breakfast program. The number of children participating in the breakfast program grew from 450,000 in 1970 to 11.7 million in 2010, and the number participating in the lunch program from 22 million to 32 million over the same period (USDA 2012c, 2012d; see table 6.A1). By 2010, spending on the two programs totaled $13.7 billion: $2.9 billion for breakfast, $10.8 billion for lunch (USDA 2012c, 2012d; see table 6.A2).

The school nutrition programs play a small but significant role in reducing poverty. Using the supplemental poverty measure, the child poverty rate in 2010 would be 1 percentage point higher—19.0 percent versus 18.2 percent—if school lunch were not counted as income (Short 2011). Although precise figures are not available, the school nutrition programs also likely contribute to reducing the poverty gap.

Although concerns have been raised about the quality of food in school meal programs, the evidence suggests that the quality is as good as or better than what children would eat in the absence of the programs (Currie 2006). Additionally, the introduction of a school breakfast program raises children's attendance and test scores (Meyers et al. 1989; Murphy et al. 1998; Currie 2006). Nevertheless, debate continues about the quality of school meals and whether school breakfast and lunch programs are improving child nutrition and well-being or instead are contributing to the rise in child obesity (Roni Rabin, "Childhood: Obesity and School Lunches." *New York Times*, February 4, 2011). More research in this area would be helpful.

Women, Infants, and Children

The special supplemental nutrition program for women, infants, and children (WIC) provides vouchers that low-income pregnant women and women with infants and toddlers can use to purchase nutritious food. WIC reduces food costs for recipients, though grant amounts are not large, and should improve nutrition because participants can use the vouchers only for approved foods.

Although introduced after the War on Poverty, in 1969, and formalized only in 1972 through an amendment to the Child Nutrition Act, WIC is clearly part of the War on Poverty legacy of food and nutrition programs. Like SNAP and school meal programs, WIC is an in-kind program designed to improve food and nutrition for a vulnerable population. However, one difference is important: WIC, unlike SNAP and school meals, is not an entitlement, so if funding runs out, not all eligible families will receive it. As of 2011, WIC expenditures totaled $7 billion, serving 9 million women, infants, and children, up from 88,000 in 1974 (USDA 2012e; see tables 6.A1 and 6.A2). The Department of Agriculture estimates that the program currently serves about 60 percent of eligible families with children (USDA 2011).

Because grant levels are modest, the program has little impact on the child poverty rate even when using the supplemental poverty measure (Short 2011); its impact on the poverty gap is small as well (Scholz, Moffitt, and Cowan 2009). The primary purpose of the program, however, is to improve the health and nutrition of women, infants, and children, and there the program seems to be a resounding success.

Many studies have examined the effects of prenatal participation in WIC. Early studies found that participation prenatally was associated with reductions in low birth weight, from 10 to 43 percent, but such studies typically did not take into account selection into the program and how that might bias estimated effects (Currie 2003). More recent studies have used rigorous methods to control for selection and confirm that WIC is associated with higher birth weight (Currie and Bitler 2004; Kowaleski-Jones and Duncan 2002). Although debate continues as to whether the effects of WIC on birth outcomes are causal (Joyce, Gibson, and Colman 2005; Currie and Bitler 2005), the evidence suggests that participating in WIC prenatally does improve birth weight. Recent historical analyses, taking advantage of the roll-out of WIC across counties, have estimated that the implementation of WIC led to a 16 to 38 gram increase in average birth weight and an 8 percent decrease in low birth weight births for less educated participants (Hoynes, Page, and Stevens 2011).

The benefits of participating in WIC postnatally have been less studied. That WIC provides coupons for infant formula has led to concerns that it may reduce breast-feeding. Recent program reforms have increased support for breast-feeding mothers, and Currie (2006) concludes that such efforts may be paying off, as one recent study finds that breast-feeding rates do not differ between WIC and non-WIC mothers (Chatterji and Brooks-Gunn 2004). Currie (2006) also reviews evidence showing that WIC improves child nutrition and reduces anemia, leading to higher scores on early vocabulary tests.

Summary Assessment

The War on Poverty's food and nutrition programs have an impressive track record. Food Stamps reach large numbers of low-income families, reduce poverty and food insecurity, and probably also improve nutrition. The smaller WIC program has less impact on poverty but a more direct effect on nutrition. The school lunch and breakfast programs have intermediate effects on poverty and nutrition. Although each program could be improved, together they have contributed to reducing poverty in the short term and improving the longer-term life chances of poor children.

CASH ASSISTANCE

Although cash assistance programs for low-income families with children predated the War on Poverty, they clearly were not enough to address the problem of poverty in America. Census data for 1959 showed that more than 20 percent of Americans were poor, and that poverty rates were higher among vulnerable groups such as children, 27 percent, and the elderly, 35 percent (Gabe 2010; see also figure 6.1). The 1959 data also showed a stark racial disparity in poverty rates, with the poverty rate for African Americans, 55 percent, three times that of whites, 18 percent (Gabe 2010; see also figure 6.2). Single-mother families also had much higher than average poverty rates (see figure 6.3).

However, expanding cash assistance was not originally a major focus of the War on Poverty. President Johnson was clear that he did not want to increase handouts. As he said at the signing of the 1964 Economic Opportunity Act, "We are not content to accept the endless growth of the relief rolls or welfare rolls. We want to offer the forgotten fifth of our people opportunity and not doles" (1964b).

In a similar vein, the 1965 *Economic Report of the President* rejected the idea of increasing cash transfers because "this 'solution' would leave untouched most of the roots of poverty" (Johnson 1964c, 77). For this reason, the War on Poverty initially stressed "a hand up, not a handout" (Davies 1996, 39).

AFDC/TANF

Aid to Dependent Children (ADC), later to become Aid to Families with Dependent Children (AFDC), was established as part of the Social Security legislation in

FIGURE 6.1 / Poverty Rates by Age

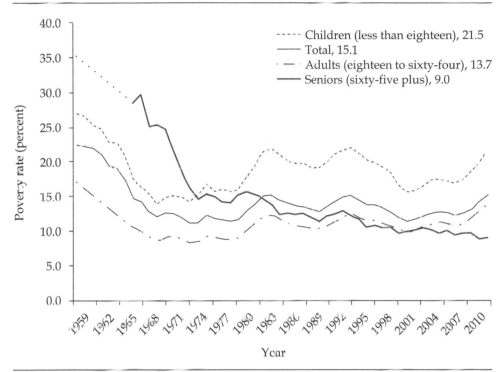

Source: Author's calculations based on U.S. Census Bureau (2012).
Note: Numbers in the labels above refer to the poverty rate in the latest year shown in the figure.

1935. Even at its inception, concerns surfaced that a cash welfare program might induce long-term dependency. President Franklin Delano Roosevelt, in his 1935 State of the Union speech, issued a memorable warning: "Continued dependence upon relief induces a spiritual and moral disintegration fundamentally destructive to the national fiber. To dole out relief in this way is to administer a narcotic, a subtle destroyer of the human spirit" (1935).

In spite of these concerns, Roosevelt and the New Deal reformers felt that "mothers' pensions" were warranted to enable women—who through no fault of their own found themselves without a male breadwinner—to support their children without having to work in the labor market. The recipient that they had in mind was a deserving widow (Skocpol 1995). Over time, however, the profile of ADC recipients changed. By the 1950s, the majority of recipients were women who had become single parents through divorce, desertion, or out-of-wedlock child-bearing (Davies 1996), and roughly 40 percent were African American (Chappell 2010). In addition, the number of recipients and the associated costs were growing rapidly. By 1957, ADC had become the largest public assistance program, surpassing even the old-age assistance program (Davies 1996). The combination of a growing welfare caseload and a growing share of African Americans within the

FIGURE 6.2 / Poverty Rates by Race and Hispanic Origin

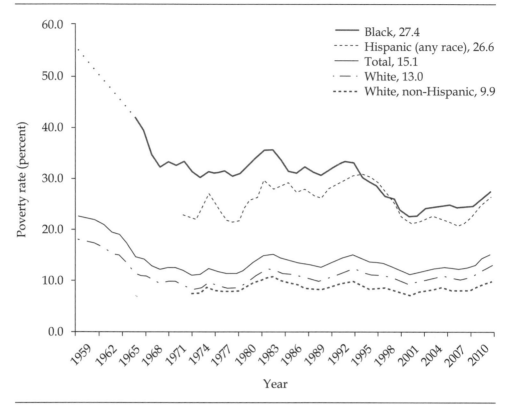

Source: Author's calculations based on U.S. Census Bureau (2012).
Note: Numbers in the labels above refer to the poverty rate in the latest year shown in the figure.

caseload led War on Poverty policymakers to feel that the program needed reform (Chappell 2010; Lynn 1977).

Against this background and in keeping with Johnson's preference for opportunities rather than handouts, the War on Poverty did not increase the generosity of the program, which in 1962 had been renamed Aid to Families with Dependent Children (AFDC). Instead, Title V of the 1964 Economic Opportunity Act introduced a work-oriented reform: setting up the Work Experience and Training Program to encourage welfare recipients to move into employment. Title V was a pilot program and served as the forerunner of the Social Security amendments of 1967, which mandated that welfare departments establish Work Incentive (WIN) programs and provide employment support, including child care. Title V and the WIN programs were offered on a voluntary basis to single mothers, but were mandatory for participants in the AFDC-unemployed parent program, which had been established in 1962 and served a small number of two-parent families. As a result, about half of those enrolled in Title V programs were men (Stats 1970). These early work incentive programs had many of the hallmarks of later welfare-to-work pro-

FIGURE 6.3 / Poverty Rates by Family Structure

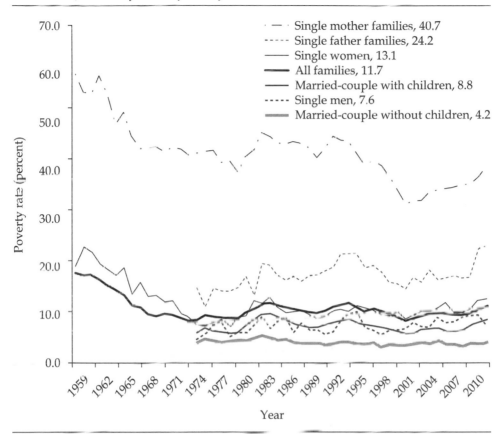

Source: Author's calculations based on U.S. Census Bureau (2012).
Note: Numbers in the labels above refer to the poverty rate in the latest year shown in the figure.

grams, including individual employability plans, job counseling and placement, and help locating and paying for child care.

The new programs did not address the long-standing problems of low benefits, and inequitable access to benefits, within the AFDC program. In the wake of riots in Watts and other urban areas, and in conjunction with the civil rights movement, these problems were drawing increasing attention. At the same time, the burgeoning civil rights movement was challenging discrimination in a host of areas, including welfare policy. Legal services lawyers and advocates successfully challenged discriminatory welfare policies that denied benefits to African American women or subjected them to greater scrutiny, and won new rights to fair hearings and appeals processes (Chappell 2010). The result was a dramatic expansion in welfare eligibility and receipt, with particularly large increases among low income African American women who had previously been underserved (Patterson 2000).

To address the problem of low benefits, key figures within the Johnson administration began to advocate for making income support programs more generous. A 1965 Interagency Task Force on Public Assistance concluded that inadequate benefit levels were the major problem facing the AFDC program (Davies 1996). Sargent Shriver, director of the Office of Economic Opportunity, and economists in the administration pressed Johnson in 1965 to introduce a negative income tax (NIT), which would replace AFDC and provide a guaranteed minimum income to all poor families (Davies 1996). A further benefit of a minimum income approach is that it would provide aid to all low-income families, regardless of family structure, addressing concerns that AFDC policies were leading to the kind of family breakdown that Daniel Patrick Moynihan had drawn attention to in his controversial report (Chappell 2010).

In 1969, Johnson's successor, President Richard Nixon, proposed a Family Assistance Plan (FAP) that would have provided a minimum income to all low-income families, including the working poor. However, FAP was defeated in 1972, opposed by conservatives, who worried that providing a minimum income would erode work incentives, and liberals, who argued that it was not generous enough, and that having no plan was better than enacting a flawed one (Chappell 2010). Brian Steensland (1998) provides more detail on this and other efforts to provide a guaranteed income.

What was the legacy of the War on Poverty in terms of the AFDC program? Certainly, caseloads and costs increased dramatically as the number of recipients more than doubled from 4.2 to 9.7 million between 1964 and 1970 (Davies 1996, 158, 215). So too did concern about the program's size and its effects on work incentives and family structure (Chappell 2010; Lynn 1977). Yet poverty among welfare recipients remained high, in spite of AFDC's burgeoning costs, because benefits continued to be low, especially in southern states.

The idea of some form of minimum income for the nonelderly poor died with the defeat of FAP. However, FAP did lead to the Supplemental Security Income program for the elderly, blind and disabled poor (discussed in the next section and in chapter 7, this volume). Future AFDC reforms would emphasize work, responding to the backlash on the part of the working poor and middle class, who resented seeing benefits go to those not working. And, in the wake of the FAP defeat, the Earned Income Tax Credit, discussed later in this chapter, emerged as an income supplement for the working poor in the early 1970s.

After the War on Poverty, AFDC continued to move in a more work-oriented direction, culminating in the passage of the Personal Responsibility and Work Opportunity Reconciliation Act (PRWORA) in 1996. PRWORA converted the open-ended AFDC program to the time-limited Temporary Assistance for Needy Families (TANF) program and further stiffened work requirements. Caseloads and expenditures on AFDC-TANF show a steep decline after 1996; by 1998, fewer people were on AFDC-TANF than had been in 1970 (Scholz, Moffitt, and Cowan 2009; Ben-Shalom, Moffitt, and Scholz 2011). Even during the Great Recession, participation in the program did not increase significantly (see tables 6.A1 and 6.A2).

It is difficult to assess how effective AFDC and its successor TANF have been in reducing poverty. Child poverty fell by nearly half from 1959 to 1969, from 27 percent to about 14 percent (see figure 6.1), with substantial reductions for the most disadvantaged groups including African Americans (figure 6.2) and single-mother families (figure 6.3). But we cannot attribute all of this reduction to the effects of AFDC. Many other factors acted to reduce poverty during this period—factors such as a strong economy, increases in social insurance benefits, and tax reductions for low-paid workers—and in many instances AFDC benefits would have been too low to move families out of poverty. Robert Plotnick and Felicity Skidmore (1975) estimate that only 5.5 percent of poor households were moved out of poverty by public assistance programs in 1972, an increase over the 2.9 percent moved out of poverty by such programs in 1965, but nevertheless a small share. We can be more confident that the availability of cash assistance reduced the depth of poverty and material hardship among the poor (Plotnick and Skidmore 1975; Smeeding 1975). However, as mentioned, TANF plays a less important role in protecting families from short-term poverty today than in the past (Scholz, Moffitt, and Cowan 2009; Ben-Shalom, Moffitt, and Scholz 2011).

At the same time, critics have argued that AFDC's provision of unconditional assistance for single-mother families increased the risk of future poverty by fostering dependency, discouraging work, and encouraging the formation of single-parent families (Murray 1984). However, the evidence suggests that any such effects on family formation (Moffitt 1998) and work effort (Ben-Shalom, Moffitt, and Scholz 2011) were small.

It is also difficult to evaluate the effects of AFDC-TANF on child outcomes. Johnson and others involved in the War on Poverty were concerned about the harmful effects for children of growing up on welfare and not having the role model of a working parent (Davies 1996; Gillette 2010). But careful econometric studies tend to find no significant effects of welfare participation on children's health and development (Currie 1995, 1997). At the same time, there is extensive evidence that children are harmed by growing up in financially insecure and poor households (Magnuson and Votruba-Drzal 2009). It therefore seems unlikely that income support from cash welfare has done children more harm than good.

Supplemental Security Income

The Supplemental Security Income program, established in 1972 after the rejection of FAP, provides a guaranteed annual income for poor families with a disabled child or adult.[2] In contrast to AFDC-TANF, SSI benefits are set by the federal government, with most states supplementing these. Benefit amounts are higher than AFDC-TANF and are raised each year to account for inflation, as Social Security benefits are. No work requirements or time limits are associated with SSI receipt.

SSI expenditures for families with disabled children rose about 50 percent from 1972 to 1990, but then rose a further 55 percent from 1990 to 1994, due to growth in the caseload following a Supreme Court decision that changed the child mental health eligibility criteria, bringing them in line with the adult criteria. After 1994, spending grew only modestly (Scholz, Moffitt, and Cowan 2009; Ben-Shalom,

Moffitt, and Scholz 2011). In 2012, 1.3 million children received SSI (Social Security Administration 2012b; see tables 6.A1 and 6.A2).

SSI has a larger effect than AFDC-TANF on reducing the depth of poverty for recipients because benefit levels are higher: Scholz and his colleagues (2009) find that SSI closed 8 percent of the poverty gap in 2004 and that AFDC-TANF closed 2.5 percent. SSI also moves some families out of poverty. Mark Duggan and Melissa Kearney (2007) find that a child becoming eligible for SSI reduces the risk of the family being in poverty by 11 percentage points. However, little research exists on the effects of SSI receipt on child health and development. This would be a useful area for future research.

Summary Assessment

The War on Poverty did have lasting effects on the cash assistance available to the poor, though not always in the way that was intended. Johnson's insistence on providing a hand up, rather than a handout, has been maintained in the post-1996 evolution of TANF. However, Johnson would not have foreseen, or intended, that the program would lose its ability to serve as a safety net for those unable to find jobs in the competitive labor market or when unemployment rates are high. As critics of PRWORA pointed out when the 1996 reforms were enacted, and as we have seen in the Great Recession, TANF provides cash assistance only to a small percentage of poor families with children, even in economic downturns. Low-income families in which parents are not able to find work in the competitive labor market but do not qualify for SSI would have received some minimal support under the post-War on Poverty AFDC program, but are left "disconnected" from both welfare and work under TANF (Blank 2007).

INCOME SUPPORT PROGRAMS TIED TO EMPLOYMENT

As discussed, the idea of providing income supplements to low-income working families dates from the War on Poverty. Work-related income support programs, however, have assumed a much more important role in recent years. The largest such program now is the EITC. Child-care subsidies have also become increasingly important.

Earned Income Tax Credit

The Earned Income Tax Credit, established in 1975 in response to the rejection of FAP, is now the single largest income support program for low-income families with children. The EITC provides families who have enough earnings in the previous year with a refundable tax credit. It is the only major safety net program administered through the tax system and is paid once a year, after tax returns are filed. The EITC was expanded several times after 1975, the most far-reaching reform occurring in 1993 when benefits were increased and indexed to inflation. Recipient families increased from 6 million in 1975 to 26 million in 2011, at a cost of nearly $60 billion per year (Internal Revenue Service 2012; see tables 6.A1 and 6.A2).

The primary goal of the EITC is to promote work and raise incomes among low-income parents. It has been effective in doing so, particularly for single parents. The effects on married parents are more ambiguous because the program also provides some disincentive to marriage as well as incentives for second earners to reduce labor supply (Dickert, Houser, and Scholz 1995; Eissa and Hoynes 2004; Hotz and Scholz 2006; Meyer and Rosenbaum 2001).

The EITC plays an important role in reducing poverty among working families (Neumark and Wascher 2001; Scholz 1994; Ben-Shalom, Moffitt, and Scholz 2011). Using the supplemental poverty measure, in 2010 the child poverty rate would be 4 percentage points higher, 22.4 percent instead of 18.2 percent, if the EITC was not counted as income (Short 2011). In addition, the EITC reduces the poverty gap, in 2004 by an estimated 4.5 percent (Scholz, Moffitt, and Cowan 2009).

The EITC also has positive effects on other child and family outcomes. William Evans and Craig Garthwaite (2010) examine the effects of the 1993 EITC expansion, taking advantage of the fact that benefits increased sharply for families with two or more children, but not for those with only one child. They find that increased EITC benefits are associated with fewer bad mental health days and a greater likelihood of being in excellent or very good health; higher benefits are also linked to a lower number of risky biomarkers, in particular, those indicative of stress. Kevin Baker (2008) finds that these EITC reforms also raised average infant birth weight. Taking advantage of variation in state EITC programs (twenty-four states plus the District of Columbia have their own EITCs in addition to the federal one) Kate Strully, David Rehkopf, and Ziming Xuan (2010) also find that higher EITC payments are linked to higher birth weights. Hilary Hoynes, Douglas Miller, and David Simon (2011), examining the effects of variation in both federal and state EITC programs, provide further evidence that higher EITC benefits are associated with reduced likelihood of low birth weight and higher average birth weights. Gordon Dahl and Lance Lochner (2012) find that income gains associated with higher EITCs are associated with higher student test scores.[3]

Child-Care Subsidies

The first provisions for helping welfare recipients with child-care costs date from the 1964 Economic Opportunity Act. Those provisions laid the groundwork for the introduction of transitional child care—for women leaving welfare for work—in the Family Support Act of 1988, which in turn set the stage for today's child-care subsidy program for low-income workers, the Child Care and Development Fund (CCDF), established in 1996.[4]

Funding for child-care subsidies more than doubled in real terms from 1996 to

2000 following welfare reform (Scholz, Moffitt, and Cowan 2009), but has been fairly flat since then; data on trends in subsidies before 1996 are not consistently available. Subsidies are not an entitlement and reach only about 30 percent of eligible families (ASPE 2008; Johnson, Ryan, and Brooks-Gunn 2012). The FY2011 budget for CCDF was $5 billion (U.S. Department of Health and Human Services 2012). In 2009, 1.6 million children received subsidized child care through CCDF; an additional 0.9 million received subsidies through TANF child-care funds and the smaller Social Services Block Grant (U.S. Department of Health and Human Services 2012).

Child-care subsidies contribute to poverty reduction in two ways: first, by providing an incentive for parents to work; and second, by offsetting the cost of child care and boosting net family income. In addition, subsidies, if they support high-quality care, can reduce poverty in the next generation by improving outcomes for low-income children.

Recent studies have begun to examine the effects of child-care subsidies on child health and development. In contrast to the large body of research showing the benefits of high-quality early childhood education and care (Ruhm and Waldfogel 2012), research on child-care subsidies tends to find either negative or neutral effects on child health and development (Herbst and Tekin 2010a, 2010b, 2011; Johnson, Ryan, and Brooks-Gunn 2012). These results likely reflect the poor quality of child care that children with subsidies receive. Further research is merited.

Summary Assessment

The EITC is now the largest income support program for low-income working families with children. It promotes work and makes work pay, reduces poverty, and leads to improved health and mental health for low-income parents and children. Nevertheless, there may be room to improve the EITC. It might be worth experimenting with different methods of administering the EITC to see whether delivering the benefit on a more regular basis might yield better outcomes for children and families. Another shortcoming of the EITC is that it is primarily limited to custodial parents and thus does not provide support to noncustodial parents, typically fathers (Mincy, Klempin, and Schmidt 2011).

Child-care subsidies also have become a more important part of the social safety net. They remain limited because, unlike the EITC, they are not an entitlement. The extent to which the care being subsidized is contributing to children's health and development is also an issue, because families may use subsidies for many different types of care and not just high-quality preschool programs.

CONCLUSIONS

The most enduring legacy of the War on Poverty's reforms to the nation's safety net derives from its expansion of food and nutrition programs for low-income families with children. Compared with the cash welfare programs, these programs have proven fairly resilient to political pressures and backlash. They have also achieved a solid track record in terms of reducing poverty and food insecurity, improving nutrition, and yielding benefits for child health and development, which may in turn lead to reductions in longer-term poverty in future.

The legacy of the War on Poverty in terms of cash welfare is more problematic. Concerns about long-term dependency culminated in the 1996 welfare reform that reduced the rolls to pre–War on Poverty levels and transformed AFDC into the time-limited and work-oriented TANF program. On a more positive note, the SSI program does provide a guaranteed annual income to low-income families with disabled children or parents. A year into the War on Poverty, Johnson and his key administrators, though favoring opportunities over handouts, were already discussing the need for some form of guaranteed minimum income for low-income families with children. This theme was picked up by Johnson's successor, Nixon, but did not come to fruition.

Fifty years later, some low-income families with children have something like a guaranteed minimum income, in the form of SNAP, plus SSI for those who are disabled, and EITC and possibly child-care subsidies for those who are working, but we have still not achieved the vision of a guaranteed minimum income (Moffitt 2003). In my view, a true guaranteed minimum income for families with children would require some form of universal child or family allowance, providing a minimum amount to all families with children regardless of family structure, disability, or employment status. This has long been the norm in other advanced industrialized countries. We have come closer to that vision with the Child Tax Credit (CTC), which provides families with children an income supplement. However, the amount is small, $1,000 per child. Moreover, the CTC is not fully refundable and thus the lowest income families do not receive any benefit from it (Harris 2012). If made more generous and fully refundable, the CTC would provide the income floor that War on Poverty planners and their successors came to see was an essential element of the nation's safety net. I can therefore think of no better way to celebrate the fiftieth anniversary of the War on Poverty than by making the CTC more generous and fully refundable, to ensure that an adequate safety net reaches all the nation's poor families with children.

However, even a universal CTC, particularly at current benefit levels, would not eliminate child poverty, which remains at unacceptably high levels. Official poverty statistics, which do not capture the full effects of the safety net, show child poverty lower today than it was fifty years ago: 20 percent versus 27 percent. Racial gaps are also smaller: the African American poverty rate twice that for whites today, versus times as high in 1959 (see figures 6.1 and 6.2). This said, it should still be unacceptable in a country as affluent and committed to equality as the United States, that one in five children, and one in four African American children, should be poor. Waging war on poverty thus remains an important imperative. Achieving that goal would require both a more generous safety net and better employment and earnings prospects, and work-family supports, for low-income families with children (Waldfogel 2009).

TABLE 6.A1 / Social Safety Net Caseloads

Year	Food Stamps	School Breakfast	School Lunch	WIC	AFDC-TANF	SSI - Child	EITC
1970	4,340	450	22,400		7,415		
1971	9,368	800	24,100		9,557		
1972	11,109	1,040	24,400		10,632		
1973	12,166	1,190	24,700		11,038		
1974	12,862	1,370	24,600	88	10,845	71	
1975	17,064	1,820	24,900	344	11,067	107	6,215
1976	18,549	2,200	25,600	520	11,386	125	6,473
1977	17,077	2,490	26,200	848	11,130	147	5,627
1978	16,001	2,800	26,700	1,181	10,672	166	5,192
1979	17,653	3,320	27,000	1,483	10,318	177	7,135
1980	21,082	3,600	26,600	1,914	10,597	190	6,954
1981	22,430	3,810	25,800	2,119	11,160	195	6,717
1982	21,717	3,320	22,900	2,189	10,431	192	6,395
1983	21,625	3,360	23,000	2,537	10,659	198	7,368
1984	20,854	3,430	23,400	3,045	10,866	212	6,376
1985	19,899	3,440	23,600	3,138	10,813	227	7,432
1986	19,429	3,500	23,700	3,312	10,997	241	7,156
1987	19,113	3,610	23,900	3,429	11,065	251	8,738
1988	18,645	3,680	24,200	3,593	10,920	255	11,148
1989	18,806	3,810	24,200	4,119	10,934	265	11,696
1990	20,049	4,070	24,100	4,517	11,460	309	12,542
1991	22,625	4,440	24,200	4,893	12,592	397	13,665
1992	25,407	4,920	24,600	5,403	13,625	556	14,097
1993	26,987	5,360	24,900	5,921	14,143	723	15,117
1994	27,474	5,830	25,300	6,477	14,226	841	19,017
1995	26,619	6,320	25,700	6,894	13,660	917	19,334
1996	25,543	6,580	25,900	7,186	12,645	955	19,464
1997	22,858	6,920	26,300	7,407	10,935	880	19,391
1998	19,791	7,140	26,600	7,367	8,790	887	20,273
1999	18,183	7,370	27,000	7,311	7,188	847	19,259
2000	17,194	7,550	27,300	7,192	6,324	847	19,277
2001	17,318	7,790	27,500	7,306	5,761	882	19,593
2002	19,096	8,150	28,000	7,491	5,656	915	21,703
2003	21,250	8,430	28,400	7,631	5,518	959	22,024
2004	23,811	8,900	29,000	7,904	5,376	993	22,270
2005	25,628	9,360	29,600	8,023	5,118	1,036	22,752
2006	26,549	9,770	30,100	8,088	4,742	1,079	23,042
2007	26,316	10,120	30,600	8,285	4,138	1,121	24,584
2008	28,223	10,610	31,000	8,705	3,993	1,154	24,757
2009	33,490	11,080	31,300	9,121		1,200	
2010	40,302	11,670	31,800	9,175		1,239	

Source: Author's compilation based on Ben-Shalom, Moffitt, and Scholz (2011); Social Security Administration (2012a, 2012b).
Note: Number of recipients, in thousands.

TABLE 6.A2 / Trends in Expenditures on the Social Safety Net

Year	Food Stamps	School Food Programs	WIC	AFDC-TANF	SSI - Child	EITC
1970	550	679		4,963		
1971	1,523	920		6,002		
1972	1,797	1,166		7,035		
1973	2,131	1,339		7,613		
1974	2,718	1,510	10	8,111	40	
1975	4,386	1,922	89	9,494	128	1,250
1976	5,327	2,162	143	10,745	176	1,295
1977	5,067	2,410	256	11,565	227	1,127
1978	5,139	2,668	380	11,869	302	1,048
1979	6,480	3,093	525	12,129	340	2,052
1980	8,721	3,617	728	13,435	397	1,986
1981	10,630	3,708	872	14,493	458	1,912
1982	10,208	3,278	949	14,613	512	1,775
1983	11,152	3,564	1,126	15,437	574	1,795
1984	10,696	3,715	1,388	16,069	659	1,638
1985	10,744	3,775	1,489	16,359	736	2,088
1986	10,605	3,958	1,583	17,195	831	2,009
1987	10,500	4,148	1,680	18,456	900	3,391
1988	11,149	4,231	1,798	19,016	955	5,896
1989	11,670	4,301	1,911	19,657	1,025	6,595
1990	14,143	4,447	2,122	21,200	1,201	7,542
1991	17,316	4,928	2,301	23,029	1,678	11,105
1992	20,906	5,365	2,601	25,087	3,158	13,028
1993	22,006	5,637	2,829	25,242	3,909	15,537
1994	22,749	5,993	3,169	26,098	4,067	21,105
1995	22,764	6,225	3,436	25,553	4,657	25,956
1996	22,440	6,490	3,695	23,677	4,947	28,825
1997	19,549	6,785	3,844	19,918	4,920	30,389
1998	16,891	7,119	3,890	16,873	4,965	32,340
1999	15,769	7,381	3,938	15,740	4,835	31,901
2000	14,983	7,557	3,982	13,482	4,789	32,296
2001	15,547	7,941	4,153	12,802	5,104	33,376
2002	18,256	8,436	4,340	12,025	5,353	38,199
2003	21,404	8,855	4,524	12,670	5,686	38,657
2004	24,619	9,416	4,887	12,668	6,036	40,024
2005	28,568	9,974	4,993	13,116	6,488	42,410
2006	30,187	10,247	5,073	12,317	6,948	44,388
2007	30,373	10,916	5,409	11,624	7,346	48,540
2008	34,608	11,699	6,190	11,226	7,831	50,669
2009	50,360	12,588	6,471	11,806	8,635	
2010	64,705	13,745	6,703		9,020	

Source: Author's compilation based on Ben-Shalom, Moffitt, and Scholz (2011); Social Security Administration (2012a, 2012b).
Note: Current dollars, in millions

This paper was prepared for the conference "The Legacy of the War on Poverty: Implications for the Future of Anti-Poverty Policies," held at the National Poverty Center, University of Michigan in Ann Arbor on June 12–13, 2012. I am grateful to Liana Fox for help preparing the figures on poverty trends, to Yonatan Ben-Shalom, Robert Moffitt, and John Karl Scholz for generously sharing their data on trends in safety net expenditures and caseloads, and to Katherine Magnuson, Alice O'Connor, Kristin Seefeldt, and the volume editors for helpful comments.

NOTES

1. Given the onerous application process and stigma associated with applying, it is also likely that potential applicants found it less worthwhile to apply if they were going to the welfare office only to get Food Stamps, rather than both welfare and Food Stamps. Conversely, when Medicaid eligibility was expanded, Food Stamp applications increased, because once parents were at the welfare office applying for Medicaid, it was worth also applying for Food Stamps (Currie 2006).
2. The disability criteria are rather strict (Social Security Administration 2012b). SSI also covers disabled adults and elderly but I focus here only on families with disabled children.
3. These positive results are consistent with earlier evidence from the Negative Income Tax (NIT) experiments. Although results varied by site and population group, most estimates point to positive impacts of the NIT on child health and educational outcomes (Currie 1997).
4. Provisions to provide tax deductions or credits for employees with child-care costs date back even further, to the 1950s. Further legislation was enacted in the 1970s, and the Dependent Care Assistance Plan (DCAP) was introduced in the 1980s. However, these provisions primarily benefit middle- and upper-income families so I do not discuss them here. I also do not discuss publicly supported preschool programs for low-income children such as Head Start (covered in chapter 2, this volume).

REFERENCES

Almond, Douglas, Hilary W. Hoynes, and Diane Whitmore Schanzenbach. 2011. "Inside the War on Poverty: The Impact of Food Stamps on Birth Outcomes." *Review of Economics and Statistics* 93(2): 387–403.

Assistant Secretary for Planning and Evaluation (ASPE). 2008. "Child Care Eligibility and Enrollment Estimates for Fiscal Year 2005." Washington: U.S. Department of Health and Human Services. Available at: http://aspe.hhs.gov/hsp/08/cc-eligibility/ib.pdf (accessed April 5, 2013).

Baker, Kevin. 2008. "Do Cash Transfer Programs Improve Infant Health? Evidence from the 1993 Expansion of the Earned Income Tax Credit." Mimeo, University of Notre Dame.

Ben-Shalom, Yonatan, Robert Moffitt, and John Karl Scholz. 2011. "An Assessment of the Effectiveness of Anti-Poverty Programs in the United States." *NPC* working paper 11-19.

Ann Arbor: University of Michigan. Available at: http://npc.umich.edu/publications/u/2011-19_NPC_Working_Paper.pdf (accessed April 5, 2013).

Berg, Joel. 2010. "Doing What Works to End U.S. Hunger: Federal Food Programs Are Effective, but Can Work Better." Washington, D.C.: Center for American Progress. Available at: http://www.americanprogress.org/wp-content/uploads/issues/2010/03/pdf/dww_hunger.pdf (accessed April 5, 2013).

Blank, Rebecca. 2007. "Improving the Safety Net for Single Mothers Who Face Serious Barriers to Work." *The Future of Children* 17(2): 183–97.

Chappell, Marisa. 2010. *The War on Welfare: Family, Poverty, and Politics in Modern America.* Philadelphia: University of Pennsylvania Press.

Chatterji, Pinka, and Jeanne Brooks-Gunn. 2004. "WIC Participation, Breast-Feeding Practices, and Well-Baby Care Among Unmarried, Low-Income Mothers." *American Journal of Public Health* 94(8): 1324–27.

Coleman-Jensen, Alisha, Mark Nord, Margaret Andrews, and Steven Carlson. 2011. "Household Food Security in the United States in 2010." *Economic Research Service* report 125. Washington: U.S. Department of Agriculture. Available at: http://www.ers.usda.gov/media/121076/err125_2_.pdf (accessed April 5, 2013).

Currie, Janet. 1995. *Welfare and the Well-Being of Children.* Chur, Switzerland: Harwood Academic.

———. 1997. "The Effect of Welfare on Child Outcomes: What We Know and What We Need to Know." *JCPR* working paper. Chicago: Northwestern University and the University of Chicago Joint Center for Poverty Research. Available at: http://www.ipr.northwestern.edu/jcpr/workingpapers/wpfiles/effectonchild.PDF (accessed April 5, 2013).

———. 2003. "Food and Nutrition Programs." In *Means-Tested Transfer Programs in the United States*, edited by Robert Moffitt. Chicago: University of Chicago Press.

———. 2006. *The Invisible Safety Net: Protecting the Nation's Poor Children and Families.* Princeton, N.J.: Princeton University Press.

Currie, Janet, and Marianne Bitler. 2004. "Does WIC Work? The Effect of WIC on Pregnancy and Birth Outcomes." *Journal of Policy Analysis and Management* 23(4): 73–91.

———. 2005. "The Changing Association Between Prenatal Participation in WIC and Birth Outcomes in New York City: What Does It Mean?" *Journal of Policy Analysis and Management* 24(4): 687–90.

Dahl, Gordon, and Lance Lochner. 2012. "The Impact of Family Income on Child Achievement: Evidence from Changes in the Earned Income Tax Credit." *American Economic Review* 102(5): 1927–956.

Davies, Gareth. 1996. *From Opportunity to Entitlement: The Transformation and Decline of Great Society Liberalism.* Lawrence: University Press of Kansas.

Dickert, Stacy, Scott Houser, and John Karl Scholz. 1995. "The Earned Income Tax Credit and Transfer Programs: A Study of Labor Market and Program Participation." *Tax Policy and the Economy* 9(1): 1–50.

Duggan, Mark, and Melissa Schettini Kearney. 2007. "The Impact of Child SSI Enrollment on Household Outcomes: Evidence from the SIPP." *Journal of Policy Analysis and Management* 26(4): 861–86.

Duncan, Gregory, and Jeanne Brooks-Gunn, eds. 1997. *The Consequences of Growing Up Poor.* New York: Russell Sage Foundation.

Eissa, Nada, and Hilary Williamson Hoynes. 2004. "Taxes and the Labor Market Participation of Married Couples: The Earned Income Tax Credit." *Journal of Public Economics* 88(9–10): 1931–958.

Evans, William, and Craig Garthwaite. 2010. "Giving Mom a Break: The Impact of Higher EITC Payments on Maternal Health." *NBER* working paper 16296. Cambridge, Mass.: National Bureau of Economic Research.

Fix, Michael, Randall Capps, and Neeraj Kaushal. 2009. "Welfare Reform and Immigrants: An Overview." In *Immigration Children and Families on Welfare Reform's 10th Anniversary*, edited by Michael Fix. New York: Russell Sage Foundation.

Food Research Action Center (FRAC). 2012. "SNAP/Food Stamp Participation 2011." Washington, D.C.: FRAC. Available at: http://frac.org/reports-and-resources/snap food-stamp-monthly-participation-data (accessed April 8, 2013).

Frongillo, Edward, Diana Jyoti, and Sonya Jones. 2006. "Food Stamp Participation Is Associated with Better Academic Learning Among School Children." *The Journal of Nutrition* 136(4): 1077–80.

Gabe, Thomas. 2010. "Poverty in the United States: 2009." Washington, D.C.: Congressional Research Service.

Gilens, Martin. 1999. *Why Americans Hate Welfare: Race, Media, and the Politics of Antipoverty Policy*. Chicago: University of Chicago Press.

Gillette, Michael. 2010. *Launching the War on Poverty: An Oral History*. Oxford: Oxford University Press.

Harris, David. 2012. "The Child Tax Credit: How the United States Underinvests in Its Youngest Children in Cash Assistance and How Changes to the Child Tax Credit Could Help." Ph.D. diss. Columbia University School of Social Work.

Herbst, Chris, and Erdal Tekin. 2010a. "Child Care Subsidies and Child Development." *Economics of Education Review* 29(4): 618–38.

———. 2010b. "The Impact of Child Care Subsidies on Child Well-Being: Evidence from Geographic Variation in the Distance to Social Service Agencies." *NBER* working paper 16250. Cambridge, Mass.: National Bureau of Economic Research.

———. 2011. "Child Care Subsidies and Childhood Obesity." *Review of Economics of the Household* 9(3): 349–78.

Hotz, Joseph, and John Karl Scholz. 2006. "Examining the Effect of the Earned Income Tax Credit on the Labor Market Participation of Families on Welfare." *NBER* working paper 11968. Cambridge, Mass.: National Bureau of Economic Research.

Hoynes, Hilary, Douglas Miller, and David Simon. 2011. "Income, the Earned Income Tax Credit, and Infant Health." Working paper. Davis: University of California. Available at: http://www.econ.ucdavis.edu/faculty/hoynes/working_papers/Hoynes-Miller-Simon-EITC.pdf (accessed April 8, 2013).

Hoynes, Hilary, Marianne Page, and Ann Stevens. 2011. "Can Targeted Transfers Improve Birth Outcomes? Evidence from the Introduction of the WIC Program." *Journal of Public Economics* 95(9–10): 813–27.

Hoynes, Hilary W., and Diane Whitmore Schanzenbach. 2009. "Consumption Responses to In-Kind Transfers: Evidence from the Introduction of the Food Stamp Program." *American Economic Journal: Applied Economics* 1(4): 109–39.

———. 2012. "Work Incentives and the Food Stamp Program." *Journal of Public Economics* 96(1–2): 151–62.

Hoynes, Hilary W., Diane Whitmore Schanzenbach, and Douglas Almond. 2012. " Long Run Impacts of Childhood Access to the Safety Net." *NBER* working paper 18535. Cambridge, Mass.: National Bureau of Economic Research.

Internal Revenue Service. 2012. "EITC Statistics." Washington: Government Printing Office. Available at: http://www.eitc.irs.gov/central/eitcstats (accessed April 8, 2013).

Johnson, Anna, Rebecca Ryan, and Jeanne Brooks-Gunn. 2012. "Child Care Subsidies: Do They Impact the Quality of Care Children Experience?" *Child Development* 83(4): 1444–461.

Johnson, Lyndon B. 1964a. "Annual Message to the Congress on the State of the Union." January 8, 1964. Washington: Government Printing Office. Available at: http://www.lbjlib.utexas.edu/johnson/archives.hom/speeches.hom/640108.asp (accessed April 8, 2013).

———. 1964b. "Remarks Upon Signing the Economic Opportunity Act." August 20, 1964. Washington: Government Printing Office. Available at: http://www.presidency.ucsb.edu/ws/index.php?pid=26452#axzz1e9o0GGSW (accessed April 8, 2013)

———. 1964c. "Economic Report of the President." Washington: Government Printing Office. Available at: http://www.presidency.ucsb.edu/economic_reports/1964.pdf (accessed April 8, 2013).

Joyce, Theodore, Diane Gibson, and Silvie Colman. 2005. "The Changing Association between Prenatal Participation in WIC and Birth Outcomes in New York City." *Journal of Policy Analysis and Management* 24(4): 661–85.

Kaushal, Neeraj. 2007. "Do Food Stamps Cause Obesity? Evidence from Immigrant Experience." *Journal of Health Economics* 26(5): 968–91.

Kowaleski-Jones, Lori, and Greg Duncan. 2002. "Effects of Participation in the WIC Program on Birthweight: Evidence from the National Longitudinal Survey of Youth." *American Journal of Public Health* 92(5): 799–804.

Lampman, Robert J. 1973. "What Does It Do for the Poor? A New Test for National Policy." *Institute for Research on Poverty* discussion paper 180-73. Madison: University of Wisconsin. Available at: http://www.irp.wisc.edu/publications/dps/pdfs/dp18073.pdf (accessed April 8, 2013).

Lee, Bong Joo, and Lucy Mackey-Bilaver. 2007. "Effects of WIC and Food Stamp Program Participation on Child Outcomes." *Children and Youth Services Review* 29(4): 501–17.

Lynn, Lawrence. 1977. "A Decade of Policy Developments in the Income-Maintenance System." In *A Decade of Federal Antipoverty Programs: Achievements, Failures, and Lessons*, edited by Robert Haveman. New York: Academic Press.

Magnuson, Katherine, and Elizabeth Votruba-Drzal. 2009. "Enduring Influences of Childhood Poverty." In *Changing Poverty, Changing Policies*, edited by Maria Cancian and Sheldon Danziger. New York: Russell Sage Foundation.

Mayer, Susan. 1997. *What Money Can't Buy.* Cambridge, Mass.: Harvard University Press.

Meyer, Bruce, and Dan Rosenbaum. 2001. "Welfare, the Earned Income Tax Credit, and the Labor Supply of Single Mothers." *Quarterly Journal of Economics* 116(3): 1063–114.

Meyers, Alan, Amy Sampson, Michael Weitzman, B. L. Rogers, and H. Kayne. 1989. "School Breakfast Program and School Performance." *American Journal of Diseases of Children* 143(10): 1234–239.

Mincy, Ronald, Serena Klempin, and Heather Schmidt. 2011. "Income Support Policies for Low-Income Men and Noncustodial Fathers: Tax and Transfer Programs." *Annals of the American Academy of Political and Social Science* 635(2011): 240–61.

Moffitt, Robert, ed. 1998. *Welfare, the Family, and Reproductive Behavior.* Washington, D.C.: National Academies Press.

——. 2003. "The Negative Income Tax and the Evolution of U.S. Welfare Policy." *Journal of Economic Perspectives* 17(3): 119–40.

Murphy, J. Michael, Maria E. Pagano, Joan Nachmani, Peter Sperling, Shirley Kane, and Ronald E. Kleinman. 1998. "The Relationship of School Breakfast to Psychosocial and Academic Functioning: Cross-Sectional and Longitudinal Observations in an Inner-City School Sample." *Archives of Pediatric and Adolescent Medicine* 152(9): 899–907.

Murray, Charles. 1984. *Losing Ground: American Social Policy, 1950–1980.* New York: Basic Books.

Neumark, David, and William Wascher. 2001. "Using the EITC to Help Poor Families: New Evidence and a Comparison with the Minimum Wage." *National Tax Journal* 54(2): 281–317.

Patterson, James. 2000. *America's Struggle Against Poverty in the Twentieth Century.* Cambridge, Mass.: Harvard University Press.

Plotnick, Robert, and Felicity Skidmore. 1975. *Progress Against Poverty.* New York: Academic Press.

Roosevelt, Franklin Delano. 1935. "Annual Message to the Congress on the State of the Union, January 1935." Washington: Government Printing Office. Available at: http://www.presidency.ucsb.edu/ws/?pid=14890 (accessed April 9, 2013)

Ruhm, Christopher, and Jane Waldfogel. 2012. "Long-Term Effects of Early Childhood Care and Education." *Nordic Economic Policy Review* 1:23–51.

Scholz, John Karl. 1994. "The Earned Income Tax Credit: Participation, Compliance, and Anti-Poverty Effectiveness." *National Tax Journal* 48(1): 59–81.

Scholz, John Karl, Robert Moffitt, and Benjamin Cowan. 2009. "Trends in Income Support." In *Changing Poverty, Changing Policies,* edited by Maria Cancian and Sheldon Danziger. New York: Russell Sage Foundation.

Short, Kathleen. 2011. "The Research Supplemental Poverty Measure: 2010." *CPS* report P60–241. Washington: U.S. Department of Commerce.

Skocpol, Theda. 1995. *Protecting Soldiers and Mothers: The Political Origins of Social Policy in the United States.* Cambridge, Mass.: Harvard University Press.

Smeeding, Timothy. 1975. "Measuring the Economic Welfare of Low-Income Households, and the Anti-Poverty Effectiveness of Cash and Non-Cash Transfer Programs." Ph.D. diss. University of Wisconsin-Madison.

Social Security Administration. 2012a. "SSI Monthly Statistics." Washington, D.C.: Government Printing Office. Available at: http://www.ssa.gov/policy/docs/statcomps/ssi_monthly/index.html (accessed April 8, 2013).

——. 2012b. "SSI Annual Report." Washington: Government Printing Office. Available at: http://www.ssa.gov/oact/ssir/SSI11/toc.html (accessed April 8, 2013).

Stats, Jeanette. 1970. *Door to Opportunity: Title V, Economic Opportunity Act.* Washington: Government Printing Office.

Steensland, Brian. 1998. *The Failed Revolution: America's Struggle over Guaranteed Income Policy.* Princeton, N.J.: Princeton University Press.

Strully, Kate, David Rehkopf, and Ziming Xuan. 2010. "Effects of Prenatal Poverty on Infant Health: State Earned Income Tax Credits and Birthweight." *American Sociological Review* 75(10): 534–62.

Swan, Patricia. 1983. "Food Consumption by Individuals in the United States: Two Major Surveys." *American Review of Nutrition* 3(July): 413–32.

U.S. Census Bureau. 2012. "Historical Poverty Tables." Washington: U.S. Department of Commerce. Available at: http://www.census.gov/hhes/www/poverty/data/historical/index.html

U.S. Department of Agriculture (USDA). 1969. "Dietary Levels of Households in the United States, Spring 1965." Washington: Government Printing Office. Available at: http://www.ars.usda.gov/SP2UserFiles/Place/12355000/pdf/6566/hfcs6566_rep_6.pdf (accessed April 8, 2013).

——— . 1985. "Dietary Levels: Households in the United States, Spring 1977." Washington: Government Printing Office. Available at: http://www.ars.usda.gov/SP2UserFiles/Place/12355000/pdf/7778/nfcs7778_rep_h-11.pdf (accessed April 8, 2013).

——— . 1994. "Food Consumption and Dietary Levels of Households in the United States, 1987–88." Washington: Government Printing Office. Available at: http://www.ars.usda.gov/SP2UserFiles/Place/12355000/pdf/8788/nfcs8788_rep_87-h-1.pdf (accessed April 8, 2013).

——— . 2011. "Special Supplemental Nutrition Program for Women, Infants, and Children (WIC) Eligibles and Coverage—2000 to 2009: National and State-Level Estimates of the Population of Women, Infants, and Children Eligible for WIC Benefits, Executive Summary." Washington: Government Printing Office. Available at: http://www.fns.usda.gov/ora/menu/published/wic/FILES/WICEligibles2000–2009Summary.pdf (accessed April 8, 2013).

——— . 2012a. "From Food Stamps to the Supplemental Nutrition Assistance Program: Legislative Timeline." Washington: Government Printing Office. Available at: http://www.fns.usda.gov/snap/rules/Legislation/timeline.pdf (accessed April 8, 2013).

——— . 2012b. "Supplemental Nutrition Assistance Program: A Short History of SNAP." Washington: Government Printing Office. Available at: http://www.fns.usda.gov/snap/rules/Legislation/about.htm (accessed April 8, 2013).

——— . 2012c. "School Breakfast." Washington: Government Printing Office. Available at: http://www.fns.usda.gov/cnd/breakfast/AboutBFast/SBPFactSheet.pdf (accessed April 8, 2013).

——— . 2012d. "National School Lunch Program." Washington: Government Printing Office. Available at: http://www.fns.usda.gov/cnd/lunch/AboutLunch/NSLPFactSheet.pdf (accessed April 8, 2013).

——— . 2012e. "WIC Program Participation and Costs." Washington: Government Printing Office. Available at: http://www.fns.usda.gov/pd/wisummary.htm (accessed April 8, 2013).

——— . 2012f. "Food Security in the United States." Washington: Government Printing Office. Available at: http://www.ers.usda.gov/topics/food-nutrition-assistance/food-security-in-the-us/key-statistics-graphics.aspx#trends (accessed April 8, 2013).

——— . 2012g. "Reaching Those in Need: State Supplemental Nutrition Assistance Program Participation Rates in 2010, Summary." Washington: Government Printing Office. Available at: http://www.fns.usda.gov/ora/menu/Published/snap/FILES/Participation/Reaching2010_Summary.pdf (accessed April 8, 2013).

U.S. Department of Health and Human Services. 2012. "Child Care and Development Fund:

FY 2012 Budget." Washington: Government Printing Office. Available at: http://www .acf.hhs.gov/programs/olab/budget/2012/cj/CCDF.pdf (accessed April 8, 2013).

Waldfogel, Jane. 2008. "Economic Dimensions of Social Policy." In *The Handbook of Social Policy*, edited by James Midgely, Martin Tracy, and Michelle Livermore. Thousand Oaks: Sage Publications.

———. 2009. "The Role of Family Policies in Antipoverty Policy." In *Changing Poverty, Changing Policies*, edited by Maria Cancian and Sheldon Danziger. New York: Russell Sage Foundation.

Wheeler, Raymond. 1967. "Hungry Children: Special Report." Atlanta, Ga.: Southern Regional Council.

Chapter 7

The Safety Net for the Elderly

Kathleen McGarry

When Lyndon Johnson declared a War on Poverty in 1964, the poverty rate was 19 percent, a rate deemed far too high for a nation with the wealth and resources of the United States. Yet far worse was the poverty rate for those age sixty-five or older, which stood at 35 percent in 1959 (data for 1964 are not available), more than twice the 17 percent rate among non-elderly adults.[1] Despite this inauspicious start, the War on Poverty has been a success for the elderly by almost any measure. In the most recent data available, the poverty rate for the elderly in 2010 was 9 percent, approximately one-quarter of what it once was and far lower than the poverty rate for children, 22 percent, or non-elderly adults, 13.7 percent.[2]

This dramatic success in reducing poverty among the elderly has spanned racial and ethnic groups and is evidenced even among the oldest-old. However, despite the impressive declines, segments of the elderly population remain who experience disproportionally high risks of poverty, suggesting there is more to do. For example, the poverty rate for elderly women living alone is nearly 20 percent—an enormous improvement from the 1965 rate of 63.3 percent, but unquestionably higher than that for many other groups.

Although the War on Poverty has produced stunning results for the elderly, these simple statistics tell only part of the story. For the elderly in particular, an income-based measure of well-being ignores many important factors. By some measures, the gain in well-being accruing to the elderly may be far less than the poverty rates indicate because items such as the soaring cost of health care are ignored. Conversely, the same numbers may mask even greater improvements in well-being because the availability of Medicare and Medicaid (see chapter 10, this volume), in-kind transfers such as Food Stamps, now the Supplemental Nutrition Assistance Program (SNAP), and the prevalence of owner-occupied homes are also ignored.

This chapter focuses on the income-related programs established or significantly expanded shortly after Lyndon Johnson's 1964 State of the Union speech.

RESOURCES OF THE ELDERLY BEFORE THE WAR ON POVERTY

The Social Security program has unquestionably played an enormously important role in improving the economic well-being of the elderly. Social Security was established in 1935 and throughout its decades of expansion the incomes of the elderly increased dramatically. Although it is impossible to say what incomes among those sixty-five or older would be without Social Security, it is clear that for low-income elderly, the program improved their standard of living relative to what it would have been in its absence and is the most important component of income by far.

Social Security is an entitlement program but it is not means tested; benefits are accrued by all those who engaged in substantial covered employment over their work life.[3] Although benefits are a function of earnings, the formula is progressive: benefits for lower-income workers replacing a larger fraction of earnings than for higher-income workers. Not only does Social Security constitute an important component of income, but as a lifetime annuity it insures against longevity risk — the prospect of living longer than expected and depleting resources. Through this insurance mechanism, Social Security provides an additional benefit over what would be an actuarial equivalent lump sum received at retirement.

Social Security also provides important insurance to spouses, widows, and dependents. Spouses who are not covered through their employment, or who have low benefits, are eligible for a spousal benefit of 50 percent of that of the covered worker. Furthermore, on the death of a covered spouse, the uncovered individual receives the full benefit to which the partner had been entitled. Spouses who have their own Social Security benefit are entitled to the larger of the benefit based on their earnings or 50 percent of their partner's benefit. Also, if they outlive their partner, they receive the maximum of their benefit or 100 percent of the deceased partner's benefit. Survivors of covered workers — widows and widowers and dependent children are entitled to survivor benefits even if the covered worker dies before claiming Social Security benefits.

Means-tested programs for the indigent elderly predate the Social Security Act, stemming back to the 1920s when various states began providing assistance to the poor elderly through Old Age Assistance Programs (OAA). By 1935, twenty-eight states had OAA programs in place (Grundmann 1985). Title 1 of the Social Security Act expanded these programs by providing federal matching funds to assist states in caring for their elderly. Although states were not required to have OAA programs, eventually all states did.

However, even with federal support, OAA benefit levels and eligibility requirements varied widely across states. As early as the 1940s, the Social Security Administration was concerned about the disparity across states and the low level of benefits in some. As Herman Grundmann notes, "In 1940 . . . payments in States with the highest payment levels were on the average about four times as high as in states with the lowest payment levels" (1985, 13). Changes in the federal matching formula instituted in 1946 that provided for higher sharing rates for states with low benefits, resulted in a decline in these differences and higher benefits overall, yet differences across states were still large. In 1960, for example, maximum OAA benefits ranged from $40 per month in Mississippi to $275 in Washington State (McGarry and Schoeni 2000). States also varied in the extent to which they placed various restrictions and limitations on benefits such as relative responsibility clauses that required children to provide financial support for their elderly parents, residency requirements limiting eligibility to those with a history of living in that state, and lien laws that allowed states to force the sale of a recipient's home at death to repay benefits. These restrictions likely limited enrollments as many elderly did not want to be a burden on their children or risk losing a family home. Finally, many state programs were underfunded and even needy elderly could fail to receive benefits or receive reduced amounts. These issues led the federal government to expand its role in reaching out and aiding the poor both by increasing Social Security benefits as described below and eventually replacing these OAA programs with the federal Supplemental Security Income (SSI) program.

Along with earnings, savings, and help from family members, the public programs of Social Security and OAA were working to begin to improve the well-being of the elderly even before the launch of the War on Poverty. Social Security in particular was expanding at a rapid pace. In 1950, at year end, 16.4 percent of the elderly population was receiving Social Security benefits and by 1965 that number had risen to 75.2 percent (Grundmann 1985). Poverty rates for the elderly had also begun to fall, declining from 35.2 percent in 1959 to 28.5 percent in 1966 (U.S. Census Bureau 2011b).[4] However, disparities across demographic groups were large, and some faced extraordinarily high rates of poverty. In 1964, for example, 59 percent of single elderly individuals living on their own were poor; this figure was even higher for women, 64 percent of whom had incomes below the poverty line (Orshansky 1967).[5]

Even in these early stages, Social Security was an important source of income for the elderly. In 1962, Social Security made up 31 percent of aggregate income for the elderly, and earnings 29 percent. Public assistance was a small component of income overall but was received by 13 percent of the elderly (Social Security Administration 2012b). However, benefits from the OAA program were typically small and incomes were thus low. Median family income among those receiving OAA benefits in 1973, the last year of the state-run OAA programs, was just $1,851 ($9,091 in 2010 dollars), far below the poverty threshold for a single person, let alone a married couple. Incomes were also low for the elderly population as a whole. The median income of families with a head age sixty-five or older in 1964 was just $3,376 ($23,747 in 2010 dollars) versus $7,752 ($54,538 in 2010 dollars) for those age forty-five to sixty-four (U.S. Bureau of the Census 1965).

Differences in well-being between whites and blacks were stark, in large part because of differences in lifetime earnings, but increases in Social Security coverage were beginning to help reduce the gap. In 1950, 21 percent of the elderly white population was receiving benefits from the Old Age, Survivors, and Disability Insurance program versus just 13 percent of the elderly black population. By 1962, these numbers had risen to 73 and 58 percent, a 3.5-fold increase for white elderly and a nearly 4.5-fold increase for blacks (Orshansky 1964). Despite the convergence in the receipt of Social Security, incomes for elderly blacks remain far behind those of whites. In 1967, the median income for elderly blacks was $8,774 (2010 dollars) and that for whites was $12,417, a 7 to 10 ratio. Although the difference in incomes was large, it was substantially less than the difference for the population as a whole, wherein the ratio of black to white income was 5.8 to 10 (Social Security Administration 2012b; U.S. Census Bureau 2010), suggesting that the progressivity of Social Security helped to reduce differences in income that were evident during the working years.

The 1964 *Economic Report of the President* defines poverty as "the inability to satisfy minimum needs" (Council of Economic Advisers 1964, 62).[6] Thus factors other than income, such as homeownership and savings, ought to inform our assessment of well-being. Asset income should be particularly important for the elderly because our life-cycle model calls for individuals to save during their working years and to spend down savings to support themselves during retirement. In 1965, the median net worth (assets less debts) for households headed by an elderly individual was $8,000, 70 percent more than the $4,700 for all households. Homeownership also plays an important role in contributing to resources, and here, too, resources were greater for the elderly. In 1970, the homeownership rate among households headed by an individual sixty-five or older was 67.5 percent, versus 41.2 percent for those younger than thirty-five (U.S. Census Bureau 2011a).

In addition to formal sources of support from Social Security, OAA, earnings and assets, poor elderly likely also received support from family. Such support was even mandated in many states by "relative responsibility" clauses included in their OAA programs. Although data do not exist on the extent of familial cash support, or even in-kind support such as caregiving or the provision of food, evidence is clear that families assisted considerably through shared housing. In 1940, just as Social Security was beginning to pay benefits, nearly 60 percent of elderly widows lived with their children. By 1960, this fraction had fallen to 40 percent, still a substantial number (McGarry and Schoeni 2000). Among all elderly individuals, the likelihood of shared residence was similarly high: 45 percent lived with relatives or unrelated individuals (Congressional Budget Office 1988). In sharing a home and thus resources, the financial situation of the elderly was better than it would have been had they been living independently. Mollie Orshansky (1965) estimates that in 1963, an additional 10 percent of elderly individuals would have been poor were it not for the income of the relatives with whom they shared a home, raising the estimated poverty rate that year from 30 to 40 percent.

WAR ON POVERTY LEGISLATION SINCE 1964

The financial situation for the elderly at the time of Johnson's declaration of the War on Poverty was obviously bleak, both at an absolute level and relative to that for the non-elderly. Not only were poverty rates extremely high, but the elderly had little hope of escaping to the ranks of the nonpoor through education or employment, some of the principal tenets of the War on Poverty. Yet, despite these difficulties, in many respects, the improvement in the financial status of the elderly is one of the great successes of the War on Poverty.

The Older Americans Act 1965

For the elderly, a central element of Johnson's War on Poverty was the Older Americans Act. This 1965 legislation explicitly stated that it was the responsibility of the government to "assist our older people to secure equal opportunity to the full and free enjoyment of the following objectives": "adequate income in retirement," "suitable housing," and "no discriminatory personnel practices because of age." Although the act explicitly mentions "discriminatory personnel practices," and Johnson's 1967 State of the Union address repeated this goal stating that "We must eliminate by law unjust discrimination in employment because of age," the Civil Rights Act of 1964 prohibited discrimination based on race, religion, or sex but not age. Age discrimination was first explicitly prohibited in 1967 when Congress passed the Age Discrimination in Employment Act, which protected workers age forty to sixty-five against discrimination in employment. Those sixty-five or older were not covered until 1986, when amendments extended the upper age to seventy.[7]

The legislation did not establish specific income maintenance programs, but instead provided for grants to be made to state and local agencies to help fund various support services, such as caregiver support, nutritional services, and social services—items that likely greatly enhanced the well-being of the elderly, despite having little direct effect on official poverty rates. However, through its stated goal of ensuring adequate income for the elderly, the Older Americans Act set the stage for increases in Social Security benefits and the establishment of SSI soon thereafter and demonstrated explicitly that the well-being of the elderly was an important national concern.

Social Security Increases Since 1965

In 1964, approximately 75 percent of the elderly were receiving Social Security benefits and the average monthly benefit for retired workers was $545 (2010 dollars). As figure 7.1 makes clear, benefits soon began to increase dramatically in real terms. The 1965 amendments to the Social Security Act launched the Medicare and Medicaid programs but also served to increase the incomes of the elderly by providing an across-the-board increase of 7 percent in Social Security benefits. In 1967, Johnson used his State of the Union address to call for additional increases in Social Security benefits as part of the continuing War on Poverty—"Let us insure that older Americans . . . share in their Nation's progress"—and proposing an increase of "at least 15 percent" for all those who were currently receiving benefits (Johnson 1967). In response, Congress approved an increase of 13 percent, in addition to the initial 7 percent increase, along with other changes, including increases in the min-

FIGURE 7.1 / Average Monthly Social Security Benefit for Retired Workers

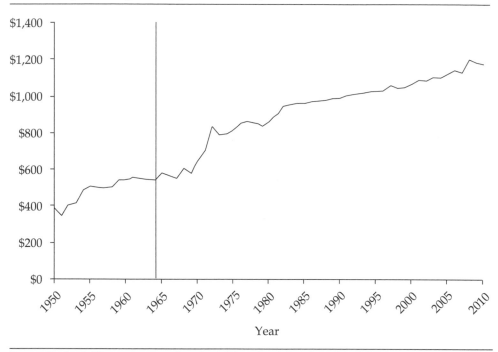

Source: Author's illustration based on Social Security Administration (2012a).

imum benefit. In signing the 1967 amendment, Johnson noted that "this means that 9 million people will have risen above the poverty line since the beginning of 1964," thus clearly demonstrating his intent to use Social Security as an important weapon in his War on Poverty (Johnson 1968).

This reliance on Social Security to improve the economic well-being of older Americans accelerated in the years following the Johnson administration. The Tax Reform Act of 1969 increased Social Security benefits by 15 percent and a second increase, of 10 percent, was added in 1971. Finally, Congress increased benefits once again in 1972, this time by 20 percent, for a total of nearly 52 percent (compounded) over the three years between 1969 and 1972. This sharp rise is readily apparent in figure 7.1 and represents an increase of nearly 100 percent from 1964 to 1972.

Partially in response to these continued ad hoc increases, Congress passed the Social Security Amendments of 1972, indexing benefits to the consumer price index (Myers 1985).[8] Retired workers were thus protected against an erosion of benefits due to inflation and not dependent on Congress to implement ad hoc increases, increases that may have been difficult to enact in times of economic downturn or when the Social Security trust fund came under financial pressure, as it soon did. Other changes enacted in 1972 included an increase in the widows' benefit, and the establishment of a special minimum benefit to provide assistance to those with low earnings but significant attachment to the labor force. These last two changes directly targeted those who were often near or below the poverty line in old age, further strengthening Social Security's role in reducing poverty among the elderly.

Supplemental Security Income

Despite the growing generosity of the Social Security program, many elderly continued to have incomes below the poverty line. These impoverished elderly were often entitled to benefits from state-run Old Age Assistance programs, programs that continued to be criticized on many fronts, including the typically low level of benefits and the variation across states in both benefits and eligibility guidelines. In addition to raising Social Security benefit levels, the 1972 amendments replaced these state-run OAA programs with the federal means-tested Supplemental Security Income program. SSI provides a guaranteed annual income floor for the elderly, the blind, and the disabled. This federal program was part of Richard Nixon's Family Assistance plan, which originally included an income guarantee for the non-elderly poor as well—a concept Congress rejected. That a guaranteed income program was successfully implemented for the elderly, blind, and disabled is noteworthy. It attests to the nation's recognition that employment was not expected from these groups and that the government would provide assistance to help meet their needs if they could not. In addition to the income guarantee, those entitled to SSI benefits are eligible for Medicaid and for Food Stamps in most states, important in-kind benefits.

The SSI program first began paying benefits in 1974 with income guarantees of $140 per month for singles and $210 for couples, indexed for inflation; in 2012, the amounts were $698 and $1,048. The magnitude of an individual's benefit is determined by subtracting countable income from the guaranteed amount. Countable income is defined as total income less a series of disregards. Thus, in most cases a beneficiary's actual income is increased to an amount slightly above the guarantee. Disregards include the first $20 of unearned income (typically Social Security) and $20 of irregularly or infrequently received income, as well as the first $65 of earned income and 50 percent of any additional earned income. Notably, these disregards are defined in nominal dollars and have not increased since the program's inception.

In addition to the income requirements, SSI includes an asset test: to be eligible for benefits, individuals must have assets below $2,000 and couples below $3,000. Again, several exclusions determine the value of assets, including life insurance, small sums for burial expenses, and, importantly, the value of an owner-occupied home.[9] These asset limits were initially set at $1,500 and $2,250—amounts that if increased for inflation would be $7,000 and $10,500 in 2012. So while the income guarantees themselves have kept up with inflation, in practice, the use of nominal amounts with respect to the income disregards and the asset test set has made the program less generous over time.[10]

States have the option of supplementing the federal SSI guarantees. In 2011, all but six states and the District of Columbia had supplemental programs—although these programs are not always targeted to the elderly and in many cases are available only to those residing in some sort of assisted living facility. However, even when states do supplement the federal income amounts, rarely do the amounts of the guarantees rise above the poverty line.[11]

The number of elderly individuals receiving SSI benefits increased sharply in the first years of the program. In 1974, 1.865 million people were receiving benefits as aged recipients. This number peaked in 1975 at 2.3 million, fell to just 1.185 million in 2009 (Trout and Mattson 1984; Social Security Administration 2012a), and will likely continue to decline as Social Security benefits increase.[12]

Despite the extremely low income levels required for eligibility, many of those who could receive benefits are not enrolled in the program. Several studies using a variety of data sets have consistently found participation rates of approximately 50 to 60 percent (Menefee, Edwards, and Schieber 1981; Warlick 1982; McGarry 1996, 2002).[13] This low participation is puzzling, particularly in the face of the numerous outreach programs that have tried, and by and large failed, to increase participation significantly (U.S. General Accounting Office 1976).[14] Explanations include lack of knowledge or understanding about the program, an individual's perception that he or she is not in need of or entitled to benefits, and the stigma of receiving welfare.[15] Studies attempting to address these issues suggest that stigma and the belief that one does not need assistance are important factors in explaining the low take-up of benefits.[16] Thus, SSI could do more to aid the low-income elderly were benefits paid to all those who are eligible to enroll.

An alternative means of reaching the elderly poor would be a minimum Social Security benefit. Such a benefit would not be affected by the low rate of take-up evident for many means-tested programs. In fact, Social Security did contain such a provision and when Social Security benefits were increased in the 1960s and early 1970s the minimum benefit was increased as well, nearly doubling from 1967 to 1972. The difficulty in addressing poverty through a minimum benefit is that because means testing is not required for eligibility, individuals with substantial income from other sources and those who have perhaps worked in uncovered employment for most of their lives, would benefit as well. In an attempt to avoid this problem, the 1972 Social Security Amendments also established a special minimum benefit for those with low Social Security benefits despite substantial histories of covered employment. Both minimum benefits gradually disappeared as wages of contributing workers grew quickly enough that regular benefits soon outstripped the legislated minimums (Myers 1985).

WHAT THESE PROGRAMS MEAN FOR WELL-BEING

Estimating the effect of Social Security and SSI on poverty rates is difficult as patterns of savings, labor force participation, and living arrangements would all have been different in absence of the programs or in the face of different benefit schedules.[17] However, the effects on well-being are undoubtedly large and have grown in importance since the War on Poverty began.

Income and Poverty

The correlation between well-being and the large increases in Social Security benefits enacted in the late 1960s and early 1970 is readily apparent in the trend in poverty, as is its continued role in income maintenance in the more recent period. Figure 7.2 illustrates that poverty rates for all age groups declined at a rapid rate throughout the 1960s as the economy grew and the War on Poverty gained steam, but that rates for the elderly declined far more sharply and continued to fall in the first half of the 1970s, whereas those for other groups remained constant. Gary Engelhardt and Jonathan Gruber call the decline in poverty "One of the most striking trends in elderly well-being in the twentieth century" (2004, 2). The authors assess the importance of Social Security income in driving the decline in poverty rates from 1967 to 2000, and conclude that increased Social Security benefits explain nearly all the decrease in poverty. The poverty rate for the elderly has continued to gradually decline over time, avoiding the recent uptick in poverty experienced by other age groups, a rise correlated with the downturns in the economy, increases in unemployment, and cutbacks in spending on public assistance programs. The divergent trends are likely attributable in large part to the protection afforded Social Security recipients from the automatic indexation of benefits, a policy that ensures that the value of Social Security does not decline in real terms during economically difficult times.

Although Social Security has improved the financial position of the elderly, SSI has also had an important effect. The transition from state OAA programs to the federal SSI program resulted in an immediate increase in income among the poorest elderly; estimates suggest that the median income of OAA recipients rose by one-third from 1973 to 1974 as recipients transitioned between programs. In addition, an estimated 2.8 million elderly people who did not qualify for benefits under state OAA programs became eligible for assistance under the new program (Burke and Burke 1974). SSI also appeared to reduce the stigma associated with welfare receipt that plagued state-run programs, thus benefiting participants and perhaps inducing greater take-up (Tissue 1978; Schieber 1978), although it is likely that some stigma remains.

However, because the federal SSI income guarantees and those in most state supplemental programs are below the poverty line, the effects of SSI on the poverty rate itself are somewhat limited. Jennifer Warlick estimates that in its first year, SSI was responsible for "lifting one in of five out of poverty" (1982, 237). A poverty rate of 12.5 percent in 1974, subsequent to the dramatic Social Security increase, would correspond to a reduction of 2.5 percentage points. Although the effect on poverty might be small, particularly relative to that of Social Security, SSI does have an important impact on the poverty gap.[18] Kathleen McGarry (2002), using data collected in 1993, finds that though SSI income reduced the poverty rate by just 1 percentage point, it reduced the poverty gap by nearly 30 percent; other estimates of the effect are even greater (Schieber 1978).

Not only did poverty fall, but incomes for the elderly also rose dramatically,

FIGURE 7.2 / Poverty Rates by Age

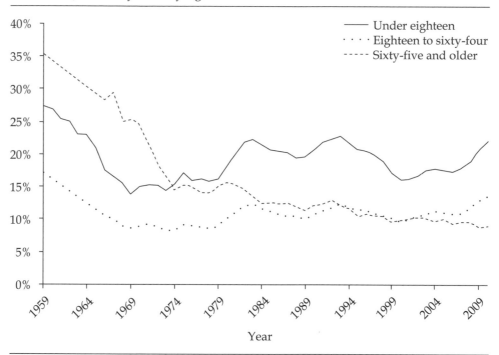

Source: Author's illustration based on U.S. Census Bureau (2011b).

doubling in real terms from 1967 to 2010. Income for married couples increased from $22,021 to $44,718 while that for unmarried individuals increased from $8,526 to $17,261 (in 2010 dollars). In contrast, median household income for the country as a whole rose by just 21 percent. As noted, Social Security played a key role in this rise as it made up nearly 40 percent of income over much of this period (Social Security Administration 2012b). In contrast, the importance of SSI and other public assistance has fallen dramatically over time from 2.7 percent of aggregate income in 1968 to just 0.6 percent in 2008 (Purcell 2009). However, among those receiving benefits from SSI, the amounts were significant, averaging $4,488 in 2008 dollars suggesting that few could have afforded to live independently absent the program (Purcell 2009).

Most striking is the difference in the importance of the various components across portions of the income distribution. As shown in figures 7.3 and 7.4, those in the bottom 25 percent of the income distribution relied on Social Security for 84 percent of income in 2008, but for those in the top quartile, it constituted just 20 percent (Purcell 2009). In fact, the Social Security Administration estimates that in 2008 benefits accounted for more than half of the income of 52 percent of couples receiving benefits and for 73 percent of unmarried individuals, and an astounding 90 percent of income for 43 percent of unmarried beneficiaries (Social Security Administration 2010). Public assistance payments were obviously restricted to

FIGURE 7.3 / Components of Income 2008, Lowest Quartile

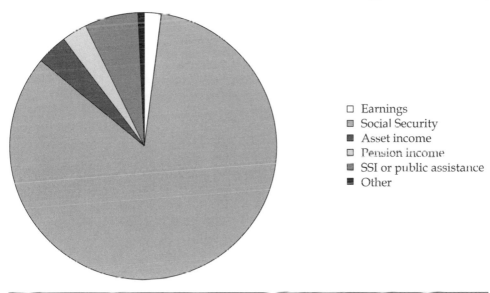

- □ Earnings
- ▣ Social Security
- ■ Asset income
- □ Pension income
- ▣ SSI or public assistance
- ■ Other

Source: Reproduced from Purcell (2009).

FIGURE 7.4 / Components of Income 2008, Highest Quartile

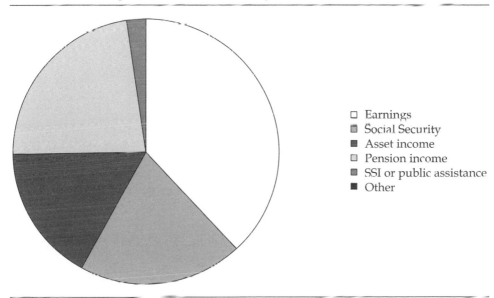

- □ Earnings
- ▣ Social Security
- ■ Asset income
- □ Pension income
- ▣ SSI or public assistance
- ■ Other

Source. Reproduced from Purcell (2009).

FIGURE 7.5 / Poverty Rates, Age Sixty-Five and Older

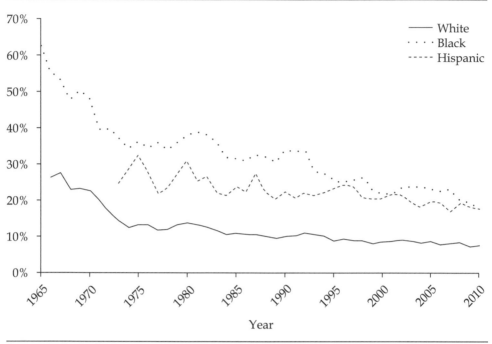

Source: Author's illustration based on U.S. Census Bureau (2011b).

those with the very lowest incomes, and thus even in the bottom quartile they make up only 6.5 percent of aggregate income—far lower than in earlier years (Purcell 2009).

The sharp declines in poverty for the elderly appear across racial and ethnic groups, but the initial difference by race persists, whites having a distinct advantage. Figure 7.5 shows the trends in poverty rates from 1965 to 2010 for whites, blacks, and Hispanics.[19] Although the differences across groups have narrowed greatly over time in absolute terms, they have changed little in relative terms; the poverty rate for blacks has remained at more than twice that of whites throughout the period. Trends in median incomes by race show a similar pattern (figure 7.6): the median income for elderly whites rose from $12,417 (2010 dollars) in 1967 to $27,214 in 2010, an increase of nearly 120 percent. Income for blacks rose from $8,774 to $16,463, or a change of just 88 percent (Social Security Administration 2012b). Thus, although income for both groups improved dramatically, blacks fell further behind whites. Differences by race in the components of income are important. For 19 percent of whites, Social Security was the only source of income; 31 percent relied on it for at least 90 percent of their income. For blacks, the percentages were 36 and 42 percent. The numbers for Hispanics were similarly high, at 36 and 38 percent. In contrast, blacks and Hispanic relied far less on income from

FIGURE 7.6 / Median Income by Race

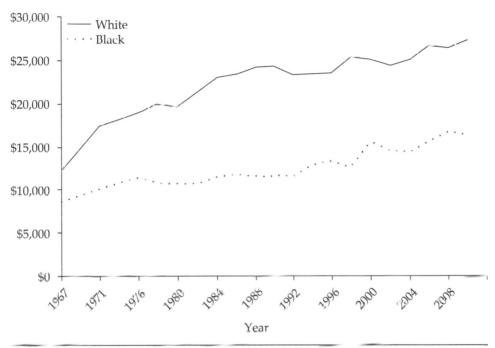

Source: Author's compilation based on Social Security Administration (2012b).
Note: In 2010 dollars.

assets, perhaps attesting to lower lifetime incomes and thus lower levels of savings (Social Security Administration 2012d).

Not shown here, because data are available only intermittently, are the shockingly high rates of poverty for some groups, such as unmarried elderly black and Hispanic women, who in 1999 had poverty rates of 26.4 and 25.4 percent respectively, and particularly among the subgroups of these women who were living alone, for whom the rates were 44 and 58 percent (Dalaker and Proctor 2000).[20]

Thus, despite the amazing gains realized by the elderly since the inception of the War on Poverty, the composition of the poor remains largely unchanged: poverty is still more likely among elderly women relative to men, among blacks relative to whites, and among unmarried relative to married individuals.

Redistribution

Because it is such an important part of the income for the elderly and because benefits have increased enormously over time, Social Security has the potential to play a significant role in not just the level of income but also in the distribution of income across various population subgroups. At first glance, Social Security would appear to redistribute income from those with high incomes to those with low incomes. The benefit formula itself is progressive, benefits replacing a larger share of former earnings for low-income retired workers relative to their high-income counterparts. The U.S. Government Accountability Office (2004) reports replacement rates for low earners at 49 percent, versus 37 percent for average earners and 24 percent for those earning the taxable maximum in each year. Because of the correlations between income and characteristics such as race and education, one would expect redistribution from whites to blacks, from high educated to low educated, and from those with a long work life to those with few years of covered employment.[21]

However, other factors offset this programmatic progressivity. Because benefits are paid as an annuity, when looking at the lifetime value of Social Security benefits, those with longer lifespans will receive a larger amount, all else held constant. Longevity is strongly positively related to income and education, and whites typically live longer than blacks, so the annuity aspect favors those with higher incomes and favors whites and thus adds a regressive component to the program (for example, Panis and Lillard 1996). However, more recent work suggests that the amount of redistribution attributable to differences in longevity is relatively small (Harris and Sabelhaus 2005; Brown, Coronado, and Fullerton 2009). Current forecasts predict that the difference between white and black life expectancy will increase over time and that that between whites and Hispanics will decline (Hendley and Bilimoria 1999). These changes may alter the importance of this mode of redistribution.

The availability of spousal benefits for spouses who have never worked or who have worked for just a few years also offset the progressivity of the program. High-income earners are more likely to have a spouse who has only a weak (if any) attachment to the labor force and such families thus benefit more from spousal and survivor benefits. On a household level then, benefits can be much more regressive with greater transfers to higher earning families (Gustman and Steinmeier 2001). This aspect of redistribution, however, will likely change as labor force participation rates rise across the board and high-income earners have spouses who also have high incomes.

Other Factors Affecting Financial Well-Being

The dramatic changes in poverty rates among the elderly observed throughout the 1960s and 1970s suggests that the income support programs targeting this group have been successful in improving their economic well-being. However, in many respects, the gains may be even greater than those based on simple comparisons of income levels over time. Benefits from in-kind transfer programs, particularly those from Medicare and Medicaid are large (see chapter 10, this volume) but the value of this insurance is not included in income measures. In addition to these health insurance programs, the low-income elderly are also likely to be eligible for

Food Stamps, also part of Johnson's War on Poverty (see chapter 6),[22] home energy assistance (specifically, the Low-Income Home Energy Assistance Program, or LIHEAP), and housing assistance. In 2010, 11.5 percent of the elderly received some sort of noncash food, housing, or energy benefit. Again, differences by race and income are substantial. Ten percent of elderly whites received such benefits, versus nearly 28 percent of blacks. Among those in the lowest income quintile, 34 percent received such benefits (Social Security Administration 2012d). Despite their importance to the low-income population, none of these benefits factor into poverty calculations.

In addition, the elderly consume very different consumption bundles or market baskets from non-elderly, making a comparison using poverty thresholds based on food consumption alone incomplete. For example, the elderly consume more medical care than the non-elderly, an expense not considered in determining the poverty thresholds or in their increase over time. Medical expenses not covered by Medicare or Medicaid are significant (Marshall, McGarry, and Skinner 2011). Similarly, the elderly are more likely than younger individuals to own their own homes: home ownership rates are over 80 percent for those sixty-five and older, compared with 50 to 60 percent for those in their thirties. The implicit value of owner-occupied homes, however, is not included in income measures, nor is the lower exposure to risk via increases in housing costs (U.S. Census Bureau 2012). The elderly also have more leisure time than working-age individuals to engage in home production, and may therefore face a lower cost of living, but because of health issues they may be constrained from tackling household chores or even completing regular errands such as grocery shopping. Driving or taking public transportation will become increasingly difficult with age, perhaps necessitating the need for — and thus expense of — taxicabs.

Recognition is widespread that the poverty measure is imperfect, but consensus on an alternative is not clear. The Census's supplemental poverty measure (SPM) explores the impacts of some alternative definitions of income, particularly the importance of out-of-pocket medical expenses and Food Stamp (SNAP) benefits, but many of the items listed above are not considered. Some of the changes implemented in the SPM lead to substantial changes in relative well-being both within and across demographic groups. For instance, changing income by varying the inclusion of benefits from programs such as SNAP and LIHEAP and by subtracting payroll taxes has little effect on the poverty rate of the elderly. Conversely, subtracting out-of-pocket medical expenses from income has a dramatic effect on the well-being of the elderly, nearly doubling the poverty rate, but has far less of an effect for younger groups. Housing assistance also plays an important role for the elderly (Short 2011) as does the value of an owner-occupied home. In an earlier series of experimental measures, the Census Bureau estimated poverty rates using various definitions of resources, some of which included the value of Medicare and Medicaid and that of an owner-occupied home. Adding the value of noncash transfers, including Medicare and Medicaid, lowers the poverty rate for the elderly in 2003 from 10.2 to 8.1 percent but perhaps surprisingly, the largest change comes from imputing a value to owner-occupied homes. This addition further decreases poverty to just 5.7 percent. For comparison, the poverty rate for those age eighteen to sixty-four falls from 10.8 to 8.5 percent with all additions and subtractions (Dalaker 2005).

The idea that items other than income affect one's well-being provides a strong argument for the notion that poverty is perhaps better measured by consumption or evidence of material hardship. The life-cycle model, for instance, predicts that elderly individuals should be decumulating assets to provide for consumption and thus any measure of well-being based solely on income is at odds with what is perhaps the fundamental model of economic behavior. David Cutler and Lawrence Katz (1991) find substantially lower poverty rates among the elderly when examining the level of consumption, the incidence of poverty in 1988 falling from 10.2 percent when based on income, to 3.8 percent based on consumption. This change is far greater than that for younger groups, as one would expect given the life-cycle model and the expectation that the elderly should be consuming from a lifetime of savings. Helen Levy (2009) uses direct measures of material hardship based on questions in the Health and Retirement Study, which ask whether an individual ever did not have enough food or medication because of the cost. She finds that material hardship exists even far above the poverty line, suggesting again that income is an imperfect measure of well-being.

Even these alternative measures may be insufficient to assess accurately the well-being of the elderly, particularly since the elderly appear to choose material hardship and lower consumption in exchange for living in their own homes. This phenomenon suggests that privacy is a valuable good, but one that is excluded from our consumption measures. Similarly, individuals may choose a lower standard of living to remain close to family members, enjoy amenities such as parks or public transportation, or better weather.

Other Changes in Well-Being

Many of these quality of life issues were recognized as important components of well-being in the programs implemented under the auspices of the Administration on Aging, established through Johnson's Older Americans Act, particularly through grants made to support state and local efforts in improving the welfare of the elderly. In his signing statement on July 14, 1965, Johnson described the Older Americans' Act as providing "seed corn" to help "expand our opportunities for enriching the lives of all citizens in this county" (1965). He noted that "the grants under this law will be modest" and that they would provide results, "at the hometown level." Grants through the Administration on Aging helped in the development of programs such as the foster grandparents program, with the Office of Economic Opportunity, nutritional programs such as meals at senior centers and home delivered meals, caregiver support programs, and other programs designed to help the elderly remain in their homes. These initiatives worked to improve the lives of the elderly, but their impact is missed when examining standard income and poverty measures. In the following section, I note some of the other less tangible improvements in the well-being of the elderly spurred on by the War on Poverty and arising in large part from the increases in income just illustrated.

Living Arrangements

The rise in the income of the elderly, particularly in the lower part of the income distribution, means that the elderly now have far more independence than they did prior to the expansion of the social support programs. In 1960, 40 percent of elderly widows lived with their children; by 1990, this figure had fallen to below 20 percent — continuing a trend started earlier in the century (McGarry and Schoeni 2000). Despite some discussion as to whether this trend is due to changes in attitudes regarding co-residence and a decline in the value of extended family (Kramarow 1995; Ruggles 1994), or to changes in income (for example, Michael, Fuchs, and Scott 1980), the most recent work indicates that Social Security played the primary role (McGarry and Schoeni 2000; Engelhardt, Gruber, and Perry 2005). If the increase in income has allowed for greater independence, focusing on measures of poverty will miss some of the improvement in well-being. Furthermore, if a portion of this newfound independence is among those who have incomes below the poverty line but who can now afford to live in their own homes, strict measures of the fraction of the elderly who are poor will understate their gains in well-being (Schwartz, Danziger, and Smolensky 1984). Given the dramatic declines in poverty, however, the changes resulting from the changes in living arrangements likely make up a relatively small component. Karen Holden (1988) estimates that the decline in poverty among elderly women would have been about 3 percentage points greater in the three decades between 1950 and 1980 had the patterns of living arrangements not changed. The observed decline over this period was nearly 36 percent.

Length of Retirement

Although one of the stated objectives of the Older Americans Act was to eliminate age discrimination in the workplace, with the goal of allowing older workers to avoid forced retirement, labor force participation of elderly men is lower today than in 1960. In 1960, the labor force participation rate of men ages sixty-five or older was 33.1 percent. By 1990, it had fallen to 16.3 percent; it has since risen to 22.1 percent in 2010, reversing the decades-old trend (Fullerton 1999; Toosst 2012).

This trend toward early retirement observed through much of this period is consistent with a wealth effect of Social Security — individuals could afford to purchase more leisure and they did — although the magnitude of the Social Security effect in driving the decline remains unclear (for example, Boskin 1977; Burtless and Moffitt 1984; Burtless 1986; Samwick 1998). The recent reversal of this trend in early retirement has also been attributed in part to changes in the Social Security program, particularly to the recent increase in the Social Security full retirement age (Gustman and Steinmeier 2009). An additional potential driver of the decline in labor force participation after age sixty-five is the value of Medicare. Not only is there a wealth effect accruing from the cash value of the insurance, but by separating health insurance from employment, Medicare allows individuals to obtain insurance coverage despite the presence of pre-existing conditions and other issues that may make health insurance purchases in the private market prohibitive for the elderly.

Length of Life

Because Social Security is a defined benefit program, it insures individuals against longevity risk, providing guaranteed income for as long as they live and ensuring a consumption floor at even the oldest ages. Over the same period that Social Security benefits increased and retirement ages decreased, life expectancy increased. Because the changes in Social Security throughout the 1960s and early 1970s left the full retirement age unchanged, the rising life expectancy led to a substantial increase both in the expected number of years for which an individual would collect Social Security as well as in the actuarial value of those benefits. One estimate puts the increase in the expected number of years of retirement at just over five years in a single generation, from the 1965 to 1970 period to the 2005 to 2010 period (Gendell 2008).

FUTURE

Despite the impressive gains experienced by the elderly over the last fifty years, the current economic environment presents substantial economic risk to the elderly, risk resulting from changes in pension plans, long-term care costs, and the likelihood of changes in both Social Security and Medicare.

In the past, most elderly had a secure source of income for as long as they lived. Social Security benefits for many were supplemented with employer-provided defined benefit pension plans.[23] These pension plans guaranteed a fixed income for life, often with ad hoc inflation adjustments. Over the last few decades, the shift from these defined benefit pension plans toward defined contribution (DC) plans, such as 401K plans and individual retirement accounts, has been dramatic. DC plans require individuals to manage their own investments over their working years and into retirement, thus incurring additional risk with regard to the rate of return and the possibility of a down market or poor investment choices. In addition, employees may fail to enroll or contribute enough funds to a plan, reducing the value at retirement directly, and potentially also reducing the amount of the employer contributions. Finally, because annuity markets are not well developed and few individuals choose to annuitize their account balances at retirement, individuals also bear significant longevity risk in the possibility that they outlive their resources. They may also have difficulty managing their funds particularly if they experience some form of cognitive decline at older ages.

As the economic downturn beginning in late 2007 has demonstrated all too well, these risks are real. Many who rely on defined contribution pension plans have seen their nest eggs shrink, and what remains now generates little income given the extremely low rates of interest in the years following the recent recession. These changes emphasize the value of the annuity aspect of social security.

Exacerbating these risks is the overall low level of asset holdings of the elderly. The Median nonhousing asset holdings of households age sixty-five or older in the 2008 Health and Retirement Study was just $61,000.[24] Differences in asset holdings by race are even more dramatic than the differences in incomes illustrated earlier. For blacks age sixty-five or older, median nonhousing wealth was just $3,700, and for whites $82,500. The limited nature of asset holdings will become of greater importance as longevity increases because the longer the retirement period, the more likely it is that these resources will be exhausted.

Even with careful management of assets, these scant resources could easily be depleted by a health or other shock. Foremost among the health-care risk is the risk of long-term care. The cost of a year in a nursing home averages over $75,000 for an individual, and the cost of formal home health care is similarly high. Yet, despite these potential expenses, few elderly purchase insurance coverage to protect against long-term care costs, suggesting that what resources the elderly do have could be quickly depleted providing for long-term care needs or other health expenses. The Medicaid program does provide coverage for long-term care expenses for the very poor and thus insures that all have access to some form of care. Furthermore, spousal impoverishment provisions in the Medicaid program can protect a portion of a couple's assets should one partner need nursing home care, also helping to stave off severe poverty among the elderly (for a discussion of this program, see chapter 10, this volume).

Policies to help the elderly deal with these risks have been and are continuing to be explored. Economists have contributed substantially, both to research on these issues and to changes in policy. Research in behavioral economics has led to proscribed changes in the defaults for pension plans under the Pension Protection Act (PPA). Employers may now automatically enroll workers in a retirement savings plan, using set contribution rates and investment choices (for an overview of the policy impact, see Beshears et al. 2008). These changes appear to have significantly increased savings in 401ks and similar pension savings vehicles. Past legislation pertaining to pension regulations, ERISA and REACT (Rapid ERISA Action Team), has addressed the disproportionately high rate of poverty among elderly women by changing the defaults in pension plans to make survivorship benefits the norm. Other changes regarding annuitization of defined contribution plan balances are being discussed, but more research is needed in understanding individual decisions regarding annuities and how annuitization might be encouraged.

With respect to the risks arising from long-term care needs, the recent Patient Protection and Affordable Care Act contained a provision to establish a federal long-term care program (CLASS ACT). However, this portion of the Affordable Care Act has since been set aside because it was found to be financially unfeasible. Other policies directed at the long-term care risk have provided for tax-advantaged long-term care insurance plans, and spurred the offering of such plans through employers. However, recent work suggests that many obstacles to expanding long-term care insurance coverage exist, including distrust of insurance companies, the cost of policies, and a preference for informal care from family members (Brown, Goda, and McGarry 2012). Understanding preferences and expectations regarding long-term care will become increasingly important as our population ages, individuals reach old age with fewer children to provide assistance, and the cost of formal care continues to rise. Relatedly, the overall cost of health care, particularly near the end of life, will likely pose problems for many. This issue is now front and center in policy discussions.

Finally, the balances in the Social Security and Medicare trust funds suggests that changes to the programs will be necessary in the coming years. While proposals for change nearly all call for protecting the current generation of retirees, the outlook for future generations is less clear. Together these factors indicate that we need to be mindful of the risks the elderly face and continue to enact appropriate policy.

CONCLUSION

The War on Poverty, as broadly defined in this chapter, has unquestionably been a success from the point of view of the elderly. Poverty rates for older Americans have fallen dramatically, with the fraction in poverty in 2010 equal to nearly one-quarter of that in 1959. Poverty rates that started out far above those for the non-elderly are now substantially below. Much of the improvement in well-being was due to Social Security, which grew into a generous pension program that provides near universal coverage not only for workers but also for their spouses and dependent children. For those with low Social Security benefits or who are not eligible for Social Security, the SSI program provides a guaranteed minimum income. Finally, in ways not captured by income measures alone, a variety of other social service programs offer assistance to the elderly poor and affect their well-being.

Other trends suggest improvements in well-being that go far beyond the financial. Recent improvements in health and declines in disability among the elderly (Freedman, Martin, and Schoeni 2002) mean more quality adjusted years of life. A reversal of the trend toward early retirement suggests that the elderly will have more resources at their disposal and a greater ability to fund a longer life span. Higher incomes, accompanied by advances in technology, make coping with everyday tasks and independent living more feasible than in the past. Also, the growing recognition in policy circles of the importance of encouraging and facilitating private savings and the need to provide for long-term care as evidenced by legislation discussed earlier, all suggest that we are moving toward mitigating some of this risk despite the difficult economic circumstances.

This paper was originally prepared for the conference "The Legacy of the War on Poverty: Implications for the Future of Anti-Poverty Policies," held at the National Poverty Center, in Ann Arbor, Michigan, on June 12–13, 2012. I am grateful to Dale Everett and Haley Horton for excellent research assistance and to Martha Bailey, Sheldon Danziger, and Helen Levy for helpful comments.

NOTES

1. The poverty thresholds used by the U.S. Census Bureau were originally developed by Mollie Orshansky of the Social Security Administration (Orshansky 1963, 1965) and were based on the cost of feeding a family using the U.S. Department of Agriculture's "economy food plan." The thresholds are scaled for family size and for inflation. Because they are based on food consumption, the poverty thresholds for the elderly were set lower than those for the non-elderly given their assumed lower caloric needs; this difference remains today. In 2010, the poverty threshold for a single elderly person was $10,458 compared to $11,344 for a non-elderly individual. As the AARP notes, if the same poverty line were used for the non-elderly as for the elderly the poverty rate be in 2008 would have been 11.5 rather than 9.7 percent (AARP Public Policy Institute 2010).

2. The experience of the elderly population over this time has been so different from that for the non-elderly that a recent symposium article, "Poverty in America" (Hoynes, Page, and Stevens 2006), noted the differing trends for the two age groups and then, calling the progress for the elderly a success, focused its discussion exclusively on issues related to the non-elderly.

3. Congress has gradually expanded the types of employees covered by Social Security so that nearly 90 percent of the workforce is now covered (Social Security Administration 2012c).

4. Rates for intervening years or before 1959 are not available.

5. Many of the governmental statistics are based on the Current Population Surveys, which pertain to the noninstitutionalized population. In 1960, 3.8 percent of those sixty-five or older were in nursing homes (Congressional Budget Office 1988). If these individuals are disproportionately low income, poverty rates may have be slightly higher than published figures indicate. Furthermore, rates of institutionalization are higher for women than men.

6. The poverty rates presented in the report are not based on the same thresholds used by the Census Bureau but instead as family income below $3,000 per year. Because family size differs with age, the methodology makes it difficult to use such statistics for a comparison between the elderly and the non-elderly.

7. Although the Older Americans Act targeted individuals age sixty or older, the discussion in this paper focuses on those age sixty-five and older because sixty-five is the age cut-off used in published statistics and in the vast majority of research on the elderly.

8. An initial period of double indexation produced by the benefit formula contained in the 1972 amendments was corrected in 1977 (for an exceptionally detailed discussion of the benefit calculation and subsequent correction, see Myers et al. 1988).

9. Additionally, spousal improverishment provisions were enacted in 1988 that protect a portion of a married couple's resources to provide for a community dwelling spouse should one spouse need to enter a nursing home. The allowances can be well over $100,000.

10. Several small changes were made in the first years of the program, including ad hoc increases in benefit levels before such levels were indexed. The exclusion of the value of a home from countable assets was added in 1976 and burial plots valued at less than $1,500 in 1982 (Trout and Mattson 1984).

11. In 2012, only five states had income guarantees above the poverty line for couples and just two for singles; California's amount above the poverty line is only for singles who are living without cooking facilities.

12. Despite the decline in elderly recipients, enrollment in the SSI program is growing and the number of disabled recipients is now far larger than the number of elderly enrolled.

13. SSI is not alone in experiencing low rates of participation. Participation rates for the elderly in the Food Stamp program are even lower with approximately 35 percent of eligible elderly households enrolled—a rate far lower than for the non-elderly (Cunnyngham 2010).

14. Attempts include special mailings from the Social Security Administration to those with low benefits who appeared likely to be eligible for SSI, saturation outreach efforts on television, radio and in newspapers, cash bounties to individuals who brought in eligible individuals who later enrolled, and door to door canvasing (U.S. General Accounting Office 1976).

15. In an effort to reduce the stigma associated with the receipt of SSI, the Social Security Administration changed the color of the checks that were sent to recipients to match that of Social Security checks. Both benefits are now paid electronically, virtually eliminating the possibility that a recipient would feel stigmatized by someone seeing the check.

16. Bruce Meyer (2002) argues that the low participation rates are due to underreporting of benefit receipt in surveys. However, the Social Security Administration itself has launched repeated outreach efforts to enroll eligible elderly suggesting that though some of the nonparticipation is likely indeed due to underreporting, there is substantial scope to increase the well-being of the poor elderly by expanding participation. John Menefee, Bea Edwards, and Sylvester Schieber (1981) use the Social Security Administration Master Beneficiary file and find similarly low rates of nonparticipation.

17. Simply excluding Social Security from income yields estimated poverty rates for the elderly of nearly 50 percent (Sherman and Shapiro 2005).

18. The poverty gap is the money needed to increase the incomes of all those in poverty to the poverty line.

19. The poverty rate of non-Hispanic whites is nearly identical to those for whites alone, but the series does not start until 1974 and therefore misses much of the decline associated with the Social Security increases of the late 1960s and early 1970s.

20. The high rates of poverty among elderly widows have several possible causes. Social Security benefits are typically reduced by 33 percent when a husband dies, but the poverty line falls by just 20 percent. Women are also less likely to have their own pensions than men are and a husband's pension may not provide for survivor benefits so this

income may be lost completely. Also, because women live longer than men, they are more likely to outlive their assets, and may incur substantial loss of wealth due to medical expense of a spouse at the end of his life (McGarry and Schoeni 2005).

21. Workers who have participated in covered employment for enough time are eligible for Social Security Disability benefits should they become unable to engage in any substantial gainful activity. Because they will receive benefits over a longer period and pay Social Security taxes over a shorter one, they too receive a greater rate of return. Blacks have higher rates of disability than do whites, this component of the Social Security program also results in redistribution by race (U.S. General Accounting Office 2003).

22. The Food Stamp Program is now call the Supplemental Nutrition Assistance Program or SNAP.

23. As recently as 1980, nearly 85 percent of those participating in a pension plan, and approximately 40 percent of all workers had a defined benefit pension plan. By 2008 these percentages had fallen to 33 and 15 percent (EBRI 2013).

24. The figures in this paragraph are the author's calculations based on the RAND version of the Health and Retirement Study.

REFERENCES

AARP Public Policy Institute. 2010. *Older Americans in Poverty: A Snapshot*. Washington, D.C.: American Association of Retired Persons.

Beshears, John, James Choi, David Laibson, Brigitte Madrian, and Brian Weller. 2008. "Public Policy and Saving for Retirement: The 'Autosave' Features of the Pension Protection Act of 2006." Paper presented at the 2008 American Economic Association Annual Meeting. New Orleans (January 5, 2008).

Boskin, Michael 1977. "Social Security and Retirement Decisions." *Economic Inquiry* 15(1): 1–25.

Brown, Jeffrey, Julia Coronado, and Don Fullerton. 2009. "Is Social Security Part of the Social Safety Net?" *NBER* working paper 15070. Cambridge, Mass.: National Bureau of Economic Research.

Brown, Jeffrey, Gopi Shah Goda, and Kathleen McGarry. 2012. "Long-Term Care Insurance Demand Limited by Beliefs About Needs, Concerns About Insurers, and Care Available from Family." *Health Affairs* 31(6): 1294–302.

Burke, Vincent, and Vee Burke. 1974. *Nixon's Good Deed: Welfare Reform*. New York: Columbia University Press.

Burtless, Gary T. 1986. "Social Security, Unanticipated Benefit Increases, and the Timing of Retirement." *Review of Economic Studies* 53(5): 781–805.

Burtless, Gary T., and Robert A. Moffitt. 1984. "The Effect of Social Security Benefits on the Labor Supply of the Aged." In *Retirement and Economic Behavior*, edited by H. J. Aaron and G. Burtless. Washington, D.C.: Brookings Institution Press.

Congressional Budget Office. 1988. *Changes in the Living Arrangements of the Elderly: 1960 2030*. Washington: Government Printing Office.

Council of Economic Advisers. 1964. *Economic Report of the President 1964*. Washington, D.C.: Government Printing Office.

Cunnyngham, Karen. 2010. "State Trends in Supplemental Nutrition Assistance Program Eligibility and Participation Among Elderly Individuals." Mathematica Policy Research Final Report to the U.S. Department of Agriculture Economic Research Service.

Cutler, David, and Lawrence Katz. 1991. "Macroeconomic Performance and the Disadvantaged." *Brookings Papers on Economic Activity* 2(1): 1–74.

Dalaker, Joseph. 2005. "Alternative Poverty Estimates in the United States: 2003." *Current Population Reports*, series P60, no. 227. Washington: U.S. Census Bureau.

Dalaker, Joseph, and Bernadette Proctor. 2000. "Poverty in the United States: 1999." *Current Population Reports*, series P60, no. 210. Washington: U.S. Bureau of the Census.

EBRI. 2013. "FAQs About Benefits—Retirement Issues." Washington, D.C.: Employee Benefit Research Institute. Available at: http://www.ebri.org/publications/benfaq/index.cfm?fa=retfaq14 (accessed January 18 2013).

Engelhardt, Gary, and Jonathan Gruber. 2004. "Social Security and the Evolution of Elderly Poverty." *NBER* working paper 10466. Cambridge, Mass.: National Bureau of Economic Research.

Engelhardt, Gary, Jonathan Gruber, and Cynthia Perry. 2005. "Social Security and Elderly Living Arrangements." *Journal of Human Resources* 40(2): 354–72.

Freedman, Vicki, Linda Martin, and Robert Schoeni. 2002. "Trends in Disability and Functioning Among Older Americans: A Critical Review of the Evidence." *Journal of the American Medical Association* 288(24): 3137–146.

Fullerton, Howard N. 1999. "Labor Force Participation: 75 Years of Change, 1950–98 and 1998–2025." *Monthly Labor Review* December: 3–12. Available at: http://www.bls.gov/mlr/1999/12/art1full.pdf (accessed April 8, 2013).

Gendell, Murray. 2008. "Older Workers: Increasing the Labor Force Participation and Hours of Work." *Monthly Labor Review* 131(1): 41–54.

Grundmann, Herman. 1985. "Adult Assistance Programs Under the Social Security Act," *Social Security Bulletin* 48(10): 10–21.

Gustman, Alan, and Thomas Steinmeier. 2001. "How Effective Is Redistribution Under the Social Security Benefit Formula?" *Journal of Public Economics* 82(1): 1–28.

———. 2009. "How Changes in Social Security Affect Recent Retirement Trends." *Research on Aging* 31(2): 261–90.

Harris, Amy Rehder, and John Sabelhaus. 2005. "How Does Differential Mortality Affect Social Security Finances and Progressivity?" Washington: Congressional Budget Office.

Hendley, Alexa, and Natasha Bilimoria. 1999. "Minorities and Social Security: An Analysis of Racial and Ethnic Differences in the Current Program." *Social Security Bulletin* 62(2): 59–64.

Holden, Karen. 1988. "Poverty and Living Arrangements Among Older Women: Are Changes in Economic Well-Being Underestimated?" *Journal of Gerontology* 43(1): s22–s27.

Hoynes, Hilary, Marianne Page, and Ann Huff Stevens. 2006. "Poverty in America: Trends and Explanations." *Journal of Economic Perspectives* 20(1): 47–68.

Johnson, Lyndon B. 1965. "Remarks at the Signing of the Older Americans Act." July 14, 1965. Santa Barbara: University of California, American Presidency Project. Available at: http://www.presidency.ucsb.edu/ws/?pid=27079 (accessed April 8, 2013).

———. 1967. "Annual Message to the Congress on the State of the Union." January 10,

1967. Santa Barbara: University of California, American Presidency Project. Available at: http://www.presidency.ucsb.edu/ws/index.php?pid=28338 (accessed April 8, 2013).

———. 1968. "Statement by the President upon Signing the Social Security Amendments and upon Appointing a Commission to Study the Nation's Welfare Programs." January 2, 1968. Santa Barbara: University of California, American Presidency Project. Available at: http://www.presidency.ucsb.edu/ws/index.php?pid=28915#axzz1vMaLw9CE (accessed April 8, 2013).

Kramarow, Ellen. 1995. "The Elderly Who Live Alone in the United States: Historical Perspectives on Household Change?" *Demography* 32(3): 335–52.

Levy, Helen. 2009. "Income, Material Hardship, and the Use of Public Programs and the Elderly." *MRRC* working paper UM09–14. Available at: http://www-personal.umich.edu/~hlevy/Helen_Levy_CV_2013_May.pdf.

Marshall, Sam, Kathleen McGarry, and Jonathan Skinner. 2011. "The Risk of Out-of-Pocket Health Care Expenditures at the End of Life." In *Explorations in the Economics of Aging.* Chicago: University of Chicago Press.

McGarry, Kathleen. 1996. "Factors Determining Participation of the Elderly in SSI." *Journal of Human Resources* 31(2): 331–58.

———. 2002. "Guaranteed Income: SSI and the Well-Being of the Elderly Poor." In *The Distributional Effects of Social Security and Social Security Reform,* edited by Martin Feldstein and Jeffrey Liebman. Chicago: University of Chicago Press.

McGarry, Kathleen, and Robert Schoeni. 2000. "Social Security, Economics Growth, and the Rise in Elderly Widows' Independence in the Twentieth Century." *Demography* 37(2): 221–36.

———. 2005. "Widow Poverty and Out of Pocket Medical Expenses Near End of Life." *Journals of Gerontology: Social Sciences* 60B(3): s160–69.

Menefee, John, Bea Edwards, and Sylvester Schieber. 1981. "Analysis of Nonparticipation in the SSI Program." *Social Security Bulletin* 44(6): 3–21.

Meyer, Bruce. 2002. "Comment on 'Guaranteed Income: SSI and the Well-Being of the Elderly Poor.'" In *The Distributional Effects of Social Security and Social Security Reform,* edited by Martin Feldstein and Jeffrey Liebman. Chicago: University of Chicago Press.

Michael, Robert, Victor Fuchs, and Sharon Scott. 1980. "Changes in the Propensity to Live Alone: 1956–1976." *Demography* 17(1): 39–56.

Myers, Robert. 1985. *Social Security.* Homewood, Ill.: Richard D. Lewin.

Myers, Robert, Gary Burtless, Suzanne Dilk, and James Kelley. 1988. *The Social Security Benefit Notch: A Study.* Washington, D.C.: National Academy of Social Insurance. Available at: http://www.nasi.org/usr_doc/Notch%20Report.PDF (accessed April 8, 2013).

Orshansky, Mollie. 1963. "Children of the Poor." *Social Security Bulletin* 26(7): 3–13.

———. 1964. "The Aged Negro and His Income." *Social Security Bulletin* 27(2): 3–13.

———. 1965. "Who's Who Among the Poor: A Demographic View of Poverty." *Social Security Bulletin* 28(7): 3–33.

———. 1967. "Counting the Poor: Before and After Federal Income-Support Programs." In *Old Age Income Assurance: A Compendium of Papers on Problems and Policy Issues in the Public and Private Pension System.* Washington: Government Printing Office.

Panis, Constantijn, and Lee Lillard. 1996. "Socioeconomic Differentials in the Returns to

Social Security." *Labor and Population Program* working paper 96–05. Santa Monica, Calif.: RAND Corporation.

Purcell, Patrick. 2009. "Income of Americans Aged 65 and Older, 1969–2008." Washington, D.C.: Congressional Research Service.

Ruggles, Steven. 1994. "The Transformation of American Family Structure." *American Historical Review* 99(1): 103–27.

Samwick, Andrew. 1998. "New Evidence on Pensions, Social Security, and the Timing of Retirement." *Journal of Public Economics* 70(2): 207–36.

Schieber, Sylvester. 1978. "First Year Impact of SSI on Economic Status of 1973 Adult Assistance Populations." *Social Security Bulletin* 41(2): 18–46.

Schwartz, Saul, Sheldon Danziger, and Eugene Smolensky. 1984. "The Choice of Living Arrangements by the Elderly." In *Retirement and Economic Behavior*, edited by Henry Aaron and Gary Burtless. Washington, D.C.: Brookings Institution Press.

Sherman, Arloc, and Isaac Shapiro. 2005. *Social Security Lifts 13 Million Seniors Above the Poverty Line: A State-by-State Analysis*. Washington, D.C.: Center on Budget and Policy Priorities.

Short, Kathleen. 2011. "The Research Supplemental Poverty Measure: 2010." *Current Population Reports*, series P60, no. 241. Washington: U.S. Census Bureau.

Social Security Administration. 2010. "Facts and Figures About Social Security 2010." Washington: Government Printing Office. Available at: http://www.socialsecurity.gov/policy/docs/chartbooks/fast_facts/2010/fast_facts10.pdf (accessed April 19, 2013).

———. 2012a. *Annual Statistical Supplement to the Social Security Bulletin, 2011*. Washington: Government Printing Office.

———. 2012b. *Income of the Aged Chartbook 2010*. Publication 13-11727. Washington: Government Printing Office. Available at: http://www.ssa.gov/policy/docs/chartbooks/income_aged/2010/iac10.pdf (accessed April 19, 2013).

———. 2012c. "Social Security Basic Facts." July 30, 2012. Washington: Government Printing Office. Available at: http://www.ssa.gov/pressoffice/basicfact.htm (accessed April 19, 2013).

———. 2012d. *Income of the Population 55 or Older, 2010*. SSA Publication 13–11871. Washington: Government Printing Office.

Tissue, Thomas. 1978. "Response to Recipiency Under Public Assistance and SSI." *Social Security Bulletin* 41(11): 3–15.

Toosst, Mitra. 2012. "Labor Force Projections to 2010: A More Slowly Growing Workforce." *Monthly Labor Review* 135(1): 43–64. Available at: http://www.bls.gov/opub/mlr/2012/01/art3full.pdf (accessed April 8, 2013).

Trout, John, and David Mattson. 1984. "A 10-Year Review of the Supplemental Security Income Program," *Social Security Bulletin* 47(1): 3–24.

U.S. Census Bureau. 1965. "Income in 1964 of Families and Persons in the United States: 1964." *Current Population Reports*, series P60, no. 47. Washington: U.S. Department of Commerce.

———. 2010. "Money Income in the United States: 1999." *Current Population Reports*, series P60, no. 209. Washington: U.S. Department of Commerce.

———. 2011a. "Historical Census of Housing Tables." Washington: U.S. Department of

Commerce. Available at: http://www.census.gov/hhes/www/housing/census/his toric/ownerchar html (accessed April 8, 2013).

———. 2011b. "Income, Poverty, and Health in the United States 2010." *Current Population Reports,* series P60, no. 239. Washington: U.S. Department of Commerce.

———. 2012. *Statistical Abstract of the United States: 2012,* 131st ed. Washington: U.S. Department of Commerce. Available at: http://www.census.gov/compendia/statab/2012 edition.html (accessed April 8, 2013).

U.S. General Accounting Office. 1976. "Efforts Made to Locate and Enroll Potential Recipients of the Supplemental Security Income Program for the Aged, Blind and Disabled." HRD-76-176. Washington: U.S. Department of Commerce.

U.S. Government Accountability Office. 2003. "Social Security Distribution of Benefits and Taxes Relative to Earnings Level." GAO-04-747. Washington: U.S. Department of Commerce.

———. 2004. "Social Security and Minorities: Earnings, Disability Incidence, and Mortality are Key Factors that Influence Taxes Paid and Benefits Received." GAO-03–387. Washington: Government Printing Office.

Warlick, Jennifer. 1982. "Participation of the Aged in SSI." *Journal of Human Resources* 17(2): 236–60.

Chapter 8

Performance and Legacy of Housing Policies

Edgar O. Olsen and Jens Ludwig

T his chapter assesses the War on Poverty's performance and legacy in the area of urban housing policy. Several decades after President Lyndon B. Johnson launched the War on Poverty, President Ronald Reagan in his own 1988 State of the Union address famously claimed that the War on Poverty represented a massive failure of government policies to achieve their goals:

> My friends, some years ago, the Federal Government declared war on poverty, and poverty won. Today the Federal Government has 59 major welfare programs and spends more than $100 billion a year on them. What has all this money done? Well, too often it has only made poverty harder to escape.

Reagan's pessimistic assessment of the War on Poverty in general, and its housing policies in particular, is at some level easy to understand. In the nearly two decades leading up to Reagan's speech, from 1970 to 1988, the official poverty rate increased slightly despite a doubling of real, inflation-adjusted spending on means-tested transfer programs (Scholz, Moffitt, and Cowan 2009, table 8A.1). Newspaper coverage in the 1970s of scandals in President Johnson's new low-income housing programs and the widely publicized demolition of thirty-three vandalized high-rise buildings in the crime-ridden Pruitt-Igoe public housing projects in St. Louis, a mere twenty years after their construction, led to negative popular perceptions about low-income housing policies. The nation's most distressed housing projects became "a notorious symbol of failed public policy and architectural hubris" ("Why the Pruitt-Igoe housing project failed," *The Economist*, October 15, 2011). Initial scholarly assessments of the first decade of the War on Poverty's housing policies were also quite negative. Phyllis Wallace argued that "the failures of the federal housing programs have been colossal" (1977, 358).

Against this backdrop of widely perceived failure, the primary purpose of this chapter is to produce a balanced account of the effects of Johnson's low-income housing initiatives. Improving the housing of the poorest families was always a high priority for Johnson, and he launched major initiatives early in his presidency. In 1968, housing became his domestic priority (Wolman 1971, 86). His goal was to ensure that all families lived in decent housing within a decade, and his term witnessed the largest number of major housing initiatives in the country's history. Although some had serious design flaws and were soon terminated, some were important successes.

Given that one of Johnson's lasting legacies was the creation of the U.S. Department of Housing and Urban Development (HUD), some readers might wonder why our focus does not include his urban development efforts as well. After all, they received about the same attention in his 1964 special message to Congress on housing and urban development and his 1965 State of the Union address, which is widely regarded as the official launch of the Great Society. Johnson did obtain the adoption of several major urban development programs. The Model Cities program (1966) was the best known and most focused on poverty alleviation. This program attempted to concentrate the assistance of existing social programs on people living in the highest-poverty neighborhoods, and over its brief history, it provided an additional $12 billion (in 2011 dollars) to local governments to improve these neighborhoods, albeit spread thinly over 150 cities. Unfortunately, the program received almost no rigorous evaluation and seems to have had no significant long-term impact. In 1974, it was replaced by the current Community Development Block Grant program, which focused less on the poorest urban neighborhoods. In contrast, President Johnson's housing initiatives have had a substantial legacy.

The evidence indicates that Johnson's housing initiatives and their direct descendants substantially increased the number of poor families receiving housing assistance. One disappointment with the War on Poverty's housing initiatives is that they did not lead to higher earnings for recipients. The central goal of the War on Poverty was to help people earn their way out of poverty. Johnson believed that living in better housing would reduce poverty to some extent by increasing the ability of people to produce goods. As he said in his 1964 State of the Union address,

> Very often a lack of jobs and money is not the cause of poverty, but the symptom. The cause may lie deeper in our failure to give our fellow citizens a fair chance to develop their own capacities, in a lack of education and training, in a lack of medical care and housing, in a lack of decent communities in which to live and bring up their children. (Johnson 1964a)

Working in the opposite direction is the fact that housing programs have usually been structured in a way that reduces the incentive for work. For most families, earning more reduces their subsidy. The empirical evidence suggests that the work disincentive effects of the subsidy formula exceed any work- and productivity-enhancing effects. Nonetheless, the housing subsidies received by the poorest families have been large, thereby reducing the material deprivation of poor families.

Johnson's most surprising legacy in the area of low-income housing policy was to increase the reliance of means-tested housing programs on the private housing market. His initiatives emphasized the construction of privately owned subsidized projects and single-family units. However, the success of one of his smallest initiatives led to the current housing voucher program, the country's largest low-income housing program. These changes greatly improved the cost-effectiveness of the system of low-income housing assistance, thereby making it possible to serve more people with a given budget. Unlike the public housing program that contributed to racial and economic segregation, Johnson's reforms modestly reduced both. Recent evidence from HUD's Moving to Opportunity study suggests that the War on Poverty's legacy of shifting housing assistance from public housing projects to privately owned existing units is unlikely to have had much effect on income poverty by changing the labor market outcomes of adults or the educational outcomes of children. It also indicates, however, that giving poor families vouchers instead of public housing units in neighborhoods with the highest poverty rates would improve their housing and neighborhood conditions with beneficial effects on their mental and physical health.

The changes President Johnson initiated in low-income housing programs, together with the provisions of the 1964 and 1968 Civil Rights Acts applicable to housing, have also arguably contributed to the overall reduction in residential segregation by race that has occurred in the United States since 1970. The available evidence makes it difficult to determine how much of the decline in segregation is due to policy changes of the 1960s, but we believe that a reasonable circumstantial case can be made that Johnson's initiatives played some role.

The next section sets the stage by describing trends in housing conditions, racial segregation and housing policy prior to the War on Poverty.

BACKGROUND

Housing conditions in the United States had improved markedly in the years following the end of World War II. According to HUD's definition, the percentage of occupied units classified as substandard declined from 36 percent to 16 percent between 1950 and 1960 (Aaron 1972, table 2-1). This extended an earlier trend (Weicher 1980, table 1) and continued up to the time of Johnson's major low-income housing initiatives (Aaron 1972, table 2-1).

Although housing conditions were improving before the War on Poverty, residential segregation by race was worsening during this time because African Americans were increasingly concentrated in the central cities of America's large metropolitan areas. This period was the end of the Great Migration of blacks from the rural South. Between 1910 and 1930, most moved to industrial cities in the Northeast and Midwest. Between 1940 and 1970, blacks also spread into large urban areas in other parts of the country. Between 1960 and 1970, the number of blacks in the central cities of metropolitan areas with populations exceeding 500,000 increased by 2.8 million, even as the white population of these areas declined by 1.9 million. In the suburbs of these cities, the white population increased 12.5 million and the black population only 0.8 million (U.S. Commission on Civil Rights 1974, 4). Indices of the degree of residential segregation by race in metropolitan areas had been rising since 1890 (Glaeser and Vigdor 2001, figures 1, 2). These trends, together with the race riots in the summers of 1965, 1966, and 1967, influenced Johnson's civil rights proposals related to housing and his reforms of low-income housing policy.

Housing and urban development policies before the 1960s contributed to improvements in housing conditions, albeit modestly, but also to increased levels of racial segregation. Between 1950 and 1960, the number of substandard units decreased by 6.7 million. Public housing and urban renewal were almost surely among the programs that had the greatest effect on this outcome. However, fewer than 300,000 additional public housing units were built over this period (HUD 1977, 124) and fewer than 170,000 units were demolished under the urban renewal program (HUD 1966, 401).

Despite these positive trends, about 8.5 million households still lived in substandard housing in 1960 (Aaron 1972, table 2-1). Housing conditions were particularly bad for African Americans. For example, 12 percent of white families but fully 31 percent of black families lived in units without a private toilet (Aaron 1972, table 2-2).

Substantial government involvement in subsidizing low-income housing began with the Public Housing Program enacted in the U.S. Housing Act of 1937. Its purpose was to increase employment during the Great Depression and improve housing conditions of low-income households. In 1964, 98 percent of the low-income households that received housing assistance lived in public housing projects that had received substantial federal subsidies for their construction but were operated by local public housing authorities. In the first public housing projects, rents varied with the size and amenities of the units, but not with the income of the tenant. As a result, many of the poorest of the poor had to increase their expenditure on housing significantly to live in these units, which in turn deterred their participation. However, by 1964, most housing authorities charged most tenants 20 percent of their income for rent, which had the effect of providing a larger subsidy for lower-income families and a smaller subsidy to higher-income families, thereby increasing the share of poor families living in such projects and reducing the revenue available to housing agencies for upkeep.

The public housing program never gained enough political support to garner the appropriations necessary to serve a significant fraction of the poorest households. In 1964, more than a quarter century after the creation of the first program intended to eliminate unsafe and insanitary housing conditions and provide decent, safe, and sanitary dwelling units for low-income families, fewer than 700,000 public housing units had been authorized — about 25,000 a year — and only 540,000 had been completed. In that year, the public housing program served fewer than 10 percent of poor families in the United States.

Another problem with public housing that was quite influential in shaping Johnson's housing policies was the long lag between congressional appropriation of funds for new housing projects and actual project completion. The median time between the start and completion of construction of 745 public housing projects surveyed from 1962 to 1964 was forty-four months (U.S. President's Committee on Urban Housing 1969, 19), and substantial additional time elapsed between congressional authorization and the beginning of construction (Edson and Lane 1972, 6:8). The time required to get local approval for public housing sites surely played an important role in these construction lags.

In the five years before Johnson took office, Congress created two new programs to deliver housing assistance to low-income households. Both subsidized selected private organizations to build and operate rental housing projects. Under the Section 202 Elderly Program authorized in 1959, nonprofit sponsors built projects for the elderly and disabled. Under the Section 221(d)(3) Below Market Interest Rate (BMIR) Program created in 1961, nonprofit organizations and limited-dividend firms built townhouses and apartments for low-income families of all types.[1]

These programs produced few units before Johnson took office, fewer than 12,000, and had other substantial shortcomings from the viewpoint of poverty alleviation. Unlike public housing, the rent charged to a tenant under these programs did not depend on the household's income. This precluded participation by the very poorest households, and the high rent and modest subsidy made them unattractive to households with somewhat higher incomes. Furthermore, the maximum income limits in the BMIR program were much higher than the public housing limits, and project managers were not required to establish preference systems that gave priority to the poorest families on their waiting lists. The result was that the BMIR program served the poorest households to a much lesser extent than public housing did. At the time, about 61 percent of public housing tenants had annual incomes less than $3,000, whereas fewer than 8 percent of BMIR participants had incomes this low (see table 8.2). Similar data for the elderly program proved elusive. However, the racial composition of its residents differed markedly from the other two programs. Only 4 percent of its residents were black, versus 41 percent for the BMIR program and 46 percent for public housing (HUD 1973, table 142). Section 202 Elderly projects served almost exclusively whites in predominantly white areas. Differential treatment of people by race more generally was a prominent feature of housing policy before the War on Poverty. For many years, some local and state governments had practiced or facilitated racial discrimination in housing (Yinger 1995, chapter 10). The U.S. Supreme Court had outlawed some of the most egregious practices long before Johnson took office. In 1917, it ruled that racial zoning ordinances were unconstitutional. In 1948, the Court concluded that it was unconstitutional for any government to enforce racially restrictive covenants. However, some local and state governments continued to support racial segregation in housing by other means, and some federal agencies still pursued policies that sustained it (Bonastia 2006, 61–65).

Before the Johnson administration, low-income housing policies had arguably contributed to racial segregation. Public housing projects exhibited high levels of

TABLE 8.1 / Johnson's Urban Housing Programs, Predecessors, and Descendants

Predecessors	
1937	Public Housing: subsidized construction, publicly owned projects, project-based assistance
1959	Section 202 Elderly: subsidized construction, privately owned projects, project-based assistance, elderly, and disabled only
1961	Section 221(d)(3) BMIR: subsidized construction, privately owned projects, project-based assistance
New programs	
1965	Rent Supplements: subsidized construction, privately owned projects, project-based assistance
1965	Section 23 Leased Existing: existing privately owned units, some project-based and some tenant-based assistance
1965	Section 23 Leased New: subsidized construction, privately owned projects, project-based assistance
1968	Section 235 Homeownership New: subsidized construction, privately owned units, project-based assistance
1968	Section 235 Homeownership Existing: existing privately owned units, assistance neither purely project- nor tenant-based
1968	Section 236 Rental: subsidized construction, privately owned projects, project-based assistance
Descendants	
1974	Section 8 Existing: existing privately owned units, tenant-based assistance
1974	Section 8 New: subsidized construction, privately owned projects, project-based assistance

Source: Authors' compilation.
Note: Unless otherwise specified, programs provided assistance for renting, and served families with children as well as elderly and disabled, though not necessarily in the same buildings. All subsidized construction programs provide subsidies to selected suppliers, and almost all funded some projects that involved substantial rehabilitation rather than new construction. Project-based assistance requires occupancy of particular dwelling unit offered. Tenant-based assistance allows the recipient to receive subsidy in any unit meeting the program's standards.

segregation. In March 1964, fully 72 percent of public housing projects were inhabited by people of a single race (Bonastia 2006, 74). Indices of black-white segregation and black isolation in public housing projects were quite high in most metropolitan areas.[2]

The high levels of racial segregation in public housing at the start of the War on Poverty resulted in part from explicit policies of some local housing authorities to assign blacks to some projects and whites to others. It also resulted in part from the location of projects in mostly white or mostly black neighborhoods combined with the preferences of potential residents concerning the race of their neighbors. For all practical purposes, local political bodies had veto power over site selection.[3] Because community opposition to building public housing projects was lowest in neighborhoods with the worst housing, it is not surprising that many public housing projects were built in the poorest neighborhoods and the neighborhoods with the highest minority concentrations. Many residents in these neighborhoods welcomed these projects because they replaced the worst slums (Hunt 2009, 112–13).

National data on the extent to which public housing projects were located in the lowest-income, racially segregated neighborhoods before the Johnson administration has not been assembled. However, Sandra Newman and Ann Schnare (1997, table 3) show that in the mid-1990s public housing units were much more concentrated in extreme-poverty areas than were the units occupied by other low-income people (those receiving cash welfare assistance). Specifically, 36 percent of public housing tenants lived in census tracts with poverty rates in excess of 40 percent, versus only 12 percent of households receiving cash welfare assistance. Similarly, 38 percent of public housing tenants lived in census tracts where more than 80 percent of residents were minorities, versus only 18 percent of households receiving cash welfare assistance.

In 1962, President Kennedy issued executive order 11063, which required federal agencies to take actions to prevent discrimination in all housing programs that received federal support. However, this order was largely ignored and the regulations needed to implement it were not completed for several decades (Yinger 1995, 188). Some states had enacted fair housing laws before the Johnson administration. However, the evidence suggests that they had little effect on black housing market outcomes or the level of residential segregation (Collins 2004). At the beginning of the Johnson administration, some state and local governments, public housing authorities, and federal agencies continued to practice racial discrimination and support racial segregation.

EXPANDING HOUSING ASSISTANCE

The primary goal of Johnson's housing policy initiatives was to ensure that all families occupy units meeting minimum housing standards (Johnson 1965, 1968). The 1937 and 1949 Housing Acts had stated a similar goal but did not set a deadline for achieving it. Johnson launched initiatives early in his presidency to reduce the number of families living in substandard housing, and the landmark 1968 Housing Act established an ambitious goal and deadline, namely, 6 million additional units meeting minimum housing standards within ten years.

Johnson's low-income housing initiatives substantially increased the number of households receiving housing assistance. In 1964, about 8 million households lived in substandard housing. Fewer than 600,000 families received low-income housing assistance, almost all in public housing projects. By 1975, almost 2.4 million households received low-income housing assistance, a threefold increase over seven years in the per-capita participation rate in low-income housing programs.[4] Less than a third of this increase (about 450,000 additional units) occurred by expanding the number of units served by the programs that he had inherited. His new programs added many more. The programs inherited by Johnson and established during his administration and their direct descendants created in 1974 now serve about 4.9 million households.[5]

Although the widely reported problems in the nation's most distressed public housing has led many people to conclude that low-income housing policies have done little good for poor families, Johnson's expansion to the size of these programs has in fact helped improve the material living conditions of poor families. This effect comes primarily from transferring substantial resources to families who participate in such programs, rather than by enabling participants to earn more in the labor market. The remainder of this section describes Johnson's initiatives and their performance with respect to poverty alleviation.

Johnson's Low-Income Housing Initiatives

Johnson's earliest initiatives in the area of low-income housing policy greatly expanded—and reformed—existing housing programs. At his request, Congress authorized about 280,000 additional public housing units during his administration. This is about 20 percent of all public housing units ever built. He also expanded the two programs that subsidized private projects by about 167,000 units. Therefore, about 447,000 additional units were authorized under existing programs during his term. To put these achievements in perspective, the construction of about 750,000 subsidized units had been approved, though not completed, before his term under the programs he inherited (HUD 1973, 1977).

The Johnson administration also instituted the most substantial reforms of the public housing program in its history to speed the delivery of housing assistance to low-income families. For example, the administration in 1966 introduced a new method for acquiring public housing projects—the *turnkey* method, which gave private developers more input on how and where housing projects were built.[6] Johnson also proposed legislation that allowed public housing authorities to pay a part of the rent in existing private units that met minimum housing standards (Johnson 1964b; Wolman 1971, 80). This 1965 amendment to the U.S. Housing Act of 1937 established the Leased Housing Program (Section 23). Under one variant of this program, housing authorities rented the units and sublet them to assisted households. Another variant allowed tenants to locate their own apartments meeting the program's minimum standards, and the family retained its subsidy if it moved to another unit. This was the first program of tenant-based housing assistance, as discussed further. Housing authorities also entered into agreements with private developers to build, or substantially rehabilitate, and manage housing projects for low-income households under this program (Edson and Lane 1972, 7:3).[7] The leased and turnkey methods spread rapidly. By 1977, 40 percent of the units added to the public housing program used the turnkey method and 23 percent used the leased method.

In 1965, Johnson developed a new program that subsidized low-income households in privately owned projects. The inherited programs of this type had several major defects from the viewpoint of achieving his primary goal of a decent home for every American. Budgetary accounting rules made funding them unattractive to members of Congress, and their minimum rents made living in them unattractive to the poorest households.[8] To overcome these shortcomings, Johnson proposed replacing the BMIR program with a rent supplement program that would award subsidies to the owners of otherwise unsubsidized projects at the time of their construction. These supplements would pay the difference between the market rents of the units and 20 percent of the countable income for some of the poorest people living in the project, and thereby provide larger subsidies to the poorest households. In the interest of promoting a mix of incomes in projects, Johnson proposed income limits greater than those for public housing in the locality.

The president's proposal encountered substantial congressional opposition. Congress authorized the rent supplement program in the 1965 Housing and Urban Development Act with many modifications and added further restrictions in the years that followed. Benefits were limited to families with incomes low enough to be eligible for public housing. Congress appropriated no money for it in its first year. At its peak in 1977, it provided subsidies of about $900 million (in 2012 dollars) on behalf of about 320,000 households (HUD 1978b, 32). About 180,000 were in otherwise unsubsidized projects (Olsen 2003, table 6.5); the rest were in projects receiving additional subsidies under Johnson's signature rental housing program introduced three years later. To put this number in perspective, public housing served about 1.2 million households in 1977 (Olsen 2003, table 6.5).

In 1968, passage of the Housing and Urban Development Act was Johnson's number one domestic priority (Wolman 1971, 86). Johnson's Committee on Urban Housing had told him that at least 6 million households would have lived in substandard housing in 1978 in the absence of additional government action. This led to Johnson's proposal to build or rehabilitate 6 million subsidized units for these households within ten years.[9]

Johnson believed that achieving this ambitious goal required the substantial involvement of private firms beyond their role as passive contractors in building public housing. He did not believe that it could be achieved by expanding existing programs that subsidized private projects (U.S. President's Committee on Urban Housing 1969, 222). In the 1968 Housing Act, Congress agreed to his goal and timetable for achieving it, and authorized the construction of many units under two new programs that relied primarily on private firms. The Section 235 Homeownership Program subsidized the construction of new units for sale to low-income households and to a lesser extent the purchase of existing houses; the Section 236 Rental Program subsidized the construction or substantial rehabilitation of rental housing projects. These two programs subsidized more low-income households than any of Johnson's other initiatives. At their peak, they served about 800,000 households. We discuss these programs in more detail in the next section. For now, we merely note that they required participants to contribute a significant minimum amount toward the cost of their housing and this deterred participation by the poorest families.

Consequences for Poor Families

What were the effects of Johnson's initiatives on poverty alleviation? Most of the available evidence on this question comes from studies of public housing. Despite the negative perception of the public housing program and the apparent failure of this program to achieve some of the key goals of the War on Poverty, such as increasing adult earnings or children's long-term life chances, Johnson's expansion of public housing nonetheless succeeded in reducing the level of material deprivation among poor households.

The main thrust of the War on Poverty as defined in the 1964 Economic Opportunity Act was to increase the productivity of the poorest members of society. The net effect of any housing program on the earnings of adults or educational outcomes and future earnings of children is ultimately empirical. A housing program could affect the mental and physical health of adults or children in either direction by affecting the quality of their housing or neighborhood environments, and thereby affect the current productivity of adults and the educational attainment and future earnings of their children. Changes in neighborhood environments might also influence these outcomes through peer influences or role model effects (Wilson 1987; Jencks and Mayer 1990). If a housing program reduces its subsidy when a recipient's income increases, the result is a reduction in the financial incentive to work.[10] In a public housing project, the family paid a higher rent for the same apartment if its earnings increased.

The available evidence indicates that public housing on net has induced adult recipients to reduce their work effort and earn less. The best evidence is that the program reduced the earnings of adult recipients by 19 percent (Susin 2005). Combining the evidence from the studies that estimate the difference in the effect of public housing and housing vouchers on labor earnings using the best methods and data (Carlson et al. 2012; Olsen et al. 2005; Sanbonmatsu et al. 2011) with the evidence on the effects of housing vouchers alone (Abt Associates et al. 2006; Carlson et al. 2012; Jacob and Ludwig 2012a) leads to the same qualitative conclusion. Specifically, housing vouchers lead to a reduction in earnings, and shifting families from the public housing program into the housing voucher program has little detectable effect on earnings, which leads us to conclude that enrolling an unsubsidized family into public housing leads to about the same reduction in labor market earnings that housing vouchers do.

Public housing might also affect the educational attainment and future earnings of children who grow up in it. The evidence on this matter is much more modest than what is known about effects on adult labor market outcomes, and is also less compelling. Janet Currie and Aaron Yelowitz (2000) find no effect of public housing occupancy on grade repetition for whites and a 19 percent reduction for blacks. Sandra Newman and Joseph Harkness (2002) estimate that children who lived in public housing for more years between 1968 and 1982 had somewhat higher employment rates and labor earnings as young adults.

Nonetheless, Johnson's expansion of the public housing program and his other low-income housing initiatives helped improve the material living conditions of poor families by simply transferring substantial resources to such households. Although newspaper and television coverage of conditions in the worst public housing projects may suggest otherwise, public housing typically led to substantial improvements in the housing conditions of its recipients. Most tenants also paid

TABLE 8.2 / Families in Low-Income Housing Programs

Annual Income Bracket	Public Housing (1970)	Section 221(d)(3) BMIR (1968)	Rent Supplements (1969)	Section 235 (1971)	Section 236 (1970)	All Households (1970)
Less than $3,000	61.3	7.5	76.1	1.1	10.7	17.8
$3,000 to $5,999	30.3	49.7	23.9	45.1	62.6	17.9
$6,000 to $8,999	8.4	39.4	0.0	49.4	26.1	18.1
More than $8,999	0.0	3.4	0.0	4.3	0.6	46.1

Source: Authors' compilation of data from Aaron (1972, tables 7-1, 8-1); U.S. Bureau of the Census (1971, table 7).
Note: All numbers in percentages.

lower rents and hence increased their consumption of other goods. Based on data from the mid-1960s through the mid-1970s for various combinations of large metropolitan areas, nine studies estimated that public housing tenants increased their consumption of housing services by between 22 and 82 percent on average, with a median of 58 percent across the studies (Olsen 2003, table 6.18). Their estimates of increased consumption of other goods ranged from 5 to 19 percent, with a median of 16 percent. The mean net benefit of these changes in consumption patterns was substantial. For example, Edgar Olsen and David Barton (1983) estimate that the mean annual net benefit to public housing tenants in New York City in the late 1960s was about $8,000 (in 2012 dollars). Michael Murray's (1975) estimate for seven unidentified cities during the same period is about $6,300 (in 2012 dollars).[11] Furthermore, net benefits are greatest for the poorest households (Olsen 2003, table 6.18). Therefore, Johnson's expansion of the public housing program significantly improved the material well-being of the poorest families lucky enough to be served by it. The limited evidence on Johnson's leased housing and rent supplement programs and his signature homeownership and rental programs (Section 235 and Section 236) indicate that they had similar effects (Mayo et al. 1980a, chap. 3; Reid 1989; HUD 1974a, chapter 4).

Because low-income housing assistance is not limited to the poor, the effect of a housing program on poverty alleviation also depends importantly on the incomes of the families served. The upper income limits for eligibility for low-income housing assistance have usually been well above the relevant poverty threshold. Table 8.2 reveals that the majority of public housing tenants around the time of the Johnson administration were reasonably poor: 61 percent of recipients had annual incomes below $3,000. Johnson's rent supplement program targeted the poorest households to an even greater extent: 76 percent had incomes below $3,000. In contrast, Johnson's signature housing programs and his expansion of the BMIR program served few poor families (see table 8.2). Only 11 percent of recipients of assistance from his signature rental program (Section 236) and 1 percent of recipients of assistance from his homeownership program (Section 235) had annual incomes below $3,000, roughly the lowest quintile of the income distribution. Johnson's earliest initiatives were his most consequential from the viewpoint of poverty alleviation. The rent supplement program accounted for half of all of the poor families served by Johnson's new programs and his expansion of existing programs. Public housing expansions accounted for about 70 percent of the rest.

INCREASED RELIANCE ON THE PRIVATE SECTOR

Johnson believed that achieving his goal of insuring that all families lived in decent housing required the substantial involvement of private firms. All of his new programs acted on this assumption. His signature programs established in the 1968 Housing Act moved the system of low-income housing assistance sharply in the direction of privately owned subsidized projects, and his smallest initiative planted the seed that led to the current housing voucher program, which relies heavily on the private market.

Johnson's signature programs suffered from highly visible scandals that led to the termination of one program in 1974 and the substantial revision of the other in 1975. However, this seeming setback did not stunt the movement of the system of low-income housing assistance toward reliance on private markets. The 1974 Housing Act replaced Johnson's signature rental program with a similar program that combined features of his earlier programs. More importantly, the success of the variant of his leased housing program—which allowed tenants to find their own housing in the private market—led to the most successful current housing program, the Housing Choice Voucher Program.

Table 8.3 describes the evolution of HUD's low-income rental housing assistance that resulted from Johnson's initiatives and their direct descendants. The share of all assisted households living in public housing declined steadily from 98 percent in 1964 to 23 percent in 2008. The share in privately owned subsidized projects jumped sharply from 2 percent in 1964 to 38 percent in 1978, reached its peak of 45 percent in 1984, and declined to 33 percent in 2008. Due to the rapid expansion of the housing voucher program after its creation in the 1974 Housing Act, housing vouchers accounted for 17 percent of all HUD-assisted households in 1978 and rose steadily to 44 percent in 2008.

The shift in the mix of housing assistance, especially toward housing vouchers, had important benefits. The Johnson initiatives and their direct descendants greatly reduced the cost of providing equally good housing, thereby making it possible to serve many more families with a given budget. They also led to significant improvements in the health and well-being of recipients compared with a simple expansion of public housing. Finally, they reduced racial and economic segregation in housing.

The next section describes Johnson's signature rental and homeownership programs, the scandals that led to their demise, the programs that replaced them, and the evidence on the effects of changing the mix of housing assistance to favor programs that relied on the private market.

TABLE 8.3 / Households Served by HUD Low-Income Rental Programs

Year	Public Housing	Private Projects	Housing Vouchers
1964	98	2	0
1978	45	38	17
1988	33	43	24
2008	23	33	44

Source: Authors' compilation. Data for 1964 are based on HUD (1973, tables 152, 156) and Aaron (1972, table D.8); data for 1978 and 1988 are based on Olsen (2003, table 6.5); data for 2008 are based on HUD's Picture of Subsidized Households available at: http://www.huduser.org/portal/picture2008/index.html (accessed June 14, 2013).
Note: All numbers in percentages.

Johnson's Signature Programs and Their Visible Shortcomings

Before the Johnson administration, no federal housing program provided deep subsidies for homeownership to poor households. To receive a large subsidy, a family had to live in a rental housing project. Johnson wanted to encourage home-ownership for the poor and embraced a homeownership program that had been developed by Senators Walter Mondale and Charles Percy (Wolman 1971, 72–80). The Section 235 Homeownership Program provided substantial subsidies on behalf of low-income families to buy a house. The larger component of this program authorized selected developers to build houses and sell them to eligible families. The smaller existing housing component provided subsidies to low-income buyers of existing houses on a first-come, first-served basis. This program was unique in that it left the responsibility for informing the public of its existence to the real estate industry. Local Federal Housing Administration (FHA) offices did not advertise the program nor seek out eligible buyers (U.S. Commission on Civil Rights 1971, 45). The program placed an upper limit on the amount of the mortgage that varied with location and family size, and its regulations required that units meet HUD's minimum property standards. The FHA insured the mortgage. Under the original program, the buyer had to put up a small down payment about equal to the security deposit on a similar rental unit. The poorest recipients made fixed mortgage payments based on a below-market interest rate, and the government paid the balance of the payment amount. Recipients with higher incomes contributed 20 percent of their adjusted income toward the mortgage payment and received a smaller subsidy. The income limits for the program were 135 percent of the public housing limits in most places and higher in others.

The 1968 Housing Act also created the Section 236 Rental Program as the primary vehicle for delivering rental housing assistance to additional low-income families. Under this program, the federal government contracted with selected private organizations to build, or substantially rehabilitate, and operate rental housing projects. In return for the subsidies, the private parties agreed to provide housing meeting certain standards at restricted rents to eligible households for a specified number of years. To try to prevent excessive taxpayer cost for the housing provided, participation was restricted to nonprofit organizations, limited-dividend corporations, and cooperatives. Limited-dividend corporations agreed to accept a cash return each year that was a fixed percentage of its certified equity in the project. It also received certain tax advantages that were not available for investments in other activities.[12] In the basic Section 236 program, the poorest households paid a below-market rent that was independent of their income—the so-called basic rent. Occupants with higher incomes paid more, specifically, 25 percent of their adjusted incomes. However, the owners of many projects received additional subsidies under the rent supplement and later programs to reduce the rents of many of the poorest households to 25 percent of adjusted income.[13]

Johnson's homeownership program was plagued by scandals and high default rates that led almost immediately to congressional hearings and staff investigations, congressionally mandated HUD and General Accounting Office investigations, and considerable media attention (see, for example, U.S. Congress, House Committee on Banking and Currency 1970, 1971; U.S. Congress, House Committee on Government Operations 1971, 1972a, 1972b; see also Edith Asbury, "F.H.A. Aide Pleads Guilty to Fraud," *New York Times*, September 13, 1972; Jerry Flint, "A Mortgage Scandal in Detroit Could Cost U.S. $200-Million," *New York Times*, December 4, 1971; Morris Kaplan, "6 Named in Indictment on Mortgage-Fraud Plot," *New York Times*, August 17, 1973). The scandals involved houses that were well below HUD's minimum property standards or bought for prices well above market levels. Because FHA insured the mortgages, its inspectors had to certify that the houses met the minimum housing standards and were priced at market levels. An early study by HUD's Internal Audit Division based on a small sample revealed that 25 percent of the houses in the new construction component of the program and 36 percent in its existing component failed to meet the minimum property standards (U.S. Congress, House Committee on Banking and Currency 1971, 17). In 1972, twenty-eight HUD officials were indicted for accepting bribes to provide false certifications, and HUD referred more than 1,300 cases of possible corruption to the Department of Justice for investigation (Bonastia 2006, 133). By 1974, at least 239 HUD employees, builders, real estate speculators, and mortgage bankers had been convicted of giving or accepting bribes or other illegal activities, and 227 had been indicted (*Newsweek*, "Housing: The FHA Scandals," May 20, 1974).

The homeownership program was suspended in 1973, reactivated with substantial modifications in 1975, and terminated in 1987.[14] Over the life of the program, it provided subsidies to more than 500,000 low-income households. The number of households receiving assistance peaked at 419,000 in 1974. By mid-1979, 20 percent of the originally subsidized households had defaulted on their loan (Weicher 1980, 124). Only 125,000 units were built under the revised program (Carliner 1998, 314).

To avoid future programs performing this poorly, it is important to understand the reasons for the disappointing performance of the homeownership program.

The minimal down payment combined with the excessive price paid for many houses could explain the high default rate. Because the down payment was minuscule and the price paid for the house often greatly exceeded its market value, many occupants had no equity in their houses. They were essentially renters who remained in their house as long as it provided services worth their subsidized monthly mortgage payment or until changing circumstances dictated moving. Otherwise, they defaulted on their mortgages. The question is why the sales price was well in excess of market value in so many cases. Because these scandals had a profound effect on the direction of low-income housing policy, this question deserves careful consideration.

Most explanations that have been offered are problematic. One popular explanation, such as that of Representative William Widnall, is that families who were eligible for this program were incompetent buyers of housing (U.S. Congress, House Committee on Banking and Currency 1971, 2–3). However, many unsubsidized households in the same income categories as program participants were homeowners. Why did program participants pay much higher prices for similar housing? Another popular explanation for the excessive prices paid for the houses is administrative failures. It is undeniable that the program had such failures. The question is whether they were due to the particular personnel involved or the design of the program. Well-designed programs minimize the incentives for corruption. Some economists have offered an explanation for overpriced houses based on a feature of the program's design, namely, that the buyers had no incentive to resist the higher price because the amount they would pay each month was the same no matter how much the seller received for it (Aaron 1972, 138–39; Quigley 2000, 61). This argument fails to recognize the buyer's incentive to get the best house possible for whatever they contribute to its cost. If the program allows an eligible family to occupy a house with a sales price up to $40,000 for a fixed payment, why buy one whose market value is only $30,000?

Jack Guttentag suggests a more likely culprit, namely, allocating subsidies to selected suppliers (1976, 1321–323). How this would lead to overpriced houses is most easily understood for the program's new construction component. Under it, selected builders were authorized to build and sell a specified number of houses to eligible families. The number of houses authorized was always a small fraction of the number of eligible families. Due to the subsidies, the number of eligible families who would have wanted to participate in the program had builders charged market prices for the houses greatly exceeded the number of houses authorized. As a result, the developers authorized to build and sell units under the program would have been able to sell their units even had they charged above-market prices. They had a captive audience. Buyers who were eligible for the program would not have received a subsidy had they bought from other suppliers. Because FHA provided mortgage insurance, it sent its appraisers to the houses to certify that the houses were not overpriced. Builders had a strong incentive to bribe the appraiser to certify prices in excess of market prices. Some builders offered, and some appraisers accepted, bribes. The result was excessive cost for the housing provided.

Overpricing also occurred in the existing component of the program. Because eligible buyers were allowed to buy from any seller, why would they agree to pay, say, $30,000 for a house with a market value of $20,000? An important part of the explanation is surely that realtors told the eligible families that a fixed amount of money was allocated to the program, and if they delayed making a decision about a house, they risked losing the subsidy.

The performance of U.S. Department of Agriculture's (USDA) Section 502 Single Family Direct Loan Program lends support to the preceding explanation for the poor performance of the Section 235 Homeownership Program. The USDA program differed from Section 235 in one important respect, and it did not suffer from scandals or high default rates (Carliner 1998). Until 1968, the subsidy under the USDA program was modest and did not depend on the household's income. It consisted of lending at the federal borrowing rate to farmers and others living in rural areas. The 1968 Housing Act authorized the USDA to pay a portion of the loan repayments for low-income households using the same subsidy formula as Section 235. The primary difference between the programs concerned the allocation of the subsidies. Unlike Section 235, eligible families applied to the USDA's local offices for assistance, and families offered assistance were free to buy any house that met the program's standards.

Although the scandals in Johnson's homeownership program attracted the lion's share of congressional and newspaper attention, his signature rental program (Section 236) also had serious problems. The default rate on its FHA-insured mortgages exceeded Section 235's rate (Weicher 1980, 46).[15] Anecdotal evidence suggested that limited dividend corporations earned large profits, despite the nominal cap on their returns, by overstating the project's cost and hence their equity in it (Downie 1974, 47–51; John Herbers, "Housing Reform Bill Lags As Nation's Crisis Grows," *New York Times*, July 24, 1972). The large number of applicants for the limited budget suggests that excess profits could be earned. Only a third of applications could be approved (Edson and Lane 1972, 2:11).

Direct Descendants of Johnson's Housing Programs

The Nixon administration and its HUD secretary George Romney initially embraced the goals in the 1968 Housing Act, and many additional units were authorized in his first term. However, scandals in Johnson's housing programs, especially his signature homeownership program, the high default rates on their insured mortgages, and their unexpectedly large cost to the government led President Nixon, on January 8, 1973, to declare a moratorium on new commitments under these programs and create a task force, the National Housing Policy Review, to study them and recommend reforms. Based in part on the results, Congress in the 1974 Housing and Community Development Act accepted the administration's proposals to replace the BMIR program that Johnson had inherited, his leased housing program, and his signature rental housing program (Section 236) with alternative programs of tenant-based and project-based rental assistance, namely, the Section 8 Existing Housing Program and Section 8 New Construction and Substantial Rehabilitation Program. These reforms had bipartisan support. The vote was 76 to 11 in the Senate and 351 to 25 in the House. Congress reactivated a substantially revised version of Johnson's homeownership program a year later.

The Section 8 Existing Housing Program (hereafter the housing voucher program) differed little from the variant of Johnson's Leased Existing Housing Program that allowed each assisted recipient to find its own unit as long as it met minimum housing standards and rented for less than a specified amount.[16] The poorest recipients were eligible for the largest subsidies; the federal government paid the entire rent for the very poorest.[17] This program has become HUD's largest low-income housing program, serving more than 2 million households.

The 1974 Housing Act also created the Section 8 New Construction and Substantial Rehabilitation Program (hereafter Section 8 New Construction Program) that combined features of Johnson's programs. This became HUD's largest program of privately owned subsidized projects. Like Section 236, it offered subsidies to selected private developers to build, or substantially rehabilitate, projects for low-income households. In addition to construction subsidies, the developer received monthly subsidies equal to the difference between a specified amount and the tenant's rent. As in Johnson's Leased New Construction Program, the tenant's rent was 25 percent of its countable income. Evidence on the Section 8 New Construction Program's excessive cost (discussed later) led to its repeal in the Housing and Urban-Rural Recovery Act of 1983. Before its termination, about 900,000 units were built or substantially rehabilitated; most have continued to serve low-income households with the help of HUD subsidies. Indeed, many units built under older programs now receive subsidies from the Section 8 Program.

The direct descendants of the Johnson initiatives remedied a major deficiency of Johnson's signature programs from the viewpoint of poverty alleviation. Like Johnson's early initiatives but unlike his signature programs, they heavily targeted the poorest households. About 70 percent of the households in the housing voucher program and 68 percent in the Section 8 New Construction Program had incomes below $3,000 in 1970 prices (HUD 1978a, tables 95, 104, 127, 134).[18] These percentages are similar to those for public housing and Johnson's rent supplement program (see table 8.2).

Consequences for Poor Households

Although several of Johnson's housing programs performed poorly, they nevertheless initiated a dramatic shift over time in the share of families living in subsidized private-market units (rather than government projects) that has benefited poor families. Specifically, the shift greatly improved the cost-effectiveness of the system of government housing programs, thereby making it possible to serve many more families with a given budget, and led to significant improvements in the health and well-being of recipients compared with what would have hap-

TABLE 8.4 / Estimated Ratio of Total Cost to Market Rent

Program	Pittsburgh	Phoenix
Public housing	2.20	1.79
Section 236	2.01	1.47
Section 23 existing	1.67	1.11
Housing allowances	1.15	1.09

Source: Adapted from Mayo et al. (1980b, table 5.1).

pened under a simple expansion of public housing. The best evidence on cost-effectiveness comes from the Experimental Housing Allowance Program (EHAP) of the 1970s, a large social experiment.[19] Stephen Mayo and his colleagues (1980b) study the cost-effectiveness of public housing (conventional and turnkey), Section 236 (new construction and substantial rehab), Section 23 Existing (Johnson's precursor to the housing voucher program), and housing allowances (minimum condition type used in EHAP and in a national housing voucher program in effect between 1983 and 1999) in Pittsburgh and Phoenix. To measure cost-effectiveness, the study compares the total cost of providing the housing under each program with the market rents of the units. Within a housing market, market rent is an index of the overall desirability of the unit including its size, quality, and amenities, the attractiveness and amenities of its neighborhood, and the convenience of its location. The predictions of the market rents of subsidized units were based on the rents of unsubsidized units in the same localities and unusually detailed information on their housing and neighborhood characteristics.

Table 8.4 reports their basic results on the ratios of total cost to the market rent of the housing provided under the programs. The results indicate that it was much less expensive to provide equally good housing in Section 236 projects than in public housing, Johnson's Leased Existing Program was even more cost-effective, and the housing allowance program in which the tenants located their own units was, by far, the most cost-effective.[20]

Another study with excellent data on the housing and neighborhood characteristics of the subsidized units produced cost-effectiveness results for the direct descendants of Johnson's programs consistent with the results for the earlier programs. James Wallace and his colleagues (1981) estimated the excessive cost of Section 8 New Construction compared with the tenant-based housing voucher program to be between 44 percent and 78 percent.

The shift that Johnson's policies helped initiate from public housing to housing vouchers also helped improve the lives of poor families in other ways such as improved health and overall well-being. For example, data from HUD's Moving to Opportunity (MTO) randomized mobility experiment found that relative to public housing, receipt of a regular housing voucher generates a decline in extreme obesity that is just below the usual thresholds for statistical significance but are very large — one-quarter to one-third — of the control group prevalence (Ludwig et al. 2011, supplemental table 3). Relative to public housing, receipt of a regular housing voucher also reduces prevalence of clinical depression or anxiety disorder by one-third to one-half (Sanbonmatsu et al. 2011, table 4.3), and increases subjective well-being—that is, happiness—by an amount equivalent to around two-thirds of the black-white gap in happiness in the United States as a whole (Ludwig et al. 2012).

Except for effects on racial segregation discussed in the next section, the change in the mix of programs has had only a modest effect on other important aspects of program performance. The best available evidence suggests that the consequences for adult productivity from changing the mix of housing programs away from public housing toward housing vouchers are modest (Carlson et al. 2012; Olsen et al. 2005; Sanbonmatsu et al. 2011; Susin 2005). Similarly, the evidence suggests on balance little difference between the effects of public housing and housing vouchers on the educational outcomes of children in recipient households, though there may be particular benefits to getting children out of the most severely distressed, dangerous housing projects (Jacob 2004; Jacob and Ludwig 2012b; Sanbonmatsu et al. 2011; Burdick-Will et al. 2011).

REDUCING RACIAL DISCRIMINATION AND SEGREGATION IN HOUSING

Johnson opposed racial discrimination in all activities. In his State of the Union address on January 8, 1964, he said, "Let me make one principle of this administration abundantly clear. All of these increased opportunities—in employment, in education, in housing, and in every field—must be open to Americans of every color. As far as the writ of Federal law will run, we must abolish not some, but all racial discrimination" (1964a).

Although Johnson considered eliminating racial discrimination as desirable for its own sake, he also believed reducing segregation would improve the economic circumstances of blacks. Johnson pursued racial and economic integration through initiatives that changed the mix of housing programs and more direct measures to fight racial discrimination and promote racial integration. His expansion of public housing might have contributed to racial segregation, but we believe that at least a circumstantial case is to be made that the net effect of all Johnson's initiatives—including civil rights legislation intended to reduce discrimination in the private housing market and laying the groundwork for a shift away from public housing projects toward subsidized private projects and housing vouchers—helped contribute to the decline in residential racial segregation that has occurred in the United States starting sometime around 1970.

Initiatives to Address Discrimination and Segregation

Johnson's major legislative initiatives, the 1964 and 1968 civil rights acts, had provisions applicable to housing discrimination. Title VI of the Civil Rights Act of

1964 prohibited discrimination based on race, color, or national origin in any program or activity receiving federal financial assistance, which obviously includes low-income housing programs. A week after the assassination of Martin Luther King Jr., Congress passed the 1968 Civil Rights Act, which had been under consideration for some time. Section VIII, known as the Fair Housing Act, broadened the scope of the 1964 act to include most housing market transactions.

Some argue that these acts provided extremely limited tools to achieve their purposes. Mainly, they allowed private fair-housing groups the right to sue alleged violators. Over time, these groups became increasingly active and effective in winning lawsuits (Massey and Denton 1993, chapter 7; Yinger 1995, chapter 10). However, this case-by-case approach arguably had limited potential to affect the overall pattern of racial segregation. Others maintain that the laws could have been used much more aggressively to promote racial integration. For example, the 1968 act required federal agencies to affirmatively further fair housing. In selecting which privately owned projects received subsidies, HUD could have given much more weight to the minority concentration in the neighborhood of the proposed project and effective affirmative marketing methods (Bonastia 2006).

Under the Johnson administration, HUD issued some regulations and directives to implement the 1964 Civil Rights Act (Bonastia 2006, 76). However, it is not clear how vigorously HUD pursued them. Opposition to racial integration in housing was substantial. Because the 1968 act occurred at the end of Johnson's term, its implementation fell to the Nixon administration.

Although President Nixon did not share his HUD Secretary George Romney's enthusiasm for government actions to promote racial integration in housing (Bonastia 2006, 108–10), he did implement the 1968 Fair Housing Act. On June 11, 1971, he issued a lengthy statement that summarized the constitutional provisions, statutes, and executive orders related to racial discrimination in housing and the policies of his administration in this regard (Nixon 1971). Soon after, HUD issued regulations for the selection of housing projects under the public housing program and programs that subsidized privately owned projects that gave some weight to providing nonsegregated housing opportunities to minorities, albeit a weight that deeply disappointed those with the greatest enthusiasm for promoting racial integration (*Federal Register* 1972). This was the most immediate direct descendant of Johnson's fair-housing initiatives. The Fair Housing Amendments Act of 1988 was an important, but much later, descendant that substantially increased the tools for enforcement (Massey and Denton 1993, 209–12; Yinger 1995, 190–93, 221–23).

In addition to his landmark civil rights laws, Johnson pursued low-income housing policies that weakened the ability of local governments to control the locational choices of subsidized households. Under his signature rental and home-ownership programs, local governments did not have the same veto power over the location of projects as they did with public housing, though they sometimes attempted to use their zoning powers and other local regulations to prevent projects at particular locations.

Effects of Johnson's Initiatives and Their Direct Descendants

Although it was not his primary motivation, Johnson's housing policies were intended to promote racial and economic integration or at the very least to avoid the ill effects of public housing in this regard. The evidence indicates that the change in the mix of housing assistance away from public housing and toward privately owned projects and dwelling units achieved this goal to some extent.

Some relevant evidence comes from EHAP's Housing Assistance Demand Experiment in the 1970s, which showed that segregation levels were higher for families when they were in public housing than when they did not participate in any low-income housing programs (Mayo et al. 1980a, chapter 5). EHAP data indicated that families moving into public housing wound up living in higher-poverty census tracts than they would have otherwise, and that black public housing tenants moved to census tracts with a significantly higher fraction black. For example, public housing tenants in the Pittsburgh EHAP site moved from census tracts with a mean low-income concentration of 37 percent to ones with 50 percent. Black public housing tenants in Pittsburgh moved from census tracts with a mean minority concentration of 52 percent to ones with 69 percent.[21] The EHAP data show that, by contrast, other housing programs like Johnson's signature Rental Housing Program (Section 236), his Leased Housing Program (Section 23), and housing allowances similar to current housing vouchers had only a small effect on economic or racial segregation relative to families not in housing programs. The implication is that shifting from public housing to other programs reduced segregation.

HUD's more recent Moving to Opportunity experiment, which included a treatment that randomly offered public housing families the opportunity to use regular Section 8 housing vouchers, also found declines in economic segregation and modest declines in racial segregation for voucher recipients relative to those living in public housing (Sanbonmatsu et al. 2011; Ludwig 2012). Moving out of public housing with a regular Section 8 voucher reduced average census tract poverty rates one year after the voucher offer by about 45 percent, about 22 percentage points compared with the average for the MTO control group of 50 percent. It also reduced the average tract poverty rate families experienced over ten to fifteen years by about 25 percent, 11 percentage points compared with a control mean of 40 percent. The effect on average tract minority share was much smaller — about 3 percentage points, compared with 88 percent for the MTO control group that did not receive help moving out of public housing.

Therefore, the limited evidence suggests the shift in the mix of housing assistance from public housing toward privately owned projects and housing vouchers that resulted from Johnson's initiatives and their descendants reduced racial and economic segregation.

Did the fair-housing provisions of the 1964 and 1968 civil rights acts also contribute to declines in the economic and racial segregation of low-income families? Direct evidence on this question is not available. William Collins (2004) examines the effects of state-level fair-housing laws enacted during the 1960s before the 1968 change in federal law. Some, but not all, states had enacted such laws. These state laws typically had broader coverage and stronger enforcement mechanisms than the 1968 Fair Housing Act (Collins 2004, 535). Although Collins finds little effect of these laws on housing conditions for blacks, his study captures fairly short-term impacts. Thus, if longer periods are required for housing market changes, they will not be reflected in his estimates. Moreover the states enacting such laws during the 1960s were almost all outside the South. Previous research has found that federal antidiscrimination laws targeted to the labor market had more pronounced effects inside the South than outside it (Donohue and Heckman 1991). The same could be true with housing.

Although responsibility for this change is difficult to apportion across policy or other social changes, it is unarguably true that America has become less racially segregated since 1970. Edward Glaeser and Jacob Vigdor (2001, 2012) document that the mean of the standard measures of racial segregation—the dissimilarity and the isolation index—across metropolitan areas had increased continuously between 1890 and sometime between 1960 and 1970 and had declined continuously since then. In 1960, about 20 percent of urban census tracts had no black residents. In 2010, only 0.5 percent had none (Glaeser and Vigdor 2012). Glaeser and Vigdor attribute some of that decline to the federal fair-housing legislation. However, based on the evidence in two major national fair-housing audits, John Yinger (1999, 95) concludes that the available evidence does not indicate a trend in discrimination between 1979 and 1989. Obviously, there is considerable uncertainty about the effects of the Johnson's initiatives to reduce racial discrimination and segregation in housing.

CONCLUSION

In the interest of improving the housing conditions of millions of the poorest families, Johnson launched the largest number of major housing initiatives in the country's history. Many people had hoped that helping poor people meet their housing needs would promote economic self-sufficiency by improving residential stability (presumably useful for getting and keeping a job) or improving the conditions in which people live. In practice, however, the subsidy discourages work and reduces labor supply. Nevertheless, the large increase in the number of poor families who received means-tested housing assistance did increase the consumption levels of poor families. These improvements in living conditions do not show up in the official poverty rate, which focuses on income rather than consumption, but the expansion of housing programs did reduce "consumption poverty."

The most surprising legacy of the War on Poverty was to begin the process of increasing the reliance of means-tested housing programs on the private housing market. Most of Johnson's initiatives emphasized the building of privately owned subsidized projects, but one of his smallest initiatives led to the creation of the tenant-based Section 8 housing voucher program. These changes in the mix of housing programs improved the efficiency of the system of low-income housing assistance in providing housing services, by reducing the total cost of providing poor families with housing of a given quality. Recent data from Moving to Opportunity and other studies suggest that this shift from public housing to vouchers, though it did not have much impact on the economic self-sufficiency of recipients or the schooling outcomes of their children, did improve the well-being of the poor by improving their health and subjective well-being—that is, their happiness.

Whether we continue the shift Johnson initiated and go even further away from project-based housing assistance to housing vouchers remains the subject of debate within the housing policy community. The available evidence suggests that relative to project-based housing, vouchers help families live in at least slightly less economically and racially segregated neighborhoods. Evidence on the older construction programs that have been studied indicate that vouchers also enable the government to provide units of a given quality to poor families at lower cost. High-quality evidence about whether vouchers are more cost-effective than current construction programs that provide project-based assistance—such as the Low-Income Housing Tax Credit, HOME (Home Investment Partnerships Program), and HOPE VI—should be one of the highest research priorities for housing policy at present.

If there is an even higher priority research question in housing policy, it is related to the common argument made for generations against exclusive reliance on tenant-based housing assistance—namely, that construction programs will work better in certain market conditions or local regulatory environments (for example, very tight housing markets). This belief is not based on any evidence on the performance of different programs in different environments. Evidence on this matter is of the utmost importance for guiding low-income housing policy moving forward.

We are grateful to Martha Bailey, Raphael Bostic, Sheldon Danziger, Michael Feinberg, Robert Haveman, Guian McKee, Alice O'Connor, John Weicher, John Yinger, and two anonymous reviewers for helpful input, and to Brett McCully for research assistance. Ludwig's work on this chapter was supported in part by visiting scholar awards from the Russell Sage Foundation and LIEPP at Sciences Po, and an investigator award in health policy research from the Robert Wood Johnson Foundation. Any errors and all opinions are, of course, those of the authors alone.

NOTES

1. Because the many housing programs that subsidize the construction of privately owned projects are intended to achieve essentially the same goals by different means that cannot be succinctly described, most are referred to by the section number of the relevant legislation. To help the reader navigate this complicated system, table 8.1 summarizes the programs discussed in this chapter.

2. On average, across fifteen of the largest metropolitan areas in 1977, about 73 percent of black families would have had to switch places with white families to achieve the same percentage black in each project in the metro area (Massey and Denton 1993, 203). The situation was surely similar at the outset of the Johnson administration.

3. Bradford Hunt (2009, chapter 4) provides an excellent account for one city. More generally, in order for a public housing project to be built in a political jurisdiction, it must establish a public housing authority (PHA). Many jurisdictions chose not to create one. Furthermore, because the PHA had to obtain the local government's signature on a co-operation agreement in order to develop public housing projects, the local government had veto power over the location of the projects. A few states required voter approval in a referendum. After 1954, building public housing required a federally certified Workable Program for community improvement (U.S. President's Committee on Urban Housing 1969, 60). Localities could prevent development of public housing projects by failing to submit one to the Housing and Home Finance Agency (HUD's predecessor).

4. In talking about any president's legacy, it is important to account for the lags between the creation of new programs and the receipt of assistance. For any new program, regulations must be written and an administrative staff must be assembled before the program can begin operation. For housing programs that have a competition for limited funds, there are inevitably long lags between the request for proposals and project completion. Even for established construction programs, the lag between congressional appropriations and units available for occupancy is substantial.

5. Two large programs that were not direct descendants serve at least a million additional households. The Low-Income Housing Tax Credit (LIHTC), authorized in 1986, and the HOME Investments Partnership Program, established in 1990, are the only two large housing programs created since 1974. Because they often combine subsidies from each other and earlier programs, it is difficult to determine their net effect on the number of households that have received low-income housing assistance. John Weicher (2012, chapter 4) reports that the LIHTC served about 1.8 million households in total in 2009, that about 1.0 million did not receive other assistance, and that the HOME program served about 1.2 million in total. Except when combined with other programs that provide deep subsidies, the LIHTC has served few poor households (U.S. Government Accountability Office 1997, 147).

6. Under the conventional approach, the PHA hired a private firm to build a well-specified project at a particular location. Under the turnkey method, the PHA solicited bids from private developers to build a project with a particular number of units on a site selected by the developer and provided minimal guidance concerning the features desired. Applicants responded with a general plan and statement of qualifications, the PHA selected a bidder to produce a detailed plan and negotiated a contract, and the developer built the project and was paid on its satisfactory completion (Edson and Lane 1972, chapter 6).

7. Tenants paid the same rent in these projects that they would in public housing, and the PHA agreed to provide subsidies for twenty years on behalf of their tenants, provided that the unit continued to meet HUD's minimum housing standards.

8. The budgetary accounting rules counted the full cost of building the project in its first year. This was offset by later payments to the federal government at below market interest rates over the term of the mortgage.

9. This goal fails to recognize that low-income housing programs have not, and arguably could not, be limited to households that would live in substandard housing in the absence of the program.

10. Barbara Schone (1992) has shown that this effect of the usual subsidy formula on labor earnings is not an implication of standard economic theory when restrictions on consumption that result from the program's all-or-nothing offer of a particular dwelling unit are taken into account.

11. These are estimates of the mean of the unrestricted cash grants that would be as satisfactory to public housing tenants as participation in the public housing program.

12. In May 1970, 52 percent of the projects were built by limited-dividend corporations, 38 percent by nonprofits, and 10 percent by cooperatives (Edson and Lane 1972, 2:8).

13. By 1980, 30 percent of households in Section 236 projects received additional subsidies from the rent supplement program or its successors (Olsen 2003, table 6.5).

14. The revised program was limited to new construction, it required a more substantial down payment, and its maximum subsidy was much smaller in real terms.

15. The default rate was higher for nonprofit sponsors, possibly reflecting their inexperience in housing development and management (U.S. General Accounting Office 1978).

16. The specified amount varies with household size and composition and across metropolitan areas and nonmetro counties. In the original Section 8 program, it was called the Fair Market Rent (FMR).

17. If a household occupied a unit renting for exactly the specified upper limit, it contributed 25 percent of its countable income toward the rent and the federal government paid the rest. If the tenant occupied a less expensive unit, it shared the saving with the government. Later versions of the program had somewhat different subsidy schemes, but the poorest recipients were eligible for the largest subsidies in all cases (Olsen 2003, 401–04).

18. The HUD *Statistical Yearbook* reports the fraction of recipients with an annual income less than $5,000 in 1978. Between 1970 and 1978, the consumer price index rose 68 percent. Therefore, $5,000 in 1978 prices corresponded to a nominal income of about $3,000 in 1970.

19. Edgar Olsen (2003, 394–99) provides a brief account of the evidence on the cost-effectiveness of low-income housing programs. In a later study, he provides a more detailed account (2009).

20. The excessive cost of public housing and subsidized private projects is usually attributed to the absence of financial incentives for good decisions on the part of civil servants who operate public housing, offering overly generous subsidies to selected developers of private projects, and subsidy formulas that favor some inputs relative to others.

21. The effects for public housing were much more modest in the Phoenix EHAP site, where Hispanics were the predominant minority.

REFERENCES

Aaron, Henry J. 1972. *Shelter and Subsidies: Who Benefits from Federal Housing Policies?* Washington, D.C.: Brookings Institution Press.

Abt Associates, Gregory Mills, Daniel Gubits, Larry Orr, David Long, Judie Feins, Bulbul Kaul, Michelle Wood, Amy Jones & Associates, Cloudburst Consulting, and QED Group. 2006. *Effects of Housing Vouchers on Welfare Families*. Washington: U.S. Department of Housing and Urban Development.

Bonastia, Christopher. 2006. *Knocking on the Door: The Federal Government's Attempt to Desegregate the Suburbs*. Princeton, N.J.: Princeton University Press.

Burdick-Will, Julia, Jens Ludwig, Stephen W. Raudenbush, Robert J. Sampson, Lisa Sanbonmatsu, and Patrick Sharkey. 2011. "Converging Evidence for Neighborhood Effects on Children's Test Scores: An Experimental, Quasi-Experimental and Observational Comparison." In *Whither Opportunity? Rising Inequality, Schools, and Children's Life Chances*, edited by Greg J. Duncan and Richard J. Murnane. New York: Russell Sage Foundation.

Carliner, Michael S. 1998. "Development of Federal Homeownership 'Policy'." *Housing Policy Debate* 9(?): 299–321.

Carlson, Deven, Robert Haveman, Tom Kaplan, and Barbara Wolfe. 2012. "Long-Term Earnings and Employment Effects of Housing Voucher Receipt." *Journal of Urban Economics* 71(1): 128–50.

Collins, William J. 2004. "The Housing Market Impact of State-Level Anti-Discrimination Laws, 1960–1970." *Journal of Urban Economics* 55(3): 534–64.

Currie, Janet, and Aaron Yelowitz. 2000. "Are Public Housing Projects Good for Kids?" *Journal of Public Economics* 75(1): 99–124.

Donohue, John J., III, and James Heckman. 1991. "Re-Evaluating Federal Civil Rights Policy." *Georgetown Law Journal* 79(6): 1713–736.

Downie, Leonard. 1974. *Mortgage on America*. New York: Praeger Publishers.

Edson, Charles L., and Bruce S. Lane. 1972. *A Practical Guide to Low- and Moderate-Income Housing*. Washington, D.C.: Bureau of National Affairs.

Federal Register. 1972, January 7. "Evaluation of Rent Supplement Projects and Low-Rent Housing Assistance Applications," vol. 37, no. 4, pp. 203–9.

Glaeser, Edward L., and Jacob L. Vigdor. 2001. *Racial Segregation in the 2000 Census: Promising News*. Washington, D.C.: Brookings Institution Press.

———. 2012. *The End of the Segregated Century: Racial Separation in America's Neighborhoods, 1890–2010*. New York: Manhattan Institute.

Guttentag, Jack M. 1976. "Direct Federal Loans Versus Interest Rate Subsidies." In *Housing in the Seventies: Working Papers*, vol. 2. National Housing Policy Review. Washington: U.S. Department of Housing and Urban Development.

Hunt, D. Bradford. 2009. *Blueprint for Disaster*. Chicago: University of Chicago Press.

Jacob, Brian A. 2004. "Public Housing, Housing Vouchers, and Student Achievement: Evidence from Public Housing Demolitions in Chicago." *American Economic Review* 94(1): 233–58.

Jacob, Brian A., and Jens Ludwig. 2012a. "The Effects of Housing Assistance on Labor Supply: Evidence from a Voucher Lottery." *American Economic Review* 102(1): 272–304.

———. 2012b. "Neighborhood Effects on Low-Income Families: Evidence from a Randomized Chicago Housing-Voucher Lottery." Working Paper, University of Michigan Ford School of Public Policy.

Jencks, Christopher, and Susan E. Mayer. 1990. "The Social Consequences of Growing Up in a Poor Neighborhood." In *Inner City Poverty in the United States*, edited by Laurence Lynn and Michael McGeary. Washington, D.C.: National Academy Press.

Johnson, Lyndon B. 1964a. "Annual Message to the Congress on the State of the Union, January 8, 1964." Washington: Government Printing Office. Available at: http://www .lbjlib.utexas.edu/johnson/archives.hom/speeches.hom/640108.asp (accessed April 4, 2013).

———. 1964b. "Special Message to the Congress on Housing and Community Development." January 27, 1964. Washington: Government Printing Office. Available at: http:// www.presidency.ucsb.edu/ws/?pid=26035 (accessed April 6, 2013).

———. 1965. "Remarks at the Signing the Housing and Urban Development Act." August 10, 1965. Washington, D.C.: Government Printing Office. Available at: http://www.pres idency.ucsb.edu/ws/?pid=27147 (accessed April 6, 2013).

———. 1968. "Remarks upon Signing the Housing and Urban Development Act of 1968." August 1, 1968. Washington: Government Printing Office. Available at: http://www .presidency.ucsb.edu/ws/?pid=29056 (accessed April 6, 2013).

Ludwig, Jens. 2012. "Guest Editor's Introduction: Special Issue on Moving to Opportunity." *Cityscape* 14(2): 1–28.

Ludwig, Jens, Greg J. Duncan, Lisa A. Gennetian, Lawrence F. Katz, Ronald C. Kessler, Jeffrey R. Kling, and Lisa Sanbonmatsu. 2012. "Neighborhood Effects on the Long-Term Well-Being of Low-Income Adults." *Science* 337(6101): 1505–510.

Ludwig, Jens, Lisa Sanbonmatsu, Lisa Gennetian, Emma Adam, Greg J. Duncan, Lawrence F. Katz, Ronald C. Kessler, Jeffrey R. Kling, Robert C. Whitaker, and Thomas McDade. 2011. "Neighborhoods, Obesity, and Diabetes: A Randomized Social Experiment." *The New England Journal of Medicine* 365(16): 1509–519.

Massey, Douglas S., and Nancy A. Denton. 1993. *American Apartheid: Segregation and the Making of the Underclass.* Cambridge, Mass.: Harvard University Press.

Mayo, Stephen K., Shirley Mansfield, David Warner, and Richard Zwetchkenbaum. 1980a. *Housing Allowances and Other Rental Assistance Programs – A Comparison Based on the Housing Allowance Demand Experiment,* part 1, *Participation, Housing Consumption, Location, and Satisfaction.* Cambridge, Mass.: Abt Associates.

———. 1980b. *Housing Allowances and Other Rental Housing Assistance Programs – A Comparison Based on the Housing Allowance Demand Experiment,* part 2, *Costs and Efficiency.* Cambridge, Mass.: Abt Associates.

Murray, Michael. 1975. "The Distribution of Tenant Benefits in Public Housing." *Econometrica* 43(4): 771–88.

Newman, Sandra J., and Joseph M. Harkness. 2002. "The Long-Term Effects of Public Housing on Self-Sufficiency." *Journal of Policy Analysis and Management* 21(1): 21–43.

Newman, Sandra J. and Ann B. Schnare. 1997. "'. . . and a Suitable Living Environment': The Failure of Housing Programs to Deliver on Neighborhood Quality." *Housing Policy Debate* 8(4): 703–41.

Nixon, Richard M. 1971. "Statement About Federal Policies Relative to Equal Housing Opportunity." June 11, 1971. Santa Barbara: University of California, The American Presidency Project. Available at: http://www.presidency.ucsb.edu/ws/?pid=3042 (accessed April 9, 2013).

Olsen, Edgar O. 2003. "Housing Programs for Low-Income Households." In *Means-Tested Transfer Programs in the United States,* edited by Robert A. Moffitt. Chicago: University of Chicago Press.

————. 2009. "The Cost-Effectiveness of Alternative Methods of Delivering Housing Subsidies." Paper presented at the Thirty-First Annual APPAM Research Conference, Washington, D.C. (November 5–7, 2009). Available at: http://economics.virginia.edu/sites/economics.virginia.edu/files/CESurvey2009.pdf (accessed April 9, 2013).

Olsen, Edgar O., and David M. Barton. 1983. "The Benefits and Costs of Public Housing in New York City." *Journal of Public Economics* 20(3): 299–332.

Olsen, Edgar O., Catherine A. Tyler, Jonathan W. King, and Paul E. Carrillo. 2005. "The Effects of Different Types of Housing Assistance on Earnings and Employment," *Cityscape* 8(2): 163–87.

Quigley, John M. 2000. "A Decent Home: Housing Policy in Perspective." *Brookings Papers on Urban Affairs* 1(1): 53–99.

Reid, William J. 1989. *A Benefit-Cost Analysis of Section 23 Leased Public Housing.* Ph.D. diss., University of Virginia.

Sanbonmatsu, Lisa, Jens Ludwig, Lawrence F. Katz, Lisa A. Gennetian, Greg J. Duncan, Ronald C. Kessler, Emma Adam, Thomas W. McDade, and Stacy Tessler Lindau. 2011. *Moving to Opportunity for Fair Housing Demonstration Program: Final Impacts Evaluation.* Washington: U.S. Department of Housing and Urban Development, Office of Policy Development and Research.

Scholz, Karl, Robert Moffitt, and Benjamin Cowan. 2009. "Trends in Income Support," In *Changing Poverty, Changing Policies,* edited by Maria Cancian and Sheldon Danziger. New York: Russell Sage Foundation.

Schone, Barbara Steinberg. 1992. "Do Means Tested Transfers Reduce Labor Supply?" *Economics Letters* 40(3): 353–58.

Susin, Scott. 2005. "Longitudinal Outcomes of Subsidized Housing Recipients in Matched Survey and Administrative Data." *Cityscape* 8(2): 189–218.

U.S. Bureau of the Census. 1971. "Income in 1970 of Families and Persons in the United States." *Current Population Reports,* series P60, no. 80. Washington: U.S. Department of Commerce. Available at: http://www2.census.gov/prod2/popscan/p60-080.pdf (accessed May 25, 2012).

U.S. Commission on Civil Rights. 1971. *Homeownership for Lower Income Families: A Report on the Racial and Ethnic Impact of the Section 235 Program.* Washington: Government Printing Office.

————. 1974. *Equal Opportunity in Suburbia.* Washington: Government Printing Office.

U.S. Congress. House Committee on Banking and Currency. 1970. *Investigation and Hearing of Abuses in Federal Low- and Moderate-Income Housing Programs: Staff Report and Recommendations.* 91st Congress, 2nd session. December. Washington: Government Printing Office.

————. 1971. *Hearing on HUD Investigation of Low- and Moderate-Income Housing Programs.* 92d Congress, 1st session. March 31. Washington: Government Printing Office.

U.S. Congress. House Committee on Government Operations, Subcommittee on Legal and Monetary Affairs. 1971. *Defaults on FHA-Insured Mortgages(Detroit).* 92d Congress, 1st session. December 2, 3, and 4. Washington: Government Printing Office.

————. 1972a. *Defaults on FHA-Insured Mortgages (Part 2).* 92nd Congress, 2d session. February 24, May 2, 3, and 4.Washington: Government Printing Office.

————. 1972b. *Defaults on FHA-Insured Mortgages(Part 3).* 92nd Congress, 2d session. May 16. Washington: Government Printing Office.

U.S. Department of Housing and Urban Development (HUD). 1966. *HUD Statistical Yearbook*. Washington: Government Printing Office.

———. 1973. *HUD Statistical Yearbook*. Washington: Government Printing Office.

———. 1974a. *Housing in the Seventies: A Report of the National Housing Policy Review*. Washington: Government Printing Office.

———. 1974b. *HUD Statistical Yearbook*. Washington: Government Printing Office.

———. 1977. *HUD Statistical Yearbook*. Washington: Government Printing Office.

———. 1978a. *HUD Statistical Yearbook*. Washington: Government Printing Office.

———. 1978b. *Programs of HUD*. Washington: Government Printing Office.

U.S. General Accounting Office. 1978. *Section 236 Rental Housing: An Evaluation with Lessons for the Future*. PAD-78-13. Washington: Government Printing Office.

U.S. Government Accountability Office. 1997. *Tax Credits: Opportunities to Improve Oversight of the Low-Income Housing Program*. GGD/RCED-97–55. Washington: Government Printing Office.

U.S. President's Committee on Urban Housing. 1969. *A Decent Home: Report of the President's Committee on Urban Housing*. Washington: Government Printing Office.

Wallace, James E., Susan Philipson Bloom, William L. Holshouser, and Shirley Mansfield. 1981. *Participation and Benefits in the Urban Section 8 Program: New Construction and Existing Housing*, vols. 1 and 2. Cambridge, Mass.: Abt Associates.

Wallace, Phyllis A. 1977. "A Decade of Policy Developments in Equal Opportunities in Employment and Housing." In *A Decade of Federal Antipoverty Programs: Achievements, Failures, and Lessons*, edited by Robert H. Haveman. New York: Academic Press.

Weicher, John C. 1980. *Housing: Federal Policies and Programs*. Washington, D.C.: American Enterprise Institute for Public Policy Research.

———. 2012. *Housing Policy at a Crossroads*. Washington, D.C.: AEI Press.

Wilson, William Julius. 1987. *The Truly Disadvantaged: The Inner-City, the Underclass, and Public Policy*. Chicago: University of Chicago Press.

Wolman, Harold. 1971. *Politics of Federal Housing*. New York: Dodd, Mead.

Yinger, John. 1995. *Closed Doors, Opportunities Lost: The Continuing Costs of Housing Discrimination*. New York: Russell Sage Foundation.

———. 1999. "Sustaining the Fair Housing Act." *Cityscape* 4(3): 93–106.

Part III

Improving Access to Medical Care and Health

Chapter 9

Health Programs for Non-Elderly Adults and Children

Barbara Wolfe

Millions of our citizens do not now have a full measure of opportunity to achieve and to enjoy good health. Millions do not now have protection or security against the economic effects of sickness. And the time has now arrived for action to help them attain that opportunity and to help them get that protection.

President Harry Truman, November 19, 1945

Almost twenty years after President Harry Truman spoke these words in his call to Congress for national health insurance, President Lyndon Johnson signed the Medicaid and Medicare bills into law. The programs were designed to provide health-care coverage for senior citizens, the disabled, children, and the poor as part of Johnson's Great Society agenda, unofficially called the War on Poverty. The legacy of Medicaid, neighborhood health centers, and other health programs introduced at this time are the focus of this chapter.

PUBLIC HEALTH CARE BEFORE THE WAR ON POVERTY

In 1960, most health care was privately financed. Health insurance financed less than 30 percent of private health spending. Private coverage for medical care was first provided by Blue Cross and then Blue Shield in the 1940s, but grew rapidly only with modifications of tax policy (Internal Revenue Service code of 1954), which allowed employers to consider health insurance premiums as costs of business on which they and their employees paid no tax. Thus, the first large expansion of public support for health insurance came in the form of tax subsidies to the private sector. Just before the War on Poverty, an estimated 70 percent of the population had hospital insurance and nearly as many had surgical insurance, but the rates varied substantially by income and race: 34 percent of those in the lowest income group (less than $2,000 per family) having coverage versus 88 percent of those in the highest income group (more than $10,000), and 74 percent of whites but only 45.5 percent of nonwhites having coverage (National Center for Health Statistics 1964).

In terms of providing access to medical care, the public sector intervened on the supply side by financing public hospitals, military health care, public medical research, school health programs, and other medical facilities. Excluding veterans' medical programs, direct public supply-side expenditures expanded from about 0.3 percent of gross domestic product (GDP) in 1929 to 1 percent of GDP in the 1970s or the early years of the War on Poverty (Fishback and Thomasson 2006).[1]

MEDICAID

The Medicaid program was signed into law on July 30, 1965. Medicare, passed at the same time, was a program directed to those sixty-five and older; Medicaid was initially designed to cover only children in low-income families, pregnant women, and parents of authorized children. Essentially, it began as hospital coverage for these categories of poor Americans. It was a program funded by general revenue and run by states.[2] Former President Truman was part of the signing-in ceremony in honor of his leadership on health insurance, which he first proposed in 1945. Table 9.A1 is an augmented version of a table from the Centers for Medicare and Medicaid Services (CMS), which documents the various stages of Medicaid legislation. Expenditures in the first year (1966) were less than $1 billion, enrollment stood at 4 million, and per enrollee spending was less than $200.

Medicaid is a joint federal-state program under which certain standards are set federally, including a minimum package of benefits. The federal government provides the majority of financial resources, though the states' contributions are a far larger share of their revenues. At the beginning, participating states received matching federal payments between 50 percent and 83 percent of their outlays, depending on per capita income. Participating states were required to cover mandatory subpopulations and services and to supplement Medicare for dual-eligible low-income seniors. States had the option to cover additional groups and services and set the income eligibility level for mandatory groups. This state-based determination of eligibility was of great concern, and Medicaid eligibility varied widely across states. Over time, federal rules regarding eligibility have expanded and now minimum eligibility standards cover children, pregnant women, and certain other groups.

Since its inception, Medicaid has grown significantly. In 2012, it covered around 60 million people, versus about 4 million in 1966, and is the largest source of financing for nursing home and community-based long-term care. Medicaid targets the neediest and most vulnerable individuals: children, pregnant women, people with disabilities and chronic health problems, and low-income seniors. Low-income adults are covered to various degrees in some states.

Medicaid is currently the third-largest domestic federal program in the budget, and in most states it is the second largest. Medicaid outlays are largely spent on a small percentage of the beneficiaries. Most of the increase in spending has been due to an increased number of enrollees, rather than expanded spending per recipient. Medicaid spending per beneficiary has grown more slowly than premiums for employer-based coverage and national health expenditures (Kaiser Family Foundation 2012).

Broad Trends in Medicaid

Initially, Medicaid program eligibility was targeted on welfare recipients—single-parent families and the aged, blind, and disabled. But there were two exceptions: *Ribicoff children*, who met the financial standards of welfare programs, but not the categorical standards because they were in two-parent families; and the *medically needy*, whose incomes were above the eligibility standards, but who had very high medical bills. Initially, states did not face an upper-income limit for eligibility for the medically needy.

The growth of Medicaid during the first six years of its existence was substantial as states gradually implemented programs. By 1971, annual spending was $6.5 billion, and enrollment 16 million. These levels were far above those initially forecast, in part because numerous states offered coverage to optional groups, such as the medically needy, and offered optional services as well.

The Social Security Act amendments of 1972 created the Supplemental Security Income (SSI) program, which federalized existing state cash assistance programs for disabled and elderly persons (see chapter 7, this volume). Because most SSI beneficiaries receive Medicaid coverage, enrollment increased substantially. These amendments also added optional Medicaid-covered services such as intermediate-care facilities for the mentally retarded and inpatient psychiatric services for beneficiaries under age twenty-two. This coverage led to substantial growth in enrollment and expenditures because disabled persons tend to be far more expensive to cover than others eligible for Medicaid. By 1976, enrollment was about 21 million. Just over 14 percent of the under-sixty-five age group remained uninsured.

Expenditures during the late 1970s to the early 1980s rose dramatically, about 7 percent per enrollee in excess of inflation, although enrollment itself did not increase. The share of GDP spent on national health expenditures (NHE) went from 8.5 percent in 1978 to 9.5 percent in 1981, and the uninsured were reduced to about 12 percent of the under-sixty-five population. With the new Republican majority in the Senate and the election of Ronald Reagan, the pressure to reduce expenditures precipitated the passage of the Omnibus Reconciliation Act of 1981 (OBRA-81), which led to three years' of reductions in both eligibility for Aid to Families with Dependent Children (AFDC) and hence Medicaid, and in federal matching rates if states' Medicaid growth exceeded specified targets. By 1983, the overall proportion of non-elderly uninsured had climbed to 14.6 percent. State flexibility increased during this period, fostering the development of alternative delivery and financing mechanisms including capitation, health maintenance organizations, prospective payments to hospitals, and a variety of state-specific waiver programs. Medicaid expenditure growth slowed and enrollment remained at about 20 million. Spending on NHE was stable between 1982 and 1984 at 10.3 percent of GDP, but the proportion of non-elderly uninsured increased.

After this reduction in the growth of Medicaid, the flattening of expenditures on NHE, the increase in uninsured, and the end of a recession, Congress reversed course and turned to expansions of Medicaid beginning in 1984. First, it expanded eligibility for children and pregnant women. These included adding options to cover pregnancy expenses for women without children who met the Aid to Families with Dependent Children (AFDC) income criteria (Currie and Gruber 1996). From 1984 to mid-1987, eligibility expanded to persons in two-parent families whose incomes met AFDC standards. In 1988, states were required to offer twelve months of transitional health-care coverage to those who lost AFDC eligibility due to earnings. This meant opening the possibility of increased earnings while maintaining eligibility for Medicaid. By 1992, states were required to cover all pregnant women and children under the age of six living in families with incomes up to 133 percent of poverty (independent of family composition), and were permitted (with federal matching funds extended) to expand coverage up to 185 percent of poverty. Federal mandates required that all children born after October 1983 be covered in families with income up to 100 percent of the federal poverty line (FPL). Then, in 1996, Congress formally severed the tie between Medicaid eligibility and cash welfare assistance. Those who would have been eligible for Medicaid under cash assistance maintained their eligibility, but eligibility was extended to infants, children under age six, and pregnant women at levels above those for cash assistance before the reforms.

These expansions, beginning in the mid-1980s, led to an increase in expenditures as enrollment reached 35.8 million by 1992 and overall NHE grew to 13.5 percent of GDP. They also led to a slight decline in the proportion uninsured (16.8 percent in 1992) as well as to problems for states in paying for their Medicaid share. To reduce costs, managed care was encouraged and sometimes mandated by states for most categories of eligibles.

By 1995, enrollment growth stopped and even declined and expenditures flattened. This was tied to welfare reform including, in particular, the need to separately sign up and establish eligibility for Medicaid. The percentage of non-elderly uninsured stood at 16.7 percent in 1996 but increased to 17.5 percent the following year. Perhaps in response to these high rates of uninsured, especially among children, a new program to cover children was passed in 1997, the State Children's Health Insurance Program (SCHIP), discussed later in this chapter. Although the proportion uninsured was reduced for children, for all non-elderly it has stayed at or above 16 percent since 1990.

In 2001, the Bush administration created a section 1115 waiver initiative, Health Insurance Flexibility and Accountability (HIFA), which increased state flexibility, allowing states to demonstrate comprehensive approaches to increase the number of individuals with health insurance coverage using current Medicaid and SCHIP

FIGURE 9.1 / Personal Health-Care Expenditures

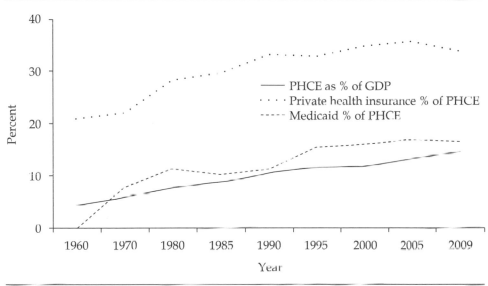

Source: Author's illustration based on Centers for Medicare and Medicaid Services (2010, table 1.1).

resources. However, as Medicaid expenditures continued to rise, reaching $271 billion and 17.1 percent of all personal health-care expenditures in 2004, Secretary Michael Leavitt of the U.S. Department of Health and Human Services established an advisory Medicaid Commission. The commission was to submit two reports. The first was to outline recommendations to achieve $10 billion in savings during the next five years and ways to begin meaningful long-term enhancements that better serve beneficiaries. The second was to provide recommendations to help ensure the long-term sustainability of Medicaid.

Figure 9.1 shows the tremendous growth of Medicaid in terms of its share of personal health-care expenditures (PHCE) beginning in 1960 at zero and continuing to 2009. Over the entire period, total PHCE increased by 9.6 percent annually in current dollars, from 4.4 percent to 14.8 percent of GDP (Centers for Medicare and Medicaid Services 2010). Medicaid increased at a greater rate than PHCE, from 8 percent of PHCE in 1970 to more than 17 percent in 2004. In comparison, between 1970 and 2009, Medicare increased from 11.5 percent of PHCE in 1970 to 19 percent in 2004 (not shown); private coverage rose from 22 percent of PHCE to 35 percent—both increasing at lower rates than Medicaid.

Medicaid provides health coverage to people who need it most and would not have it on their own. In the United States, most individuals with private health insurance are covered through employer-sponsored plans. Individuals or their parents who cannot work because of a long-term health condition, whose employer does not offer a company plan (because the worker is a part-time employee or because the firm is a small business, for example), or who are simply unemployed may find it difficult or extremely expensive to get health insurance on their own. Many of these individuals are also likely to have the most serious health needs.

Medicaid is a countercyclical program, so its expenditures and effects are larger during economic recessions. The Kaiser Family Foundation (KFF) estimates that from June 2007 to June 2011, during the most recent recession, Medicaid enrollment grew by more than 10 million, reaching 52.6 million: more than 27 million nondisabled children and nearly 25.4 million adults, including at least 725,000 adults without children, a group traditionally not covered by Medicaid. The 2010 Affordable Care Act (ACA) opens the door to a major expansion of coverage, at state option, to 133 percent of the FPL for everyone regardless of family status.[3]

Both the numbers enrolled and expenditure growth of Medicaid suggest that the expansion of public coverage under Medicaid was far more comprehensive than originally envisioned in the War on Poverty–era legislation, when only limited groups were made eligible for the program. However, the remaining high rate of the uninsured suggests a continuing issue of access to care among those with low incomes, especially childless adults. Perhaps what was also not envisioned in 1964 and 1965 is the tremendous growth in what medical care can do and its very high cost.

The ACA, formally known as the Patient Protection and Affordable Care Act, signed into law on March 23, 2010, is designed to tackle the high proportion of uninsured as well as improve the efficiency of the health-care system. In some ways, it moves from what was passed in the War on Poverty closer to Johnson's hopes for universal coverage. It was passed along largely party lines, first by the Senate in December 2009 and then by the House in March 2010. Numerous states filed legal actions in federal courts challenging the constitutionality of the law, and among the outcomes of this are limits on the federal government's ability to require all states to expand Medicaid to cover all those with incomes below 133 percent of the FPL. In addition to expanding Medicaid, the ACA creates an individual mandate for all persons to have health insurance, with an exemption for financial hardship; establishes state insurance exchanges to improve the functioning of the private insurance market; eliminates pre-existing condition clauses, thus improving the insurability of and lowering the cost for those with such conditions; expands family coverage to include children up to age twenty-six; sets up numerous incentives to experiment with ways to improve access and reduce costs of care; and establishes an essential benefits package (for a longer discussion, see Haveman and Wolfe 2010).

What Is the State of the Evaluation Literature?

Because of the variation in Medicaid programs across states, most evaluations of the program are either at the state level or, if across states, focus on the success of a particular program specification. Studies of different Medicaid programs since the program's inception in the 1960s are numerous.

One example is an evaluation of the BadgerCare Medicaid demonstration in Wisconsin (Wolfe et al. 2006). BadgerCare, launched in 1999, is a public health insurance program focused on low-income families without health insurance, especially those making the transition from welfare to work. BadgerCare expands eligibility to families with incomes up to 185 percent of the FPL, eliminates the asset test for eligibility, provides family coverage, charges monthly premiums for families with incomes above 150 percent of FPL, subsidizes purchase of employer-sponsored health insurance, and encourages qualified families to participate. BadgerCare has succeeded in achieving its main objective of bridging the gap between Medicaid and private insurance for the working poor. For example, the rate of uninsured among the non-elderly in Wisconsin was 10.6 percent in 2009 to 2010, but 18.5 percent in the rest of the nation; the difference among non-elderly adults, the target of expanded BadgerCare, was even more stark: 13 percent in Wisconsin versus 22 percent nationally.

A second type of evaluation is the ongoing study of the Oregon Medicaid initiative. This study is based on a state lottery in which adults between nineteen and sixty-four, with family income below the FPL, and uninsured for at least six months were given a chance to apply for Medicaid, a subset of whom were selected. Those selected who then applied, were found eligible, and enrolled pay a low premium ($0 to $20 per month) and no co-pays for receipt of covered services. After one year, those selected by the lottery and enrolled were found to have higher medical care use as measured by hospital admissions (2 percentage points or 30 percent) and prescription drug use (15 percent); an increase in outpatient visits of more than 50 percent; and better general health and less depression than those who signed up for the lottery but were not selected (Finkelstein et al. 2011). Thus the Oregon study provides the first strong evidence of both health especially mental health and use gains for low-income adults not previously covered. It is a strong endorsement of the potential of Medicaid expansion for improving health as well as access of the poor.[4]

A third approach to evaluation has been to compare the mortality experience of poor adults in states that offer Medicaid with their counterparts in neighboring states that do not. Benjamin Sommers, Katherine Baicker, and Arnold Epstein (2012) compare the experience of adults age twenty to sixty-four in three states that expanded Medicaid with those in neighboring states without expansions; the study covered a decade including five years prior to the expansions. The primary outcome variable is annual county-level all-cause mortality rates, though the study also collected data on insurance coverage and those in the top two categories of general self-reported health. The study finds a substantial decline in all-cause mortality due to expansions of Medicaid of about 6 percent; the reduction in mortality was larger in counties with higher proportions of poor and among nonwhites and older adults. Sensitivity analysis suggested some difference in states prior to expansions, but differences in mortality largely remained even after statistical analysis attempted to take them into account.

Medicaid's Shortcomings

For all of the gains from Medicaid, problems continue (much of this discussion is based on Wolfe 1994). Many of these are expected to be eliminated or at least reduced by the Affordable Care Act. The first problem is that coverage varies by state. Eligibility levels, the coverage of optional groups, and the components of medical care covered all continue to vary. This creates inequity and for some an inducement to move. As discussed later in this chapter, this problem may be exacerbated as some states choose not to implement the Medicaid expansion included in the ACA.

A second problem is that low reimbursement rates have led some providers to refuse to serve Medicaid recipients. This appears to especially be the case with specialists and oral health-care providers. Low reimbursement, or other rules to reduce costs, limits access and thus may have health consequences. A third problem also tied to access is the mandated use of managed care for most Medicaid recipients; although it reduces costs, this policy may limit access either because of distance to a covered provider or because managed care limits the pool of doctors and thus may exclude those who previously provided care to these individuals.

A final problem is that the Medicaid system, along with SCHIP, functions as a substitute for private coverage, and its availability may induce people to turn down coverage at their place of employment. This situation is more likely if the employee has to pay sizeable premiums plus co-payments when care is received. It is hoped that the subsidies offered through the planned exchanges, based on family income relative to the poverty line, will greatly reduce this problem, termed *crowd-out*.

WHAT DOES THE EXPERIENCE WITH MEDICAID MEAN FOR THE ACA REFORM?

The 2010 Affordable Care Act includes many provisions to reform Medicaid. In the bill as passed, income eligibility was to be made uniform across states, based on a modified adjusted gross income (MAGI) without income disregards or an asset or resource test. This approach simplifies the process of determining eligibility, and gives states less leeway to limit the populations they cover.

The original ACA Medicaid reform required states to cover all adults, regardless of whether they have children or chronic health conditions, up to 133 percent of the federal poverty level. The federal government will initially absorb the costs of the new enrollees, but states will be required to take on a share of the costs after 2016, paying 10 percent of these costs. ACA Medicaid reform will also establish minimum coverage thresholds for children age six to nineteen and parents with incomes up to 133 percent of the FPL. However, because the Supreme Court decision prevented federal government withholding of all Medicaid funds as a punishment if states do not expand coverage to these uniform levels, disparities across states may become even larger than in the past. This is especially likely for childless adults who are currently covered only in a few states under waivers. For those currently not covered and with incomes below the poverty line, no other form of subsidy is available; these individuals are likely to remain uninsured in states that do not follow the planned expansion of Medicaid.

One major hurdle facing the expansion of Medicaid in the ACA is how to meet the increased level of demand for health services. A shortage in supply of physicians and other health professionals is possible. The supply of medical specialists available to Medicaid patients is a particular concern, because the ACA does not extend payment boosts to compensate beyond primary care. Another area of concern is the potential shortage of mental health specialists. All of these may exacerbate the second problem with Medicaid, of low reimbursement rates and refusal to serve Medicaid recipients.

Some experts believe that new provisions of the ACA give states incentives to cover patients through a Medicaid Managed Care (MMC) system. The planned expansions of the ACA create a larger and more diverse population of Medicaid recipients, and a managed care structure will allow such varied needs to be addressed more efficiently. However, in certain cases, mandating managed care is an issue, as noted earlier.

It is also not clear whether MMCs are ideal for a *churning* Medicaid population—people constantly being disqualified and requalified for coverage. This problem of churning is also an issue for those who need steady treatment for chronic conditions. Unless states are aware of patients potentially falling through gaps, and guarantee twelve-month coverage intervals for adults as well as children, the problem could be significant. Individuals who do not qualify for Medicaid under the ACA are required to obtain insurance privately through one of the newly created exchanges. The people who move in and out of Medicaid will probably also be moving in and out of these exchanges. Policymakers overseeing the new health system face a challenge in making the coverage and information sharing between these two systems as seamless as possible. It will be problematic if low-income individuals are treated by two health systems that do not communicate with one another. States that do not expand Medicaid to at least 100 percent of the FPL will create an extremely inequitable situation in which those from 100 to 400 percent of the FPL are subsidized, but some of those under 100 percent receive no assistance.

Innovations funded by Medicaid may improve health-care delivery far beyond the population covered by Medicaid. The ACA funds new demonstration projects in Medicaid that make bundled payments for episodes of care that include hospitalizations, make global capitated payments to safety net hospital systems (five states), allow pediatric medical providers organized as accountable care organizations to share in cost savings, and provide Medicaid payments to institutions of mental disease for adult enrollees who require stabilization of an emergency condition (Bazelon Center for Mental Health Law 2010). These demonstrations will test different methods of payments to providers, in an effort to improve health quality outcomes, provider performance, and cost-effectiveness. The demonstrations are tied to considering new ways to pay for health care over the coming decades, and should provide data on the more efficient ways to improve the health of low-income populations.

The ACA creates a new option for states to permit Medicaid enrollees with at least two chronic conditions—or one serious and persistent mental health condition—to designate a provider as their "health home." Providers can be a physician, clinic, home health agency, or others deemed qualified by the state. States that exercise this option would receive 90 percent Federal Medical Assistance Percentage (FMAP) for those patients' health-related services for the first two years of the program. This provision is a start to improving the efficiency and effectiveness of care for patients with extensive health needs. The health-home model is designed to centralize the care of patients in one place, to improve the coordination of treatments across physicians and service providers, and to improve patients' access to care by simplifying access for them. Health-home models so far have been moderately successful in achieving these goals, specifically for high-needs patients. It is worth remembering that Medicaid spending is concentrated largely among the neediest patients, so any improvement in efficiency or savings for this subpopulation would be significant for Medicaid as a whole.

CHILDREN'S HEALTH INSURANCE PROGRAM

The State Children's Health Insurance Program, now the Children's Health Insurance Program (CHIP), was initiated in 1997 and has been reauthorized through 2019. CHIP is designed to meet the needs of low-income children who do not have a means of accessing affordable private insurance and whose family income does not qualify them for Medicaid. Many states have extended CHIP to include coverage for otherwise uninsured pregnant mothers and low-income parents.

CHIP is supported at both the state and federal levels. States design and administer the program independently, subject to programmatic guidelines set at the federal level. States may offer the CHIP program as an extension of the state Medicaid program (seven states), as a separate program in both administration and design (seventeen states), or as some combination of these two options (twenty-six states).

CHIP experienced substantial growth in children's enrollment during the early years of the program. Since 2003, growth in enrollment has slowed but continues to demonstrate an overall upwards trend. Figure 9.2 depicts the number of children ever enrolled annually from 1998 through 2010.

Primary challenges to the CHIP program have been low take-up, churning enrollment, and concerns with crowd-out, that is, parents dropping private coverage of their children or the entire family in response to eligibility for CHIP. Some states have undertaken rigorous efforts to effectively reach and serve the population targeted by CHIP. States have also adopted program features to help ensure that those already enrolled in the program do not inadvertently transition out of the program because of the procedural burdens of the reenrollment process.

Besides establishing program policies aimed at increasing enrollment and retention among the program-eligible, states have also had to meet the challenges of containing program costs and ensuring that CHIP enrollment—funded by state and federal dollars—is not substituted for private coverage among those with access to an (affordable) employer offer—that is, crowd-out. In some instances, states

FIGURE 9.2 / Children Ever Enrolled in CHIP

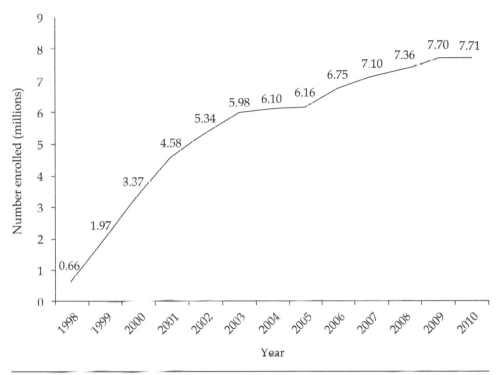

Source: Author's illustration based on Centers for Medicare and Medicaid Services (2011).

have implemented an enrollment freeze. This reached seven states in July of 2004 and seventeen from 2003 to January 2011 (Heberlein, Brooks, and Guyer 2011, table A, 27).

Literature on the Effectiveness of CHIP

Margo Rosenbach and her colleagues find that CHIP has been successful in "contributing to recent improvements in children's health insurance coverage, including substantial reductions in both the number and rate of uninsured children" (2007, 70). The authors estimate that from 1997 to 2003 lack of insurance among children fell from 11.7 to 9.9 million. This drop occurred among children below 250 percent of the FPL, but non-elderly adults saw an increase, of 2 percentage points.

Several studies examine the effects of CHIP enrollment on the use patterns of program enrollees. Genevieve Kenney (2007) finds improvement in the likelihood of office visit, preventive care, dental care, and specialty care among children enrolled in CHIP. Laura Shone and her colleagues (2005) document a CHIP-associated decrease in disparities in care access and continuity among racial-ethnic groups. However, take-up is incomplete: as of 2009, the national take-up rate among children eligible for Medicaid-CHIP was 84.8 percent (KFF 2011). Reaching the coverage-eligible and ensuring retention of the coverage-eligible remain challenging (Sommers 2010).

Disparities in access to care, including in particular specialty care, remain problematic. For example, although Shone and her colleagues (2005) document a decrease in racial disparities in access and improvements in care quality regardless of race and ethnicity tied to CHIP, they also find that racial and ethnic disparities in care quality persist.

Joanna Bisgaier and Karin Rhodes (2011) examine differences in appointment scheduling by insurance status, private versus Medicaid-CHIP, and document significant discrepancies in access to specialty services. Among the scheduling attempts where callers assumed the role of the mother of a Medicaid-CHIP-covered child, 66 percent of all phone calls resulted in appointment denial, versus 11 percent for scheduling attempts where callers assumed the role of the mother of a privately insured child. The average wait time to appointment for clinics scheduling appointments was twenty-two days longer for the Medicaid-CHIP caller scenarios. This suggests the reluctance of providers to see Medicaid-CHIP-covered children, perhaps due to low reimbursements, higher probabilities of patient no-shows, or other obstacles.

Overall, the State Children's Health Insurance Program has improved access to health services for poor and near-poor children. However, as with Medicaid, the poor do not fare as well as their counterparts.

NEIGHBORHOOD HEALTH CENTERS

Neighborhood health centers (NHCs), which take a supply-centered approach to providing increased access to health care among low-income populations, were another major component of the War on Poverty. Now known as community health centers (CHCs), NHCs were first funded in 1964 under the Economic Opportunity Act to provide health and social services access points in poor and medically underserved communities, both urban and rural, and to promote community empowerment. By the early 1970s, about 100 health centers had been established; in 1975 Congress authorized NHCs to become community and migrant health centers. At about this time, a new focus on access to care for the poor was to influence NHCs. In 1973, the Health Maintenance Organization Act called for identifying medically underserved areas (MUA). Classifying such areas included the percentage of the population below the FPL, the infant mortality rate, the percentage of elderly, and the primary care physician to population ratio. Beginning in 1975, the MUA designation was required to qualify areas to be eligible for a CHC grant. MUAs became health professional shortage areas (HPSA) and this designation is still used to determine a variety of federal assistance programs in addition to funding of CHCs (Ricketts et al. 2007). In 1989, Congress created the federally qualified health center (FQHC), which changed the options for financing and permitted cost-based reimbursement. This was largely in response to low Medicaid reimbursement rates paid in some states, which led to federal funds designated to cover poor uninsured persons being used to cover costs of care of Medicaid patients using CHCs. Community health centers provide family-oriented primary and preventative health care and serve populations with limited access to health care, including low-income populations, the uninsured, those with limited English proficiency, migrant and seasonal farmworkers, the homeless, and those living in public housing. CHCs are unique among primary care providers for the array of enabling services they offer, which include case management, translation, outreach, eligibility assistance, and health education.

Since 1996, health centers have been redefined and include public and nonprofit community-based health-care organizations defined within the Public Health Service Act. In 2010, health centers served 19.5 million patients. CHC patients are primarily low income, 92.8 percent at or below 200 percent of FPL and 71.8 percent at or below the FPL; 37.5 percent of patients were uninsured; 38.5 percent were Medicaid recipients; and 7.5 percent were Medicare recipients. Health center patients tend to be relatively young, which leads to a high demand for obstetric-gynecologic, family practice, and pediatric services (U.S. Department of Health and Human Services 2011).

Currently, health center budgets consist of a variety of funding sources. Federal grants make up about a quarter of overall CHC revenue, state and local grants an additional 12 percent, and Medicaid and Medicare reimbursements 37 percent and 6 percent, respectively. Community health centers must meet specific program requirements found in Section 330 of the Public Health Services Act to be entitled to cost-based reimbursement through Medicare and Medicaid. The federal 330 grant program has grown significantly in terms of both grantees and funds since funding was approved for the first two neighborhood health centers in 1965. In 2003, this number had reached 890 federally funded health center grantees, providing care to more than 12.4 million patients, and by 2010 grantees numbered 1,124, providing care to 19.5 million patients.

The literature on community health centers is extensive, reaching back to the 1970s. Evaluations of CHCs on measures of quality of care, improving access, reducing disparities, and cost-effectiveness are overwhelmingly favorable. CHCs are credited with reducing the nationwide infant mortality rate, as well as the incidence of low birth weight (Goldman and Grossman 1988). A higher proportion of Hispanic, African American, and poor women using health centers are up to date on cancer screening than comparable women not using health centers are (Dor et al. 2008). Reviews of Medicaid claims have shown that FQHCs have the highest proportion of pediatric patients who have received preventive services (Stuart et al. 1995), and that FQHC patients have the lowest rate of ambulatory care sensitive hospitalizations (Reynolds and Javorek 1995). CHC Medicaid patients have lower hospitalization rates and fewer per patient annual hospital days (Rothkopf et al. 2011; Freeman, Kiecoult, and Allen 1982). The costs of medical care for CHC patients are lower than comparable patients using other providers. More than half the cost reductions are thought to result from reduced inpatient care (Duggar et al. 1994). Evidence also indicates that CHCs decrease the mortality rate of the older poor, that is, those age fifty and older (Bailey and Goodman-Bacon 2012).

A 2000 Institute of Medicine report identified increasing demand for care by the uninsured and uncertain public support as the primary challenges faced by safety net providers such as CHCs. Federal health center funding has not kept pace with the costs of care. The number of health centers has greatly expanded, along with the number of uninsured patients served. Meanwhile, between 1985 and 2006, real per capita health center appropriations steadily decreased (Kaiser Family Foundation 2009).

The Affordable Care Act includes a number of provisions that will affect community health centers. The ACA allocates $11 billion for broad health center expansion over five years, and has an ultimate goal of increasing the number of patients served. In addition, $1.5 billion is appropriated for the National Health Service Corps (NHSC), which is a source of staffing for many health centers. The planned Medicaid expansions to all individuals below 133 percent of the federal poverty level, along with the creation of health insurance exchanges, will have a major impact on the insurance status of CHC patients. Finally, the current Medicare payment cap will be eliminated, and a Medicare prospective payment system for CHCs will be developed.

Despite the ACA's investment in community health centers, a number of concerns will need to be addressed moving forward. First, health centers have struggled with recruiting and retaining health professionals since their inception, and CHCs are finding it increasingly difficult to keep up with growth in demand (National Association of Community Health Centers 2008). Funded-staff vacancies are common in CHCs, particularly those in rural areas. One-third of rural grantees have been recruiting for a family physician for more than seven months, and one-half of rural grantees have been recruiting for a dentist for just as long (Rosenblatt et al. 2006). FQHC grantees rely on workforce programs, such as the NHSC and J-1 visa waivers. Further, 37.6 percent of rural CHCs have physician staff who are international medical graduates, and 32.6 percent of rural dentists are either previous recipients of NHSC scholarships or are currently receiving loan repayment from state or federal governments (Rosenblatt et al. 2006).

The ACA includes $1.5 billion in funding for NHSC program expansions; it is not clear, however, that the supply of medical professionals will be able to keep pace with planned health center expansions. That so many health centers currently have funded vacancies is a hurdle for policy goals to enhance the capacity of existing sites—such as increased hours or a broader range of services—while adding new health center grantees.

Under the ACA, it is anticipated that service capacity will reach up to 44 million patients by 2015 and up to 50 million patients by 2019 (Ku et al. 2010). This is a huge increase from the 19.5 million patients served in 2012. To reach 30 million patients by 2015, it is estimated that health centers would need at least an additional 15,585 primary care providers—which includes physicians, nurse practitioners, physician assistants, and certified midwives—along with another 11,553 to 14,397 nurses (National Association of Community Health Centers 2008).

Additional efforts will need to be made to recruit individuals to provide services. Such efforts may include exposing more students to these care environments while they are still in medical school and additional increases to NHSC funding. Although NHSC participants often leave their initial placement at the conclusion of their service requirements, they are more likely to continue working in medically underserved areas, so expanding NHSC may be viewed as more than just a short-term fix. In the past, health centers have relied on international medical graduates to address shortages in physician staff, but currently no such visa waiver program for dentists is in place.

Another concern is ensuring that health center patients have access to the full spectrum of care. Health center medical directors report major problems obtaining access to specialized medical and mental health services for uninsured patients and those covered by Medicaid. Given the finding that previous federal expansions of CHC sites "have not led to a substantial increase in the availability of many on-site specialty services, the problem of difficult access for services may increase if additional resources and planning are not devoted to assuring access to outside special services or bringing a greater array of services to CHCs" (Cook et al. 2007, 1465). The Medicaid expansions and insurance exchanges outlined in the ACA will extend insurance coverage to far greater numbers of health center patients. However, if specialized medical and mental health providers are reluctant or unwilling to accept referred Medicaid patients, it is not clear that the extended coverage will lead to adequate access beyond primary care for this subgroup. CHCs affiliated with a medical school or hospital report greater access to specialty medical care (Cook et al. 2007). Establishing networks and referral arrangements may be the best option for ensuring that health center patients have access to the full spectrum of care.

The ACA recognizes the central role that community health centers have played as an access point for individuals in traditionally underserved areas, and makes a multifaceted investment in health centers moving forward. Increased funding and expansions of the NHSC should increase service capacity, allowing community health centers to serve more patients and, ideally, offer a broader array of services. Major challenges remain in meeting the goals of more than doubling the number of patients served and providing access to the full spectrum of care.

PROGRAMS INFLUENCING THE SUPPLY OF PROVIDERS

The National Health Service Corps was established in 1970 to increase the availability of medical personnel to "medically underserved areas." It offers financial assistance to medical school students and others in exchange for service in underserved areas. There are now two types of programs: one in which a student gets a full scholarship and for each year of scholarship must serve a year in an approved underserved site or two; and a program that reduces student loans, again tied to years of service in an underserved area. From the beginning of the program through 1998, nearly 14,000 physicians and osteopaths were enrolled. The NHSC received $1.5 billion in funding from the 2010 health-care reform law and the 2009 stimulus bill and was able to expand from 3,600 clinicians in 2008 to more than 10,000 in 2010. The expansion of the student loan program goes part of the way to meet the new demands for medical care under the ACA. This is especially so for the anticipated expansion of CHCs, nearly all of which are qualified sites for persons covered by NHSC.

The NHSC has established a new Students to Service Loan Repayment Program (S2S LRP) that awards $120,000 to fourth-year medical students entering their first year of residency (over four years) in exchange for three years of NHSC service. The ACA expands the benefits and flexibility of the scholarship and loan repayment programs including moving from a full-time practice requirement to permitting practice on a half-time basis (at double the number of years) and the loan repayment up to $50,000 per year. Today about 60 percent of the NHSC serve in rural areas and 40 percent in inner-city areas; approximately 30,000 clinicians altogether have participated.

Some question whether the NHSC adequately increases the supply of medical providers to underserved areas. That is, are NHSC personnel likely to stay in service in the areas in which they meet their obligation or even move to other underserved areas, or do they just spend their required time in these communities and then move to more affluent and less rural areas? Research has suggested mixed answers: medical personnel under the NHSC do not seem likely to stay in their initial area of service. George Holmes (2004) finds that they are more likely to serve in traditionally underserved areas, however, suggesting that the NHSC is a way to improve the distribution of medical personnel and increase access.

IMPROVED ACCESS AND HEALTH?

Perhaps the most direct indicator of the success of these War on Poverty programs is the proportion of the poor or low-income population who now have health insurance coverage. According to Rosemary Stevens (1996), in 1965, just before the passage of Medicaid and Medicare, more than 70 percent of the population had some form of coverage for hospital care and 67 percent had surgical insurance, but few had coverage for out-of-hospital care. According to analysis of the National Health Survey, differences by race and income in the proportion without hospital insurance were huge in 1962 and 1963. In the lowest income group, earning less than $2,000 in that year and less than $3,000 in 1968, 65–66 percent were without coverage, versus 12 percent of those in the highest income group, earning more than $10,000. For whites, the proportion without hospital coverage was 26 percent. For nonwhites, it was nearly 54 percent. By 1968, when some states had instituted Medicaid, these proportions changed to 63.7 and 7 percent, respectively, for the lowest and highest income groups, and 18.6 and 44 percent, respectively, for the

FIGURE 9.3 / Rate of Uninsured

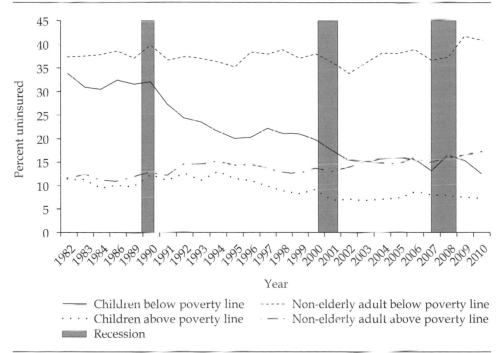

Source: Author's illustration based on Minnesota Population Center and State Health Access Data Assistance Center (2012).

two racial groups. Clearly, more progress was made for nonwhites than for those with very low incomes (U.S. Department of Health and Human Services 1964, 1972). By 1974, when Medicaid and CHCs were established, more people had some form of coverage; overall, the proportion without any coverage was about 20 percent. Children and those younger than twenty-five were more likely to be un-insured than adults; by 1974 this percentage was just above 24 percent. Big differences by income remained, however, though those defined by race declined. About 60 percent of the lowest income group were without coverage, versus fewer than 8 percent among the highest income group; by race the rate of no coverage was about 17 percent for whites and 39 percent for nonwhites (U.S. Department of Health and Human Services 1977). Figure 9.3 provides an overall picture on the proportion without coverage from 1982 onward. Official records of the uninsured were not kept earlier; rather, data were kept on numbers with policies and as-sumptions having to be made on overlap to estimate those without coverage.

In figure 9.3, two things become clear: many remain uninsured even today, and the proportion uninsured increases during recession periods. In 1982, 34 percent of those in families below the poverty line were uninsured, as were 10 percent of those in higher-income families. In 1987, 12.9 percent of the overall population was uninsured—the lowest rate over the entire period. But even then, more than 30 percent of the poor were not covered. In 2010, 16.3 percent of the overall population was uninsured, one of the highest percentages over the period; this included 29 percent of the poor and 13 percent of the nonpoor. Medicaid covered an increasing proportion of the population over this period. In 1987, 8.4 percent were covered by Medicaid, which increased steadily to the mid-1990s, when it reached 12.2 percent. Then, after declining to 9.9 percent in 1999, the proportion has steadily increased, reaching 15.9 percent in 2010, approximately 50.5 million persons (U.S. Census Bureau 2011, table C-1).

From 1987 to 2010, private employer-based coverage decreased from 62.1 percent to 55.3 percent (U.S. Census Bureau 2011). These overall numbers mask big differences by age. Figure 9.3 shows the rate of uninsured among children and non-elderly adults from 1982 onward. The pattern here is quite impressive: over time an ever-shrinking percentage of children living in poor families are without coverage—declining from 34 percent to 13 percent between 1982 and 2010. The biggest declines are in the 1990s, when the tie between Medicaid and AFDC was broken and Medicaid eligibility was extended to all poor children, and in the period after CHIP was passed and implemented. By contrast, the rate of uninsured among children in higher-income families was a much lower 11 percent in 1982, then increased through the 1990s before declining to 7 percent in about 2001. The latter figure likely also reflects the passage of CHIP and its implementation.

Figure 9.3 also shows that since 1982 the percentage of uninsured among non-elderly adults has not improved. Indeed, the percentage among the poor is higher in 2009 and 2010 than in any year since 1982. The rate for non-elderly adults in higher-income families also rose steadily throughout this period, beginning at 12 percent in 1982 and increasing to 17 percent by 2010. The age breakdown shows the success in terms of increasing coverage among children, the targeted age group, compared with adults, who lost some private coverage and gained only limited eligibility for publicly provided programs such as Medicaid. As of 2010, fewer than 10 percent of all children (9.8 percent) under age eighteen were uninsured, nearly 35 percent (34.8 percent) covered by Medicaid—the targeting of this group as previously discussed was clearly successful in reducing the percentage of children without coverage (U.S. Census Bureau 2011, table C-3).

By contrast, a high proportion of young adults are uninsured: as of 2010, 27.2 percent of those age eighteen to twenty-four and 28.4 percent of those age twenty-five to thirty-four. ACA targets coverage for the eighteen- to twenty-six-year-old population. Those in the next age group had higher rates of coverage: 21.8 percent for those age thirty-five to forty-four, 18 percent for those age forty-five to fifty-four, and 14.4 percent for those age fifty-five to sixty-four. Not surprisingly, those age sixty-five and older who are eligible for Medicare had the lowest percentage without coverage, at 2 percent.

The probability of being uninsured remains largely tied to income. Many low-income prime age adults are not employed, are not offered employer-based options, or believe they cannot afford it. Those with children may also recognize that in the event of a major episode of illness, and corresponding loss of income, they would obtain publicly provided coverage. And many who are eligible for public

FIGURE 9.4 / Visited a Doctor in Previous Year

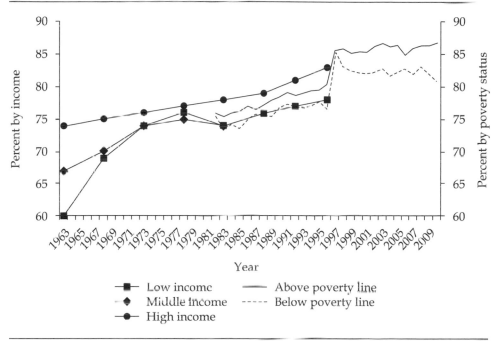

Source: Author's illustration based on Minnesota Population Center and State Health Access Data Assistance Center (2012).

coverage, especially children in low-income families, are enrolled in neither Medicaid nor SCHIP even though they are eligible. In 2010, 27 percent of families with incomes below $25,000 were not covered, nor were 22 percent of families with incomes between $25,000 and $50,000. By contrast, only 8 percent of those with incomes over $75,000 were not covered (U.S. Census Bureau 2011, table 8).

Thus those with low incomes are much more likely to not have coverage even after the expansion of War on Poverty-tied programs, particularly working-age adults. Empirical evidence is strong of a link between insurance coverage and use of health care. Those with insurance use more care, controlling for health, age, and location, than those without coverage; those with more extensive coverage tend to use more care than those with more limited coverage (see, for example, Newhouse and the Insurance Experiment Group 1993).

Coverage is one objective measure of the success of the War on Poverty medical programs, but it is also important to ask, did they increase and equalize use of care? As shown in figure 9.4, improvement in use of medical care by those in low-income families has been dramatic. In 1963, only 60 percent of low-income family members had visited a doctor in the previous year. But others in the population also did not do well: 67 percent of moderate- or middle-income families had visited a doctor, meaning that 33 percent had not, and nearly 75 percent of those in

FIGURE 9.5 / Twenty-Eight-Day Infant Mortality

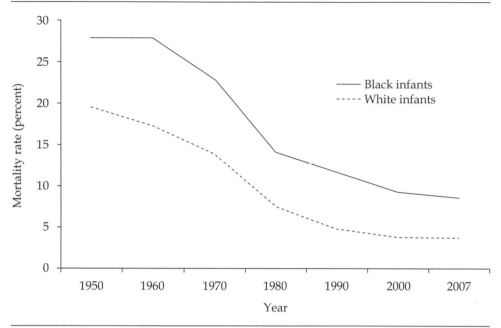

Black infants
White infants

Source: Author's illustration based on National Center for Health Statistics (2011, table 17).

high-income families had done so, meaning that 25 percent had not. Still, the poor had less access.

Since the implementation of the War on Poverty programs, access to care has improved, especially for those in low-income families. As early as 1973, the rate of having had a doctor visit in the previous year was nearly identical for the low- and middle-income families.

Coverage and use are direct measures of success of the War on Poverty programs, but what about the core objective of improving and equalizing health? Our first measure is of infant mortality, depicted in figure 9.5, and life expectancy, depicted in figure 9.6. By both measures, health has improved substantially overall, as we can see from the trend of decreasing twenty-eight-day infant mortality and increased life expectancy for both sexes and both races. Both figures also show that the gaps have decreased across the races. This suggests that the War on Poverty programs, including many beyond those studied in this chapter, may have reduced these gaps and led to improvements in health. One explanation for these changes has to do with the civil rights component of the War on Poverty. According to Douglas Almond, Kenneth Chay, and Michael Greenstone (2006), the rapid decline in post-neonatal mortality rates for blacks in the rural South beginning in 1966 is tied to the passage of Title VI of the Civil Rights Act of 1964, which prohibited discrimination and segregation in institutions receiving federal funds. When combined with the new Medicare program implemented in 1966, this meant that

FIGURE 9.6 / Life Expectancy at Birth

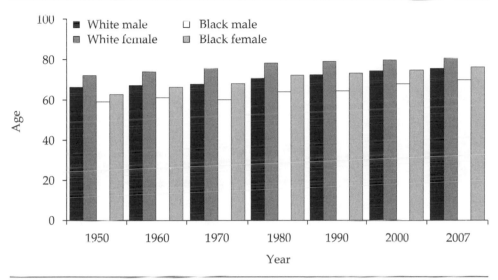

Source: Author's illustration based on National Center for Health Statistics (2011, table 22).

hospitals had to eliminate discrimination in order to receive payment, so hospitals in the South opened up to nonwhites. This end of white only hospitals improved medical care access to southern blacks and led to a major decrease in black infant mortality rates. In contrast, these authors suggest that the initial decline in post-neonatality mortality among black infants is not tied to Medicaid, because the decline occurred before Medicaid was introduced in Mississippi.

Beyond mortality, health was unequally distributed in 1963, before the War on Poverty and the start of these programs, as shown in figure 9.A1. Among those in the lowest annual income group, 14.7 percent reported having four or more conditions, versus 4.7 percent of those in the highest income group. If we use another indicator of health, those who report being bedridden for fourteen or more days in the previous year, the figure is 1.8 percent for the lowest income group and 0.7 percent for the highest, as shown in figure 9.A2. Twenty years later, with the War on Poverty programs in effect, among those in the lowest income group, a much lower 8.3 percent, versus 14.7 percent in 1963, reported having four or more conditions, compared with 1.9 percent of those in the highest income group. Clearly, the health of those in the lowest income groups improved over this period even though a measure of relative inequality, the ratio—now 4 to 1—grew.

As of 1996, the last date for which we have this measure, 1.2 percent of the low-income population reported more than fourteen days bedridden, evidence that health clearly improved for the low-income population. Bedridden days also were improved among the other income groups, 0.5 and 0.4 percent—middle and high income, respectively—reporting fourteen or more days by 1973. Here, too, however, our relative measure of inequality increased, from 2.5 in 1963 to 3.3 in 1973.

FIGURE 9.7 / Health Status and Poverty Threshold

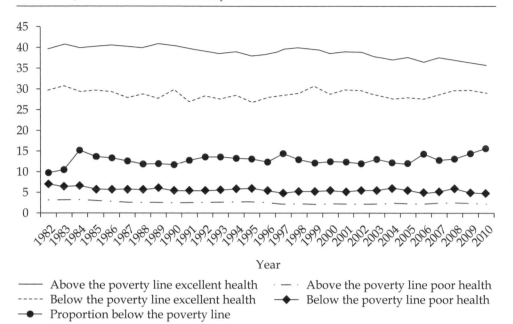

Year

—— Above the poverty line excellent health · — · Above the poverty line poor health
- - - - - Below the poverty line excellent health ◆— Below the poverty line poor health
—●— Proportion below the poverty line

Source: Author's illustration based on Minnesota Population Center and State Health Access Data Assistance Center (2012).

By both measures, then, absolute health improved among those with the lowest incomes as it did for those with higher incomes. By 1996, thirteen years later, and with changes in the categories marking income groups, the proportion of the lowest income group reporting more than four conditions remained relatively constant, at 8.85 percent in 2010. Again, the proportion in the highest income groups dropped slightly. For those reporting fourteen or more days bedridden, health appears to have improved, "only" 1.2 percent of the lowest income group reporting so many days bedridden versus 0.2 percent of those in the highest income group, again suggesting improved health though greater relative inequality in health. The relative measure will increase as the denominator decreases even if the absolute decline is equal across the income groups, or somewhat greater among the low-income group. For this reason, we pay more attention to the absolute declines.

Other related trends in health by income to 2010 shown in figure 9.7 suggest a reduction in the income gap in health, a trend that is likely attributable in part to these War on Poverty health programs. The figure shows little change in self-reports of poor health for those above or below the FPL since 1996. However, the pattern also suggests a slight decrease in the income-health gap as captured by the proportion reporting excellent health (a lower proportion of the nonpoor report excellent health) perhaps due to the aging of the population, a change in the composition of those poor and not poor, and the recent recession.

CONCLUSION

Just before the War on Poverty, most health care was privately financed; few among the poverty population had hospital insurance, the dominant form of health insurance. The federal government subsidized the purchase of employer-sponsored health insurance coverage through taxes and thus this aid was targeted to the nonpoor. Supply-side public-sector programs—such as the Hill Burton Act, military health care, school health programs, and so on—provided subsidies to institutions for providing care to the poor. The full set of these programs increased from about 0.3 percent of GDP to 1 percent from 1929 to the 1970s. Use of health care was unequal. Nearly 4 percent of the low-income population but 1 percent of middle and 0 percent of higher-income persons had never seen a doctor; 9 percent of low-income persons but less than 5 percent of middle- and higher-income populations had their last doctor visit more than five years earlier; and only 60 percent of the low-income but 74 percent of the high-income population had had at least one doctor visit in the last year, all as of 1963. The combination of limited health insurance and lower use rates were accompanied by unequal health. The infant mortality rate differed considerably by income and race, as did life expectancy.

If the War on Poverty was to be successful in reducing poverty and creating equal opportunity, clearly health was a vital part.

The core program to increase access to health care was Medicaid, but it was initially targeted only on a limited group of people—low-income children in single-parent families and their resident parent. Soon after low-income persons with disabilities were added; still, many of the poor were not covered by Medicaid. States were free to set income eligibility thresholds for these children and parents, but the services to be covered were set federally. States could also cover some additional groups but such coverage still largely excluded adults without children unless the adult was disabled. Slowly, coverage was expanded to children in two-parent low-income families and to low-income pregnant women. The required tie between participation in cash assistance and eligibility for Medicaid was eliminated, improving the potential for Medicaid to cover more of the targeted population of children in single-parent households. A new program, the State Children's Health Insurance Program, then further expanded public insurance to low-income children and in some states to their parents using an enhanced match. That is, a greater contribution of the federal government to encourage states to both participate and expand eligibility. Still, major differences in eligibility and take-up remain with inequality across states.

In terms of the direct goals of the Medicaid component of the War on Poverty, it is largely a success. More low-income children are covered; indeed the rate of coverage of children is higher than for all other groups of non-elderly. The combination of federal funding of the majority of the cost and the defining of a benefit package appears to have led to a great deal of success in coverage of the target group of low-income children. A far greater proportion of low-income children are covered—those in two-parent families—than were part of the initial design of the program. Program expansions that required coverage of all children below specific income levels reduced inequality of eligibility, and hence coverage, across states.

Defining a benefit package and payment for the majority of the expanded coverage by the federal government are part of the design of the Affordable Care Act. The initial legislation also established minimum eligibility levels, 133 percent of the FPL, for Medicaid for all persons regardless of family status. This, however, was not upheld by the Supreme Court. Depending on states' responses to the option of expanding to cover all residents with incomes below 133 percent of the FPL, some low-income individuals and couples may be without coverage, thus perpetuating the existing cross-state inequality for these groups.

The second major part of the medical component of the War on Poverty was establishment of neighborhood, now community, health centers. These are located in low-income and rural underserved areas with a goal of improving access to care. Evidence suggests that low-income persons in communities with a CHC indeed have access, at least to primary care, and that care that is available is both high quality and efficiently delivered. Indeed, these centers may be the key to providing access to care in states that do not expand Medicaid to all those with incomes below the FPL. Again, evidence suggests CHCs should be viewed as a successful part of the War on Poverty. Although it took longer than anticipated to establish a sizeable number of them, CHCs are viewed today as part of the plan under the ACA to provide care to those newly covered. A continuing issue with CHCs is staffing. The National Health Service Corps was established after the first few years of the War on Poverty to try to increase the supply of providers to CHCs and underserved areas more generally. The expansion of this program is another component of the ACA in its attempt to both increase coverage and access to medical care for those in lower-income families. Providing access to specialists including oral health providers has been far more difficult to accomplish.

Major components of the ACA appear to be built on the successful components of the Medicaid and CHC programs of the War on Poverty. Additionally, major additions of the ACA appear built on the recognition of problems these War on Poverty programs encountered. Clearly coverage will be increased, the proportion uninsured decreased, and access equalized. What is far more difficult to accomplish is reducing disparities in health, although clearly the health of the poor improved dramatically since the start of the War on Poverty. Eliminating disparities is far more difficult, because health insurance and access to care are only two elements in influencing health; knowledge, resources, health-related behaviors, and security purchased through higher incomes are clearly other important determinants. Some of the redesign of Medicaid and CHIP, further pursued in the ACA, removes disincentives to work, which may improve family incomes and thus health. Other components of the War on Poverty–type programs, including those tied to early childhood, education, training, and making work pay — the Earned Income Tax Credit or EITC, for example — may all need to work together with health-care programs to achieve greater equality in health. Ultimately, health insurance should only be expected to increase access to health care and reduce financial uncertainty tied to health; in these terms, the health components of the War on Poverty should be viewed as largely successful.

TABLE 9.A1 Medicaid's Milestones

Year	Milestone
July 30, 1965	The Medicaid program, authorized under Title XIX of the Social Security Act, was enacted to provide health-care services to low-income children deprived of parental support and their caretaker relatives, the elderly, the blind, and individuals with disabilities.
1967	The Early and Periodic Screening, Diagnostic, and Treatment (EPSDT) comprehensive health services benefit for all Medicaid children under age twenty-one was established.
1972	The newly enacted federal Supplemental Security Income (SSI) program provided states with the opportunity to link to Medicaid eligibility for elderly, blind, and disabled residents.
1981	Freedom of choice waivers (1915b) and home and community-based care waivers (1915c) were mandated. States were required to pay hospitals treating a disproportionate share of low-income patients—called disproportionate share hospitals (DSH)—additional payments.
1986	Medicaid coverage for pregnant women and infants (age one year or under) whose family income was at or below 100 percent of the federal poverty line (FPL) was established as a state option.
1988	The Qualified Medicare Beneficiary (QMB) eligibility rule required states to provide Medicaid coverage for pregnant women and infants whose family income was at or below 100 percent of the FPL. The criteria established special eligibility rules for institutionalized persons whose spouse remained in the community to prevent "spousal impoverishment."
1989	EPSDT requirements were expanded. Medicaid coverage of pregnant women and children under age six whose family income was at or below 133 percent of the FPL was mandated.
1990	The Medicaid prescription drug rebate program was enacted. The Specified Low-Income Medicare Beneficiary (SLMB) eligibility group was established to provide Medicaid coverage for children ages six through eighteen whose family income was at or below 100 percent of the FPL.
1991	DSH spending controls were established, provider donations were banned, and provider taxes were capped.
1996	The Aid to Families with Dependent Children (AFDC) entitlement program was replaced by the Temporary Assistance for Needy Families (TANF) block grant. The welfare link to Medicaid was severed and enrollment or termination of Medicaid was no longer automatic with the receipt (or loss) of welfare cash assistance.
1997	The Balanced Budget Act of 1997 (BBA) created the State Children's Health Insurance Program (SCHIP). Under this new state-based program, new managed care options were established. DSH payment limits were revised.
1999	The Ticket to Work and Work Incentives Improvement Act of 1999 (TWWIIA) expanded the availability of Medicare and Medicaid for certain disabled beneficiaries who return to work. The Medicare, Medicaid, and SCHIP Balanced Budget Refinement Act of 1999 stabilized the SCHIP allotment formula and modified the Medicaid DSH program.

continued

TABLE 9.A1 Continued

Year	Description
2000	The Benefits Improvement and Protection Act of 2000 (BIPA) modified the DSH program and modified SCHIP allotments. The Breast and Cervical Cancer Treatment and Prevention Act of 2000 allowed states to cover uninsured women with breast or cervical cancer regardless of income or resources at enhanced SCHIP federal matching rate. The Medicare, Medicaid, and SCHIP Benefits Improvement and Protection Act directs the Secretary of the U.S. Department of Health and Human Services (HHS) to issue regulations tightening upper payment limits (UPLs). This continued a trend of the federal government clamping down on state financing practices.
2001	The Bush administration announces the section 1115 waiver initiative, Health Insurance Flexibility and Accountability (HIFA), allowing states to demonstrate comprehensive state approaches that would increase the number of individuals with health insurance coverage using current-level Medicaid and SCHIP resources.
2003	The Jobs and Growth Tax Relief Reconciliation Act of 2003 raises all state Medicaid matching rates by 2.95 percentage points for the period April 2003 through June 2004 tied to the downturn in the economy. Congress recognized that state revenue collection had declined just when Medicaid programs were facing increased enrollment by low-income families. Medicaid drug coverage for dual eligibles, those who qualify for both Medicaid and Medicare, is transferred to Medicare effective January 1, 2006. Congress raises state-specific DSH allotments by 16 percent for FY 2004 for all states, through FY 2009 for low-DSH states (states that historically had not been large users of DSH).
2005	Congress passes a budget resolution requiring $10 billion in cost savings from the Medicaid program.
2009	The Children's Health Insurance Program (CHIP) reauthorized through FY 2013 under Children's Health Insurance Program Reauthorization Act, phases out coverage for parents by 2014.
2010	The Patient Protection and Affordable Care Act (PPACA) expands Medicaid to nearly all individuals under age sixty-five with incomes up to 133 percent of the federal poverty line (FPL). It is due to go into effect in 2014. As originally passed, PPACA expected to increase enrollment in Medicaid by 15.9 million. It also increases payments for primary care services to 100 percent of the Medicare payment rates for 2013 and 2014, and requires all states to extend levels of CHIP coverage eligibility in place at the time of the Affordable Care Act passage through 2019.
2012	The Supreme Court ruled that the federal government could not use the threat of loss of all federal funding to force states to expand Medicaid, saying this threat was too coercive. This leaves a substantial likelihood of continued inequality in eligibility for coverage.

Source: Author's compilation based on Centers for Medicare and Medicaid Services n.d. and Medicaid and CHIP Payment and Access Commission (2011).

FIGURE 9.A1 / Four or More Health Conditions

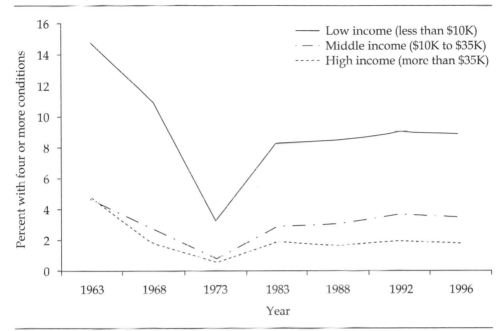

Source: Author's calculations based on data from Minnesota Population Center and State Health Access Data Assistance Center (2012).

FIGURE 9.A2 / Bedridden for Fourteen Days

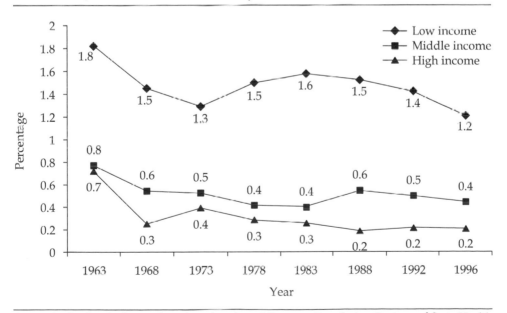

Source: Author's calculations based on data from Minnesota Population Center and State Health Access Data Assistance Center (2012).

NOTES

1. These included expenditures by the U.S. Children's Bureau to promote maternal and infant health spurred by the Shephard-Towner Maternity and Infancy Act of 1921 (see Fishback and Thomasson 2006, 714–15); expenditures under worker's compensation; funding to improve hospital and nursing home facilities under the Hill Burton Act of 1946, which included an obligation to provide services to those unable to pay and provided funds until 1997; and direct expenditures on medical research following World War II, reaching $1 billion in 1957 and $5 billion by 1966 (in 1992 dollars).
2. The core idea of Medicaid was a Republican alternative to Johnson's initial plan calling for compulsory health insurance (see Boyer 2001).
3. In the original ACA as passed, all persons who are citizens and have family incomes below 138 percent of the federal poverty line were to be covered. With the Supreme Court decision on ACA, this can no longer be enforced by the federal government and numerous states have elected not to expand their Medicaid programs.
4. One possible issue with the study is that, except for the hospital admissions data, all other outcomes are based on survey data.

REFERENCES

Almond, Douglas, Jr., Kenneth Y. Chay, and Michael Greenstone. 2006. "Civil Rights, the War on Poverty and Black-White Convergence in Infant Mortality in the Rural South and Mississippi." *MIT Department of Economics* working paper 07-04. Cambridge, Mass.: MIT Press.

Bailey, Martha J., and Andrew Goodman-Bacon. 2012. "The War on Poverty's Experiment in Public Medicine: Community Health Centers and the Mortality of Older Americans." March. Unpublished paper. University of Michigan, Ann Arbor. Available at: http://www-personal.umich.edu/~baileymj/Bailey_Goodman-Bacon.pdf (accessed April 9, 2013).

Bazelon Center for Mental Health Law. 2010. "How Will Health Reform Help People with Mental Illnesses?" Washington, D.C.: Author.

Bisgaier, Joanna, and Karin V. Rhodes. 2011. "Auditing Access to Specialty Care for Children with Public Insurance." *New England Journal of Medicine* 364(24): 2324–333.

Boyer, Paul S. 2001. "Medicare and Medicaid." *The Oxford Companion to United States History. Encyclopedia.com*. Available at: http://www.encyclopedia.com (accessed July 12, 2012).

Centers for Medicare and Medicaid Services. 2010. "Medicare and Medicaid Statistical Supplement." *CMS.gov*. Available at: http://www.cms.gov/Research-Statistics-Data-and-Systems/Statistics-Trends-and-Reports/MedicareMedicaidStatSupp/2010.html (accessed April 9, 2013).

———. 2011. "CHIP Enrollment Trends." *CMS.gov*. Available at: http://www.medicaid.gov/Medicaid-CHIP-Program-Information/By-Topics/Childrens-Health-Insurance-Program-CHIP/Childrens-Health-Insurance-Program-CHIP.html (accessed April 9, 2013).

———. n.d. "Medicaid's Milestones." Available at: http://www.cms.gov/about-cms/agency-information/history (accessed April 10, 2012).

Cook, Nakela, LeRoi S. Hicks, A. James O'Malley, Thomas Keegan, Edward Guadagnoli, and Bruce E. Landon. 2007. "Access to Specialty Care and Medical Services in Community Health Centers." *Health Affairs* 26(5): 1459–468.

Currie, Janet, and Jonathan Gruber. 1996. "Health Insurance Eligibility, Utilization of Medical Care, and Child Health." *Quarterly Journal of Economics* 111(2): 431–66.

Dor, Avi, Yuriy Pylypchuck, Peter Shin, and Sara Rosenbaum. 2008. "Uninsured and Medicaid Patients' Access to Preventive Care: Comparison of Health Centers and Other Primary Care Providers." Research Brief 4. New York: RCHN Community Health Foundation.

Duggar, B., K. Keel, B. Balicki, and E. Simpson. 1994. "Utilization and Costs to Medicaid of AFDC Recipients in New York Served and Not Served by Community Health Centers." Washington, D.C.: Heritage Foundation Center for Health Policy Studies.

Finkelstein, Amy, Sarah Taubman, Bill Wright, Mira Bernstein, Jonathan Gruber, Joseph P. Newhouse, Heidi Allen, and Katherine Baicker. 2011. "The Oregon Health Insurance Experiment: Evidence from the First Year." NBER working paper 17190. Cambridge, Mass.: National Bureau of Economic Research. Available at: http://www.nber.org/papers/w17190.pdf (accessed April 9, 2013).

Fishback, Price V., and Melissa Thomasson. 2006. "Social Welfare: 1929 to the Present." In *Historical Statistics of the United States: Millennial Edition*, vol. 2, edited by Susan Carter, Scott Gartner, Michael Haines, Alan Olmstead, Richard Sutch, and Gavin Wright. New York: Cambridge University Press.

Freeman, Howard E., K. Jill Kiecoult, and Harris M. Allen. 1982. "Community Health Centers: Making Health Care Less Expensive and More Accessible." *Public Affairs Report* 23(4): 1–7.

Goldman, Fred, and Michael Grossman. 1988. "The Impact of Public Health Policy: The Case of Community Health Centers." *Eastern Economic Journal* 14(1): 63–72.

Haveman, Robert H., and Barbara L. Wolfe. 2010. "U.S. Health Care Reform: A Primer and an Assessment." *CESifo DICE Report* 8(3): 53–60.

Heberlein, Martha, Tricia Brooks, and Jocelyn Guyer. 2011. "Holding Steady, Looking Ahead: Annual Findings of a 50-State Survey of Eligibility Rules, Enrollment and Renewal Procedures, and Cost Sharing Practices in Medicaid and CHIP, 2010–2011." Washington, D.C.: Henry J. Kaiser Family Foundation. Available at: http://www.kff.org/medicaid/upload/8130.pdf (accessed April 9, 2013).

Holmes, George M. 2004. "Does the National Health Service Corps Improve Physician Supply in Underserved Locations?" *Eastern Economic Journal* 30(4): 563–81.

Kaiser Family Foundation (KFF). 2009. "Community Care of North Carolina: Putting Health Reform Ideas into Practice in Medicaid." Policy Brief 7899. Washington, D.C.: Henry J. Kaiser Family Foundation. Available at: http://www.kff.org/medicaid/7899.cfm (accessed April 9, 2013).

———. 2011. "Children's Medicaid/CHIP Participation Rates, 2009." Washington, D.C.: Henry J. Kaiser Family Foundation. Available at: http://www.statehealthfacts.org/comparemaptable.jsp?ind=868&cat=4 (accessed April 9, 2013).

———. 2012. "Medicaid Enrollment: June 2011 Data Snapshot." Washington, D.C.: Henry J. Kaiser Family Foundation. Available at: http://www.kaiserfamilyfoundation.files.wordpress.com/2013/01/8050-05.pdf (accessed April 9, 2013).

Kenney, Genevieve. 2007. "The Impacts of the State Children's Health Insurance Program on Children Who Enroll: Findings from Ten States." *Health Services Research* 42(4): 1520–543.

Ku, Leighton, Patrick Richard, Avi Dor, Ellen Tan, Peter Shin, and Sara Rosenbaum. 2010. "Strengthening Primary Care to Bend the Cost Curve: The Expansion of Community Health Centers Through Health Reform." Policy Research Brief 19. Washington, D.C.: George Washington University, School of Public Health and Health Services.

Medicaid and CHIP Payment and Access Commission. 2011. Report to the Congress on Medicaid and CHIP. Washington.

Minnesota Population Center and State Health Access Data Assistance Center. 2012. *Integrated Health Interview Series: Version 5.0.* Minneapolis: University of Minnesota, Minnesota Population Center. Available at: http://www.ihis.us (accessed April 9, 2013).

National Association of Community Health Centers. 2008. "Access Transformed: Building a Primary Care Workforce for the 21st Century." Washington, D.C.: George Washington University, School of Public Health and Health Services. Available at: http://www.nachc.com/access-reports.cfm (accessed April 9, 2013).

National Center for Health Statistics. 1964. Health Insurance Coverage, United States, July 1962–June 1963, series 10, no. 11. Washington: U.S. Government Printing Office (August).

———. 2011. Health, United States, 2010, with Special Feature on Death and Dying. DHHS pub. no. 2011-1232. Washington: U.S. Department of Health and Human Services (February).

Newhouse, Joseph P., and the Insurance Experiment Group. 1993. *Free for All? Lessons from the RAND Health Insurance Experiment.* Cambridge, Mass.: Harvard University Press.

Reynolds, Reid T., and Frank J. Javorek. 1995. "Medicaid's Primary Care Physician Initiative and Ambulatory Care Sensitive Hospitalizations." Denver: Colorado Department of Health Care Policy and Financing.

Ricketts, Thomas C., III, Laurie J. Goldsmith, George M. Holmes, Randy Randolph, Richard Lee, Donald H. Taylor Jr., and Jan Ostermann. 2007. "Designating Places & Populations as Medically Underserved: A Proposal for a New Approach." *Journal of Health Care for the Poor and Underserved* 18(3): 567–89.

Rosenbach, Margo, Carol Irvin, Angela Merrill, Shanna Shulman, John Czajka, Christopher Trenholm, Susan Williams, So Sasigant Limpa-Amara, and Anna Katz. 2007. "National Evaluation of the State Children's Health Insurance Program: A Decade of Expanding Coverage and Improving Access." Washington, D.C.: Mathematica Policy Research. Available at: http://www.mathematica-mpr.com/publications/pdfs/schipdecade.pdf (accessed April 9, 2013).

Rosenblatt, Roger A., C. Holly A. Andrilla, Thomas Curtin, and L. Gary Hart. 2006. "Shortages of Medical Personnel at Community Health Centers: Implications for Planned Expansion." *Journal of the American Medical Association* 295(9): 1042–49.

Rothkopf, Jennifer, Katie Brookler, Sandeep Wadhwa and Michael Sajovetz. 2011. "Medicaid Patients Seen at Federally Qualified Health Centers Use Hospital Services Less than Those Seen by Private Providers." *Health Affairs* 30(7): 1335–342.

Shone, Laura P., Andrew W. Dick, Jonathan D. Klein, Jack Zwanziger, and Peter G. Szilagyi. 2005. "Reduction in Racial and Ethnic Disparities after Enrollment in the State Children's Health Insurance Program." *Pediatrics* 115(6): e697–705.

Sommers, Benjamin D. 2010. "Enrolling Eligible Children in Medicaid and CHIP: A Research Update." *Health Affairs* 29(7): 1350–355.

Sommers, Benjamin D., Katherine Baicker, and Arnold M. Epstein. 2012. "Mortality and Access to Care Among Adults After State Medicaid Expansions." *New England Journal of Medicine* 367 (September): 1025–35. Available at: http://www.nejm.org/doi/full/10 .1056/NEJMsa1202099#t=articleBackground (accessed April 9, 2013).

Stevens, Rosemary A. 1996. "Health Care in the Early 1960s." *Health Care Financing Review* 18(2): 11–22.

Stuart, Mary E., Donald Steinwachs, Barbara Starfield, Suezanne Orr, and Ann Kerns. 1995. "Improving Medicaid Pediatric Care." *Journal of Public Health Management Practice* 1(2): 31–38.

Truman, Harry S. 1945. "Special Address to the Congress Recommending a Comprehensive Health Program, November 19, 1945." In *Public Papers of the Presidents: Harry S. Truman, 1945–53*. Independence, Mo.: Harry S. Truman Library and Museum. Available at: http:// www.trumanlibrary.org/publicpapers/index.php?pid=483 (accessed April 9, 2013).

U.S. Census Bureau. 2011. *Income, Poverty, and Health Insurance Coverage in the United States: 2010*. Washington: Government Printing Office. Available at: http://www.census.gov/ prod/2011pubs/p60-239.pdf (accessed April 9, 2013).

U.S. Department of Health and Human Services. 1964. "Health Insurance Coverage, United States, July 1962–June 1963." *NCES* series 10, no. 11. Washington: Government Printing Office. Available at: http://www.cdc.gov/nchs/data/series/sr_10/sr10_011acc.pdf (accessed April 9, 2013).

———. 1972. "Hospital and Surgical Insurance Coverage, United States–1968." *NCES* series 10, no. 66. Washington: Government Printing Office. Available at: http://www.cdc .gov/nchs/data/series/sr_10/sr10_066acc.pdf (accessed April 9, 2013).

———. 1977. "Hospital and Surgical Insurance Coverage United States-1974." *NCES* series 10, no. 117. Washington: Government Printing Office. Available at: http://www.cdc .gov/nchs/data/series/sr_10/sr10_117.pdf (accessed April 9, 2013).

———. 2011. "2010 National Data." *Primary Care: The Health Center Program*. Washington: Government Printing Office. Available at: http://bphc.hrsa.gov/uds/view.aspx?year =2010 (accessed April 9, 2013).

Wolfe, Barbara L. 1994. "Reform of Health Care for the Non-Elderly Poor." In *Confronting Poverty: Prescriptions for Change*, edited by Sheldon H. Danziger, Gary D. Sandefur, and Daniel H. Weinberg. Cambridge, Mass.: Harvard University Press.

Wolfe, Barbara L., Robert H. Haveman, Thomas Kaplan, and Yoonyoung Cho. 2006. "SCHIP Expansion and Parental Coverage: An Evaluation of Wisconsin's BadgerCare." *Journal of Health Economics* 25(6): 1170–192.

Chapter 10

Medicare and Medicaid

Katherine Swartz

The War on Poverty created two health insurance programs, Medicare and Medicaid, which have had profound effects on the elderly and non-elderly (for details about both programs, see box 10.1). The War on Poverty also created community health centers (CHC) to expand the supply of physicians, nurses, and dentists in rural and low-income areas where assuring financial access to health care would not be enough to increase use.

With these programs, the War on Poverty's architects hoped to reduce documented disparities in use of care—among the elderly and between the elderly and non-elderly. Differences in access to health care between the elderly and non-elderly were an increasing concern by 1960 as more non-elderly workers obtained employer-sponsored health insurance but only half of the elderly had hospital insurance (Council of Economic Advisors 1964). Additionally, differences in use among the elderly by income, race, and region of the United States were a concern; three-fourths of the elderly poor did not have insurance (Council of Economic Advisors 1964, 67). By providing insurance similar to that held by many non-elderly, Medicare was expected to provide the elderly with the same access to health care that the non-elderly had, and to reduce income and racial disparities in the use of health care among the elderly. Medicaid's role for the elderly was to complement Medicare for the elderly poor by paying cost-sharing required by Medicare. Beyond this, initial expectations for Medicaid's impact on the elderly poor were small. A disproportionate share of the elderly poor lived in the South, and the southern states were slow to implement Medicaid and restricted Medicaid eligibility to people with incomes well below the poverty level. Medicare, as a federal program, was expected to have a greater impact on elderly across the country, especially the elderly poor.

The primary objective of these programs was achieved within a decade: poor and near-poor elderly were obtaining medical care at rates very similar to those of elderly with higher incomes. In 1964, low-income elderly had 22 percent fewer physician office visits than higher-income elderly; within ten years, they were as likely as higher-income elderly to see a physician (Davis and Schoen 1978, 42). The narrowing of the income gap in access to physicians has continued in the decades since, although disturbing differences in the use of specific medical services have been documented within the past decade.

The most significant outcome of these programs is that they drastically reduced what had been a common fear for older people in the years before the War on Poverty: that they would not be able to obtain medical care because they could not afford it. Medicare also reduced individuals' risk of financial ruin due to high medical costs in old age. Substantially reducing the elderly's risk of financial ruin from expensive medical care is a profound change and is perhaps the greatest effect of the War on Poverty for all Americans. As a result, current cohorts of elderly—all of whom were younger than sixty-five when Medicare and Medicaid were implemented—and their children have lived far differently during their income-earning years than earlier generations. Most have not saved (or worried about saving) for the costs of medical care in their retirement years. This low level of savings for medical costs in old age may come to haunt retirees in the next decade or two. As we discuss later in this chapter, the dramatic rise in the costs of medical care during the past fifty years is challenging Medicare and Medicaid's ability to prevent future generations from being afraid that they will not be able to pay for medical care.

Medicare produced another significant outcome that is often overlooked today: the racial integration of hospitals. Before 1965, virtually all the hospitals in the South and in many northern cities had separate floors for blacks and whites, and black physicians were denied hospital staff privileges. By December 1966, six months after Medicare was operational, racially segregated hospital areas were gone and staff privileges were given to black physicians. The speed with which this transformation occurred is breathtaking—particularly in comparison with the integration of schools and employment practices. This outcome was produced by a combination of two forces (Reynolds 1997; Quadagno 2000). One was money—any hospital not in compliance with integration and civil rights guidelines would not be eligible for Medicare payments. The second was the persistence and hard work of key people within the Department of Health, Education, and Welfare who created a strategy of reaching out to hospitals and political leaders in southern states and pressed them to comply (Reynolds 1997; Quadagno 2000). The strategy worked—and it contains lessons for current efforts to implement the Affordable Care Act's insurance exchanges.

In this chapter, we explore what is known about the effects of Medicare and Medicaid and of community health centers. The focus is on their effects on the elderly in general and low-income elderly in particular. Three points need to be remembered. First, in the years before the War on Poverty, information about the elderly (especially who was poor and who was not) and their use of medical care and health was crude by today's standards. Improvements over the past five decades in the level of detail we gather about people's characteristics and their medical care and health outcomes have enabled researchers to produce more nuanced analyses of the programs' effects. Second, the elderly population of today is differ-

---

Box 10.1 The War on Poverty's Health Programs for the Elderly

Medicare covers much of the health-care costs of almost all people sixty-five years of age and older. Since 1972, it also covers people younger than sixty-five who have end-stage renal disease, amyotrophic lateral sclerosis (ALS), or otherwise meet the eligibility criteria for disability under the Social Security Act. In 2011, about 41 million elderly and 8 million non-elderly Americans were covered by Medicare (Kaiser Family Foundation 2011b). The program is a federal program and funded by payroll taxes, premiums paid by beneficiaries, and federal general revenues; general revenues account for 43 percent of the total Medicare expenditures (Kaiser Family Foundation 2011a). In 2010, 20 percent of all U.S. health-care spending was paid for by Medicare (Martin et al. 2012). After fifty years, Medicare is perhaps the most popular government program the United States has ever created.

Medicaid is a joint federal-state, means-tested program to cover health-care expenses of poor and near-poor people of all ages. States can opt to increase the income eligibility maximum for different categories of eligible people, and have discretion over providing some services. Medicaid accounted for 15.5 percent of all health-care spending in 2010. In 2008, the program covered almost 60 million people, about 10 percent of whom are sixty-five and older and eligible for both Medicare and Medicaid because they have incomes below 125 percent of the federal poverty level (Young et al. 2012). The poor elderly account for two-thirds of the "dual eligibles," as they are known. Medicaid's role in underwriting long-term care services for the elderly is substantial. More than 33 percent of all Medicaid expenditures are for long-term care services, provided both in nursing homes and in beneficiaries' homes; 43 percent of all long-term care services are paid for by Medicaid; and 70 percent of all nursing home residents are Medicaid beneficiaries (the elderly and non-elderly disabled).

Although Medicaid is frequently the target of state politicians' budget cuts, Medicaid pays for home- and community-based long-term care services and nursing home care for many frail elderly who have exhausted their savings.[15] Medicaid enables many formerly middle-class people to remain in their homes when they need assistance with activities of daily living.

Community health centers were funded initially through the Office of Economic Opportunity and were seen as integral to the development of neighborhood efforts to address needs of low-income people. In particular, CHCs were created because low-income people of all ages living in rural areas and nonwhites living in the South had far fewer physician visits than those with higher incomes, whites, and people living in the other three regions of the country. Originally known as neighborhood health centers, CHCs were launched with eight demonstration centers funded in 1965. Building and staffing was slow: by 1975, only about 130 CHCs were operating, serving an estimated 1.3 million people (Reynolds 1976).[16] Political and financial support for CHCs has waxed and waned over the last fifty years. In inflation-adjusted dollars, funding was cut in the 1980s and 1990s, then significantly increased during the Bush administration and again in the first years of the Obama administration so that in 2010, funding was just 10 percent higher than in 1980 (Shin, Rosenbaum, and Paradise 2012). In 2010, CHCs received about 6 percent of their total funding from Medicare and 38 percent from Medicaid (Shin, Rosenbaum, and Paradise 2012); in 2003, about 7 percent of their patients were elderly (Taylor 2004). In 2011, about 1,200 CHCs served an estimated 20 million people (National Association of Community Health Centers 2012).

ent from the elderly of twenty or thirty or sixty years ago. Today's elderly are more educated, live longer, and a far smaller fraction are poor than fifty years ago (see Box 10.2). These changes matter when it comes to examining the effects of the health programs on the elderly—especially the elderly poor—because changes in the elderly population are in part due to some War on Poverty programs reviewed in other chapters of this book (see chapters 4, 5, and 7). Third, the health programs themselves changed substantially after they were implemented. The changes reflect evaluations of the programs' effects in the early years as well as new options for treating diseases and medical conditions. Many of the new treatment options were created in large part because Medicare's reimbursements of hospitals and physicians encouraged the development of new medical technologies without regard to their costs. Medicaid now pays for home- and community-based long-term care services that were not even in the lexicon of long-term care services in 1965. Because of all these changes, conclusions about the programs' effects on the elderly and the elderly poor must be placed in the context of specific time periods.

The effects of Medicare and Medicaid since the War on Poverty was launched reflect the continued interaction between analyses and program changes. In the next section, I briefly describe what was known about the elderly and elderly poor's access to and use of health care before 1965. The elderly poor's difficulties in obtaining care were central to the shaping of the War on Poverty health programs, and any evaluation of their effects must be mindful of this background.

THE ELDERLY'S HEALTH AND USE OF HEALTH CARE BEFORE THE WAR ON POVERTY

An evaluation of the effects of the War on Poverty's health programs on the elderly and elderly poor requires a short review of the health care available to the elderly and their general health in the 1950s and early 1960s.

Health of the Elderly

A simple measure of health is life expectancy at age sixty-five—the number of additional years a person can expect to live conditional on reaching age sixty-five. In 1950 and 1960, an American who reached sixty-five could expect to live another 13.9 and 14.3 years, respectively, and, by 2011, 19.2 years (Hoyert and Xu 2012, table 6). This rapid increase coincides with the elderly's increased access to medical care provided by Medicare—but the relationship, as we will see, is far more complex than one of simple causality. Before 1965, heart disease, stroke, and cancers were the leading causes of death, especially for older people, and medical care at that time could do little to reduce mortality rates attributable to these causes. Within three decades of the War on Poverty's beginning, enormous advances in medicine turned these terminal diagnoses into chronic diseases.

In the early 1960s, however, early research results from the Framingham Heart

---

Box 10.2. Income and Health Interactions for the Elderly

Income and health interact and often determine each other. People in good health can earn higher incomes and people in poor health frequently cannot work. People with higher incomes can afford to live in better houses and eat healthier diets than people with lower incomes. This interrelationship poses potential problems for distinguishing the effects of Medicare and Medicaid on the elderly poor's use of health care relative to the elderly who are not poor. Some economists have tried to minimize this problem by using educational attainment as a proxy for income, so that people with less than high school were defined as poor. However, the relationships among retirement income, preretirement income, education, health, and life expectancy at age sixty-five were very different during at least the first thirty years of Medicare and Medicaid than today. In 1959, 35 percent of the elderly were poor and fewer than 4 percent had a four-year college degree. In 1995, fewer than 15 percent of the elderly had four-year college degrees. The incomes of many men with only a high school diploma or less were solidly middle class during their working years in the 1940s through the early 1980s. When they retired, they made up the majority of the elderly between 1965 and at least 1995.

Most retirees did not have pensions (see chapter 7, this volume), and thus their retirement income was comprised of Social Security and personal savings. As a result, the income distribution of the elderly has long been skewed toward lower incomes, without much variation of income by education until very recently. This has been the case especially for older women. Poverty among the elderly—as measured by income—declined rapidly after 1965 as a result of the introduction of Supplemental Security Income in 1972 and the indexing of Social Security benefits to inflation rather than any sudden increase in the elderly's educational attainment. Thus, education as a proxy for income does not effectively identify the elderly poor before the mid-1990s. Therefore, in this chapter the elderly poor are defined by specific income thresholds or the census income measure of poverty, recognizing that analyses of Medicare and Medicaid's impacts since 1965 need to be interpreted in the context of all the changes among the elderly and health care that have occurred since then.

Study and several other large-scale population studies strongly suggested that smoking, poor diets, and lack of exercise were leading risk factors for these diseases (Remington and Brownson 2011). The timing of these studies is important. First, these risk factors are not easily reversed in a few years—so we should not expect the War on Poverty to have an immediate impact on the health of the elderly, especially as measured by a reduction in mortality rates or a sudden increase in life expectancy. Second, the *Surgeon General's 1964 Report on Smoking and Health* (Terry et al. 1964) was published just two years before Medicare was implemented, making it difficult to disentangle the effects of reducing smoking and Medicare. More critically, smoking reductions occurred more dramatically among more educated and higher-income non-elderly than among the poor in the decades after 1965, so Medicare and Medicaid's effect on the health of the elderly poor is confounded by the continued smoking behaviors of lower-income people before they reached age sixty-five.

Additionally, the rapid increase in life expectancy at age sixty-five after roughly 1970 is not unique to the United States. Karen Eggleston and Victor Fuchs (2012) document that sixteen other industrial countries have virtually identical patterns of life expectancy at age sixty-five since 1900, and in all the countries the rapid increase in life expectancy at age sixty-five occurred around 1970. All of these countries have national health insurance, but the similar patterns of life expectancy among these countries and the United States even before the War on Poverty suggest that other factors beyond health insurance are at work.

As a result, we pay less attention to life expectancy as a measure of Medicare and Medicaid's effects on the health of the elderly. Instead, we focus primarily on Medicare and Medicaid's effects on the elderly's use of health-care services, particularly visits to a physician, number of hospitalizations per thousand people, and length of stay per hospitalization. Even though mortality rates are used to calculate life expectancy, we occasionally note changes in mortality rates because for some health conditions access to hospital treatments could reduce mortality rates. Similarly, changes in disability rates, days of inactivity or bed rest, and the share of the population who are in poor or fair health are occasionally used to measure the effects of the two programs on health. In general, however, rates of use of physician and hospital services along with spending on such services have been the primary measures of the effects of Medicare and Medicaid on the elderly, the elderly poor, and elderly blacks.

What Was Known Before 1965 About Health Care Use by the Elderly

Information provided in congressional hearings about Medicare and Medicaid provided a bleak picture of how poor elderly individuals fared in obtaining health care. For example, the 1964 *Economic Report of the President* reported that just over half of people age sixty-five and older, and three-fourths of the elderly poor, did not have hospital insurance (Stevens 1996, 67). Much also was made of the poverty rates and difficulty in obtaining medical care of rural elderly and black elderly. Hospital use was a particular focus of concern. Nearly a quarter of the hospitalized elderly in 1962 reported that they asked for assistance to meet the costs of hospital care.[1] Hospital data from 1963, analyzed several years after Medicare was enacted, showed a clear income gradient describing the number of stays per 100 elderly persons in short-stay hospitals (Loewenstein 1971, table 2). Black elderly were found to have far fewer stays per 100 persons than white elderly. Medical charges per person followed similar patterns, strongly suggesting that lower-income and black elderly had difficulties obtaining hospital care.

The best physician visit information available at the time showed that people sixty-five and older had more physician visits per person than other age groups (U.S. Bureau of the Census 1964, 70). Although it seems obvious now that health-care needs increase with age, it was not so clear earlier. When the number of physician visits of the elderly were analyzed by the elderly's income, a clear income gradient appeared: elderly individuals with annual incomes below $2,000 had 6.5 visits per year compared with 8.7 for those with incomes at $7,000 and above.

The lack of detailed data on the elderly's use of physician visits meant that policymakers and analysts paid more attention to hospital use data, already available from hospital discharges. As Rosemary Stevens commented in a thirty-year retrospective on health care in the early 1960s, "The debates that led up to Medicare focused almost entirely on providing income to hospitals and on easing the burdens (or lack) of hospital insurance for the elderly" (1996, 15).[2] There also were concerns that there was a shortage of physicians in areas where poor people lived. Community health centers were part of the War on Poverty's health programs to improve access to physicians for elderly poor in rural areas and nonwhite elderly in southern states. Analyses of the limited data available indicated that access to primary medical care for people in these areas was due at least as much to the shortage of health-care providers and discriminatory practices as it was to low income (Davis and Schoen 1978).

Finally, an estimated 460,000 people age sixty-five or older (2.6 percent of the elderly) were living in nursing homes or personal care homes in 1964 (Mathis 1973). In general, nursing homes and personal care homes in the 1950s and 1960s were places people tried hard to avoid and moved into only if they did not have relatives who could care for them.

EARLY EFFECTS OF MEDICARE, MEDICAID, AND CHCS

In the initial decade after Medicare and Medicaid were implemented, research on their effects focused on access to care measures that were available—numbers of physician office visits and hospitalizations during the year, lengths of stay for a hospitalization, and health-care expenses per year.

Earliest Analyses: Before and After Comparisons

The first analyses of the effects of Medicare focused primarily on changes in the elderly's use of care before and after 1965 rather than on comparisons between the elderly and non-elderly. The first analysis, based on two samples of elderly in 1965 and 1967, showed that use of short-stay hospitals by the elderly (measured as days of care per enrolled person) increased by 25 percent—largely because the average length of stay rose from 14.2 days to 15.9 (Loewenstein 1971). Use of long-term medical institutions did not change, though use did shift from nursing homes to extended-care rehabilitation facilities, which were covered by Medicare after at least a three-day stay in the hospital. The percent of elderly having ambulatory visits did not change, although visits per person declined slightly, from 6.6 to 6.1 (Loewenstein 1971). When the short-stay hospital use data were analyzed by beneficiaries' income (for those living in one-person families and two-person families), "no clear pattern of differences in the use of short-stay hospitals was discernible" (Loewenstein 1971, 7). In contrast, the income gradient found for ambulatory care visits in 1965 had not changed significantly by 1967. Declines in the percentages of elderly blacks relative to whites having ambulatory visits in clinics, however, were significant and substantial, as were those of elderly rural residents relative to urban elderly having clinic visits (Loewenstein 1971). This shift in where elderly blacks and rural residents saw physicians was assumed to be due to Medicare paying for visits in physician offices so people no longer had to rely on public or charity clinics. It also could have been due to more black physicians being given staff privileges at southern hospitals after 1966 so they could see patients in hospital outpatient settings (Quadagno 2000).

Total expenditures for Medicare grew far more rapidly in the first five years than had been projected: from $3.4 billion in the first fiscal year to $7.9 billion in 1971 (West 1971). This increase has long been attributed to Medicare suddenly increasing the number of elderly with insurance, and was viewed as a negative effect of Medicare because health-care costs for the non-elderly also increased. However, Theodore Marmor (1970) noted that hospitals and physicians may have taken advantage of administrative start-up issues with processing claims and determining reimbursements, and raised fees in anticipation of regulated reimbursements. Hospital spending per Medicare enrollee doubled and physician fees rose almost 26 percent between 1967 and 1971 (West 1971). Medicare's reimbursement regulations for physicians were tightened significantly at the end of 1970. In fiscal years 1969 and 1970, expenditures for physician services had increased 20 percent from the previous year, but with the new regulations in place in 1971, the rate of increase fell to 2.8 percent (West 1971).[3]

An early concern with the initial pre-post Medicare comparisons of the elderly's use of health care was that data from 1967 might not reflect longer-term use patterns given that half of the elderly did not have hospital insurance before Medicare. These previously uninsured seniors might have had unmet medical needs before Medicare, and those with insurance before Medicare might have postponed hospital care assuming it would cost them less under Medicare. Julian Pettengill (1972) analyzed the elderly's hospital use between 1967 and 1971, and concluded that a major share of the increase in hospital use was directly due to the Medicare program given that hospital use continued to increase through 1971.[4] He also concluded that "There does not seem to be any evidence that the medical needs of the average aged person have increased in the last few years" (8). Because Pettengill did not analyze the hospital use data by income or race, we do not know whether or how much of the increased use through 1971 was due to the elderly poor or blacks.

Early Concerns About Medicare Cost-Sharing Effects

Medicare Part A is financed primarily by a payroll tax, and Part B is financed by premiums paid by the elderly and general revenues. Part A has a deductible equal to an average day's stay in a short-term hospital for each hospitalization; Part B has an annual deductible plus 20 percent coinsurance payments are required for most covered services.[5] Originally, the Part B premium was to equal half of all the expected expenditures per Part B enrollee.[6] Medicaid regulations required states to pay at least the premium for Part B for very poor elderly (those receiving Supplemental Security Income [SSI]) under what was known as a "buy in" provision. States also had the option of paying the premium for medically indigent — that is, medically needy — elderly who were not eligible for SSI. As of 1975, forty-six states, the District of Columbia, Guam, and the Virgin Islands paid premiums for 13 percent of all Part B enrollees, and 97.4 percent of the elderly who were enrolled in Medicare Part A were also enrolled in Part B (Gornick 1976).

By the early 1970s, the rapid growth in health-care costs were raising concerns about whether Medicare was living up to one of its goals — reducing disparities by income and race in access to health care. The higher costs together with Medicare's cost-sharing requirements were thought to have reduced the elderly poor's access to health care relative to the nonpoor. Karen Davis and Roger Reynolds (1975) used 1969 data to analyze the payments per Medicare beneficiary and the relationship between the distribution of use of covered services and Medicare's cost-sharing requirements. They found significant disparities in payments for Part B services per person by income: higher-income enrollees received more reimbursable services and were charged more (Davis and Reynolds 1975, table 1). They suggested that the greater use of physician visits by higher-income persons occurred either because the cost-sharing was "less of a deterrent" as income rises or because higher-income elderly had supplementary insurance and paid lower net prices for physician services (370). One finding provided an exception to their conclusion that inequities by income still remained in 1969: the elderly on public assistance, who were likely to have Medicaid paying the cost-sharing, had 30 to 40 percent more Part B services than low-income elderly not receiving public assistance, controlling for health status, age, gender, white-nonwhite, and education. Hospitalizations were not affected by Medicaid: differences between elderly public assistance recipients and other low-income elderly in use of hospital care were not significant. Davis and Reynolds also analyzed racial disparities in use, and concluded that elderly blacks in the South faced discrimination in obtaining health care: "While other groups are generally not deprived of care on the basis of income, Southern blacks receive substantially less care than others for any degree of need" (375).

Analyses with Mid-1970s Data

Some worried that even 1969 was too early to reflect a mature Medicare program. Charles Link, Stephen Long, and Russell Settle (1982) analyzed changes in health-care use from the late 1960s to the mid-1970s to see how Medicare's effects might have changed as providers, administrators, and the elderly learned about covered services and cost-sharing rules. Using 1976 data, Link and his colleagues concluded that the income-related disparities reported by Davis and Reynolds (1975) had disappeared by 1976. However, Link and his colleagues found that among the elderly who did not have chronic health conditions (some 22 percent of the elderly), higher-income elderly had more physician visits than the lowest-income elderly, and the difference was statistically significant. Their analyses also showed that racial differences in inpatient hospital use in the South had narrowed but continued to be statistically significant, whereas racial differences in ambulatory care use in the South were no longer statistically significant.

In a later paper with 1977 Medicare data, Stephen Long and Russell Settle concluded that income-related disparities in access to physicians and hospital care had "disappeared" by 1977 (1984, 644). They found that racial differences in health-care use were not statistically significant among the elderly without chronic health problems. However, among the elderly with chronic conditions requiring some inpatient care during 1977, ambulatory service use among Southern blacks was only 81 percent that of whites. More troubling was Long and Settle's finding that the hospital "admission rate among Southern whites was almost twice . . . that of Southern blacks, after adjusting for other determinants of hospital utilization" even though they had similar lengths of stay once admitted (631). As they noted, this is consistent with the racial disparities in inpatient use found by Davis and Reynolds and themselves earlier, and suggested that more efforts were needed to reduce barriers to health care among southern elderly blacks.

Effects of Medicaid on Elderly Poor in the 1970s and 1980s

Unlike Medicare, Medicaid is a federal-state partnership and the states did not implement their Medicaid programs all at once. It was not until 1974 that all of the states — except Arizona, which did not start its Medicaid program until 1982 — had functioning Medicaid programs. The poor elderly were categorically eligible for Medicaid if they were receiving cash assistance. However, significant cash assistance was not available to the very poor elderly until 1972, when the federal Supplemental Security Income program was established. Although SSI recipients were eligible for Medicaid, many states required them to make separate applications for Medicaid. As a result, there was (and still is) great variation across states in Medicaid enrollment of the elderly poor.

Medicaid's effects on the elderly poor in the early decades were not well documented beyond the analyses of Davis and Reynolds (1975) and Davis and Cathy Schoen (1978). Even analyses of nursing home expenditures by Medicaid rarely separated the elderly from the non-elderly disabled. Nonetheless, two significant changes to Medicaid in the 1980s directly affected the elderly poor. In 1981, Congress authorized the home and community-based Medicaid waiver program, known as 1915(c) waivers. This program permits states to use federal Medicaid matching funds to pay for home and community-based long-term care services for individuals who otherwise would receive such care in nursing homes. The waiver program was established to address complaints that demand for nursing home beds was greater than the supply[7] and the quality of care provided to Medicaid beneficiaries in nursing homes was poor. Many also thought Medicaid's costs of caring for a person would be less if the person could live at home. Such costs had become a significant concern by the late 1970s, when nursing home care accounted for almost half of all Medicaid spending (Holahan and Cohen 1986).

The second change was the expansion of eligibility for poor Medicare beneficiaries. Growing concerns about the elderly poor's eroding ability to access care because of the growth in medical costs since 1966 finally led in 1986 to the expansion of Medicaid eligibility for Medicare beneficiaries with incomes below the federal poverty level. The expansions initially were optional for states and then states were required to cover the elderly poor by January 1992. For these dual eligibles, Medicaid pays the Medicare Part B premium, Medicare's cost-sharing, and covers services that Medicare does not but Medicaid does, such as vision services. In addition, states have the option of using federal Medicaid funds with state funds to create a Medicaid medically needy program. Under this option, Medicaid covers people whose income minus their medical expenses is below the state's medically needy income limit. Of the fifty states plus the District of Columbia, thirty-four have medically needy programs. This program enables most elderly who do not meet income definitions of poverty but are poor by medical need standards to receive long-term care services through Medicaid.

These changes clearly helped the elderly poor. More became eligible for Medicaid, which paid the Medicare Part B premium and other cost-sharing. Many were able to receive home and community-based services (HCBS) rather than having to move to nursing homes when they needed long-term care (LTC). The waivers for HCBS, however, also created a large benefit for middle-class elderly who needed LTC and did not have enough savings to pay for many weeks of such care. States with medically needy Medicaid programs could allow people to qualify for Medicaid coverage of HCBS if they have very few assets (beyond their home) and their income minus the costs of LTC services is below the eligibility income limit. That has made it possible for many nonpoor elderly to receive LTC at home and have better health outcomes during their last years of life. It is not easy to determine how many of the elderly who receive HCBS services would be poor if Medicaid were not paying for their LTC.

Community Health Centers' Effects on Elderly Poor

In striking contrast to the amount of research focused on Medicare and Medicaid's early effects on access to care by the elderly poor, little is known about the community health centers' effects on the elderly poor per se. One reason for the lack of information is that CHCs were intended to provide care to poor people of all ages. Reynolds concluded that "the most important policy question unanswered about [CHCs] is whether they have made care more accessible among groups that have been traditionally deprived of care" (1976, 54). A household baseline survey, completed in 1972, of twenty-one neighborhoods with CHCs showed that center users tended to be younger and include more blacks than the eligible population around the centers (Reynolds 1976). Martha Bailey and Andrew Goodman-Bacon (2012) reviewed the early research on the effects of CHCs and concluded that, over the first fifteen years of the program, CHCs reduced age-adjusted mortality rates among poor people fifty and older. This conclusion implies that access to primary care can avert early deaths among people with relatively asymptomatic conditions, such as diabetes and heart disease, that are fatal if left untreated.

Medicare's Effects on Health-Care Spending in First Three Decades

Since at least 1960, health-care spending has grown by an average 2.5 percentage points faster than gross domestic product (GDP) (Social Security Advisory Board 2009). Even though the rate of growth in spending per Medicare beneficiary was lower than the growth in spending per privately insured person between 1970 and 2000 (Boccuti and Moon 2003), Medicare was often cited in the media as the reason health-care spending had grown from about 5 percent of GDP in 1960 to 12.5 percent in 1990 and 13.8 percent in 2000 (Hartman et al. 2013). It is, however, important to remember that during the 1960s and 1970s, many non-elderly workers gained employer-sponsored health insurance (ESI). In 1963, 25 percent of working adults age nineteen to sixty-four were uninsured, versus just 11.5 percent in 1979 (Swartz 1984). Although Medicare and Medicaid expanded access to health care for millions of elderly and poor people, the relationship between Medicare and the growth in health-care spending has far more to do with the way Medicare paid hospitals than with expanding access to care. Moreover, the growth in health-care costs affected people of all ages—not just the elderly—so it is important to understand how Medicare affected spending.

Technological change in medical care is widely accepted as the primary driver of the growth in spending. As Joseph Newhouse (1992) showed, when other factors that changed between 1950 and 1990 are accounted for—such as an aging population, rising incomes, and more people with health insurance—perhaps half of the increased medical spending is accounted for, with technological change credited with the rest. The real cost, after accounting for price inflation, of a day in the hospital nearly quadrupled between 1965 and 1986, though admission rates were no higher than in 1960 and length of stay among those hospitalized was shorter (Newhouse 1992). Hospital spending has consistently been the largest component of total health spending since 1960. Further support for concluding that technological change was the primary source of the growth in medical spending in the 1970s comes from the growth in more expensive new diagnostic and surgical procedures by 1982 (Showstack, Stone, and Schroeder 1985).

Technological change is often directed by incentives toward areas of greatest potential profit. Between 1966 and 1983, Medicare paid hospitals retrospectively: that is, hospitals were reimbursed for any allowable costs associated with the care of a patient (Davis et al. 1990). The retrospective system lacked any incentives for hospitals to provide care efficiently or for innovators to be cost-conscious when developing new technologies or procedures. To create incentives for health-care providers to be cost-conscious, in the fall of 1983 Medicare replaced the retrospective reimbursements for inpatient care with a prospective payment system (PPS), which pays hospitals a predetermined amount that depends on a patient's diagnosis. The reimbursement amount is equal, with some adjustments, to the average costs of treating people with similar diagnoses. All possible diagnoses have been grouped into about 550 diagnosis related groups (DRGs). The prospective payments were (and still are) expected to provide an incentive for hospitals to be more efficient in how they provided treatments. The notion is that hospitals will have higher profit margins if they can deliver the same quality care at lower cost.

It turned out, however, that the PPS contained incentives for hospitals to continue investing in costly technologies. Mark McClellan (1996) analyzed hospitals' investments in technology in the 1980s after Medicare implemented the PPS. His findings strongly suggested that hospitals invested in technologies that enabled them to provide more intensive treatments—particularly surgeries—because such treatments were different enough from those provided for the basic DRG that they were given an alternative DRG for the disease. Because these more intensive treatments were new, the new DRG payments were greater than marginal costs—creating a profit. In contrast, when a patient had a disease or condition for which there was only one DRG, the payment was closer to the marginal cost of treating the patient. McClellan argued that greater use of specific intensive procedures, especially surgical procedures, accounted for all of the growth in Medicare's spending on hospital care between 1983 and 1988. David Cutler and McClellan (1996) developed this line of investigation by examining the use of different treatments provided to elderly people hospitalized with a heart attack between 1984 and 1991. They found that the DRG payments for three intensive cardiac procedures were enough to be profitable for the marginal patient, and hospitals had an incentive to do more of them. Although Medicare payments for the procedures were essentially constant between 1984 and 1991, the use of intensive cardiac procedures rose markedly and changed how heart attacks were treated. Cutler and McClellan estimated that the expanded use of these cardiac treatment procedures accounts for almost all of the growth in Medicare spending on heart attack patients between 1984 and 1991.[8]

Thus it is not a coincidence that, in the late 1980s and early 1990s, significant advances in surgical techniques were introduced, making surgery—such as laparoscopic—less invasive and far safer for people who in earlier years would have been deemed poor candidates for surgery.[9] The benefits of such advances are huge, of course. However, as the studies just cited have shown, because Medicare and insurers in general were paying high reimbursements for the new advances in surgery, surgeons and hospitals did not have an incentive to demand that manufacturers look for cheaper ways of making the devices that made the new techniques possible. Similarly, the use of diagnostic radiological scans grew dramatically after the first commercially available magnetic resonance imaging (MRI) machines were introduced in 1983. Medicare's high reimbursement rates for scans encouraged hospitals to use scans far more than Medicare anticipated when it set the rates; the rates also encouraged the manufacturers to create new versions of the machines without constraints on their costs (Medicare Payment Advisory Commission 2006).

Thus, Medicare's role in the growth of health-care costs is not a simple story of expanded insurance coverage reducing the effective price of health care to a large number of people who then increased their demand for care, driving up prices. The story is more complicated. Medicare's reimbursement policies have encouraged the development of new treatment options without regard to their cost. Many of these new options have made it possible to diagnose conditions without surgery and to treat many more people who would not be able to survive previous ways of treating conditions or diseases. As a result, more people are being treated for particular diagnoses — driving up expenditures. Thus, Medicare has provided benefits to people of all ages — not just the elderly. Unfortunately, the benefits also came at high costs that have affected everyone.

RECENT RESEARCH ON THE EFFECTS OF MEDICARE

Between 1967 and 1996, Medicare spending grew, in 1996 dollars, from $16 billion to $203 billion (West 1971; Levit et al. 1998). This dramatic increase occurred in spite of Medicare's changes during the 1980s in the way hospitals and physicians were paid, and in spite of changes affecting Medicare cost-sharing that caused beneficiaries to pay an increasing share of their incomes for medical care. Even though many more elderly of different ages and incomes were benefitting from the new medical treatment options, questions were raised as to whether Medicare was continuing to meet its early objectives of reducing income inequality in access to health care and health outcomes among the elderly (Moon 1993, 1996). Such questions were asked also because several studies in the late 1980s and early 1990s showed that people who were nonwhite or of lower socioeconomic status (SES) were receiving fewer health services than those who were white or of higher SES when they had the same medical condition (see, for example, Wenneker and Epstein 1989; Escarce et al. 1993). Moreover, research was showing that although mortality rates had declined overall between 1960 and 1986, mortality rates had declined relatively more for higher-income and more educated people than lower-income and less-educated people of all ages (Pappas et al. 1993).

All these findings led to a renewed interest in analyzing whether Medicare — after thirty years — was providing greater benefit to higher-income elderly than lower income elderly.[10] The research sparked by this interest can be categorized as focusing on three questions. One is whether Medicare has been like a rising tide that lifts all boats or has redistributed resources from higher-income people to the elderly poor. A second set of research has used recently released data from the 1960s to determine whether greater access to health services — especially hospital care — led to improved health outcomes for the elderly who were poor or nonwhite during the first few years after Medicare was implemented. The third set of research has focused on analyzing medical treatment patterns of people with the same conditions and comparing the treatments of those who are recently eligible for Medicare — that is, a few years older than sixty-five — with people who are not quite sixty-five. The analyses have tried to determine whether the elderly poor in the 1990s and 2000s have treatment patterns similar to those of higher-income elderly.

The findings from these different studies suggest that although Medicare (and Medicaid) increased the elderly poor's access to health care, it has not led to equity in treatment patterns. It is far from clear why differences continue in treatment patterns and health outcomes that seem to be related to income and education. In reviewing the more recent research, we start with the question of whether Medicare has had any redistributional effects.

Redistributional Effects

Because higher-income people pay more through higher payroll tax contributions to Medicare and higher income taxes than low-income people do, it is commonly believed that Medicare is a progressive social insurance program.[11] To put it another way, many assume that Medicare is transferring resources from wealthier people to lower-income elderly because higher-income people pay more taxes to finance Medicare. But as we noted, although Medicare greatly reduced income-based disparities in health-care access and use among the elderly by 1969, Davis and Reynolds (1975) found that high-income elderly used more Part B services. Almost twenty-five years later, in 1993, Medicare was spending significantly more per person on elderly beneficiaries with the highest incomes than on those with lower incomes (Gornick et al. 1996). These results did not match the general assumption that Medicare was a program redistributing resources to elderly poor individuals from their higher-income counterparts.

A simple accounting framework — with flows of all the Medicare-related taxes paid by people during their working years and retirement years compared with flows of spending by Medicare on their behalf — has been used in several studies (Lee, McClellan, and Skinner 1999; McClellan and Skinner 2006; Bhattacharya and Lakdawalla 2006). However, the studies' estimates provide a mixed picture of Medicare's redistributional effects without a clear direction of the transfer of resources. McClellan and Skinner acknowledged that the accounting framework was not a satisfactory approach to measuring Medicare's redistributional effects. When they accounted for the insurance value of Medicare, they claimed that "the lowest income groups benefit the most from the imputed value of Medicare; . . . the intragenerational transfers are tilted toward lower-income [people]" (McClellan and Skinner 2006, 270).

Amy Finkelstein and Robin McKnight (2005, 2008) also argued that Medicare's redistributional effects come about through its role as an insurance program. Medicare's inherent insurance value is its ability to reduce a person's risk of significant out-of-pocket medical expenses. Finkelstein and McKnight used data from the early years of Medicare and compared health-care expenses of the elderly — those between sixty-five and seventy-four — with expenses of the near-elderly — those between fifty-five and sixty-four — in 1963 and 1970. It is important to recall that the distribution of health-care spending in the United States for any group of people is highly skewed. For the entire U.S. population, those in the top decile of the distribution have accounted for about 70 percent of all expenditures since 1977; in 1963 they accounted for 59 percent and in 1970 for 66 percent of all expenditures (Berk and Monheit 2001). Finkelstein and McKnight found no evidence of an impact of Medicare on out-of-pocket spending for people in the bottom three quartiles of the distribution of out-of-pocket spending. For people in the top quartile —

people with the highest medical bills—the insurance benefits of Medicare are clear, however: on average, Medicare is associated with a 40 percent decline in out-of-pocket spending. For people in the top 10 percent of the distribution, Medicare is associated with an almost 50 percent drop. Finkelstein and McKnight reframed the question of how Medicare redistributes resources, and their findings are a reminder that Medicare is an insurance plan. Unfortunately, their results do not provide an indication of whether the elderly with higher medical expenses are also poor or are a mix of elderly by income or socioeconomic status.

As Jonathan Skinner and Weiping Zhou (2006) pointed out, expenditures for health care are a result of a person's health status, preferences for health care, availability of particular health services, and financial resources (including insurance). It could be that the elderly poor are not receiving treatments thought to be effective even though they have Medicare, and thus they may not even have higher expenditures that would place them in the upper quartile or decile of the spending distribution. Skinner and Zhou examined the utilization rates of a limited set of treatments that have well-established benefits: mammography screening among women sixty-five to sixty-nine years old, eye examinations for diabetics, smoking cessation advice, and treatments following a heart attack. An advantage of using these treatments is that controlling for health status is not an issue—anyone in the relevant group of people for them should be receiving the treatments. Skinner and Zhou found that elderly in the highest income decile had significantly higher rates of effective care use than their counterparts in the lowest income decile. So although the elderly poor had Medicare and received some effective care treatments, they were not obtaining such care at the same rates as higher-income elderly—providing an indication that income-based inequalities in use of effective care remain among elderly Medicare beneficiaries in spite of Medicare's insurance role.

Thus, on balance, Medicare has not substantially redistributed resources from the high-income elderly to the low-income elderly.[17] When the insurance aspects of Medicare are included in analyzing Medicare's effects, it is clear that Medicare has done what many hoped it would: it has provided relief from high out-of-pocket expenses for medical care and reduced the elderly's fear of not being able to have medical care because of its cost. However, Skinner and Zhou's study raises concerns that low-income elderly may still not be receiving the same level of care as their higher-income counterparts.

Effects on Health

Access to health care is thought to be important for reducing morbidity and mortality rates, and improving quality of life, especially for people in their later years of life. However, trying to identify Medicare and Medicaid's effects on health outcomes is quite difficult. Health insurance cannot be expected to have immediate or even near-term effects on mortality rates except when access to a hospital and all the treatment options available at a hospital could reduce the likelihood of death.

In recent years, researchers have taken advantage of new data to try to determine whether Medicare improved the health of the elderly poor. One group of studies has returned to examining data on mortality and morbidity rates from the years just before and soon after the War on Poverty began. A second group of studies focused on Medicare's effects when a person becomes eligible for Medicare at age sixty-five. Such studies analyze how health-care use among people who have just become sixty-five differs from that of those who are not quite sixty-five, controlling for specific health conditions. In general, the findings from all these studies provide evidence that Medicare has improved the health of the elderly but only weak evidence that the elderly poor have benefitted especially.

Pre-Post 1965 Analyses   Two studies suggest that Medicare's effects on the health of the elderly came primarily through Medicare's effects on hospital use, but neither study provides strong evidence that Medicare had particularly positive effects on the elderly poor's health. In addition to examining Medicare's role in reducing high out-of-pocket medical expenditures, Finkelstein and McKnight (2005, 2008) investigated whether insurance (Medicare) or access to hospitals, brought about by integration of hospitals, was associated with a decline in mortality rates among the elderly after Medicare was implemented. They analyzed annual age-specific mortality data from 1952 to 1975 and variation in the timing of Medicare's implementation in the twenty-five counties of the Mississippi Delta region where most hospitals were desegregated between 1967 and 1969. The assumption behind their analyses is that in Medicare's first decade, hospitals were more effective at treating acute illnesses, such as pneumonia, than chronic conditions, such as coronary heart disease. Thus, if Medicare were to have an impact on the elderly's mortality rates, it would be by expanding access to hospitals for elderly poor and black beneficiaries. Finkelstein and McKnight concluded that there was no "discernible" impact of Medicare on the mortality rates of all of the elderly in the Mississippi Delta counties during Medicare's early years. However, they found a statistically significant but substantively small decline in pneumonia mortality rates among the nonwhite elderly and no decline in pneumonia mortality among the white elderly in the same counties. They also did not find a decline in elderly mortality rates for any other cause of death for nonwhites or whites. Although their analysis is limited to the twenty-five counties in the Mississippi Delta region, the finding suggests that Medicare increased access to hospitals for blacks by forcing the integration of hospitals. The white elderly (even poor white elderly) already could seek care at southern hospitals before Medicare. The implication is that Medicare improved the health of elderly blacks by reducing their mortality rates from acute illnesses that can be fatal without inpatient medical intervention.

Kenneth Chay, Daeho Kim, and Shailender Swaminathan (2011) analyzed two measures of health, rates of restricted activity and mortality, and then compared changes in these outcomes between the pre- and post-Medicare years for individuals who were eligible for Medicare and those who were younger than sixty-five. They found some evidence that restricted activity rates fell for people between sixty-five and sixty-nine in the years after Medicare was implemented. They also estimated that an additional twenty-eight people per 1,000 in the same age range were discharged from a hospital in 1968 and 1969 compared with the pre-Medicare period of 1964 to 1966; and during this time the hospital discharge rate for the non-elderly did not change. They concluded that their finding of thirty-five fewer deaths per 10,000 individuals among the elderly age sixty-five to sixty-nine compared with the non-elderly during the same years must be due to Medicare's enabling greater use of hospital care by the elderly. Chay and colleagues were unable to examine Medicare's effects on the elderly by income. However, given the earlier findings in the 1970s that Medicare did not reduce income disparities in hospital use, their results suggest that the early reductions in restricted activity days and mortality were not coming from the elderly poor.

Changes Due to Coverage by Medicare at Age Sixty-Five   David Card, Carlos Dobkin, and Nicole Maestas (2008) took advantage of the fact that when people reach age sixty-five, they are eligible for Medicare coverage and almost everyone who is eligible for Medicare enrolls in it. The authors analyzed data from people age fifty-six through seventy-four who were interviewed for one of the National Health Interview Surveys conducted between 1992 and 2003, and hospital discharge data from California, Florida, and New York between 1992 and 2003. They do not have an income variable or a separate Medicaid coverage variable to indicate who is poor; instead, they use minority status and less education variables as proxies. They found that the use of low-cost services, such as routine physician visits, increased when people reached sixty-five, and that the increases are relatively larger for less-educated and minority groups who had lower use rates before they were sixty-five. In contrast, the use of high-cost services, which generally also involved hospitalizations for procedures such as coronary artery bypass (CABG) surgery or hip replacements, increased primarily among more educated people. They also found overall a 10 percent increase in hospitalization rates at age sixty-five, though the increases are larger for the better-educated whites—a 20 percent jump—than for the other groups. These findings suggest continued income and race-based disparities in access to health care that can have beneficial effects on health outcomes and quality of life for the elderly.

Michael McWilliams and his colleagues (2009), using National Health and Nutrition Examination Surveys (NHANES) data collected between 1999 and 2006, examined health outcome measures that generally indicate control of cardiovascular disease and diabetes. They compared these outcomes among a group of people who were just younger than sixty-five and another group who were just older than sixty-five, and analyzed differences by race, ethnicity, and education. They found that control of blood pressure, glucose, and cholesterol levels improved between 1999 and 2006 among both age groups of adults with cardiovascular disease and diabetes, but racial, ethnic, and education differences in these measures did not improve. However, significant "narrowing" of these differences did occur among those older than sixty-five, presumably because of Medicare coverage and access to health-care providers.

Sandra Decker (2005) investigated how Medicare eligibility at age sixty-five affects the use of health services and outcomes related to breast cancer. Medicare began covering the cost of mammography for beneficiaries every two years in 1991, and then annually in 1998. Decker used data from the Behavioral Risk Factor Surveillance System (BRFSS) from 1991 through 2002, and restricted her sample to women age fifty to eighty. She found that the probability of using health services increases discontinuously at age sixty-five, and the use increases the most for women who did not finish high school. Although the probability of having had a recent mammogram increases after age sixty-five for women with less than a high school diploma, the difference in probabilities of having a mammogram between these women and those with more education remains "very substantial" (Decker 2005, 955). She also found a modest decrease in the probability of late-stage breast cancer diagnosis after age sixty-five, which suggests that Medicare makes a difference in the chances that a woman diagnosed with breast cancer will survive another five or more years.

As Card, Dobkin, and Maestas noted in the introduction to their 2009 paper on Medicare's effects, although Medicare had been shown to increase the rates of use of health care, "the health impact of these additional services remains uncertain" (597). In this study, they focused on differences in mortality rates among people who were between sixty and seventy, severely ill, and admitted to hospitals through the emergency department for "nondeferrable" conditions. These conditions account for 12 percent of hospital admissions and 25 percent of all deaths among people in this age range. Whether someone has health insurance is not likely to affect a decision to go to a hospital emergency department when symptoms of one of these conditions are evident. Because insurance coverage is known to affect the types of treatment provided to people, the question motivating Card and his colleagues is whether Medicare enabled people to have more hospital procedures that also reduced mortality rates. They found a clear drop in mortality rates among those sixty-five to seventy compared with those younger than sixty-five. Their results suggest that the additional treatment options provided to those with Medicare has a positive impact on survival rates. Although they did not directly answer the question of whether Medicare improves the health of the elderly poor, their findings provide a hint that this is the case. People between sixty and sixty-four who were uninsured were more likely to be low income. The drop in mortality among people sixty-five to seventy thus suggests that Medicare's effect was particularly noticeable among poorer elderly who would be uninsured if Medicare did not exist.

All of these studies of Medicare's effects on the health of beneficiaries, especially the elderly poor, are tantalizing. They suggest that Medicare covers medical treatments that people younger than age sixty-five, especially those who are most likely to be poor, are unlikely to receive, and that such treatments can reduce mortality rates for people with health problems that require hospitalizations. However, it also is clear that higher-income and more educated beneficiaries are more likely to have procedures that improve a person's quality of life. Why this is the case is unknown but it surely deserves more attention.

THE NEXT DECADE: INTERACTIONS WITH THE ACA AND FISCAL SUSTAINABILITY

Looking to the next decade (and beyond), two significant issues will affect the country's ability to reduce income disparities in health-care access and outcomes among the elderly. One is the impact of the Affordable Care Act (ACA) and the other is how the country chooses to restructure Medicare and Medicaid so they are financially sustainable for future generations.

It is likely to be at least a decade before the ACA's effects on the elderly poor's access to health care and health outcomes will be known. Some reforms in the ACA will affect low-income people before they reach sixty-five and other reforms are directed at improving the care of elderly poor more immediately. Starting in 2014, almost all Americans younger than sixty-five will have health insurance because of the ACA. The expectation is that with insurance, the low-income non-elderly will seek medical care—especially preventive care—and thereby reduce the current disparities in health and access to health among the elderly. In particular, if health insurance causes low-income non-elderly to obtain better health care, perhaps some of the unexplained disparities in health-care use and health outcomes among the elderly will be reduced in another decade. Perhaps also the prevalence of costly medical conditions will be reduced in the future because people will have obtained care before they become elderly. But we do not know how the elderly's use of health care and health outcomes will change as a result of people having health insurance during their younger years. If low-income non-elderly people have trouble accessing health care even after the ACA is fully implemented, we could continue to see income disparities among the elderly in their health outcomes and use of health care. It will be some time—probably not until the 2030s—before enough elderly will have been covered by health insurance during their younger years for us to know whether such coverage reduces current disparities in health-care use and outcomes among the elderly.

The ACA also contains two changes directed at Medicare and Medicaid that could have more immediate impacts on the elderly poor. Medicare and Medicaid payments to primary care physicians will be increased. And, as part of a strategy to improve care for the elderly poor, the ACA created a new office within the Centers for Medicare and Medicaid Services (CMS) to seek efficiencies and higher quality of care for Medicare-Medicaid dual eligibles. Because Medicare and Medicaid currently pay primary care physicians less than commercial insurers do, it is often difficult for the elderly—especially those who are poor—to receive the coordinated attention needed for several chronic medical problems. Whether the higher payments will provide the elderly poor with greater access to treatments that improve quality of life is a question for future research.

Making Medicare and Medicaid financially sustainable for future generations is the other significant issue the country needs to address in this decade if it wants to continue to help the elderly and elderly poor obtain health care. To ensure the financial sustainability of both programs involves efforts on two fronts: substantially slowing the growth in health-care spending and restructuring the financing of the programs. Adjusting for inflation, health-care spending per person in the United States more than tripled between 1970 and 2011 (Levit et al. 1998; Hartman et al. 2013). For at least the last five decades, health-care spending per capita has been growing at a rate about 2.5 percentage points faster than gross domestic product (GDP) has been. To see the effects of this, in 1970 Medicare accounted for 0.7 percent of GDP, in 2010 for 3.5 percent, and it is projected by 2020 to account for 4 percent (Medicare Payment Advisory Commission 2012). If health-care spending were to grow by just 1 percent faster than GDP, one estimate is that 40 percent of per capita income growth will be spent on health care between 2010 and 2050 (Chernew, Hirth, and Cutler 2009). It is clear that the current growth in health-care spending is not sustainable, particularly given that median household income for people of all ages has not kept pace with the increase in health spending. Adjusting for inflation, median household income has increased by only 22.5 percent between 1975 and 2011 (U.S. Census Bureau 2012).

Policy options for quickly slowing health-care spending are limited. They include reducing payments to hospitals, physicians and other health-care providers, and increasing the cost-sharing required of patients when they use care. However, if Medicare and Medicaid reduce payments to health-care providers, many providers might refuse to care for some people, most likely low-income and elderly people with complex medical needs. Similarly, requiring patients to pay higher cost-sharing for services could result in lower-income people, especially poor elderly, not seeking essential care. Clearly, without protections for low-income people, such options could send the country backward in terms of providing assistance to low-income people, a large share of whom are elderly.

Other options for slowing health-care spending are aimed at reducing inefficiencies and waste in health care. The extent of inefficiencies and waste is estimated to be between 20 and 30 percent of total U.S. health-care spending (Berwick and Hackbarth 2012; Institute of Medicine 2012). For comparison, Medicare accounted for 21 percent of all U.S. health care spending in 2011 (Hartman et al. 2013). Under the ACA, the federal government is providing significant funding for information technology investments (including greater use of electronic health records), and demonstrations to learn what types of Medicare payment incentives will reduce unnecessary spending. Private insurers also are pursuing organizational changes to increase efficiency in the delivery of care. These efforts are beginning to create major changes in the health-care market. Whether they will reduce enough unnecessary spending to slow health-care spending growth to less than the growth of GDP, however, will not be known for several years.

Restructuring the financing of Medicare and Medicaid is also necessary if both programs are to be available in the future. Since 1990, the proportion of the population sixty-five or older has ranged from 12.5 percent to 13.0 percent, after increasing from 9.8 percent in 1970 to 11.3 percent in 1980. Americans are used to thinking of the elderly as accounting for about 10 percent of the population. By 2030, the figure will be about 20 percent (U.S. Census Bureau 2008). Significantly, recent projections indicate that large numbers of people approaching retirement do not have enough savings to pay for years of life expectancy at age sixty-five (Munnell 2012). Moreover, as more employers are cutting back on retiree health benefits, it is highly probable that more elderly may become poor as they live longer and run down their savings paying higher shares of their incomes for health care. The restructuring of how Medicare is financed should include a mechanism that provides prefunding of a larger portion of Medicare's projected expenses (as the Part A payroll tax does) to help assure younger cohorts that the program will exist when they retire. Similarly, if the income distribution continues to grow more unequal, raising taxes on unearned income is another option that must be considered.

Current fears about becoming impoverished in old age because one does not have enough savings to pay for medical care and long-term care services are similar to those people had in the decades before Medicare and Medicaid were established. Younger cohorts, who have been mostly insulated from the costs of health care for their elderly relatives because of Medicare and Medicaid, are increasingly anxious about having to pay higher taxes to support Medicare and Medicaid and wondering if the programs will be there for them. Research that simulates likely effects of various ways of financing Medicare and Medicaid is urgently needed to reduce such fears and anxieties.

CONCLUSIONS AND IMPLICATIONS FOR THE FUTURE

As with all long-lived programs, changes in the three War on Poverty health programs inevitably occurred. Some change came in response to research showing that the programs also had unintended consequences, as with the rapid increase in health-care costs. Some came in response to changes in the elderly population and their preferences for how services are delivered, such as home- and community-based long-term care services rather than only nursing home care. Thus, a fifty-year evaluation of the effects of these programs should include an analysis of the many different aspects of the programs that changed in response to changes in the elderly and in the health-care delivery system.

The preponderance of the evidence is that Medicare has been enormously beneficial to the elderly for the past fifty years. Almost all the elderly have health insurance today, which almost certainly would not have happened if the U.S. had relied on a market for individual private insurance. The health insurance provided by Medicare and Medicaid have removed most financial barriers to obtaining medical care, enabling the elderly to obtain treatments that are now regarded as standard care for many conditions. Without these programs, the elderly could not possibly afford such care. Even so, it also is clear that income and race-based disparities (and to some extent geographic residence disparities) in the elderly's use of medical care still exist, and in some cases may be widening. As the costs of health care continue to grow faster than GDP, Medicare's cost-sharing requirements are causing more lower-income elderly to face financial difficulties paying for care. Moreover, given the gains in life expectancy since 1965, a rising proportion of older people are at risk of not having enough income when they are eighty years old and older to pay for Medicare Part B premiums and long-term care services.

Medicare also is associated with historic benefits for the country as a whole. It was a significant factor in the racial integration of hospitals and the removal of barriers that had prevented nonwhite physicians from admitting patients to hospitals. It fostered the development of numerous medical treatment options: some of these have transformed previously fatal conditions into chronic conditions; others have greatly improved the quality of life for millions of people, both elderly and non-elderly. Medicare also has provided a less obvious benefit—as the single largest payer of health care, it can initiate changes in how health care is delivered. Insurers and large employers are individually too small as purchasers of health care to effect much change. Medicare, however, can introduce changes in payments or regulations that may improve quality of care or reduce inefficiencies and waste in the delivery of care. The demonstration projects funded by the ACA are just the latest in a series of Medicare initiatives that affect everyone's health care.

Medicaid, particularly its medically needy program option that allows states to cover the elderly who spend down their income paying for medical bills, is the "sleeper" program in terms of its effects on the elderly poor. Most research on people who have both Medicaid and Medicare coverage has not distinguished between the elderly and non-elderly, making it difficult to know what Medicaid's effects have been on the elderly poor.[13] Many elderly who are eligible for Medicaid do not know they are eligible or are discouraged from enrolling because the process is difficult in a number of states. Access to Medicaid for the elderly poor differs across the country. Thus, in theory Medicaid is there to assist the elderly poor with health-care expenses but in reality many of them are doing without.[14] At the same time, other elderly with incomes above the federal poverty level are Medicaid beneficiaries receiving long-term care services because they live in states that have medically needy programs. Under these programs, if a person's income less the costs of services would cause him to be eligible for Medicaid, the person is eligible. This provision has prevented many elderly and their families from becoming poor—a benefit recognized by many middle-class families but often forgotten in political debates about Medicaid.

Finally, the undisputed greatest effect of the War on Poverty's health programs is that they have significantly reduced what had been a common fear for older people in the years before the War on Poverty: that they would not be able to obtain medical care because they could not afford it. Substantially reducing the elderly's risk of financial ruin due to the high costs of medical care is a profound change, especially for elderly poor people. Looking to the future, the biggest challenge facing these programs is how to make them financially sustainable for future generations so current cohorts of younger people will not have the fears that people had before Medicare and Medicaid were launched.

I am grateful to Martha Bailey, Sheldon Danziger, Michael Chernew, Frank Levy, David Mechanic, two anonymous reviewers, and other conference participants for helpful comments; they are not to blame for errors that remain.

NOTES

1. The 1964 *Economic Report of the President* reported that the savings and financial resources of the elderly were "typically inadequate to cover the costs of a serious illness" (Council of Economic Advisors 1964, 68).
2. As Stevens also said, Medicare would enable the elderly to become "paying consumers of hospital services" (1996, 14). There is a striking similarity between this argument and another in support of requiring everyone to have health insurance under the Affordable Care Act: health-care providers will receive payments rather than providing uncompensated care.
3. This change in reimbursement for physician claims is important because it affects the interpretation of Medicare's effects on the costs of care for the elderly in the years immediately following the implementation of Medicare.
4. Pettengill also noted that "the extent to which hospitalization was actually postponed is unknown. That it did occur is suggested by the fact that the discharge rate among aged patients for the treatment of cataracts—generally considered elective care—rose 52 percent between 1965 and 1967" (1972, 6).
5. In the early years of Medicare, the Part A deductible was $92 for the first sixty days of hospital care, and the Part B cost-sharing consisted of a $60 annual deductible and 20 percent coinsurance of allowable charges. In 2012, the Part A deductible was $1,156, and the Part B deductible was $140.
6. Since legislation passed in 1982, with a few years of exceptions in the early 1990s, the Part B premium has been set to 25 percent of total expected expenditures for Part B services; general revenues have paid for the difference between premium payments and total expenditures (Moon 1996).
7. States controlled nursing home expenditures by limiting the supply of beds (Scanlon 1980; Feder and Scanlon 1980; Holahan and Cohen 1986).
8. In a later paper, Michael Chernew, Gautam Gowrisankaran, and Mark Fendrick (2002) took a different approach to analyze Medicare's payment effects on the use of high tech procedures. They estimated the returns—financial and other benefits—to California hospitals for providing coronary artery bypass graft (CABG) surgery by observing the increase in hospitals providing CABG between 1984 and 1994. Their results suggest that hospitals did indeed begin to offer CABG when they could earn positive returns.
9. Personal communication with Atul Gawande, MD.
10. Such questions also were being debated by researchers involved in the National Academy of Science Panel on Poverty Measurement and Family Assistance, which was debating how to impute the value of public and private health insurance to individuals and families (Citro and Michael 1995). Although panel members agreed that the value

of health insurance should be included in alternative poverty measures from the Census Bureau, they did not agree on the details of how to impute the value (Betson 2012).

11. The two taxes that fund most of Medicare are the payroll tax dedicated to Medicare Part A's Trust Fund and federal income taxes and other taxes that go into general revenues. Currently, the payroll tax is 2.9 percent—half paid by an employer and half paid by an employee—of a person's wages and salary, without any upper limit on income to which the tax is applied. The payroll tax has increased several times since 1965 but has not been raised since 1986 with one exception: since January 2013, individuals earning more than $200,000 and couples filing joint income tax returns with more than $250,000 of earned income pay an additional 0.9 percent, for a total tax rate of 2.35 percent. Medicare Part B is financed primarily by federal income taxes and other taxes that go into general revenues and by premiums paid by enrollees. Originally, the premiums were set to equal half of expected expenditures under Part B divided by the number of enrollees. However, the fraction of expected expenditures covered by the premiums has declined over time; in 2009 the premiums accounted for 22 percent and general revenues accounted for 74 percent of Part B spending (Potetz, Cubanski, and Neuman 2011). Medicare Part D relies even more on general revenues: 83 percent of Part D expenditures are financed by general revenues (Kaiser Family Foundation 2011c). The relatively small share of Medicare funding paid by beneficiaries via Part B premiums is indicative of how much income is being transferred to the elderly from younger generations to finance Medicare spending.

12. A political benefit of the conclusion that Medicare was not redistributing resources from the higher-income to lower-income elderly is that it is easier to justify raising Medicare Part B premiums for the very high-income elderly and to increase the Medicare payroll tax on earned income for high-income people.

13. The non-elderly dual eligibles have Medicare coverage because they meet the Medicare disability criteria, but their medical needs and expenses are often very different from those of the elderly dual eligibles.

14. Recent estimates of the Medicaid take-up rate among community-dwelling elderly who are eligible for Medicaid are lacking, but Aaron Yelowitz (2000) and Liliana Pezzin and Judith Kasper (2002) reported estimates of only about 50 percent. The two papers used different data; Yelowitz relied on the 1987–1995 Survey of Income and Program Participation panels, and Pezzin and Kasper used the 1996 Medicare Current Beneficiary Survey (MCBS).

15. In January 2011, 59 percent of Americans said that "Medicaid is very important or somewhat important to them and their family" in response to a Kaiser Family Foundation/Harvard School of Public Health survey.

16. The first two neighborhood health center demonstration projects opened in Boston (1965) and Mississippi (1967).

REFERENCES

Bailey, Martha J., and Andrew Goodman-Bacon. 2012. "The War on Poverty's Experiment in Public Medicine: Community Health Centers and the Mortality of Older Americans."

Presented at the West Coast Poverty Center Seminar Series on Poverty and Policy. University of Washington. Seattle (May 7, 2012). Available at: http://depts.washington.edu/wcpc/events/seminar/archive/2012_05_07_Bailey_Goodman-Bacon (accessed April 9, 2013).

Berk, Mark L., and Alan C. Monheit. 2001. "The Concentration of Health Care Expenditures, Revisited." *Health Affairs* 20(2): 9–18.

Berwick, Donald M., and Andrew D. Hackbarth. 2012. "Eliminating Waste in U.S. Health Care." *Journal of the American Medical Association* 307(14): 1513–516.

Betson, David M. 2012. "Medical Care and Poverty Measurement." Unpublished paper, University of Notre Dame.

Bhattacharya, Jay, and Darius Lakdawalla. 2006. "Does Medicare Benefit the Poor?" *Journal of Public Economics* 90(1–2): 277–92.

Boccuti, Christina, and Marilyn Moon. 2003. "Comparing Medicare and Private Insurers: Growth Rates in Spending over Three Decades." *Health Affairs* 22(2): 230–37.

Card, David, Carlos Dobkin, and Nicole Maestas. 2008. "The Impact of Nearly Universal Insurance Coverage on Health Care Utilization: Evidence from Medicare." *American Economic Review* 98(5): 2242–258.

———. 2009. "Does Medicare Save Lives?" *Quarterly Journal of Economics* 124(2): 597–636.

Chay, Kenneth Y., Daeho Kim, and Shailender Swaminathan. 2011. "Health Insurance, Hospital Utilization and Mortality: Evidence from Medicare's Origins." Working paper. Montréal: HEC Montréal. Available at: http://www.hec.ca/iea/seminaires/120418_chay_kenneth.pdf (accessed April 9, 2013).

Chernew, Michael, Gautam Gowrisankaran, and A. Mark Fendrick. 2002. "Payer Type and the Returns to Bypass Surgery: Evidence from Hospital Entry Behavior." *Journal of Health Economics* 21(3): 451–74.

Chernew, Michael E., Richard A. Hirth, and David M. Cutler. 2009. "Increased Spending on Health Care: Long-Term Implications for the Nation." *Health Affairs* 28(5): 1253–255.

Citro, Constance F., and Robert T. Michael, eds. 1995. *Measuring Poverty: A New Approach.* Washington, D.C.: National Academy Press.

Council of Economic Advisors. 1964. *Economic Report of the President, 1964.* Washington: Government Printing Office. Available at: http://www.presidency.ucsb.edu/economic_reports/1964.pdf (accessed April 9, 2013).

Cutler, David M., and Mark McClellan. 1996. "The Determinants of Technological Change in Heart Attack Treatment." *NBER* working paper 5751. Cambridge, Mass.: National Bureau of Economic Research.

Davis, Karen, Gerard F. Anderson, Diane Rowland, and Earl P. Steinberg. 1990. *Health Care Cost Containment.* Baltimore, Md.: Johns Hopkins University Press.

Davis, Karen, and Roger Reynolds. 1975. "Medicare and the Utilization of Health Care Services by the Elderly." *Journal of Human Resources* 10(3): 361–77.

Davis, Karen, and Cathy Schoen. 1978. *Health and the War on Poverty: A Ten-Year Appraisal.* Washington, D.C.: Brookings Institution Press.

Decker, Sandra L. 2005. "Medicare and the Health of Women with Breast Cancer." *Journal of Human Resources* 40(4): 948–68.

Eggleston, Karen N., and Victor R. Fuchs. 2012. "The New Demographic Transition: Most

Gains in Life Expectancy Now Realized Late in Life." *Journal of Economic Perspectives* 26(3): 137–56.

Escarce, Jose J., Kenneth R. Epstein, David C. Colby, and J. Sanford Schwartz. 1993. "Racial Differences in the Elderly's Use of Medical Procedures and Diagnostic Tests." *American Journal of Public Health* 83(7): 948–54.

Feder, Judith, and William Scanlon. 1980. "Regulating the Bed Supply in Nursing Homes." *Milbank Memorial Fund Quarterly* 58(1): 54–88.

Finkelstein, Amy, and Robin McKnight. 2005 "What Did Medicare Do? (And Was It Worth It?)" *NBER* working paper 11609. Cambridge, Mass.: National Bureau of Economic Research.

———. 2008. "What Did Medicare Do? The Initial Impact of Medicare on Mortality and Out of Pocket Spending." *Journal of Public Economics* 92(7): 1644–668.

Gornick, Marian. 1976. "Ten Years of Medicare: Impact on the Covered Population." *Social Security Bulletin* 39(7): 3–21.

Gornick, Marian E., Paul W. Eggers, Thomas W. Reilly, Renee M. Mentnech, Leslye K. Fitterman, Lawrence E. Kucken, and Bruce C. Vladeck. 1996. "Effects of Race and Income on Mortality and Use of Services Among Medicare Beneficiaries." *New England Journal of Medicine* 335(11): 791–99.

Hartman, Micah, Anne B. Martin, Joseph Benson, Aaron Catlin, and the National Health Expenditure Accounts Team. 2013. "National Health Spending in 2011: Overall Growth Remains Low, but Some Payers and Services Show Signs of Acceleration." *Health Affairs* 32(1): 87–99.

Holahan, John F., and Joel W. Cohen. 1986. *Medicaid: The Trade-off between Cost Containment and Access to Care*. Washington, D.C.: Urban Institute Press.

Hoyert, Donna L., and Jiaquan Xu. 2012. "Deaths: Preliminary Data for 2011." *National Vital Statistics Reports* 61(6): 1–51. Available at: http://www.cdc.gov/nchs/data/nvsr/nvsr61/nvsr61_06.pdf (accessed April 9, 2013).

Institute of Medicine. 2012. "Best Care at Lower Cost: The Path to Continuously Learning Health Care in America." Report Brief, September. Washington, D.C.: National Academies of Science. Available at: http://www.iom.edu/bestcare (accessed April 9, 2013).

Kaiser Family Foundation. 2011a. "Medicare Spending and Financing." Fact Sheet, September. Washington, D.C.: The Henry J. Kaiser Family Foundation. Available at: http://www.kff.org/medicare/upload/7305-07.pdf (accessed April 9, 2013).

———. 2011b. "Medicare at a Glance." Fact Sheet, November. Washington, D.C.: The Henry J. Kaiser Family Foundation. Available at: http://www.kff.org/medicare/upload/1066-15.pdf (accessed April 9, 2013).

———. 2011c. "The Medicare Prescription Drug Benefit." Fact Sheet, November. Washington, D.C.: The Henry J. Kaiser Family Foundation. Available at: http://www.kff.org/medicare/upload/7044-12.pdf (accessed April 9, 2013).

Lee, Julie, Mark McClellan, and Jonathan Skinner. 1999. "The Distributional Effects of Medicare." In *Tax Policy and the Economy*, vol. 13, edited by James M. Poterba. Cambridge, Mass.: MIT Press. Available at: http://www.nber.org/chapters/c10922 (accessed April 9, 2013).

Levit, Katharine R., Helen C. Lazenby, Bradley R. Braden, and the National Health Accounts Team. 1998. "National Health Spending Trends in 1996." *Health Affairs* 17(1): 35–51.

Link, Charles R., Stephen H. Long, and Russell F. Settle. 1982. "Equity and the Utilization of Health Care Services by the Medicare Elderly." *Journal of Human Resources* 17(2): 195–212.

Loewenstein, Regina. 1971. "Early Effects of Medicare on the Health Care of the Aged." *Social Security Bulletin* 34(4): 3–20, 42.

Long, Stephen H., and Russell F. Settle. 1984. "Medicare and the Disadvantaged Elderly: Objectives and Outcomes." *Milbank Memorial Fund Quarterly* 62(4): 609–56.

Marmor, Theodore R. 1970. *The Politics of Medicare.* London: Routledge.

Martin, Anne B., David Lassman, Benjamin Washington, Aaron Catlin, and the National Expenditure Accounts Team. 2012. "Growth in U.S. Health Spending Remained Slow in 2010; Health Share of Gross Domestic Product Was Unchanged from 2009." *Health Affairs* 31(1): 208–19.

Mathis, Evelyn S. 1973. "Characteristics of Residents in Nursing and Personal Care Homes, United States—June-August 1969." *Vital and Health Statistics* series 12, no. 19. Publication HSM 73-1704. Washington: U.S. Department of Health, Education, and Welfare.

McClellan, Mark. 1996. "Medicare Reimbursement and Hospital Cost Growth." In *Advances in the Economics of Aging*, edited by David A. Wise. Chicago: University of Chicago Press.

McClellan, Mark, and Jonathan Skinner. 2006. "The Incidence of Medicare." *Journal of Public Economics* 90(1–2): 257–76.

McWilliams, J. Michael, Ellen Meara, Alan M. Zaslavsky, and John Z. Ayanian. 2009. "Differences in Control of Cardiovascular Disease and Diabetes by Race, Ethnicity, and Education: U.S. Trends from 1999 to 2006 and Effects of Medicare Coverage." *Annals of Internal Medicine* 150(8): 505–15.

Medicare Payment Advisory Commission. 2006. *Report to the Congress: Increasing the Value of Medicare.* Washington, D.C.: MedPac. Available at: http://www.medpac.gov/documents/jun06_entirereport.pdf (accessed April 9, 2013).

———. 2012. *A Data Book: Health Care Spending and the Medicare Program.* Washington, D.C.: MedPac. Available at: http://www.medpac.gov/documents/Jun12DataBookEntireReport.pdf (accessed April 9, 2013)

Moon, Marilyn. 1993. *Medicare Now and in the Future.* Washington, D.C.: Urban Institute Press.

———. 1996. *Medicare Now and in the Future,* 2nd ed. Washington, D.C.: Urban Institute Press.

Munnell, Alicia H. 2012. "2010 SCF Suggests Even Greater Retirement Risks." *Center for Retirement Research* brief 12–15. Boston, Mass.: Boston College. Available at: http://crr.bc.edu/wp-content/uploads/2012/08/IB_12-15.pdf (accessed April 9, 2013).

National Association of Community Health Centers. 2012. "About Our Health Centers." Bethesda, Md.: NACHC. Available at: http://www.nachc.com/about-our-health-centers.cfm (accessed April 9, 2013).

Newhouse, Joseph P. 1992. "Medical Care Costs: How Much Welfare Loss?" *Journal of Economic Perspectives* 6(3): 3–21.

Pappas, Gregory, Susan Queen, Wilbur Hadden, and Gail Fisher. 1993. "The Increasing Disparity in Mortality Between Socioeconomic Groups in the United States, 1960 and 1986." *New England Journal of Medicine* 329(2): 103–09.

Pettengill, Julian H. 1972. "Trends in Hospital Use by the Aged." *Social Security Bulletin* 35(7): 3–15.

Pezzin, Liliana E., and Judith D. Kasper. 2002. "Medicaid Enrollment Among Elderly Medicaid Beneficiaries: Individual Determinants, Effects of State Policy, and Impact on Service Use." *Health Services Research* 37(4): 827–47.

Potetz, Lisa, Juliette Cubanski, and Tricia Neuman. 2011. "Medicare Spending and Financing: A Primer." Washington, D.C.: The Henry J. Kaiser Family Foundation. Available at: http://www.kff.org/medicare/upload/7731-03.pdf (accessed April 9, 2013).

Quadagno, Jill. 2000. "Promoting Civil Rights through the Welfare State: How Medicare Integrated Southern Hospitals." *Social Problems* 47(1): 68–89.

Remington, Patrick L., and Ross C. Brownson. 2011. "Fifty Years of Progress in Chronic Disease Epidemiology and Control." Centers for Disease Control and Prevention *Morbidity and Mortality Weekly Report* 60(4)(Supplement, October): 70–77.

Reynolds, P. Preston. 1997. "The Federal Government's Use of Title VI and Medicare to Racially Integrate Hospitals in the United States, 1963 Through 1967." *American Journal of Public Health* 87(11): 1850–858.

Reynolds, Roger A. 1976. "Improving Access to Health Care Among the Poor—The Neighborhood Health Center Experience." *Milbank Memorial Fund Quarterly: Health and Society* 54(1): 47–82.

Scanlon, William. 1980. "A Theory of the Nursing Home Market." *Inquiry* 17(1): 25–41.

Shin, Peter, Sara Rosenbaum, and Julia Paradise. 2012. "Community Health Centers: The Challenge of Growing to Meet the Need for Primary Care in Medically Underserved Communities." Kaiser Commission on Medicaid and the Uninsured Issue Paper (March), Washington, D.C.: The Henry J. Kaiser Family Foundation. Available at: http://www.kff.org/uninsured/upload/8098-02.pdf (accessed April 9, 2013).

Showstack, Jonathan A., Mary Hughes Stone, and Steven A. Schroeder. 1985. "The Role of Changing Clinical Practices in the Rising Costs of Hospital Care." *New England Journal of Medicine* 313(19): 1201–207.

Skinner, Jonathan, and Weiping Zhou. 2006. "The Measurement and Evolution of Health Inequality: Evidence from the U.S. Medicare Population." In *Public Policy and the Income Distribution,* edited by Alan J. Auerbach, David Card, and John M. Quigley. New York: Russell Sage Foundation.

Social Security Advisory Board. 2009. "The Unsustainable Cost of Health Care." Washington, D.C.: Social Security Advisory Board. Available at: http://www.ssab.gov/documents/TheUnsustainableCostofHealthCare_graphics.pdf (accessed April 9, 2013).

Stevens, Rosemary. 1996. "Health Care in the Early 1960s." *Health Care Financing Review* 18(2): 11–22.

Swartz, Katherine. 1984. "Who Has Been Without Health Insurance? Changes Between 1963 and 1979." Unpublished Urban Institute working paper 3308-01. Washington, D.C.: Urban Institute.

Taylor, Jessamy. 2004. "The Fundamentals of Community Health Centers." *National Health Policy Forum* background paper. Washington, D.C.: National Health Policy Forum.

Terry, Luther, et al. 1964. *Smoking and Health: Report of the Advisory Committee to the Surgeon General of the United States.* Public Health Service publication 1103. Washington: U.S. Department of Health, Education, and Welfare. Available at: http://profiles.nlm.nih.gov/ps/access/NNBBMQ.pdf (accessed April 9, 2013).

U.S. Bureau of the Census. 1964. *Statistical Abstract of the United States: 1964.* Washington:

Government Printing Office. Available at: http://www2.census.gov/prod2/statcomp/documents/1964-01.pdf (accessed April 9, 2013).

U.S. Census Bureau. 2008. "U.S. Population Projections Based on 2000 Census." Washington: Government Printing Office. Available at: http://www.census.gov/population/www/projections/summarytable s.html (accessed April 9, 2013).

——. 2012. "Historical Income Tables: Households, table H-6. Regions – All Races by Median and Mean Income: 1975 to 2011." Washington: Government Printing Office. Available at: http://www.census.gov/hhes/www/income/data/historical/household (accessed April 9, 2013).

Wenneker, Mark B., and Arnold M. Epstein. 1989. "Racial Inequalities in the Use of Procedures for Patients with Ischemic Heart Disease in Massachusetts." *Journal of the American Medical Association*, 261(2): 253-57.

West, Howard. 1971. "Five Years of Medicare – A Statistical Review." *Social Security Bulletin* 34(12): 17-27.

Yelowitz, Aaron S. 2000. "Public Policy and Health Insurance Choices for the Elderly: Evidence from the Medicare Buy-In Program." *Journal of Public Economics* 78(3): 301-24.

Young, Katherine, Rachel Garfield, MaryBeth Musumeci, Lisa Clemans-Cope, and Emily Lawton. 2012. "Medicaid's Role for Dual Eligible Beneficiaries." Kaiser Commission on Medicaid and the Uninsured Issue Paper (April). Washington, D.C.: The Henry J. Kaiser Family Foundation. Available at: http://www.kff.org/medicaid/upload/7846-03.pdf (accessed April 9, 2013).

Index

Boldface numbers refer to figures and tables.

Index

Index